Schooling and Capitalism

The Open University
Faculty of Educational Studies

The Schooling and Society course team

Colin Brown (*staff tutor*)
Heather Cathcart (*course assistant*)
Ben Cosin (*unit author*)
Roger Dale (*unit author*)
Geoff Esland (*unit author*)
Ken Giles (*staff tutor/unit author*)
Martyn Hammersley (*unit author*)
Keith Harry (*liaison librarian*)
Richard Hoyle (*designer*)
Jack Jones (*staff tutor*)
Ken Little (*BBC*)

Madeleine MacDonald (*unit author*)
Donald Mackinnon (*unit author*)
Gill Mason (*editor*)
Edward Milner (*BBC*)
Robert Nicodemus (*IET*)
Maggie Preedy (*editor*)
Don Swift (*unit author*)
Vi Winn (*research officer*)
Peter Woods (*unit author*)
Ray Woolfe (*staff tutor/unit author*)

Reader prepared with the editorial assistance of Dawn Bramer

Schooling and Capitalism
A sociological reader

edited by
Roger Dale,
Geoff Esland
and Madeleine MacDonald
for the Schooling and Society Course
at The Open University

London and Henley
Routledge & Kegan Paul
in association with The Open University Press

The Open University Press

First published in 1976
by Routledge & Kegan Paul Ltd
39 Store Street,
London WC1E 7DD and
Broadway House,
Newtown Road,
Henley-on-Thames,
Oxon RG9 1EN
Set in Monotype Times by
Kelly, Selwyn & Co., Melksham, Wiltshire
Printed in Great Britain by
Billing & Sons Ltd, Guildford, London and Worcester

ISBN 0 7100 8493 5 (c)
    0 7100 8494 3 (p)

Contents

Acknowledgments

The Open University and the publishers would like to thank the following for permission to reproduce copyright material. All possible care has been taken to trace ownership of the selections included and to make full acknowledgment for their use.

Reading 1 Copyright © 1972 by President and Fellows of Harvard College.

2 © 1973 by Rand McNally Publishing Company, Chicago.

3 Copyright © 1975, by M. Carnoy. Reprint permission by David McKay publishers.

4, 7, 15 © Routledge & Kegan Paul Ltd, 1976.

5 By permission of the authors and Sage Publications Ltd, Beverly Hills and London.

6 © The Open University, 1976.

8 By permission of the editor, *History of Education Quarterly*, 1972.

9 By permission of Routledge & Kegan Paul Ltd, 1974.

10 Copyright 1972 by Social Policy Corporation.

11 By permission of *This Magazine*, 1974.

12 © P. Bourdieu and Éditions du Centre National de la Recherche Scientifique de Paris, 1966, reprinted by permission of Methuen & Co. Ltd, 1974; originally published as 'L'école conservatrice: les inégalités devant l'école et devant la culture', *Revue française de Sociologie*, 7 (3), July–September 1966, pp. 325–47.

13 Reprinted by permission of Macmillan London and Basingstoke.

14 By permission of the editor, *Educational Theory*, 1972.

16 By permission of Dr Ingleby and Cambridge University Press, 1974.

17 Copyright © 1973 Hard Cheese Publications and P. S. Wilson.

18 By permission of the American Sociological Association, 1972.

19 Copyright © 1975 by the Association for Supervision and Curriculum Development.

20 By permission of Michael F. D. Young and the editor, *Educational Studies*, 1975.

21 Reprinted by permission of Unesco, © Unesco 1967.

22 By permission of the editor, *New Left Review*, 1973.

23 Copyright © 1964 by Herbert Marcuse, reprinted by permission of Routledge & Kegan Paul Ltd and Beacon Press, Boston.

24 By permission of Lawrence & Wishart Ltd, 1971.

25 By permission of the editor, *Hard Cheese*, 1971.

Introduction

Sociology has traditionally conceived of itself as elaborating through its theoretical and empirical research a critical analysis of both social beliefs and actions, and the sociology of education to greater or lesser extent has located itself within this tradition. With the expansion, diversification and multiplication of educational institutions within this country, educational theories and research have proliferated. The work of sociologists has provided alternatively critiques and legitimations of political practice. Proposed solutions to problems of social stability, of social improvement and social change have more often than not educational policies at their core.

Under a capitalist mode of production there is an unequal distribution of power. It is therefore in the interest of those who hold power to ensure the perpetuation of capitalism. The maintenance of existing social relations of production is crucial and is achieved not only through direct work experience but also through the whole range of social institutions, which take their basic form from the contribution they make to such reproduction. This collection of papers is assembled to show how the capitalist mode of production influences one social institution, schooling.

Schooling is not just one among many of the social institutions which contribute to the perpetuation of the capitalist mode of production, it is arguably the most important. We find lodged within political manifestos and educational policies a plurality of ideologies, each presenting programmes of action not merely to define the nature of our school experience but also to direct and transform the quality of our lives. Schools are commonly seen as a central aspect of our social formation. Children are assumed to achieve both knowledge and skills, and through their directed self-development to be educated in the culture of their society. As an active agent in both the formation and transformation of social beings, the educational system has been credited with the power to aid economic progress, to alleviate social ills, and develop and push forward our cultural heritage while providing for the fulfilment of the individual.

The rationale for this collection of articles takes as its central purpose a critique of this, liberal, ideology and its practice. Although liberalism is not presented as the only ideological basis of education policies, and it cannot be viewed as unitary and homogeneous, our view is that its assumptions and dimensions have penetrated patterns of educational thinking and informed educational practice more decisively than any other ideology.

Perhaps the single most important plank of the liberal ideology of education is that education creates and sustains progressive social change. This faith rests on a number of critical assumptions. It is basically from a belief that these assumptions are not valid that we have assembled this collection of readings, the majority of which start from a similar belief.

What are these assumptions which underlie the liberal ideology of education? The first is that schooling critically affects the level of economic growth and social progress through its link with technology. The level of technological growth is taken to determine the level of economic growth and is itself seen to be dependent on the level of schooling. The education system provides personnel both to push back the frontiers of technical knowledge and to consolidate these advances and bring them into our everyday lives. Through manpower planning, the apparent imperatives of the technical production process exert pressure upon the school system to produce a diversely skilled and qualified workforce. The expansion and differentiation of educational institutions is underpinned by a belief in the supportive role education can play in technological growth, and this has led not only to the rapid growth of higher education in the 1960s but also to the continuing stress on technical and business education.

The second assumption involves a view of education as capable of redressing social inequalities, of over-coming—through the equalisation of educational opportunity—the unfair distribution of life chances. The education system is seen as providing a ladder and an avenue for social mobility, implementing objective selection procedures for the establishment of a meritocracy, in which the only qualification for personal advancement is 'ability'. The education system becomes the key mechanism of social selection, to the benefit of both society and the individual.

Finally, education and the culture it both produces and transmits are viewed as independent and autonomous features of our society. Educational policies are directed towards the production of both knowledge and knowledgeable individuals through the sponsoring of academic research and curriculum reform. The idealism within the liberal tradition presents both culture and schooling as politically neutral forces for social change.

Increasing interest in Marxism, both within this country and abroad, has given central importance to the problem of relating both the institutions and ideologies of the superstructure to its economic base. The cultural and educational apparatuses, together with their ideological assumptions, are presented as part of a theory of social control. From the premise that social being determines consciousness, the intermediary intervention of educational and intel-lectual structures has become a major concern for analysis. We have now a range of analyses of the superstructure with theories of cultural production, reproduction and transmission.

Moreover, in making such analyses, there is an increased interest in understanding the ways, implicit or explicit, in which culture and education may act as a means of social reproduction of the class structure. We are learning to identify the structures, and the relations of production, not just within the economic sphere but in the symbolic, and to recognise the existence of cultural as opposed to economic capital, of educational and symbolic property. By so doing we are moving closer to an understanding of how 'forms of consciousness' are created and re-created across generations.

The first two sections of the book contain the kernel of the critique of the first assumption of the liberal ideology, about the central importance of education in economic growth. This assumption rests on the view that the level of technological expertise in a society determines its level of economic and social progress. The social relations of production are seen to arise in response to the demands of technology. Samuel Bowles and Herbert Gintis in their articles start from the opposing position that it is the social relations of production which determine the nature of the technology to be employed. The consequences of this for their view of schooling[1] are that the main function of schooling in capitalist

society (for it is capitalism as a mode of production rather than production techniques as such which this approach places at the centre of the stage) is not in the provision of technical expertise (beyond a general level of literacy and numeracy) but in the provision of particular types of people. The social relations of schooling are best seen, according to Gintis and to Bowles, as reproducing the social relations of capitalist production, and thus the sort of personality attuned to working contentedly under that mode of production.

Bowles and Gintis mount their criticism of the liberal ideology of education from the basis of a 'political economy' approach. The other major source of the critique of the liberal ideology of education has been the American radical historians. Although they cannot be described as a uniform group, they all see the history of education as basically about control rather than about progress. They are repre-sented in this volume by Clarence Karier, who argues in 'Business Values and the Educational State' that the link between man's production and his education 'is obvious with respect to training skilled workers to man the machines; it is subtle with respect to inculcating the important social-psychological values requisite to the maintenance of a particular economic social system.' Karier examines particularly the attempts to organise schooling on a business-like footing and the consequences of these attempts.

The effect of these approaches is to direct attention to the 'hidden' rather than the 'overt' curriculum of schooling. In a paper tracing the career of the hidden curriculum, Elizabeth Vallance suggests that:[2]

the functions of the hidden curriculum have been variously identified as the inculcation of values, political socialization, training in obedience and docility, the perpetuation of the class structure-functions that may be characterized generally as social control. I use the term to refer to those non-academic but educationally significant consequences of schooling that occur systematically but are not made explicit at any level to the public rationales for education.

Furthermore, Vallance argues, what we now call the hidden curriculum in fact represents the prior function of schooling. Schooling has always been primarily concerned with social control. It is not this concern that has changed, but rather the language of justifica-tion. As she expresses it:[3]

the function of the hidden curriculum had been explicit from the beginning, it gained in salience as formal education became legitimate, and ... it went underground only when schooling as a social institution was secure enough to turn for its justification from the control of groups to the welfare of individuals. The hidden curriculum became hidden only when people were satisfied that it was working.

In Section II the basic theme of control is developed and specified in relation to the growth of English education. It was the industrial revolution which created the social changes and social problems to which mass schooling was one of the major responses. Critically, the breakdown of feudalism had created social uncertainty and removed the basis on which people knew their place. Richard Johnson argues in his 'Notes on the Schooling of the English Working Class, 1780–1850' that class control was reasserted largely through mass schooling. The working class as a whole was to be 'civilised' through its children. Schooling involved more than control—it was to bring about the *transformation* of the working class. 'The school and schoolteacher must take the child from home and prepare it for work and loyal citizenship.' This was to be achieved at least as much through the process as the content of schooling.

Steven Shapin and Barry Barnes, in 'Science, Nature and Control: Interpreting Mechanics' Institutes', examine the reasons behind the formation of Mechanics' Institutes which were aimed at the more advanced sections of the working classes. Here the need for control was explicitly recognised and it was sought by means of the curriculum. The effectiveness of old religious explanations and justifications of the natural and social worlds was being eroded with the development of new science-based techniques for use in industry, and Shapin and Barnes show how the curriculum of the Mechanics' Institutes was directed at filling the potentially dangerous gap which such erosion might create, especially in the minds of those most intimately concerned with the new ways of controlling nature.

Adopting the categories used by the American revisionist historian Michael Katz in his study of the nature and types of control over schooling in nineteenth-century Massachusetts, Dennis Smith provides a valuable comparison between Boston and Birmingham. He traces the history of groups whose desire to influence the pattern of education was not necessarily informed by a desire to control the school population and shows how a particular form and philosophy of educational administration came to predominate in late-nineteenth-century Birmingham.

Dave Harris and John Holmes examine the question whether any radical potential which the Open University conception may have possessed has been weakened by the practical imperatives with which it is confronted. As they indicate, the claimed openness of the university in entrance as well as in its curricula and pedagogy is considerably modified by the bureaucratic/technological means it has chosen by which to purvey its materials and to evaluate its students. As they put it:

[In the Open University] open-ness can lead to the establishment of new and more rational hierarchies, individualisation can produce a profound anonymity and alienation, liberal means can exist only in so far as they can be accommodated within authoritarian structures, tentative means can become final ends in themselves to which the original ends have to be fitted.

In Section III the covert but very powerful control implications of liberal ideology are analysed in a variety of contexts. The idea of equality of opportunity, the drive to establish a meritocracy based upon ability, while compensating those deprived of opportunity to participate in the movement towards upward social mobility, are shown neither to threaten nor to replace the essential economic structures of society.

In 'Liberalism and the Quest for Orderly Change', Clarence Karier outlines the development of liberalism from its early classical formulations to its new pragmatic and progressive ideals as exemplified in the works of Dewey (*the* philosopher of liberalism in education). With the development of corporate managerialism, of scientifically organised technology and computer-managed bureaucracy, the rhetoric of the new liberalism has reflected a key concern for more effective and efficient means of social control. The new welfare liberalism stressed stability, predictability and a controlled rational process of social change. Education within this context was to fulfil the need in society for citizens capable of adjusting to the necessities of an industrial system, of respecting the expertise and authority which sustained the emerging corporate society.

In their discussion of the development of criminology and deviance theory in Britain, Ian Taylor, Paul Walton and Jock Young analyse the emergence and characteristics of the Fabian project. Here, too, one may see the social democratic opposition to the traditional laissez-faire ideology as representing a new and more rational, meritocratic, form of conservatism. In proposing new forms of social control, new involvement of the state in welfare programmes, and more equality of opportunity, the Fabians were concerned 'not with a critique of capitalism as a mode of social and industrial organization, but with the inequality of access to participate in such a society'.

The essentially conservative implications of the liberal approach to one of the most pressing educational issues of the day is revealed in Stanley Aronowitz's article, 'The Trap of Environmentalism'. In their very acceptance of the grounds of the debate over the contribution of genetic or environmental factors to IQ scores, the liberal critics of genetic determinism have also accepted the underlying ideology of meritocracy and have left unchallenged the social order which requires the very category of measurable intelligence.

George Martell, in 'The Politics of Reading and Writing', offers a critique of the Hall–Dennis Report, which may be considered a Canadian equivalent of the Plowden Report in its belief in education's role to provide for individual fulfilment and personal growth. Within the ideology of corporate liberalism, new forms of social control through 'state therapy' hide the implicit function of schooling which, according to Martell, is to fit children into the occupational hierarchy of modern capitalism. One of the major mechanisms by which schools reinforce the existing class system is through the relationship of different social classes to the language of the school. Learning to be middle class requires an ability to handle reading and writing and, through differing success rates, pupils are distributed into the social hierarchy.

The ability to cope with the middle-class culture of the school is seen as crucial by Pierre Bourdieu. In 'The School as a Conservative Force', he points out that through an apparently neutral process of inculcation and selection, schools reproduce the social hierarchies of the class structure. By taking all children as equal, while implicitly favouring those who have already acquired the linguistic and social competences to handle a middle-class culture, schools take as natural what is essentially a social gift, i.e. cultural capital. Like economic capital, cultural capital (good taste, knowledge, ability, language) is unequally distributed throughout society and by selecting for such properties, schools serve to reproduce the distribution of power within the society.

The readings in Section IV explore the ways in which many of the structures of schooling have become ideologically underpinned by the theories and methods of 'scientific psychology'. A theme which occurs in all of them is that the processes of control and differentiation which operate in the school and ultimately the reproduction of the class structure itself have become legitimated by the rationality and authority which now permeate the practices of educational psychology. During the twentieth century, schools—along with other institutions—have come to regard psychology as an important source of knowledge and technique which may be applied to the social, political and organisational problems with which they are faced. Indeed, the occupations which are responsible for utilising this knowledge are involved in the assessment and treatment of behaviour over a wide area of social life. Educational as well as social and judicial decisions which relate to the competence and personal adequacy of individuals are now grounded in and filtered through the criteria and diagnostic frameworks which form the ideological substance of these occupations. The converse of this is that they have a professional right to label and in some cases stigmatise, and their mandate for this is embodied in the professional licence and curriculum. The task of a sociological critique of the social uses of psychology is, therefore, to bring to the foreground the inherently political nature of its practices.

This task forms the basis of Steven and Hilary Rose's paper, 'The Politics of Neurobiology'. Although it is primarily directed at various forms of biological theory and research, it also includes within its critique certain areas of psychological practice. The central theme of the paper is that a good deal of scientific research in the West is characterised by *reductionism*—that is, the tendency to reduce problems which are identified in 'higher level' disciplines (such as economics and sociology) to the methodologies and procedures of 'lower level' sciences (for example, biology and physics). The particular form of reductionism which is explored in their paper is 'biologism'—a phenomenon which they define as

the attempt to locate the cause of the existing structure of human society, and of the relationships of individuals within it, in the biological character of the human animal. For biologism, all the richness of human experience and the varying historical forms of human relationships merely represent the product of underlying biological structures . . . In a word, the human condition is reduced to mere biology, which in its turn is no more than a special case of the laws of chemistry and hence of physics.

During the course of their paper they argue that the reduction of social and political issues to the principles of biology has led to their becoming 'locked into the processes of social control'. They then go on to provide a number of examples of biological reductionism in which there has been considerable research investment in attempts to discover biological causes of, and sometimes solutions to, problems which are essentially moral and political. One which is particularly striking concerns the recently-diagnosed condition of 'minimal brain dysfunction'. Here up to 250,000 American schoolchildren who have been diagnosed as 'hyperactive' are given daily doses of the amphetamine drug Ritalin.

Karier's article 'Testing for Order and Control in the Corporate Liberal State' provides some well-documented analysis of the growth of psychological testing of schoolchildren in the United States. He argues that the rise of the intellectual testing of children and the institutionalisation of vocabularies relating to IQ and achievement can be regarded as an expression of capitalist economic logic. According to Karier, intelligence tests were seen explicitly by early educational planners as a means of legitimating and preserving middle-class control of the higher status occupations. A crucial part of his argument rests on his evidence that the educational foundations—such as the Carnegie Foundation—sponsored by corporate industry, spent large sums supporting and promoting the work on testing of such people as Terman and Thorndike.

It was men like Thorndike, Terman and Goddard, supported by corporate wealth, who successfully persuaded teachers, administrators and lay school boards to classify and standardize the school's curriculum with a differentiated track system based on ability and values of the corporate liberal society . . .

The many varied tests, all the way from IQ to personality and scholastic achievement, periodically brought up-to-date, would serve a vital part in rationalizing the social class system. The tests also created the illusion of objectivity which on the one side served the needs of the 'professional' educators to be 'scientific,' and on the other side served the need of the system for a myth which could convince the lower classes that their station in life was part of the natural order of things.

Paul Henderson's paper, 'Class Structure and the Concept of Intelligence', makes a number of similar points. After tracing certain ideological continuities between the work of the nineteenth-century writer Francis Galton and the twentieth-century psychometricians, he develops the argument that the grading of children by intelligence testing can be seen in terms of the protection of middle-class culture during the rise of mass education. The notion of IQ effectively legitimated the middle-class curriculum and downgraded working-class culture.

The implicit political nature of psychology forms the theme of David Ingleby's paper 'The Psychology of Child Psychology'. Here Ingleby argues that it is the dominance of the scientific world-view in psychology which has effectively depoliticised its apparent purpose; this is particularly true of conceptions of the child, his development, his social situation, his relationship with parents, and so on, which are contained in it:

child psychology has not looked at its subject-matter in the light of the political system in which it is found: the political order is usually seen as a source of extraneous variance which must be partialled out of the data to make them truly 'psychological'.

. . . the 'scientific' label is a device for throwing us, ideologically speaking, off the scent: for that which is 'scientific', by definition, does not depend for its authority on the political loyalties implicit in it. My contention was that the social function which determines the spirit of inquiry in psychology—whatever convictions psychologists may have about it—is the maintenance of the *status quo* . . .

Wilson's paper 'Plowden Children' is an attempt to examine the dominance of certain of the psychological theories which are contained in the Plowden Report. In the first place they are the products of an expert group which in some senses can be seen as alien to the work of teachers, and second, Wilson argues, they are based on a 'physicalistic' model of the child. She is critical of the mechanistic objectivism of these psychological theories and suggests that they are far from adequate as a basis for formulating a 'child-centred' education.

The third assumption of liberalism, a belief in the autonomy and independence of knowledge as a force for social change is seen most clearly in the prevailing attitudes to both culture and schooling. The reluctance to allow material concerns to infiltrate the world of thought underlies the traditional British segregation of theoretical and practical, of abstract and technical knowledge. Institutionalised in different educational agencies, supported by the division of knowledge and the structure of academic practice, the distinction between mental and manual labour is replicated.

Similarly the divorce between the world of ideas and that of man's existence can be seen in the lack of analysis of the relationship between culture and its external material base. Thus we have been taught to make distinct and separate the understanding of the forces of economic and social production from that of the cultural. The separate existence and development of academic disciplines, each with its own form of discourse, perpetuate a tendency to reveal more often than not the autonomous nature of their subject matter. Physically distinct departments and exclusive forms of analysis inhibit both the unification of cultural forms and the identification of common features. Thus paradoxically we find that the rules for understanding education's transmission of culture become mutually exclusive of the rules for analysing the content of cultural forms.

Furthermore, the research within each area, be it philosophy, science, 'high' culture or education, reveals in the history of each discipline through its inception, development and accumulation an internally governed logic. The cultural workmen are portrayed in the whole range of knowledge and cultural production as isolated and privatised actors on the cultural stage. The recognition of the similarities and homologies between their products are put down to the cohesion and internal consistency of their field.

By alienating cultural goods and their producers from both the social condition of their existence and the patterns of cultural production and consumption, we are presented with a view of their impeccable neutrality. Similarly we find the ideology of political neutrality applied to education, the agency for both cultural creation and dissemination. Seen as objective, apolitical and internally governed, the selection, modification and transmission of a cultural heritage, through the curriculum and pedagogical practice of education, is assigned more often than not a total autonomy from the society of which it is part. Academic freedom, teacher autonomy, the denial of censorship and bias are all called in to support the view of a world in which the free flow of ideas is beyond ideological control.

In Section V, the authors take a more critical stance towards both the overt and hidden features of the curriculum and the culture it transmits. The construction and reform of the curriculum revealed in the articles presented implicit assumptions which serve to reproduce both the political and ideological structures of society.

In 'The Organization Child', Rosabeth Moss Kanter discusses some of the implications of a neo-Freudian psychological approach in the nursery school. While it is true that this approach does not obviously prepare children for the typical structure of manual work, Kanter suggests that it does reproduce in school many of the central characteristics of bureaucracy, for instance in its stress on security and rationality, and in its reduction of personal accountability.

Michael Apple shows in 'Commonsense Categories and Curriculum Thought' how difficult it is to break out of 'conventional' ways of thinking about the curriculum and argues that those who have attempted curriculum reform have failed to do so. He stresses that the conventional way of looking at the curriculum and the 'scientific' stance sought by curriculum theorists are not politically neutral but are conservative in their implications, while 'one important latent function of schooling seems to be the distribution of forms of consciousness, often quite unequally, to students.'

Michael Young takes up similar problems in looking at the 'curriculum as fact' and comparing it with a possible 'curriculum as practice'. ' "Curriculum as fact" presents education as a thing, hiding the social relations between those who collectively produce it . . . [while] the basic premise of "curriculum as practice" is how men collectively attempt to order their world and in the process produce knowledge.' He argues that both these views obscure the political and economic character of education: the curriculum as fact takes for granted what its task as theory is to explain—curriculum as practice invalidly locates the possibilities for change primarily in teachers' practices. Thus there are shortcomings to both in their possibilities as a theory of change.

Pierre Bourdieu, concerned with the elitist nature of the French educational system and its stress on intellectual and scholastic excellence, analyses the formation, and transmission by education, of a cultural code which unifies cultural projects and their producers. In 'Systems of Education and Systems of Thought', the importance of the code, as an internalised grammar of thought and practice, lies in a theory of cultural reproduction and of social control.

The selection of readings we present in Section VI constitutes an important part of the material so far produced in the Marxist tradition. Although each is distinct in terms of the subject matter and form of the analysis, the central problem of the superstructure provides their unity. The articles in this final section illustrate both the consistency of a cross-cultural sociological tradition and the distinctiveness of each theory in relation to the social context of its author.

Raymond Williams, while responding to the British tradition of literary criticism, argues for a more complete analysis of both base and superstructure to include an understanding of the totality of a hegemonic culture, and the ways in which social change through cultural forms is expressed; the key problems he delineates cover the extent to which the 'hegemony' or dominant culture may incorporate new and even contradictory cultural forms, the use of residual legacies of past cultures and bind together both the creative and recreative aspects of education and culture.

In *One-Dimensional Man*, written in the early 1960s, Marcuse presents us with insights derived from his experience of the totalitarian effects of American technology. He argues that the technological order, with its political and intellectual coordination, incorporates or represses all forms of opposition. The ideology of technical rationality and efficiency becomes, he argues, part of men's thought and behaviour; where even such concepts as liberty, free choice and needs symbolise not freedom but subservience to the established social division of labour. The likelihood of transcending the pressures of domination through the economic and superstructural levels becomes in such a case barely a possibility.

The extracts from Gramsci's *Prison Notebooks* reveal, on the other hand, a belief in the political role of intellectuals and in their potential to provide an ideological counter-attack to the social hegemony and state domination of the existing social hierarchy. Although extensive translations have only recently become available in this country, Gramsci provides a unique finely-worked-out analysis of the role of the superstructure in relation to the class structure.

We conclude the Reader with a note of optimism from Paulo Freire. Like Gramsci, Freire takes the position that theoretical 'consciousness-raising' activities (for instance, most sociology) have meaning only when united with action. The insights which he puts forward, derived from his experience of teaching literacy programmes in Brazil—though while perhaps appearing utopian in the context of industrial society—reveal to us not only the myths and paradoxes of our belief in education as a liberating force but also the futility in merely denouncing oppression without any attempt to announce and enact a future.

Notes

1 These are expanded considerably in their book, *Schooling in Capitalist America*, Routledge & Kegan Paul, 1976, also a Set Book for this course.

2 'Hiding the hidden curriculum: an interpretation of the language of justification in nineteenth-century educational reform', *Curriculum Theory Network*, 4 (1), 1974, p. 13.

3 ibid., p. 14.

Section I Education, work and the class structure

1 Towards a political economy of education: a radical critique of Ivan Illich's *Deschooling Society**

Herbert Gintis

Ivan Illich's *Deschooling Society*, despite its bare 115 pages, embraces the world. Its ostensible focus on education moves him inexorably and logically through the panoply of human concerns in advanced industrial society—a society plainly in progressive disintegration and decay. With Yeats we may feel that 'things fall apart/The centre cannot hold', but Illich's task is no less than to discover and analyze that 'centre.' His endeavor affords the social scientist the unique and rare privilege to put in order the historical movements which characterize our age and define the prospects for a revolutionary future. Such is the subject of this essay.

This little book would have been unthinkable ten years ago. In it, Ivan Illich confronts the full spectrum of the modern crisis in values by rejecting the basic tenets of progressive liberalism. He dismisses what he calls the Myth of Consumption as a cruel and illusory ideology foisted upon the populace by a manipulative bureaucratic system. He treats welfare and service institutions as part of the problem, not as part of the solution. He rejects the belief that education constitutes the 'great equalizer' and the path to personal liberation. Schools, says Illich, simply must be eliminated.

Illich does more than merely criticize; he conceptualizes constructive technological alternatives to repressive education. Moreover, he sees the present age as 'revolutionary' because the existing social relations of economic and political life, including the dominant institutional structure of schooling, have become impediments to the development of liberating, socially productive technologies. Here Illich is relevant indeed, for the tension between technological possibility and social reality pervades all advanced industrial societies today. Despite our technological power, communities and environment continue to deteriorate, poverty and inequality persist, work

remains alienating, and men and women are not liberated for self-fulfilling activity.

Illich's response is a forthright vision of participatory, decentralized, and liberating learning technologies, and a radically altered vision of social relations in education.

Yet, while his *description* of modern society is sufficiently critical, his *analysis* is simplistic and his program, consequently, is a diversion from the immensely complex and demanding political, organizational, intellectual, and personal demands of revolutionary reconstruction in the coming decades. It is crucial that educators and students who have been attracted to him—for his message does correspond to their personal frustration and disillusionment—move beyond him.

The first part of this essay presents Illich's analysis of the economically advanced society—the basis for his analysis of schools. Whereas Illich locates the source of the social problems and value crises of modern societies in their need to reproduce alienated patterns of *consumption*, I argue that these patterns are merely manifestations of the deeper workings of the economic system. The second part of the essay attempts to show that Illich's over-emphasis on consumption leads him to a very partial understanding of the functions of the educational system and the contradictions presently besetting it, and hence to ineffective educational alternatives and untenable political strategies for the implementation of desirable educational technologies.

Finally, I argue that a radical theory of educational reform becomes viable only by envisioning liberating and equal education as serving and being served by a radically altered nexus of social relations in *production*. Schools may lead or lag in this process of social transformation, but structural changes in the educational process can be socially relevant only when they speak to potentials for liberation and equality in our day-to-day labors. In the final analysis 'de-schooling'

Source: *Harvard Educational Review*, 42 (1), 1972, pp. 70–96.

is irrelevant because we cannot 'de-factory,' 'de-office,' or 'de-family,' save perhaps at the still un-envisioned end of a long process of social reconstruction.

The social context of modern schooling: institutionalized values and commodity fetishism

Educational reformers commonly err by treating the system of schools as if it existed in a social vacuum. Illich does not make this mistake. Rather, he views the internal irrationalities of modern education as reflections of the larger society. The key to understanding the problems of advanced industrial economies, he argues, lies in the character of its consumption activities and the ideology which supports them. The schools in turn are exemplary models of bureaucracies geared toward the indoctrination of docile and manipulable consumers.

Guiding modern social life and interpersonal behavior, says Illich, is a destructive system of 'institutionalized values' which determine how one perceives one's needs and defines instruments for their satisfaction. The process which creates institutional values insures that all individual needs—physical, psychological, social, intellectual, emotional, and spiritual—are transformed into demands for goods and services. In contrast to the 'psychological impotence' which results from institutionalized values, Illich envisages the 'psychic health' which emerges from self-realization—both personal and social. Guided by institutionalized values, one's well-being lies not in what one *does* but in what one *has*—the status of one's job and the level of material consumption. For the active person, goods are merely means to or instruments in the performance of activities; for the passive consumer, however, goods are ends in themselves, and activity is merely the means toward sustaining or displaying a desired level of consumption. Thus institutionalized values manifest themselves psychologically in a rigorous fetishism—in this case, of commodities and public services. Illich's vision rests in the negation of commodity fetishism:[1]

> I believe that a desirable future depends on our deliberately . . . engendering a life style which will enable us to be spontaneous, independent, yet related to each other, rather than maintaining a life style which only allows us to make and unmake, produce and consume. (*Deschooling Society*, hereafter *DS*, p. 52)

Commodity fetishism is institutionalized in two senses. First, the 'delivery systems' in modern industrial economies (i.e., the suppliers of goods and services) are huge, bureaucratic institutions which treat individuals as mere receptors for their products. Goods are supplied by hierarchical and impersonal corporate enterprises, while services are provided by welfare bureaucracies which enjoy 'a professional, political and financial monopoly over the social

imagination, setting standards of what is valuable and what is feasible . . . A whole society is initiated into the Myth of Unending Consumption of services' (*DS*, p. 44).

Second, commodity fetishism is institutionalized in the sense that the values of passive consumerism are induced and reinforced by the same 'delivery systems' whose ministrations are substitutes for self-initiated activities.

> . . . manipulative institutions . . . are either socially or psychologically 'addictive.' Social addiction . . . consists in the tendency to prescribe increased treatment if smaller quantities have not yielded the desired results. Psychological addiction . . . results when consumers become hooked on the need for more and more of the process or product. (*DS*, p. 55)

These delivery systems moreover 'both invite compulsively repetitive use and frustrate alternative ways of achieving similar results.' For example, General Motors and Ford

> . . . produce means of transportation, but they also, and more importantly, manipulate public taste in such a way that the need for transportation is expressed as a demand for private cars rather than public buses. They sell the desire to control a machine, to race at high speeds in luxurious comfort, while also offering the fantasy at the end of the road. (*DS*, p. 57)

This analysis of addictive manipulation in private production is, of course, well-developed in the literature.[2] Illich's contribution is to extend it to the sphere of service and welfare bureaucracies:

> Finally, teachers, doctors, and social workers realize that their distinct professional ministrations have one aspect—at least—in common. They create further demands for the institutional treatments they provide, faster than they can provide service institutions. (*DS*, p. 112)

The well-socialized naturally react to these failures simply by increasing the power and jurisdiction of welfare institutions. Illich's reaction, of course, is precisely the contrary.

The political response to institutionalized values

As the basis for his educational proposals, Illich's overall framework bears close attention. Since commodity fetishism is basically a psychological stance, it must first be attacked on an individual rather than political level. For Illich, each individual is responsible for his/her own demystification. The institutionalization of values occurs not through external coercion, but through psychic manipulation, so its rejection is an apolitical act of individual will. The movement for social change thus becomes a cultural one of raising consciousness.

But even on this level, political action in the form of *negating* psychic manipulation is crucial. Goods and services as well as welfare bureaucracies must be *prohibited* from disseminating fetishistic values. Indeed, this is the basis for a political program of deschooling. The educational system, as a coercive source of institutionalized values, must be denied its preferred status. Presumably, this 'politics of negation' would extend to advertising and all other types of psychic manipulation.

Since the concrete social manifestation of commodity fetishism is a grossly inflated level of production and consumption, the second step in Illich's political program is the substitution of leisure for work. Work is evil for Illich—unrewarding by its very nature—and not to be granted the status of 'activity':

> . . . 'making and acting' are different, so different, in fact, that one never includes the other. . . . Modern technology has increased the ability of man to relinquish the 'making' of things to machines, and his potential time for 'acting' has increased. . . . Unemployment is the sad idleness of a man who, contrary to Aristotle, believes that making things, or working, is virtuous and that idleness is bad. (*DS*, p. 62)

Again, Illich's shift in the work-leisure choice is basically apolitical and will follow naturally from the abolition of value indoctrination. People work so hard and long because they are taught to believe the fruits of their activities—consumption—are intrinsically worthy. Elimination of the 'hard-sell pitch' of bureaucratic institutions will allow individuals to discover *within themselves* the falsity of the doctrine.

The third stage in Illich's political program envisages the necessity of concrete change in social 'delivery systems.' Manipulative institutions must be *dismantled*, to be replaced by organizational forms which allow for the free development of individuals. Illich calls such institutions 'convivial,' and associates them with leftist political orientation.

> The regulation of convivial institutions sets limits to their use; as one moves from the convivial to the manipulative end of the spectrum, the rules progressively call for unwilling consumption or participation . . . Toward, but not at, the left on the institutional spectrum, we can locate enterprises which compete with others in their own field, but have not begun notably to engage in advertising. Here we find hand laundries, small bakeries, hairdressers, and—to speak of professionals—some lawyers and music teachers. . . . They acquire clients through their personal touch and the comparative quality of their services. (*DS*, pp. 55–6)

In short, Illich's Good Society is based on small scale entrepreneurial (as opposed to corporate) capitalism, with perfectly competitive markets in goods and services. The role of the state in this society is the prevention of manipulative advertising, the development of left-convivial technologies compatible with self-initiating small-group welfare institutions (education, health and medical services, crime prevention and rehabilitation, community development, etc.) and the provisioning of the social infrastructure (e.g., public transportation). Illich's proposal for 'learning webs' in education is only a particular application of this vision of left-convivial technologies.

Assessing Illich's politics: an overview

Illich's model of consumption-manipulation is crucial at every stage of his political argument. But it is substantially incorrect. In the following three sections I shall criticize three basic thrusts of his analysis.

First, Illich locates the source of social decay in the autonomous, manipulative behavior of corporate bureaucracies. I shall argue, in contrast, that the source must be sought in the normal operation of the basic *economic* institutions of capitalism (markets in factors of production, private control of resources and technology, etc.),[3] which consistently sacrifice the healthy development of community, work, environment, education, and social equality to the accumulation of capital and the growth of marketable goods and services. Moreover, given that individuals must participate in economic activity, these social outcomes are quite insensitive to the preferences or values of individuals, and are certainly in no sense a reflection of the autonomous wills of manipulating bureaucrats or gullible consumers. Hence merely ending 'manipulation' while maintaining basic economic institutions will affect the rate of social decay only minimally.

Second, Illich locates the *source* of consumer consciousness in the manipulative socialization of individuals by agencies controlled by corporate and welfare bureaucracies. This 'institutionalized consciousness' induces individuals to choose outcomes not in conformity with their 'real' needs. I shall argue, in contrast, that a causal analysis can *never* take socialization agencies as basic explanatory variables in assessing the overall behavior of the social system.[4] In particular, consumer consciousness is generated through *the day-to-day activities and observations* of individuals in capitalist society. The sales pitches of manipulative institutions, rather than *generating* the values of commodity fetishism, merely *capitalize* upon and *reinforce* a set of values derived from and reconfirmed by daily personal experience in the social system. In fact, while consumer behavior may seem irrational and fetishistic, it is a reasonable accommodation to the options for meaningful social outlets *in the context* of capitalist institutions. Hence the abolition of addictive propaganda cannot 'liberate' the individual to 'free choice' of personal goals. Such choice is still conditioned by the pattern of social processes which have historically rendered him or her amenable to 'institutionalized values.' In fact, the likely outcome of de-manipulation of values would be no significant alteration of values at all.

Moreover, the ideology of commodity fetishism not only *reflects* the day-to-day operations of the economic system, it is also *functionally necessary* to motivate men/women to accept and participate in the system of alienated production, to peddle their (potentially) creative activities to the highest bidder through the market in labor, to accept the destruction of their communities, and to bear allegiance to an economic system whose market institutions and patterns of control of work and community systematically subordinate all social goals to the criteria of profit and marketable product. Thus the weakening of institutionalized values would in itself lead logically either to unproductive and undirected social chaos (witness the present state of counter-culture movements in the United States) or to a rejection of the social relations of capitalist production along with commodity fetishism.

Third, Illich argues that the goal of social change is to transform institutions according to the criterion of 'non-addictiveness,' or 'left-conviviality.' However, since manipulation and addictiveness are not the sources of social decay, their elimination offers no cure. Certainly the implementation of left-convivial forms in welfare and service agencies—however desirable in itself—will not counter the effects of capitalist development on social life. More important, Illich's criterion explicitly accepts those basic economic institutions which structure decision-making power, lead to the growth of corporate and welfare bureaucracies, and lie at the root of social decay. Thus Illich's criterion must be replaced by one of democratic, participatory, and rationally decentralized control over social outcomes in factory, office, community, schools, and media. The remainder of this essay will elucidate the alternative analysis and political strategy as focused on the particular case of the educational system.

Economic institutions and social development

In line with Illich's suggestion, we may equate individual welfare with the pattern of day-to-day *activities* the individual enters into, together with the personal *capacities*—physical, cognitive, affective, spiritual, and aesthetic—he or she has developed toward their execution and appreciation. Most individual activity is not purely personal, but is based on social interaction and requires a social setting conducive to developing the relevant capacities for performance. That is, activities take place within socially structured domains, characterized by legitimate and socially acceptable roles available to the individual in social relations. The most important of these activity contexts are work, community, and natural environment. The character of individual

participation in these contexts—the defining roles one accepts as worker and community member and the way one relates to one's environment—is a basic determinant of well-being and individual development.

These activity contexts, as I shall show, are structured in turn by the way people structure their *productive relations*. The study of activity contexts in capitalist society must begin with an understanding of the basic economic institutions which regulate their historical development.

The most important of these institutions are: (1) *private ownership* of factors of production (land, labor, and capital), according to which the owner has full control over their disposition and development; (2) *a market in labor*, according to which (a) the worker is divorced, by and large, from ownership of non-human factors of production (land and capital), (b) the worker relinquishes control over the disposition of his labor during the stipulated workday by exchanging it for money, and (c) the price of a particular type of labor (skilled or unskilled, white-collar or blue-collar, physical, mental, managerial, or technical) is determined essentially by supply and demand; (3) *a market in land*, according to which the price of each parcel of land is determined by supply and demand, and the use of such parcels is individually determined by the highest bidder; (4) income determination on the basis of the *market-dictated returns to owned factors* of production; (5) *markets in essential commodities*—food, shelter, social insurance, medical care; and (6) *control of the productive process by owners of capital* or their managerial representatives.[5]

Because essential goods, services, and activity contexts are marketed, income is a prerequisite to social existence. Because factors of production are privately owned and market-determined factor returns are the legitimate source of income, and because most workers possess little more than their own labor services, they are required to provide these services to the economic system. Thus control over the developing of work roles and of the social technology of production passes into the hands of the representatives of capital.

Thus the activity context of work becomes alienated in the sense that its structure and historical development do not conform to the needs of the individuals it affects.[6] Bosses determine the technologies and social relations of production within the enterprise on the basis of three criteria. First, production must be flexibly organized for decision-making and secure managerial control from the highest levels downward. This means generally that technologies employed must be compatible with hierarchical authority and a fragmented, task-specific division of labor.[7] The need to maintain effective administrative power leads to bureaucratic order in production, the hallmark of modern corporate organization. Second, among all technologies and work roles compatible with secure and flexible control from the top, bosses choose those which minimize costs and maximize profits. Finally, bosses determine product attributes—and hence the 'craft rationality' of production—according to their contribution to gross sales and growth of the enterprise. Hence the decline in pride of workmanship and quality of production associated with the Industrial Revolution.

There is no reason to believe that a great deal of desirable work is not possible. On the contrary, evidence indicates that decentralization, worker control, the reintroduction of craft in production, job rotation, and the elimination of the most constraining aspects of hierarchy are both feasible and potentially efficient. But such work roles develop in an institutional context wherein control, profit, and growth regulate the development of the social relations of production. Unalienated production must be the result of the revolutionary transformation of the basic institutions which Illich implicitly accepts.

The development of communities as activity contexts also must be seen in terms of basic economic institutions. The market in land, by controlling the organic development of communities, not only produces the social, environmental, and aesthetic monstrosities we call 'metropolitan areas,' but removes from the community the creative, synthesizing power that lies at the base of true solidarity. Thus communities become agglomerates of isolated individuals with few common activities and impersonal and apathetic interpersonal relations.

A community cannot thrive when it holds no effective power over the autonomous activities of profit-maximizing capitalists. Rather, a true community is *itself* a creative, initiating, and synthesizing agent, with the power to determine the architectural unity of its living and working spaces and their coordination, the power to allocate community property to social uses such as participatory childcare and community recreation centers, and the power to insure the preservation and development of its natural ecological environment. This is not an idle utopian dream. Many living-working communities do exhibit architectural, aesthetic, social, and ecological integrity: the New England town, the Dutch village, the moderate-sized cities of Mali in sub-Saharan Africa, and the desert communities of Djerba in Tunisia. True, these communities are fairly static and untouched by modern technology; but even in a technologically advanced country the potential for decent community is great, given the proper pattern of community decision mechanisms.

The normal operation of the basic economic institutions of capitalism thus render major activity contexts inhospitable to human beings. Our analysis of work and community could easily be extended to include ecological environment and economic equality with similar conclusions.[8]

This analysis undermines Illich's treatment of public service bureaucracies. Illich holds that service agencies (including schools) fail because they are manipulative, and expand because they are psychologically addictive. In fact, they do not fail at all. And they expand because they exist as integral links in the larger institutional allocation of unequal power and income. Illich's simplistic treatment of this area is illustrated in his explanation for the expansion of military operations:

> The boomerang effect in war is becoming more obvious: the higher the body count of dead Vietnamese, the more enemies the United States acquires around the world; likewise, the more the United States must spend to create another manipulative institution—cynically dubbed 'pacification'—in a futile effort to absorb the side effects of war. (*DS*, p. 54)

Illich's theory of addiction as motivation proposes that, once begun, one thing naturally leads to another. Actually, however, the purpose of the military is the maintenance of aggregate demand and high levels of employment, as well as aiding the expansion of international sources of resource supply and capital investment. Expansion is not the result of addiction but a primary characteristic of the entire system.[9]

Likewise from a systematic point of view, penal, mental illness, and poverty agencies are meant to contain the dislocations arising from the fragmentation of work and community and the institutionally determined inequality in income and power. Yet Illich argues only:

> . . . jail increases both the quality and the quantity of criminals, that, in fact, it often creates them out of mere nonconformists . . . mental hospitals, nursing homes, and orphan asylums do much the same thing. These institutions provide their clients with the destructive self-image of the psychotic, the overaged, or the waif, and provide a rationale for the existence of entire professions, just as jails produce income for wardens. (*DS*, p. 54)

Further, the cause of expansion of service agencies lies *not* in their addictive nature, but in their failure even to attempt to deal with the institutional sources of social problems. The normal operation of basic economic institutions progressively aggravates these problems, hence requiring increased response on the part of welfare agencies.

The roots of consumer behavior

To understand consumption in capitalist society requires a *production* orientation, in contrast to Illich's emphasis on 'institutionalized values' as basic explanatory variables. Individuals consume as they do—and hence acquire values and beliefs concerning consumption—because of the place consumption activity holds among the constellation of available alternatives for social expression. These alternatives directly involve the quality of basic activity contexts surrounding social life—contexts which, as I have argued, develop according to the criteria of capital accumulation through the normal operation of economic institutions.

What at first glance seems to be an irrational preoccupation with income and consumption in capitalist society, is seen within an activity context paradigm to be a logical response on the part of the individual to what Marx isolated as the central tendency of capitalist society: the transformation of all complex social relations into impersonal *quid-pro-quo* relations. One implication of this transformation is the progressive decay of social activity contexts described in the previous section, a process which reduces their overall contribution to individual welfare. Work, community, and environment become sources of pain and displeasure rather than inviting contexts for social relations. The reasonable individual response, then, is (a) to disregard the development of personal capacities which would be humanly satisfying in activity contexts which are not available and, hence, to fail to demand changed activity contexts and (b) to emphasize consumption and to develop those capacities which are most relevant to consumption *per se*.

Second, the transformation of complex social relations to exchange relations implies that the dwindling stock of healthy activity contexts is parceled out among individuals almost strictly according to income. High-paying jobs are by and large the least alienating; the poor live in the most fragmented communities and are subjected to the most inhuman environments; contact with natural environment is limited to periods of *vacation*, and the length and desirability of this contact is based on the means to pay.

Thus commodity fetishism becomes a *substitute* for meaningful activity contexts, and a *means of access* to those that exist. The 'sales pitch' of Madison Avenue is accepted because, in the given context, it is true. It may not be much, but it's all we've got. The indefensibility of its more extreme forms (e.g., susceptibility to deodorant and luxury automobile advertising) should not divert us from comprehending this essential rationality.

In conclusion, it is clear that the motivational basis of consumer behavior derives from the everyday observation and experience of individuals, and consumer values are not 'aberrations' induced by manipulative socialization. Certainly there is no reason to believe that individuals would consume or work much less were manipulative socialization removed. Insofar as such socialization is required to *stabilize* commodity fetishist values, its elimination might lead to the overthrow of capitalist *institutions*—but that of course is quite outside Illich's scheme.

The limitations of left-convivial technologies

Since Illich views the 'psychological impotence' of the individual in his/her 'addictedness' to the ministrations of corporate and state bureaucracies as the basic problem of contemporary society, he defines the desirable 'left-convivial' institutions by the criterion of 'non-addictiveness.'

Applied to commodities or welfare services, this criterion is perhaps sufficient. But applied to major contexts of social activities, it is inappropriate. It is not possible for individuals to treat their work, their communities, and their environment in a simply instrumental manner. For better or worse, these social spheres, by regulating the individual's social activity, become a major determinant of his/her psychic development, and in an important sense define *who* he/she is. Indeed, the solution to the classical 'problem of order' in society[10] is solved only by the individual's becoming 'addicted' to his/her social forms by *participating through them.*[11] In remaking society, individuals do more than expand their freedom of choice—they change *who they are*, their self-definition, in the process. The criticism of alienated social spheres is not simply that they deprive individuals of necessary instruments of activity, but that in so doing they tend to produce in all of us something less than *we intend to be*.

The irony of Illich's analysis is that by erecting 'addictiveness vs. instrumentality' as the central welfare criterion, he himself assumes a commodity fetishist mentality. In essence, he posits the individual *outside* of society and using social forms as instruments in his/her preexisting ends. For instance, Illich does not speak of work as 'addictive,' because in fact individuals treat work first as a 'disutility' and second as an instrument toward other ends (consumption). The alienation of work poses no threat to the 'sovereignty' of the worker because he is not addicted to it. By definition, then, capitalist work, communities, and environments are 'non-addictive' and left-convivial. Illich's consideration of the capitalist enterprise as 'right-manipulative' only with respect to the consumer is a perfect example of this 'reification' of the social world. In contrast, I would argue that work is *necessarily addictive* in the larger sense of determining who a man/woman is as a human being.

The addictive vs. instrumental (or, equivalently, manipulative vs. convivial) criterion is relevant only if we posit an essential 'human nature' prior to social experience. Manipulation can then be seen as the perversion of the natural essence of the individual, and the de-institutionalization of values allows the individual to return to his/her essential self for direction. But the concept of the individual prior to society is nonsense. All individuals are concrete persons, uniquely developed through their particular articulation with social life.

The poverty of Illich's 'addictiveness' criterion is dramatized in his treatment of technology. While he correctly recognizes that technology can be developed for purposes of either repression or liberation, his conception requires that the correct unalienated development of technological and institutional forms will follow from a simple aggregation of individual preferences over 'left-convivial' alternatives.

The same analysis which I applied to the atomistic aggregation of preferences in the determination of activity contexts applies here as well: there is no reason to believe that ceding control of technological innovation and diffusion to a few, while rendering them subject to market criteria of success and failure, will produce desirable outcomes. Indeed this is *precisely* the mechanism operative in the private capitalist economy, with demonstrably adverse outcomes. According to the criterion of left-conviviality, the historical development of technology in *both* private and public spheres will conform to criteria of profitability and entrepreneurial control. Citizens are reduced to *passive consumers*, picking and choosing among the technological alternatives a technological elite presents to them.

In contrast, it seems clear to me that individuals must exercise direct control over technology in structuring their various social environments, thereby developing and coming to understand their needs through their exercise of power. The control of technical and institutional forms must be vested directly in the group of individuals involved in a social activity, else the alienation of these individuals from one another becomes a *postulate* of the technical and institutional development of this social activity— be it in factory, office, school, or community.

In summary, the facile criterion of left-conviviality must be replaced by the less immediate—but correct— criterion of *unalienated social outcomes*: the institutionally mediated allocation of power must be so ordered that social outcomes conform to the wills and needs of participating individuals, and the quality of participation must be such as to promote the full development of individual capacities for self-understanding and social effectiveness.

Schooling: the pre-alienation of docile consumers

Everywhere the hidden curriculum of schooling initiates the citizen to the myth that bureaucracies guided by scientific knowledge are efficient and benevolent. . . . And everywhere it develops the habit of self-defeating consumption of services and alienating production, the tolerance for institutional dependence, and the recognition of institutional rankings. (*DS*, p. 74)

Illich sets his analysis of the educational system squarely on its strategic position in reproducing the economic relations of the larger society. While avoiding the inanity of reformers, who see 'liberated education' as compatible with current capitalist political and economic institutions, he rejects the rigidity of old-style revolutionaries, who would see even more repressive (though different) education as a tool in forging 'socialist consciousness' in the Workers' State.

What less perceptive educators have viewed as irrational, mean, and petty in modern schooling, Illich views as merely reflecting the operation of all manipulative institutions. In the first place, he argues, the educational system takes its place alongside other service bureaucracies, selling a manipulative, pre-packaged product, rendering their services addictive, and monopolizing all alternatives to self-initiated education on the part of individuals and small consenting groups.

Yet, argues Illich, schools cannot possibly achieve their goal of promoting learning. For as in every dimension of human experience, learning is the result of personal *activity*, not professional ministration:

> Most learning is not the result of instruction.
> It is rather the result of unhampered participation
> in a meaningful setting. Most people learn best
> by being 'with it,' yet school makes them identify
> their personal, cognitive growth with elaborate
> planning and manipulation. (*DS*, p. 39)

Thus, as with all bureaucratic service institutions, schools fail by their very nature. And true to form, the more they fail, the more reliance is placed on them, and the more they expand:

> Everywhere in the world school costs have risen
> faster than enrollments and faster than the
> GNP, everywhere expenditures on school fall
> even further behind the expectations of parents,
> teachers, and pupils . . . School gives unlimited
> opportunity for legitimated waste, so long as its
> destructiveness goes unrecognized and the cost of
> palliatives goes up. (*DS*, p. 10)

From the fact that schools do not promote learning, however, Illich does not conclude that schools are simply irrational or discardable. Rather, he asserts their central role in creating docile and manipulable consumers for the larger society. For just as these men and women are defined by the quality of their *possessions* rather than of their *activities*, so they must learn to 'transfer responsibility from self to institutions . . .'

> Once a man or woman has accepted the need for
> school, he or she is easy prey for other
> institutions. Once young people have allowed
> their imaginations to be formed by curricular
> instruction, they are conditioned to institutional
> planning of every sort. 'Instruction' smothers the
> horizon of their imaginations. (*DS*, p. 39)

Equally they learn that anything worthwhile is standardized, certified, and can be purchased.

Even more lamentable, repressive schooling forces commodity fetishism on individuals by thwarting their development of personal capacities for autonomous and initiating social activity:

People who have been schooled down to size let unmeasured experience slip out of their hands . . . They do not have to be robbed of their creativity. Under instruction, they have unlearned to 'do' their thing or 'be' themselves, and value only what has been made or could be made . . . (*DS*, p. 40)

Recent research justifies Illich's emphasis on the 'hidden curriculum' of schooling. Mass public education has not evolved into its present bureaucratic, hierarchical, and authoritarian form because of the organizational prerequisities of imparting cognitive skills. Such skills may in fact be more efficiently developed in democratic, non-repressive atmospheres.[12] Rather, the social relations of education produce and reinforce those values, attitudes, and affective capacities which allow individuals to move smoothly into an alienated and class-stratified society. That is, schooling reproduces the social relations of the larger society from generation to generation.[13]

Again, however, it does *not* follow that schooling finds its predominant function in reproducing the social relations of *consumption per se*. Rather, it is the social relations of *production* which are relevant to the form and function of modern schooling.

A production orientation to the analysis of schooling—that the 'hidden curriculum' in mass education reproduces the social relations of production—is reinforced in several distinct bodies of current educational research. First, economists have shown that education, in its role of providing a properly trained labor force, takes its place alongside capital accumulation and technological change as a major source of economic growth.[14] Level of educational attainment is the major non-ascriptive variable in furthering the economic position of individuals.

Second, research shows that the type of personal development produced through schooling and relevant to the individual's productivity as a worker in a capitalist enterprise is primarily *non-cognitive*. That is, profit-maximizing firms find it remunerative to hire more highly educated workers at higher pay, essentially *irrespective* of differences among individuals in cognitive abilities or attainments.[15] In other words, two individuals (white American males) with identical cognitive achievements (intelligence or intellectual attainment) but differing educational levels will not command, on the average, the same income or occupational status. Rather, the economic success of each will correspond closely to the average for his educational level. All individuals with the same level of educational attainment tend to have the same expected mean economic success (racial and sexual discrimination aside). This is not to say that cognitive skills are not necessary to job adequacy in a technological society. Rather, these skills either exist in such profusion (through schooling) or are so easily developed on the job that they are not a criterion for

hiring. Nor does this mean that there is no correlation between cognitive attainments (e.g., IQ) and occupational status. Such a correlation exists (although it is quite loose),[16] but is almost totally mediated by formal schooling: the educational system discriminates in favor of the more intelligent, although its contribution to worker productivity does not operate primarily *via* cognitive development.[17]

Thus the education-related worker attributes that employers willingly pay for must be predominantly *affective* characteristics—personality traits, attitudes, modes of self-presentation and motivation. How affective traits that are rewarded in schools come to correspond to the needs of alienated production is revealed by direct inspection of the social relations of the classroom. First, students are rewarded in terms of grades for exhibiting the personality characteristics of good workers in bureaucratic work roles— proper subordinancy in relation to authority and the primacy of cognitive as opposed to affective and creative modes of social response—above and beyond any actual effect they may have on cognitive achievement.[18] Second, the hierarchical structure of schooling itself mirrors the social relations of industrial production: students cede control over their learning activities to teachers in the classroom. Just as workers are alienated from both the *process* and the *product* of their work activities, and must be motivated by the external reward of pay and hierarchical status, so the student learns to operate efficiently through the external reward of grades and promotion, effectively alienated from the process of education (learning) and its product (knowledge). Just as the work process is stratified, and workers on different levels in the hierarchy of authority and status are required to display substantively distinct patterns of values, aspirations, personality traits, and modes of 'social presentation' (dress, manner of speech, personal identification, and loyalties to a particular social stratum),[19] so the school system stratifies, tracks, and structures social interaction according to criteria of social class and relative scholastic success.[20] The most effectively indoctrinated students are the most valuable to the economic enterprise or state bureaucracy, and also the most successfully integrated into a particular stratum within the hierarchical educational process.[21]

Third, a large body of historical research indicates that the system of mass, formal, and compulsory education arose more or less directly out of changes in productive relations associated with the Industrial Revolution, in its role of supplying a properly socialized and stratified labor force.[22]

The critical turning points in the history of American education have coincided with the perceived failure of the school system to fulfil its functional role in reproducing a properly socialized and stratified labor force, in the face of important qualitative or quantitative changes in the social relations of production. In these periods (e.g., the emergence of the common school system) numerous options were open and openly discussed.[23] The conflict of economic interests eventually culminated in the functional reorientation of the educational system to new labor needs of an altered capitalism.

In the mid- to late 19th century, this took the form of the economy's need to generate a labor force compatible with the factory system from a predominantly agricultural populace. Later, the crisis in education corresponded to the economy's need to import peasant European labor whose social relations of production and derivative culture were incompatible with industrial wage-labor. The resolution of this crisis was a hierarchical, centralized school system corresponding to the ascendance of corporate production. This resolution was not without its own contradictions. It is at this time that the modern school became the focus of tensions between work and play, between the culture of school and the culture of immigrant children, and between the notion of meritocracy and equality. Thus while Illich can *describe* the characteristics of contemporary education, his consumption orientation prevents him from understanding how the system came to be.

It seems clear that schools instill the values of docility, degrees of subordination corresponding to different levels in the hierarchy of production, and motivation according to external reward. It seems also true that they do not reward, but instead penalize, creative, self-initiated, cognitively flexible behavior. By inhibiting the full development of individual capacities for meaningful individual activity, schools produce Illich's contended outcomes: the individual as passive receptor replaces the individual as active agent. But the articulation with the larger society is *production* rather than *consumption*.

If the sources of social problems lay in consumer manipulation of which schooling is both an exemplary instance and a crucial preparation for future manipulation, then a political movement for de-schooling might be, as Illich says, 'at the root of any movement for human liberation.' But if schooling is both itself an *activity context* and preparation for the more important activity context of work then personal consciousness arises not from the elimination of outside manipulation, but from the experience of solidarity and struggles in remolding a mode of social existence. Such consciousness represents not a 'return' to the self (essential human nature) but a *restructuring* of the self through new modes of social participation; this prepares the individual for itself.

Of course this evaluation need not be unidirectional from work to education. Indeed, one of the fundamental bases for assessing the value of an alternative structure of control in production is its compatibility with intrinsically desirable individual development through education. In so far as Illich's left-convivial concept is desirable in any ultimate sense, a reorganization of production should be sought conformable to it. This might involve the development of a vital craft/artistic/technical/service sector in production organized along master-apprentice or group-control lines open to *all* individuals. The development of unalienated work technologies might then articulate harmoniously with learning-web forms in the sphere of education.

But a reorganization of production has other goals as well. For example, any foreseeable future involves a good deal of socially necessary and on balance personally unrewarding labor. However this work may be reorganized, its accomplishment must be based on individual values, attitudes, personality traits, and patterns of motivation adequate to its execution. If equality in social participation is a 'revolutionary ideal,' this dictates that all contribute equally toward the staffing of the socially necessary work roles. This is possible only if the hierarchical (as opposed to social) division of labor is abolished in favor of the solidary cooperation and participation of workers in control of production. Illich's anarchistic notion of learning webs does not seem conducive to the development of personal characteristics for this type of social solidarity.[24]

The second setting for a politics of education is the *transitional society*—one which bears the technological and cultural heritage of the capitalist class/caste system, but whose social institutions and patterns of social consciousness are geared toward the progressive realization of 'ideal forms' (i.e. revolutionary goals). In this setting, the social relations of education will themselves be transitional in nature, mirroring the transformation process of social relations of production.[25] For instance, the elimination of boring, unhealthy, fragmented, uncreative, constraining, and otherwise alienated but socially necessary labor requires an extended process of technological change in a transitional phase. As we have observed, the repressive application of technology toward the formation of occupational roles is not due to the intrinsic nature of physical science nor to the requisites of productive efficiency, but to the political imperative of stable control from the top in an enterprise. Nevertheless, the shift to automated, decentralized and worker-controlled technologies requires the continuous supervision and cooperation of workers themselves. Any form this takes in a transitional society will include a constant struggle among three groups: managers concerned with the development of the enterprise, technicians concerned with the scientific rationality of production, and workers concerned with the impact of innovation and management on job satisfaction.[26] The present educational system does not develop in the individual the capacities for cooperation, struggle, autonomy, and judgment appropriate to this task. But neither does Illich's alternative which avoids the affective aspects of work socialization totally, and takes technology out of the heads of learners.

In a transitional setting, liberating technologies cannot arise in education, any more than in production, spontaneously or by imposition from above. The social relations of unalienated education must evolve from conscious cooperation and struggle among educational administrators (managers), teachers (technicians), and students (workers), although admittedly in a context of radically redistributed power among the three. The outcome of such a struggle is not only the positive development of education but the fostering of work-capacities in individuals adequate to the task of social transition in work and community life as well.[27]

The inadequacy of Illich's conception of education in transitional societies is striking in his treatment of China and Cuba. It is quite evident that these countries are following new and historically unprecedented directions of social development. But Illich argues the necessity of their failure from the simple fact that they have not de-schooled. That they were essentially 'de-schooled' *before* the revolution (with no appreciable social benefits) does not faze him. While we may welcome and embrace Illich's emphasis on the social relations of education as a crucial variable in their internal development toward new social forms, his own criterion is without practical application.

The third setting in which the politics of education must be assessed—and the one which would most closely represent the American reality—is that of capitalist society itself. Here the correspondence principle implies that educational reform requires an *internal failure* in the stable reproduction of the economic relations of production. That is, the idea of liberating education does not arise spontaneously, but is made possible by emerging contradictions in the larger society. Nor does its aim succeed or fail according as its ethical value is greater or less. Rather, success of the aim presupposes a correct understanding of its basis in the contradictions in social life, and the political strategies adopted as the basis of this understanding.

The immediate strategies of a movement for educational reform, then, are political: (a) understanding the concrete contradictions in economic life and the way they are reflected in the educational system; (b) fighting to insure that consciousness of these contradictions persists by thwarting attempts of ruling elites to attenuate them by co-optation; and (c) using the persistence of contradictions in society at large to expand the political base and power of a revolutionary movement, that is, a movement for educational reform must understand the social conditions of its emergence and development in the concrete conditions of social life. Unless we achieve such an understanding and use it as the basis of political *action*, a functional reorientation will occur vis-à-vis the present crisis in education, as it did in earlier critical moments in the history of American education.

In the present period, the relevant contradiction involves: (a) Blacks moved from rural independent agriculture and seasonal farm wage-labor to the urban-industrial wage-labor system; (b) middle-class youth with values attuned to economic participation as entrepreneurs, elite white-collar and professional and technical labor, faced with the elimination of entrepreneurship, the corporatization of production, and the proletarianization of white-collar work;[28] and (c) women, the major sufferers of ascriptive discrimination in production (including household production) in an era where capitalist relations of production are increasingly legitimized by their sole reliance on achievement (non-ascriptive) norms.[29]

This inventory is partial, incomplete, and insufficiently analyzed. But only on a basis of its completion can a successful educational strategy be forged. In the realm of contradictions, the correspondence principle must yet provide the method of analysis and action. We must assess political strategies in education on the basis of the single—but distressingly complex—question: will they lead to the transitional society?

I have already argued that de-schooling will inevitably lead to a situation of social chaos, but probably not to a serious mass movement toward constructive social change. In this case the correspondence principle simply fails to hold, producing at best a temporary (in case the ruling elites can find an alternative mode of worker socialization) or ultimately fatal (in case they cannot) breakdown in the social fabric. But only if we posit some essential pre-social human nature on which individuals draw when normal paths of individual development are abolished, might this lead in itself to liberating alternatives.

But the argument over the sufficiency of de-schooling is nearly irrelevant. For schools are so important to the reproduction of capitalist society that they are unlikely to crumble under any but the most massive political onslaughts. 'Each of us', says Illich, 'is personally responsible for his or her own de-schooling, and only we have the power to do it.' This is not true. Schooling is legally *obligatory*, and is the *major means of access* to welfare-relevant activity contexts. The political consciousness behind a frontal attack on institutionalized education would necessarily spill over to attacks on other major institutions. 'The risks of a revolt against school,' says Illich,

> ... are unforeseeable, but they are not as horrible as those of a revolution starting in any other major institution. School is not yet organized for self-protection as effectively as a nation-state, or even a large corporation. Liberation from the grip of schools could be bloodless. (*DS*, p. 49)

This is no more than whistling in the dark.

The only presently viable political strategy in education—and the precise *negation* of Illich's recommendations—is what Rudi Dutschke terms 'the long march through the institutions,' involving localized struggles for what André Gorz calls 'non-reformist reforms,' i.e., reforms which effectively strengthen the power of teachers vis-à-vis administrators, and of students vis-à-vis teachers.

Still, although schools neither can nor should be eliminated, the social relations of education *can* be altered through genuine struggle. Moreover, the experience of both struggle and control prepares the student for a future of political activity in factory and office.

In other words, the correct immediate political goal is the nurturing of individuals both liberated (i.e., demanding control over their lives and outlets for their creative activities and relationships) *and* politically aware of the true nature of their misalignment with the larger society. There may indeed be a bloodless solution to the problem of revolution, but certainly none more simple than this.

Conclusion

Illich recognizes that the problems of advanced industrial societies are institutional, and that their solutions lie deep in the social core. Therefore, he consciously rejects a partial or affirmative analysis which would accept society's dominant ideological forms and direct its innovative contributions toward marginal changes in assumptions and boundary conditions.

Instead, he employs a methodology of total critique and negation, and his successes, such as they are, stem from that choice. Ultimately, however, his analysis is incomplete.

Dialectical analysis begins with society as is (thesis), entertains its negation (antithesis) and *overcomes* both in a radical reconceptualization (synthesis). Negation is a form of demystification—a drawing away from the immediately given by viewing it as a 'negative totality.' But negation is not without presuppositions, is not itself a form of liberation. It cannot 'wipe clean the slate' of ideological representation of the world or one's objective position in it. The son/daughter who acts on the negation of parental and societal values is not free—he/she is merely the constrained negative image of that which he/she rejects (e.g., the negation of work, consumption order, and rationality is not liberation but negative un-freedom). The negation of male dominance is not women's liberation but the (negative) affirmation of 'female masculinity.' Women's liberation in dialectical terms can be conceived of as the overcoming (synthesis) of male dominance (thesis) and female masculinity (antithesis) in a new totality which rejects/embodies both. It is this act of overcoming (synthesis, consciousness) which is the critical and liberating aspect of dialectical thought. Action lies not in the act of negation (antithesis, demystification) but in the act of overcoming (synthesis/consciousness).

The strengths of Illich's analysis lie in his consistent and pervasive methodology of negation. The essential elements in the liberal conceptions of the Good Life—consumption and education, the welfare state and corporate manipulation—are demystified and laid bare in the light of critical, negative thought. Illich's failures can be consistently traced to his refusal to pass *beyond* negations—beyond a total rejection of the appearances of life in advanced industrial societies—to a higher synthesis. While Illich should not be criticized for failing to *achieve* such a synthesis, nevertheless he must be taken seriously to task for mystifying the nature of his own contribution and refusing to step—however tentatively—beyond it. Work is alienating—Illich rejects work; consumption is unfulfilling—Illich rejects consumption; institutions are manipulative—Illich places 'non-addictiveness' at the center of his conception of human institutions; production is bureaucratic—Illich glorifies the entrepreneurial and small-scale enterprise; schools are dehumanizing—Illich rejects schools; political life is oppressive and ideologically totalitarian—Illich rejects politics in favor of individual liberation. Only in one sphere does he go beyond negation, and this defines his major contribution. While technology is in fact dehumanizing (thesis), he does *not* reject technology (antithesis). Rather he goes beyond technology *and* its negation towards a schema of liberating technological forms in education.

The cost of his failure to pass beyond negation in the sphere of social relations in general, curiously enough, is an implicit affirmation of the deepest characteristics of the existing order.[30] In rejecting work, Illich affirms that it *necessarily* is alienating—reinforcing a fundamental pessimism on which the acceptance of capitalism is based; in rejecting consumption, he affirms either that it is inherently unfulfilling (the Protestant ethic), or would be fulfilling if unmanipulated; in rejecting manipulative and bureaucratic 'delivery systems,' he affirms the *laissez-faire* capitalist model and its core institutions; in rejecting schools, Illich embraces a commodity-fetishist cafeteria-smorgasbord ideal in education; and in rejecting political action, he affirms a utilitarian individualistic conception of humanity. In all cases, Illich's analysis fails to pass beyond the given (in both its positive and negative totalities), and hence affirms it.

The most serious lapse in Illich's analysis is his implicit postulation of a human 'essence' in all of us, preceding all social experience—potentially blossoming but repressed by manipulative institutions. Indeed, Illich is logically compelled to accept such a conception by the very nature of his methodology of negation. The given is capitalist (or state socialist) socialization—repressive and dehumanizing. The antithesis is no socialization at all—individuals seeking independently and detached from any mode of social integration their personal paths of development. Such a view of personal growth becomes meaningful in human terms only when anchored in some absolute human standard within the individual and anterior to the social experience that it generates.

In such a conception of individual 'essence,' critical judgment enters, I have emphasized, precisely at the level of sensing and interpreting one's pre-social psyche. This ability requires only demystification (negation); hence a methodology of negation is raised to a sufficient condition of a liberating social science. Dialectical analysis, on the other hand, takes negation (demystification) as the major *precondition* of liberation, but not its sufficient condition. Even the most liberating historical periods (e.g., the Reformation, the French and American Revolutions), despite their florid and passionately idealistic rhetoric, in fact responded to historically specific potentials and to limited but crucial facets of human deprivation. Dialectical analysis would view our present situation as analogous and, rejecting 'human essence' as a pre-social driving force in social change, would see the central struggles of our era as specific negations *and their overcoming* in localizable areas of human concern—while embracing the ideologies that support these struggles.

The place of critical judgment (reason) in this analysis model lies in a realistic visionary annihilation of both existing society *and* its negation-in-thought in a new, yet historically limited, synthesis. I have argued that this task requires as its point of departure the core economic institutions regulating social life—first in coming to understand their operation and the way in which they produce the outcomes of alienating work, fragmented community, environmental destruction, commodity fetishism, and other estranged cultural forms (thesis), and then in entertaining how we might negate and overcome them through political action and personal consciousness. Illich, in his next book, might leave the security and comfort of negation, and apply his creative vitality to this most demanding of tasks.

Acknowledgment

The ideas in this paper were developed in cooperation with Samuel Bowles, whose help in preparing this manuscript was integral.

Notes

* Calder & Boyars, 1971.
1 Illich himself does not use the term 'commodity fetishism.' I shall do so, however, as it is more felicitous than 'institutionalized values' in many contexts.
2 See for instance: Herbert Gintis, 'Commodity Fetishism and Irrational Production', Cambridge, Mass., Harvard Institute for Economic Research, 1970; 'Consumer behavior and the concept of sovereignty', *American Economic Review*, forthcoming; 'A radical analysis of welfare economics and individual development', *Quarterly Journal of Economics*, forthcoming; John K. Galbraith, *The New Industrial State*, Penguin, 1968; Herbert Marcuse, *One-Dimensional Man*, Routledge & Kegan Paul, 1964.
3 Throughout this paper, I restrict my analysis to *capitalist* as opposed to other economic systems of advanced industrial societies (e.g., state-socialism of the Soviet Union type). As Illich suggests, the *outcomes* are much the same, but the *mechanisms* are in fact quite different. The private-administrative economic power of a capitalist elite is mirrored by the public-administrative political power of a bureaucratic elite in state-socialist countries, and both are used to reproduce a similar complex of social relations of production and a structurally equivalent system of class relations. The capitalist variety is emphasized here because of its special relevance in the American context.
4 Gintis, 'Consumer behavior and the concept of sovereignty'.
5 The arguments in this section are presented at greater length in Gintis, 'Power and alienation', in *Readings in Political Economy*, ed. James Weaver, Rockleigh, N. J., Allyn & Bacon, 1972, and 'Consumer behavior and the concept of sovereignty'.
6 This definition conforms to Marxist usage in that 'alienation' refers to *social processes*, not psychological states. For some discussion of this term in Marxist literature, see Gintis, 'Power and alienation', and 'Consumer behavior and the concept of sovereignty'.
7 See Stephen Marglin, 'What do bosses do?', *Review of Radical Political Economics*, 6 (2), 1974.
8 See Michael Reich and David Finkelhor, 'The military-industrial complex', in *The Capitalist System*, ed. Richard C. Edwards, Michael Reich and Thomas Weisskopf, New York, Prentice-Hall, 1972.
9 See Gintis, 'Power and alienation', for a concise summary.
10 Talcott Parsons, *The Structure of Social Action*, Allen & Unwin, 1949.
11 Karl Marx, *The Economic and Philosophical Manuscripts of 1844*, Moscow, Foreign Language Publishing House, 1959, and Karl Marx and Friedrich Engels, *The Germany Ideology*, New York, International Publishers, 1947.
12 The literature on this subject is immense. Illich himself is quite persuasive, but see also Charles E. Silberman, *Crisis in the Classroom*, New York, Random House, 1970, for a more detailed treatment.
13 Gintis, 'Contre-culture et militantisme politique', *Les Temps modernes*, February 1971; 'New working class and revolutionary youth', *Socialist Revolution*, May 1970; and 'Education and the characteristics of worker productivity', *American Economic Review*, May 1971; David Cohen and Marvin Lazerson, 'Education and the corporate order', *Socialist Revolution*, March 1972; Clarence Karier, 'Testing for order and control',† *Educational Theory*, 22, 1972; Michael B. Katz, *The Irony of Early School Reform*, Harvard University Press, 1968, and 'From voluntarism to bureaucracy in American education', *Sociology of Education*, 44,

summer 1971; Joel Spring, 'Education and progressivism', *History of Education*, spring 1970; and Robert Dreeben, *On What Is Learned in Schools*, Reading, Mass., Addison-Wesley, 1968.

14 See Edward F. Denison, *The Sources of Economic Growth in the United States and the Alternatives Before Us*, New York, Committee for Economic Development, 1962; and Theodore Schultz, *The Economic Value of Education*, Columbia University Press, 1963.

15 This surprising result is developed in Gintis, 'Education and the characteristics of worker productivity', and is based on a wide variety of statistical data. It is validated and extended by Christopher Jencks *et al.*, *Education and Inequality*, New York, Basic Books, 1972.

16 See, e.g., Jencks *et al.*

17 For more extensive treatment, see Jencks *et al.* and Gintis, 'Education and the characteristics of worker productivity'.

18 For an analysis of relevant data and an extensive bibliography, see Gintis, 'Education and the characteristics of worker productivity' and 'Alienation and Power', dissertation, Harvard University, 1969.

19 This phenomenon is analyzed in Claus Offe, *Leistungsprinzip und Industrielle Arbeit*, Frankfurt, Europaïsche Verlaganstalt, 1970.

20 See Merle Curti, *The Social Ideas of American Educators*, Chicago, Scribner, 1935; Gintis, 'Contre-culture et militantisme politique'; Gorz, 'Capitalist relations of production and the socially necessary labor force', in *All We Are Saying . . .*, ed. Arthur Lothstein, New York, Putnam, 1970, and 'Technique, techniciens, et lutte de classes'; Samuel Bowles, 'Unequal education and the reproduction of the social division of labor',† in *The Capitalist System*, ed. Edwards, Reich and Weisskopf; and 'Contradictions de l'enseignement supérieure', *Les Temps modernes*, August–September 1971; and David Bruck, 'The Schools of Lowell', unpublished honors thesis, Harvard University, 1971.

21 This statement is supported by the statistical results of Richard C. Edwards, dissertation, Department of Economics, Harvard University, in progress.

22 Katz, *The Irony of Early School Reform* and 'From voluntarism to bureaucracy in American education'; Lawrence Cremin, *The Transformation of the School*, New York, Knopf, 1964; Raymond E. Callahan, *Education and the Cult of Efficiency*, University of Chicago Press, 1962; Curti; Bowles, 'Unequal education and the reproduction of the social division of labor'; Spring; Cohen and Lazerson.

23 See David B. Tyack, *Turning Points in American Educational History*, Boston, Ginn, 1967; and Katz, op. cit.

24 The main elements in Illich's left-convivial 'learning web' alternative to manipulative education are all fundamentally dispersive and fragmenting of a learning community:

1 Reference Services to Educational Objects—which facilitate access to things or processes used for formal learning. Some of these things can be reserved for this purpose, stored in libraries, rental agencies, laboratories, and showrooms like museums and theaters; others can be in daily use in factories, airports, or on farms, but made available to students as apprentices or on off-hours.
2 Skill Exchanges—which permit persons to list their skills, the conditions under which they are willing to serve as models for others who want to learn these skills, and the addresses at which they can be reached.
3 Peer-Matching—a communications network which permits persons to describe the learning activity in which they wish to engage, in the hope of finding a partner for the inquiry.
4 Reference Services to Educators-at-Large—who can be listed in a directory giving the addresses and self-descriptions of professionals, paraprofessionals, and free-lancers, along with conditions of access to their services.

25 Bowles, 'Cuban education and the revolutionary ideology', *Harvard Educational Review*, 41 (4), November 1971.

26 Marco Maccio, 'Parti, technicien et classe ouvrière dans la révolution chinoise', *Les Temps modernes*, August–September 1970; Gorz, 'Techniques, techniciens et lutte de classes'.

27 The theory of political organization which takes *contradictions* among the interests of the various groups participating in the control of a social activity context as central to social development, underlies my argument. This theory is well developed in Chinese Communist thought, as presented in Mao Tse Tung, 'On Contradiction', in *Selected Works*, Peking, Foreign Language Press, 1952, and Franz Schurmann, *Ideology and Organization in Communist China*, Berkeley, University of California Press, 1970. In terms of this 'dialectical theory of political action', the reorganization of power in education in a transitional society must render the contradictions among administrators, teachers, and students *non-antagonistic*, in the sense that the day-to-day outcomes of their struggles are the positive, healthy development of the educational system, beneficial to all parties concerned.

28 Bowles, 'Contradictions de l'enseignement supérieure'; and Gintis, 'Contre-culture et militantisme politique' and 'New working class and revolutionary youth'.

29 For a general discussion of these issues, see *The Capitalist System*, ed. Edwards, Reich and Weisskopf.

30 Indeed to stop one's analysis at negation normally leads to implicit affirmation. For a discussion of this, see 'The affirmative character of culture', in Herbert Marcuse, *Negations*, Boston, Beacon Press, 1968.

† In this volume.

2 Business values and the educational state

Clarence J. Karier

The school, as a formal vehicle of education, exists as an instrument of social and economic power for the most influential elite groups as much as for the political and social organizations through which the society is managed. Thus, in the twentieth century, schools became important instruments of power under capitalism and fascism, as well as under communism. The educational state that emerged in twentieth-century America did so ultimately as an instrument of those economic and political elites who managed the American corporate state. The values and attitudes making up the complicated matrix of that school system are, to a considerable extent, products of the economic and social development in American culture. Although none of the authors of these essays* accepts an economic deterministic position, they do agree that economic concerns have played a major role in shaping our values and attitudes which, in turn, shape our perception of ourselves and our community.

Perhaps Karl Marx was never more insightful than when he pointed to the intimate relationship between man's production and his life-style:[1]

As individuals express their life, so they are. What they are, therefore, coincides with their production both with what they produce and with how they produce. The nature of individuals thus depends on the material conditions determining their productions.

Not only *what* men produce, but *how* they produce is important in considering the creative act of production in which men create themselves as they shape their environment. In the most profound sense, both play and work enter into man's productions and represent the ways in which man recreates himself

Source: C. J. Karier, P. Violas and J. Spring, eds, *Roots of Crisis: American Education in the Twentieth Century*, Rand McNally, 1973, pp. 6–29.

and his world. Whether we consider education as a process of creating a free man in the full dimension of that term, or merely one of training him for specified tasks, the link between man's production and his education is simultaneously obvious and subtle. It is obvious with respect to training skilled workers to man the machines; it is subtle with respect to inculcating the important social-psychological value requisite to the maintenance of a particular economic social system.

American education in general has provided an effective service function to the business community in the training of both producers and consumers. It also has served as the vehicle through which the basic values of a commercial culture are transmitted from generation to generation. Although peripheral values have come and gone and the schools and the business community have changed during the past century, the basic values transmitted have remained fairly constant. When peripheral values change there is social reform; when basic values change there is social revolution. This nation has never undergone a social revolution. Even though America has moved from a *laissez-faire* capitalism to a state welfare capitalism, and the norms of this society have changed from those of producers to those of consumers, the basic values necessary for the maintenance of a capitalist society remain the same. It is my contention that the schools throughout the history of American education have been used as instruments to teach the norms necessary to adjust the young to the changing patterns of the economic system as well as to the society's more permanent values. I further contend that much of the historical evidence seems to indicate that if any major change in the basic core values occurs, it will result from a fundamental shift in the economic system. Starting, then, with the assumption that work and education are fundamentally linked, I intend to trace historically certain selected relationships between the business community and the education of youth so as to delineate some of the key problems now emerging.

Considering the long span of history, there have been relatively few periods in which a basic transformation of values has occurred. In the West, the last such transformation took place during the Reformation. Within that period, one can identify a fundamental change in attitude toward poverty, work, and wealth. In a society of economic scarcity, controlling institutions may reconcile themselves to the economic realities and operate a social system in such a way as to help people accept limitations. Or they may attempt to mobilize the energy of the people to overcome them. The former approach is best represented by the medieval church's caution against fretting about tomorrow and its advocation of the model of God, who through nature takes care to 'feed the birds and clothe the lilies of the field.' The latter approach is best represented by John Calvin, preaching at Geneva the gospel of work, sobriety, and diligence. The difference represents a profound transformation of values ushering in a capitalistic era. Attitudes toward poverty, work, and wealth, premised on scarcity and shaped during the Reformation, have remained the cornerstone of much of American educational practice.

Increasingly, however, many of these values are becoming irrelevant, especially to those groups that have overcome the original problem of scarcity. For the children of those groups, reared in an affluent environment free from the older system's moral demands, the possibility of a fundamental transformation of values exists. Given the likelihood of affluence for greater numbers, we may be on the verge of a transformation of values unparalleled since the Protestant Reformation.[2] The moral demand system premised on scarcity cannot survive in an affluent age.[3] To whatever extent capitalist economics demands a value system premised on scarcity, one is forced to conclude, paradoxically, that the success of capitalism will be responsible for its demise. The possibility of such a demise represents the real danger as well as the promise for the last third of this century —danger, because out of fear or panic those in power may erect a repressive regime against those who threaten the security of those holding the traditional value system; promise, because of the possibility of developing an economic and social system that enhances something other than men's materialistic competitiveness.

The schools and the Puritan ethic

The early development of modern capitalism was tied largely to the new urban bourgeoisie that found expression for its life-style in the church. Especially in Calvinist urban centers, the new business class struggled to find a kind of political and social environment conducive to its own world view. Education always has been the concern of the domin-

ant institution. Therefore, education remained largely a church function until the rise and consolidation of the nation-state.[4] The major transformation of values from a medieval to a capitalistic ethic therefore took place within a religious institution that used education to foster the ethical values of the new business elites.

Both the medieval Catholic church and the Puritans who reflected the new business ethic appreciated the sinful nature of man. The medieval church was reluctant, however, to support the businessman's quest for material goods and capital, whereas Calvin and most Puritans who followed him looked upon this quest as a possible way of honoring and glorifying God. If the community could maintain tight control over the uses of wealth, and if the individual's self-interest was harnessed to a keen sense of duty to God and community, the City of God might yet rise in this world. Always suffering from the acute tension between the ideal and the real, the Puritans hammered out both the logical and the psychological values that came to undergird a capitalistic nation.

Accumulation of capital requires savings. Such savings might be achieved by overt, coercive government action through forced savings—as in the contemporary case of the Soviet Union—or it might be achieved by a more subtle, manipulative approach —through education. By inculcating in each individual a fear of poverty, a desire for wealth, a respect for work, a need for thrift, and a keen sense of duty to be a productive, useful citizen of the community, education produces an ethic conducive to the accumulation of capital. When poverty was no longer seen as a virtue but a vice, a fundamental shift in values had occurred. 'Begging,' one result of the medieval attitude towards poverty, and once seen as a fruitful lesson in humility and charity by members of medieval mendicant orders, now came to be viewed as self-destructive and antisocial. The Puritan knew that God, in His almighty wisdom, had predestined some men to heaven and some to eternal damnation. He also knew that only God knew who was saved. Never certain of salvation, but always looking for a sign, the Puritan acted as though he were a child of the elect. From this point, it was not hard to go on to read the hand of God into one's material success. While wealth was viewed as a sign of election by some, others recognized the dangers to the spirit of religion that might result if community controls over the uses of wealth were ever relaxed. John Wesley put it well when he said:[5]

I fear wherever riches have increased, the essence of religion has decreased in the same proportion. Therefore I do not see how it is possible, in the nature of things, for any revival of true religion to continue long. For religion must necessarily produce both industry and frugality, and these cannot but produce riches. But as riches increase, so will pride, anger, and love of the world in all its branches.

By the end of the eighteenth century, Puritanism as an organized religious influence had all but disappeared in America. What remained was a secularized way of life for an emerging capitalistic nation. Brought up in the Puritan tradition by a strict Calvinist father, Benjamin Franklin personified the secularization of the Puritan tradition and its blend with the Yankee dream of success. Franklin lived in the shadow of the biblical injunction: 'Seest thou a man diligent in his business? He shall stand before kings' (Prov. 22:29). Franklin did indeed stand before kings. With his pen and wit, Franklin captured the core of the American dream of success and those perennial values that underlie the basic structure of this society. His Poor Richard maxims pointed the way to economic success. He, like so many educators before and after him, equated wealth with virtue. As he said, 'Industry multiplied by Frugality gives the product Wealth, which equals Virtue'.[6] It was very much in the Franklin tradition that Edward L. Thorndike and other educators in the twentieth century drew 'scientific' correlations between men of wealth and good character.[7]

The Franklin maxims 'time is money,' 'credit is money,' and 'money is of a prolific generating nature' also taught that work and thrift are rewarded by wealth, which is the keystone to success in any capitalistic society. Franklin argued that begging was to be shunned and poverty despised. Values expounded by Franklin reappeared again and again in children's readers as well as in popular adult literature throughout the nineteenth and twentieth centuries. America was, after all, a capitalistic society, and the values necessary to sustain a competitive materialistic world view for both producer and consumer were necessarily a fundamental part of a citizen's education.

The establishment of common schools followed the triumph of the nation-state. Their mission was to impart the new common values in order to prevent political, social, or economic revolution. The common school was, in fact, perceived by many as a form of police action to protect the system. Daniel Webster said public education is a 'wise and liberal system of police by which property, and life, and the peace of society are secured.'[8] Horace Mann, a key proponent of the common school, viewed its chief social and economic function as 'a balance wheel of the social machinery,' balancing conflicting interests and thus preventing violent revolution. The common school would protect the rights of property, first by teaching the children of the propertyless to believe that the economic system was reasonable and just, rewarding people according to natural abilities and for real contributions to society, and second by teaching that if the student practiced Puritan virtues, he, too, could be successful.[9] Horace Mann, himself a Whig politician and a former corporation lawyer, was very clear about the social impact such a school might have on revolutionaries. In making his case for common schools to the business community, he said:[10]

Finally, in regard to those who possess the largest shares in the stock of worldly goods, could there, in your opinion, be any police so vigilant and effective, for the protection of all the rights of person, property and character, as such a sound and comprehensive education and training as our system of common schools could be made to impart; and would not the payment of a sufficient tax to make such education and training universal, be the cheapest means of self-protection and insurance?

Mann repeatedly reacted to the danger that illiterate Irish immigrants might destroy the business and social institutions of Massachusetts by arguing that the best insurance policy would be an effective common school. The state would use public education as a vehicle of social control and order. Repeatedly the American public turned to the public school to inculcate the common elements of American culture into the children of the 'strangers in the land,' whether those strangers were Irish, Indian, black, southern European, or simply Catholic. This cultural indoctrination was, in fact, what the King Kleagle, Pacific Domain of the Knights of the Ku Klux Klan, had in mind in 1922 when during the Oregon parochial school controversy he said:[11]

it is the settled policy of the Ku Klux Klan and with its white-robed sentinels keeping watch, it shall for all time, with its blazing torches as signal fires, stand guard on the outer walls of the temple of liberty, cry out the warning when danger appears and take its place in the front rank of the defenders of the public schools.

Religious values taught in the common school were Protestant; social values, white Anglo-Saxon; and economic values, Puritan. Little wonder that the KKK would be such a staunch defender of the common school.

Teaching by testing

Although the economic and social situation changed and the role of public education was dramatically extended, schools nevertheless continued to transmit the values necessary for the maintenance of a business ethic. Evidence of this abounds in the texts and tests used in schools, businesses, and the armed forces. The army Alpha Test, used to classify over 1.7 million men in World War I, included questions explicitly reflecting the business ethic. For example, although a medieval mendicant might have difficulty with the following question, neither Franklin nor a graduate of the common school would.

Form D. 10. Why should you not give money to beggars on the street? Because
it breaks up families
it makes it hard for the beggar to get work

it takes away the work of organized charities

☐ it encourages living off of others

Reminiscent of Poor Richard saying, 'Sloth makes all things difficult, but Industry all things easy,' the army tester asked:

Form E. 1   If a man gets tired of his work, he should throw it up

☐ keep at it till the work is done
run away and loaf
make someone else do it

Poor Richard said, 'An Honest Man will receive neither Money nor Praise that is not his due.' The army tester asked:

Form D. 6.   If the grocer should give you too much money in making change, what is the thing to do?
take the money and hurry out

☐ tell him of his mistake
buy some candy with it
give it to the next poor man you meet

In good Puritan fashion, the army tester was concerned about keeping one's accounts straight right to the grave as he asked:

Form C. 4.   If a man knew he would die in two weeks, he should
blow in all his money

☐ make his will and straighten out his accounts
go dig his grave
start out on a sight-seeing trip[12]

Most intelligence tests utilized in schools and factories in America in the twentieth century broadly reflect the dominant Puritan ethic. For example, the Stanford-Binet, a commonly used intelligence test, counts the following answers as 'plus' to the question, What is the difference between work and play?[13]

You work to earn money and you play for fun. One is for amusement and the other for a living. Play is a pleasure and work is something you should do, your duty. Work is energy used for doing something useful and play is just wasting energy. One's recreation—and one's labor. I mean play is an enjoyment and work is something you have to do. Sometimes you enjoy it and sometimes you don't. When you're working you're generally doing something that has to be done—when you're playing you're just doing what you feel like. One is something that most people like to do and the other is a duty. The attitude towards whatever you're doing—if you're playing baseball and don't like to play baseball then it's work—if you're working at mathematics and you like to do it—then it's not work to you anymore. Work you take seriously and play you don't.

The youngster who answers the question correctly must view work as a means of earning money, as distasteful labor, irksome, serious, useful, and duty bound. He must associate play with fun, and view it as amusement, pleasure, a waste of energy, enjoyment, and lacking in seriousness. The correct answer clearly reflects a Puritan ethical attitude toward work and play that has persisted throughout the history of this society. The Stanford-Binet test, far from being culture free, is in fact a clear reflector of the common elements of American culture. It is an accurate predictor of success in a system of education based on these same common cultural elements.

Schools not only help perpetuate those attitudes toward work, wealth, and success necessary in a materialistic, competitive society; they also serve to rationalize and justify the current class system. One second-grade social studies text used in American schools today summarizes the lessons taught as follows:[14]

What did we learn?

1 We go to school to learn about other people.
2 We learn that people look different from each other.
3 People speak different languages.
4 Some people have more than others. Some have less.
5 Some people know more than others. Some know less.
6 Some people can learn a lot. Some people can learn only a little.

From this the second-grade child learns that some people look different and speak differently from others, and that some know more, learn more, and have more wealth than others. Differences in wealth seem to be associated with both knowledge and ability, and they are treated as phenomena as natural as differences in speech or appearance. If the second grader learns this lesson well, he has taken an important step in his socialization—the acceptance and justification of an economically determined social system. The school in both the nineteenth and twentieth centuries not only taught those values that normally sustain a commercial culture, but it also effectively taught the social myths necessary to maintain the social-class system that was a product of the economic order.

The school and its functions

The Marxian thesis holding that changes in the means of production result in significant changes in social institutions and life-styles is demonstrated in American educational history. The growth of large urban centers after the Civil War; the development of the American high school (an urban school); the decline of the academy (appropriate for a rural environment); the development of industrial education, manual training, and vocational guidance and training, as well as the decline of the apprenticeship system; and the enactment of child labor and compulsory education legislation—all are historic developments directly traceable to the newer forms of production that this society adopted.

The creation of a system of mass education followed the shift from handicraft to mass production and the adoption of production-line techniques. Before the turn of the century, the common school was sufficient to maintain what Mann considered the necessary 'balance within the social machinery.' After the turn of the century, there was an extensive consolidation of capital[15] and a tremendous growth of mass production industries. These events in turn stimulated urbanization, the importation of cheap labor from southern Europe, and the growth of urban ghettos. It was apparent that a new 'balance' within the social machinery was needed, one that could provide a systematic and rationalized control of the labor force. Child labor legislation went hand in hand with increased determination to enforce compulsory education laws, many of which were revised upward. Regular school attendance by masses of students in America, however, is a relatively recent phenomenon. In 1900, for example, approximately 10 percent of the high school age group (14–17) was in school; but by 1970, approximately 90 percent of that age group was in school. By then, too, although the compulsory education laws did not extend beyond high school, increasing occupational requirements had made college compulsory in fact for a large number of youth.

The American system of mass education functioned along three distinct but overlapping lines. First, there was the training function. This, in cooperation with business and industry, assisted youth to fulfill occupational requirements in an increasingly complex system. Second, there was the testing and sorting function, an operation based on economic privilege, a fact fairly well obscured by various myths propounded by the educational testers. Third, there was the holding function. The school not only kept children off the labor market, but it also maintained a viable manpower pool for almost every conceivable occupation. In *What Doctrines to Embrace*, Merle Borrowman and Charles Burgess persuasively argue that the rhetoric of educational reform in the twentieth century shifts from consumer to producer values as shortages occur in the total manpower pool.[16] When, for example, the reformer's rhetoric advocates a child oriented–consummatory function, he is serving, in effect, the need of the system to hold potential workers in the educational institution and off the production line. When, however, the rhetoric advocates a society oriented–productive function, he is serving the need of the system for trained personnel on the production line. In either case the educational reformer is a servant of the system. If one considers

this thesis in the light of demographic projections of manpower surplus in the decade of the seventies, one might expect the reform rhetoric to be child oriented–consummatory. Despite its intentions, however, the school is having increasingly serious difficulty maintaining its holding function. The increased numbers of 'phantom' schools[17] in large urban areas is empirical testimony to the difficulty of pursuing the holding function when myths involving academic achievement and occupational opportunities are no longer considered credible.

Although schools have always played some role in training and selection for the economic and social system, it was not until the latter part of the nineteenth century in Germany and the first half of the twentieth century in America that they became the major vehicle for economic and political control. With the unification of the German states, it was clear that the newly industrialized nation had ignored von Humboldt's warning about the dangers to human freedom inherent in the positive state.[18] The new Germany used coercive political machinery to resolve all sorts of economic and social problems created by new mass production industries. The idea of the compulsory state and its corollary, compulsory education, was born in Germany. The many thousands of American students who attended German universities in the nineteenth century carried it to America. In Germany, political leaders used state power to head off radical socialist demands by ameliorating the condition of the workers. In America, state authority was utilized to curb radical populism[19] as well as radical labor agitation.[20] The major impetus of progressive reform, whether political or educational, was to make the system work efficiently and effectively. Progressives were willing to use the compulsory power of the state to achieve that end. Progressive reform was indeed conservative.[21] So, for that matter, were many state socialists. They were conservative in their quest for efficiency and orderly change and in their desire to maintain the system. By World War I much of the progressive reformers' work had been institutionalized in the form of government regulation of commerce, labor, industry, and banking.

Like members of the eighteenth-century Enlightenment, twentieth-century progressives called not only for improvement of the economic-political system, but also for the perfectibility of the race. Laws prohibiting racial intermarriage increased as sterilization of the mentally unfit and the criminally insane also became part of the twentieth-century progressive reform era.[22] The eugenic movement in America, very much an outgrowth of the progressive era, was functionally related to the testing movement that proved its utility during World War I. From testing the mentally unfit and criminally insane, testers moved to testing army officers and to classifying over 1.7 million men. After the war, men like Thorndike, Goddard, Terman, and Yerkes applied what they had learned to millions of children in the rapidly expanding public school system. Under the guise of 'scientific objectivity' the testers measured millions of students against their own peculiar model of a successful man. The model usually turned out to be white, Protestant, and middle class. The early testing movement reflected the strong elitist and racist values of the testers[23] as well as of the general culture. The testers repeatedly found strong correlation between intelligence, wealth, and character. Little wonder! Thorndike best represented that tendency when he said, 'To him that hath a superior intellect is given also on the average a superior character; the quick boy is also in the long run more accurate; the able boy is also more industrious.'[24] 'Scientific' testers also helped standardize and rationalize the school along business lines. The business community used their work to classify and manage labor,[25] and Congress found it useful in developing a rationale for restricting the immigration of southern Europeans in 1924.[26] In teacher education, the test and measurement movement helped develop and perpetuate the myth of 'scientific professionalism' as well as the use of the IQ test as a device for organizing schools along social-class lines.

Utilizing the works of Lester F. Ward, Albion Small, and E. A. Ross, such educators as George D. Strayer (school administration),[27] David Snedden (vocational education),[28] and Frank Parsons (vocational guidance)[29] sought to develop education for social efficiency. By the 1920s, industrial education as well as general education was organized and developed along lines of social efficiency and control.[30] Tester, administrator, and guidance counselor—all seemed dedicated to rationalizing and standardizing the system of mass education, adjusting the child to the needs of the system. Throughout the early decades of the twentieth century, most guidance counselors considered it their chief function to match native and acquired talents with the system's manpower needs, thus increasing the efficiency of both the individual and the system. Frank Parsons said:[31]

> Superior efficiency flows from natural fitness—education, special and general, physical, intellectual and moral—and the influence of feelings which produce enthusiastic and painstaking labor. A sensible industrial system will therefore seek to make these feelings factors in every piece of work, to put men, as well as timber, stone, and iron, in the places for which their natures fit them—and to polish and prepare them for efficient service with at least as much care as is bestowed upon clocks, electric dynamos, or locomotives.

Industry, allied with schools, would 'polish and prepare' the young for efficient service. Owing to the difficulty of providing up-to-date training in a rapidly changing industrial system, while some youth received skill training in vocational technical schools, most were trained on the jobs. Actually, American industry operated the largest vocational technical-training school in the world. Although the extreme efficiency rhetoric of the earlier part of the century became subdued during the depression of the 1930s, public schools, from the kindergarten through the vocational technical and graduate schools, continued to serve the manpower needs of the business community by providing large numbers of trainable people who would easily fit into the industrial system.

Maintaining the system

The development of the Cold War and the creation of the military-industrial complex caused an acute shortage of skilled manpower. Now a second phase of the social efficiency movement in American education emerged. Those persons who once thought in terms of social efficiency now talked of manpower models, as they saw the school at all levels as an instrument to serve the manpower needs of a new technetronic society. Just as the stopwatch and Taylor symbolized the early efficiency movement, so the computer, cybernetics, Norbert Wiener, and systems analysis came to symbolize the new efficiency thrust. Among those who thought in terms of the overall needs of society during the Cold War, James B. Conant was perhaps the most influential figure. His influence was due partly to his prestigious career, and partly to his association with the Carnegie Foundation and the role that foundation had played in shaping educational policy at all levels of education. Foundations have played a major role in maintaining the corporate liberal state as well as in shaping educational policy to serve the interests of that state.[32] In virtually all of his published work on education in the post-World War II period, including *The American High School*, *The Junior High School*, and *Slums and Suburbs*, Conant repeatedly expressed his central concern for the maintenance of what he perceived as a democratic society. Reflecting the new efficiency values, Conant called for a national testing program that could provide an educational achievement index that was much like a gross national product.

Conant's educational recommendations directly followed from his conception of the good society. That was the competitive, open society where hard, honest work would be rewarded. Conant personified those Franklin virtues of work and diligence as well as a sense of calling and duty to the larger community. He was a Yankee pragmatic liberal who, like John Dewey and others, reflected the strength as well as the weakness of the liberal tradition. As an astute student of the possible, Conant turned moral questions into tactical survival problems. Avoidance of moral issues by emphasizing practical expediency was, however, as American as *Poor Richard's Almanac*. American pragmatic philosophy was functionally useful in developing a capitalistic system, but it failed to deal with the moral issues of the day. Thus Dewey did not find a moral issue in reporting how to effectively manipulate the Polish laborer in the national economic interest any more than Conant found a moral issue in the development of gas as a lethal weapon, or the dropping of the atomic bomb on Hiroshima. Pragmatism was a philosophy dedicated to the system's survival. Although some people questioned Conant's judgment, no one impugned his loyalty to the system and his dedication to making it work. His recommendations in *The American High School* and *The Junior High School* and *Slums and Suburbs* were to make the schools more vocationally efficient and more effective in sorting and holding students. Thus, Conant called for increased federal support for vocational guidance.

Turning to the problem of the urban ghetto, Conant again saw vocational training and guidance as solutions to problems. Very much like Horace Mann a hundred years before, Conant argued that if the ghetto dweller could be trained and guided into the mainstream of American economic life, the 'social dynamite' might be defused and the system saved from serious disruption. Interlaced throughout the discussion of American racism during the sixties was Conant's argument about cooling off the social dynamite through training for economic opportunity. The Kerner Report, for example, clearly and decisively indicted white America as racist, then failed to take the next logical step and call for an effective educational program for the children of white Americans in order to eliminate that racism. Instead, the Report proposed special education for black children.[33] One might conclude from the Kerner Report simply that the problem was not white racist attitudes, but rather black failure to meet sufficient standards to enter the economic system.[34] The burden of performance thus fell on black children. Interestingly, the economic opportunity argument could be used not only to support the idea of cooling off social dynamite, but also to transfer guilt within the system from those who held power to those who were victimized by that power.

By the end of the 1960s, both conservatives and liberals joined in common cause to protect and maintain the system. One could observe such a strange phenomenon as Milton Friedman (an avowed conservative economist) advocating such liberal, if not socialist, measures as guaranteed minimum family incomes in the interest of the system's maintenance. When both economists and manpower experts began to speak of an 'acceptable' level of unemployment,[35] it was evident not only that unemployment was here to stay, but even more important, that managers considered it essential to the efficient operation of the system. The unemployment pool was, in effect, a shock absorber for the economic system. For that shock absorber to function effectively, certain conditions were necessary. Those unfortunate enough to be caught in the pool had to be actively striving for employment, thus guaranteeing employers a ready and eager labor supply. In order to facilitate that condition, a graduated income was proposed. Employers of both production and service industries could then readily obtain employees and release them to the pool whenever their services were no longer required. In an interesting way, Conant's manpower-oriented educational proposal for urban slum dwellers was the complement of Milton Friedman's welfare proposal. Both served to create a manpower pool that would efficiently serve the system, and at the same time defuse the social dynamite with the least possible disruption. Neither proposal was seriously designed to eliminate the urban ghetto or the unemployment pool itself. The major threat to the system came when the Black Panthers and black nationalists generally refused to be co-opted. These groups then represented an uncontrollable threat, and therefore came under direct police action.

A key Conant recommendation for the American high school was the establishment of extensive vocational guidance services. When federal funds were increased over the following decade, they were used to support a guidance movement that increasingly directed its major efforts at psychological therapy rather than vocational guidance. The difference between the work of Frank Parsons in vocational counseling and Carl Rogers in nondirective therapy is indicative of that trend.

Individual as well as group therapy was used to overcome the alienation and depersonalization resulting from the workings of the complex bureaucratic machinery. By the late fifties and early sixties, sensitivity training as developed by such educators as Benne, Bradford, and Lippitt was found useful in overcoming and alleviating some of the personnel problems in industry and education, as well as in the churches.[36] Problems of alienation in the technetronic world were acute. Few workers—production-line, blue-collar, or white-collar—were fortunate enough to find their work intellectually, socially, and psychologically satisfying. For most, 'work' was a period of lost time, an experience from which one needed periodic escapes. The schools reflected the meaninglessness and helplessness that infected the world of technetronic change.

A high percentage of the 59 million students now in school have learned to live by the bell and passively tolerate boredom, irrelevance, and absurdity in their educational lives in order to achieve future material rewards accruing from selected occupations. Some thinkers have suggested that students therefore have been well trained and effectively prepared for the life they will be expected to live within the system. Many observers reject such preparation as a goal and argue for a more relevant curriculum and better teachers. The problem lies deeper than that. It lies in the very nature of this particular culture, in its values, and in the way it uses its educational system. For example, there may be something inherently contradictory between trying to 'educate' for individual growth, and at the same time trying to select the 'best' for the economic system. Karl Popper suggests that the latter is an impossible task with which an educational system should never be burdened. As he said:[37]

> This should never be made their task. Their tendency transforms our educational system into a race-course, and turns a course of studies into a hurdle-race. Instead of encouraging the student to devote himself to his studies for the sake of studying, instead of encouraging in him a real love for his subject and for inquiry, he is encouraged to study for the sake of his personal career; he is led to acquire only such knowledge as is serviceable in getting him over the hurdles which he must clear for the sake of his advancement. In other words, even in the field of science, our methods of selection are based upon an appeal to personal ambition of a somewhat crude form. (It is a natural reaction to this appeal if the eager student is looked upon with suspicion by his colleagues.) The impossible demand for an institutional selection of the intellectual leaders endangers the very life not only of science, but of intelligence.

Schools from the kindergarten to the university in the twentieth century negated the goal of educating for personal growth by playing a selecting and sorting role. More disturbing still, they became a manpower holding institution for the economic community. It is probably no overstatement to suggest that of the 59 million students now in school, at least 20 million are physically and mentally capable of manning most of the occupations that now exist. We have reached the absurd height of requiring twelve years of formal schooling for such occupations as clerk or night watchman. Such was not the case in the world of Benjamin Franklin. The young Franklin could move from occupation to occupation with relative ease. To be sure, in the two centuries that separate Franklin from the youth of today, American society has created a complicated technological system with a vast array of specialties. Most of these specialties, however, require minimal skills that can be learned in a relatively short time. Educational requirements are usually grossly inflated. They are concocted more in the interest of controlling labor supply than in satisfying job requirements. Employers have used inflated job requirements also to veil racial discrimination. The cooperation of educational institutions to inflate job requirements in order to delay entrance into the world of adult work creates a kind of institutional hypocrisy that seriously impairs the role of the school as a credible vehicle of education. To many students and observers, the school has become a part of the overall bureaucratic structure that imprisons people's lives. Youthful protest literature often repeats the theme of imprisonment.

For example:[38]

> the grammar school—high school—university mass education—death trip. Little classrooms, cramped with sitting, suffocating children. 'Don't talk, children, sit there and listen to me for the next six hours, for the next five days, for the next forty weeks. If you successfully pass through the first eight years imprisonment, you can do four more years in high school. Then, if you are intelligent, fortunate, and have money enough, you can do four more years in a university. Then you can graduate and proudly be imprisoned in offices, factories, and institutions throughout the world until, at long last, you are sixty-five. Then you are free to take off more than two weeks in a row.' ('Don't ask stupid questions')
> ('I'm busy right now')
> 'Amen brother.'

Delaying the young's entry into adult life produces profound social-psychological consequences. Franklin knew no adolescent culture, largely because he lived in a society that put youth into the labor market as quickly as possible. 'Youth culture,' with its unique psychology, sociology, economic needs, and tastes, is largely a by-product of the social conditioning used to delay entrance into adult life. The youth culture phenomenon is related to the needs of an industrial society to delay adulthood and increasingly to standardize, control, and create consumer demands among various discrete age groups from childhood to adulthood. The decline of the family as an educational unit, the rise of the peer group, as well as the proliferation of offerings through the mass media are all parts of the youth culture syndrome. The process, it seems, is one of creating, through means of mass media, a self-image and a set of behavioral expectations that effectively set the age group apart from the control of the adult. The process replaces adult control with peer group control, which is fairly susceptible to commercial manipulation. Here, again, as in the earlier efficiency movement, psychologists and sociologists played a facilitating role. While psychologists developed their own psychology of adolescence, educational sociologists such as Robert J. Havighurst spoke of 'developmental tasks.' Presumably based on both the psychological and sociological life of the child, each age group had its own tasks to be learned. Here, then, was an educational ladder up which the young might slowly climb out of the immature status to which the overall system had confined them. Each rung of that ladder was polished with the success-oriented achievement values of middle-class America, all of which held little meaning for children of the rich or the poor.

Children at both the top and the bottom of the socioeconomic ladder threatened Havighurst's middle-class world. Children of the affluent, free from the threatening sanctions of the system, found they could afford the luxury of their ideals. Radical white youth challenged the system by arguing that institutions, like men, ought to behave with moral purpose. The suggestion, for example, that the university was a moral institution and ought therefore to be self-conscious about the moral implications of its decisions seemed to strike fear in the hearts and confusion in the minds of trustees and administrators of most institutions of higher learning. Affluence not only led radical youth to question some of the basic Franklin virtues of success, but it also provided freedom from the controlling demands of career preparation. Radical questioning of the system occurred in the arts colleges, seldom in the professional schools, mainly because of the conservative effect of the latter's vocational orientation. People bending every effort to make it within a system cannot afford the luxury of criticizing that system. They may well put their careers in jeopardy. The arts college student, all other things being equal, was in a considerably freer position than other university students.

Means become ends

For most Americans, the possibility of gaining the economic and social requisites to exercise independent social criticism remained little more than a distant hope. The desire to maintain the economic-social value system without serious confrontation with its moral bearings continued to be an important characteristic of this society. American society, driven by anxious materialistic private-profit motives and narrow self-interest, did not disappear with the prosperity of the post-World War II period, nor did a transformation of values occur. On the contrary, World War II and the Cold War that followed gave birth to the warfare state. This phenomenon had the effect of postponing any serious confrontation with the system's purposes. The economic system was now maintained by a kind of military capitalism which under the guise of public interest, increasingly developed a larger control, not only over foreign affairs, but over the internal economic and social affairs of the nation.[39] With military expenditures at well over $1,000 billion in the postwar period and with 63 percent of all American scientists, engineers, and technicians working on defense projects, by 1970 it was clear that the American economy depended on a military budget for its survival. If peace broke out and military spending halted, it has been estimated that the unemployment rate of 5 percent would increase to approximately 15 percent—a level fairly close to that of 1939.[40] Since universities were the prime source of power directing the scientific and technological developments in the Cold War decades, their interests intertwined with those of government and industry.[41] With scientists employed by the industrial-military complex for national security reasons, the question of a society driven by private profit motives and its self-destructive character seemed irrelevant. Increasingly, many observers came

to agree with Michael Harrington that things seemed out of control and that this has been *The Accidental Century*—a century driven by the apparent necessities of technical efficiency, yet guided by no overriding humane philosophy. All kinds of artists in the post-war era repeatedly expressed the despair, chaos, and helplessness of man in a technocracy substantially out of human control.[42] A society driven by anticommunist hatreds and guided by the technologically possible had little inclination to reflect in terms of a philosophy of man or society.

The alliance of industry, government, the military, and education produced an age of considerable affluence for an ever larger middle class. As America both ideologically and practically out-materialized the Soviet Union, the American way of life came to mean little more than a vast and continuous consumption of goods and services. Fewer and fewer voices in the great middle class—most members of which existed as kept agents of the system—were heard asking the naive question, What truly humane purposes does the system serve? Most people seemed concerned only with keeping the system going and extending its co-opting benefits to minority groups that remained outside.

As population and cybernation increased, many thinkers envisioned an educational state processing people from the cradle to the grave by the end of the century. Thus, by the late sixties, Xerox, RCA, General Learning Corporation, CBS, IBM, and many other corporations entered the 'knowledge industry' field, eager to capture a share of a market estimated at possibly $50 billion a year.

The new efficiency movement emerging served both the industrial-military complex and the educational establishment. In this movement, Rand and Systems Development Corporation played an active role. Fresh from his experiences with Systems Development, Robert Boguslaw wrote about *The New Utopias* (1965) he envisioned. There was no need, he argued, for concern with the nature of man or, for that matter, his psychological needs. Simply plug man into the system and he would adjust to whatever demands the system makes. Boguslaw went on to point out that the purpose of human engineering was to eliminate the human factor as much as possible. Along the same lines, Norbert Wiener earlier suggested that the question of human purposes might also be settled by engineering techniques. Wiener argued, 'As engineering technique becomes more and more able to achieve human purposes, it must become more and more accustomed to formulate human purposes.'[43] Perceptively describing modern society, Jacques Ellul, in his *Technological Society*, pointed out that gradually the overall system takes over and techniques do become ends in themselves.

Means had become ends and the perfection of technique, not the perfection of man, had become the standard. As their lives increasingly became objectified, depersonalized, and systematized, and as the technological system was used more and more not only to create means, but also ends, independent of human will, Americans reached a critical stage in the idea of enlightened progress. The materialism that gave meaning to an earlier generation now appeared not only crass, but without meaning to some of the younger generation. The revolt of the younger generation became, in part, a revolt against the meaninglessness of middle-class life measured in terms of material fulfillment without human purpose. And that revolt holds the greatest promise for a transformation of values necessary for a humane age.

Historically, however, this has been a society that has rather consistently avoided examining its moral roots. If it had examined them, it might have pondered the wisdom of consistently respecting and honoring those who, from Franklin on, found success in materialistic, competitive, cunning, and self-seeking behavior. These are the Franklin virtues undergirding a capital-producing society that the schools, down to the present, have reinforced rather effectively. These values were productive in the development of the wealthiest technological state in the world, but counter-productive concerning development of a moral culture based on humane considerations. So we have both dilemma and promise in the present age. American society may yet move from the materialistic spirit of capitalism to a transformation of values. There might still be the time and the possibility in the affluent cybernated age of the future to usher in a humane age that will enhance the dignity of man.

Notes

1 Quoted in Erich Fromm, *Marx's Concept of Man*, New York, Ungar, 1961, p. 10.
2 See Paul Goodman, 'The new reformation', *New York Times*, 14 September 1969. To be sure, other nations have achieved varying degrees of affluence by following other historical routes than that utilized in the West. See, for example, David C. McClelland, *The Achieving Society*, Princeton, N.J., Van Nostrand, 1961. My discussion here, however, is confined to the historical development of American capitalism.
3 See Philip Rieff, *The Triumph of the Therapeutic*, New York, Harper & Row, 1966. See also Charles A. Reich, *The Greening of America*, New York, Random House, 1970.
4 This occurred at different times in different nations. In most cases when it occurred, heresy ceased to be a crime punishable by death. Treason took its place.
5 Max Weber, *The Protestant Ethic and the Spirit of Capitalism*, New York, Scribner's, 1958, p. 175.
6 Benjamin Franklin, *Poor Richard's Almanac*, New York, Doran, 1928, p. xvii.
7 See Merle Curti, *The Social Ideas of American Educators*, New York, Scribner's, 1935.
8 As quoted by Charles Burgess in 'The Educational State in America', PhD dissertation, University of Wisconsin, 1962, p. 146.
9 See Horace Mann, *Twelfth Annual Report* (1848).
10 Quoted in Lawrence A. Cremin, *The Republic and the School*, New York, Bureau of Publications, Teachers College, Columbia University, 1951, p. 53.
11 David Tyack, 'The perils of pluralism: the background of the Pierce case', *American Historical Review*, 74, October 1968, 74–98.
12 Robert M. Yerkes, *National Academy of Sciences—Memoirs XV*, Washington, D.C., US Government Printing Office, 1921, p. 215.
13 Lewis M. Terman and Maud A. Merrill, *Stanford-Binet Intelligence Scale*, Boston, Houghton Mifflin, 1960, p. 213.
14 Lawrence Senesh, *Our Working World: Neighbors at Work*, Chicago, Science Research Associates, 1965, pp. 177–8.
15 In 1897, the total capitalization of all corporations individually valued at a million dollars or more came to only $170 million. Three years later, the same figure for total capitalization stood at $5 billion, and in 1904 at over $20 billion. Charles Forcey, *The Crossroads of Liberalism*, Oxford University Press, 1961, p. xiv.
16 Glenview, Ill., Scott, Foresman, 1969, pp. 113–37.
17 Phantom schools are those schools with an absentee rate so high that they operate most of the year without students.
18 See Wilhelm von Humboldt, *Limits of State Action*, ed. J. W. Burrow, Cambridge University Press, 1969.
19 See Norman Pollack, *The Populist Response to Industrial America*, New York, Norton, 1962. See also William Appleman Williams, *The Roots of the Modern American Empire*, New York, Random House, 1969.
20 See James Weinstein, *The Corporate Ideal in the Liberal State, 1900–1918*, Boston, Beacon Press, 1968.
21 See Gabriel Kolko, *The Triumph of Conservatism*, New York, Free Press, 1965.
22 See Mark H. Haller, *Eugenics: Hereditarian Attitudes in American Thought*, Rutgers University Press, 1963, p. 158.
23 For one example, see Edward L. Thorndike, 'The psychology of the half-educated man', *Harper's*, 140, April 1920, 666–7.
24 Edward L. Thorndike, 'Intelligence and its uses', *Harper's*, 140, January 1920, 233.
25 See Loren Baritz, *The Servants of Power: A History of the Use of Social Sciences in American Industry*, New York, Wiley, 1960.
26 For the extremely questionable data and its use, see Kimball Young, 'Intelligence of certain immigrant groups', *Scientific Monthly*, 15, 1922, 444; H. H. Laughlin, *An Analysis of America's Melting Pot*, House Committee on Immigration and Naturalization, 68th Congress, 1st session, 8 March 1929, p. 1311; House Committee on Immigration and Naturalization, *Europe as an Emigrant-Exporting Continent and the United States as an Immigrant-Receiving Nation*, by H. H. Laughlin, 68th Congress, 1st session, 8 March 1924, p. 1311. For the inferiority of the racial groups, see T. R. Garth, 'The intelligence of Mexican school children', *School and Society*, 27, 20 June 1928, 794; also R. A. Schwegler, 'A comparative study of the intelligence of white and colored children', *Journal of Educational Research*, 2, December 1920, 846.

27 See Raymond E. Callahan, *Education and the Cult of Efficiency*, University of Chicago Press, 1932.

28 See Walter H. Drost, *David Snedden and Education for Social Efficiency*, University of Wisconsin Press, 1967.

29 See Howard V. Davis, *Frank Parsons*, Southern Illinois University Press, 1969.

30 See Bernice M. Fisher, *Industrial Education*, University of Wisconsin Press, 1967.

31 *The City for the People*, Philadelphia, C. F. Taylor, 1900, p. 68.

32 See David W. Eakins, 'The Development of Corporate Liberal Policy Research in the United States, 1885–1965', PhD dissertation, University of Wisconsin, 1966. Also see Merle Curti and Roderick Nash, *Philanthropy in the Shaping of American Higher Education*, Rutgers University Press, 1965.

33 See Bernard Spodek, 'So it doesn't whistle', *Illinois Schools Journal*, 49, spring 1969, 49.

34 For an interesting discussion of the way Americans implement their commission findings, see Catherine Caldwell, 'Social science as ammunition', *Psychology Today*, 4, September 1970, 38ff.

35 One always wonders, 'acceptable' to whom? For an interesting analysis of the relationship of unemployment and education, see Willard Wirtz, 'Remarks of the Honorable W. Willard Wirtz', in *Proceedings* of the Symposium on Employment, Washington, D.C., 1964, sponsored by the American Bankers' Association.

36 See Leland P. Bradford, J. R. Gibb, and K. D. Benne, eds, *T-Group Theory and Laboratory Method: Innovation and Re-education*, New York, Wiley, 1967. See also Chris Argyris, *Explorations and Issues in Laboratory Education*, Washington, D.C., National Training Laboratories, NEA, 1966.

37 *The Open Society and Its Enemies*, Routledge & Kegan Paul, 5th ed., 1966, vol. 1, pp. 135–6.

38 Jesse Kornbluth, *Notes from the New Underground*, New York, Viking Press, 1960.

39 For an interesting discussion of this problem, see Ithiel de Sola Pool's article in *Scientific Research*, 15 September 1969.

40 See Seymour Melman, *Pentagon Capitalism: The Political Economy of War*, New York, McGraw-Hill, 1970.

41 See James Ridgeway, *The Closed Corporation*, New York, Random House, 1968.

42 Interestingly, even our utopian literature has become antiutopian. Aldous Huxley's *Brave New World* and George Orwell's *1984* were both a warning and a prediction of things to come. The future they projected held little hope for individual dignity and freedom. Most disturbing, however, was the fact that Huxley's world of 'soma' and 'test-tube babies' and Orwell's world of 'double-think' became more and more a part of the social reality of twentieth-century man.

43 *God and Golem, Inc.*, MIT Press, 1964, p. 64.

* In *Roots of Crisis*

3 Unequal education and the reproduction of the social division of labor

Samuel Bowles

The ideological defense of modern capitalist society rests heavily on the assertion that the equalizing effects of education can counter the disequalizing forces inherent in the free-market system. That educational systems in capitalist societies have been highly unequal is generally admitted and widely condemned. Yet educational inequalities are taken as passing phenomena, holdovers from an earlier, less enlightened era, which are rapidly being eliminated.

The record of educational history in the United States, and scrutiny of the present state of our colleges and schools, lend little support to this comforting optimism. Rather, the available data suggest an alternative interpretation. In what follows I argue that schools have evolved in the United States not as (1) part of a pursuit of equality, but rather to meet the needs of capitalist employers for a disciplined and skilled labor force, and to provide a mechanism for social control in the interests of political stability; (2) that as the economic importance of skilled and well-educated labor has grown, inequalities in the school system have become increasingly important in reproducing the class structure from one generation to the next; (3) that the US school system is pervaded by class inequalities, which have shown little sign of diminishing over the last half century; and (4) that the evidently unequal control over school boards and other decision-making bodies in education does not provide a sufficient explanation of the persistence and pervasiveness of inequalities in the school system. Although the unequal distribution of political power serves to maintain inequalities in education, the origins of these inequalities are to be found outside the political sphere, in the class structure itself and in the class subcultures typical of capitalist societies. Thus, unequal education has its roots in the very class structure which it serves to legitimize and reproduce. Inequalities in education are part of the web of capitalist society, and are likely to persist as long as capitalism survives.

The evolution of capitalism and the rise of mass education

In colonial America, and in most pre-capitalist societies of the past, the basic productive unit was the family. For the vast majority of male adults, work was self-directed, and was performed without direct supervision. Though constrained by poverty, ill health, the low level of technological development, and occasional interferences by the political authorities, a man had considerable leeway in choosing his working hours, what to produce, and how to produce it. While great inequalities in wealth, political power, and other aspects of status normally existed, differences in the degree of autonomy in work were relatively minor, particularly when compared with what was to come.

Transmitting the necessary productive skills to the children as they grew up proved to be a simple task, not because the work was devoid of skill, but because the quite substantial skills required were virtually unchanging from generation to generation, and because the transition to the world of work did not require that the child adapt to a wholly new set of social relationships. The child learned the concrete skills and adapted to the social relations of production through learning by doing within the family. Preparation for life in the larger community was facilitated by the child's experience with the extended family, which shaded off without distinct boundaries, through uncles and fourth cousins, into the community. Children learned early how to deal with complex relationships among adults other than their parents, and children other than their brothers and sisters.[1]

Source: M. Carnoy, ed., *Schooling in a Corporate Society: the Political Economy of Education in America*, David McKay, 1972, pp. 36–46, 48–52, 54–64.

Children were not required to learn a complex set of political principles or ideologies, as political participation was limited and political authority unchallenged, at least in normal times. The only major socializing institution outside the family was the church, which sought to inculcate the accepted spiritual values and attitudes. In addition, a small number of children learned craft skills outside the family, as apprentices. The role of schools tended to be narrowly vocational, restricted to preparation of children for a career in the church or the still inconsequential state bureaucracy.[2] The curriculum of the few universities reflected the aristocratic penchant for conspicuous intellectual consumption.[3]

The extension of capitalist production, and particularly the factory system, undermined the role of the family as the major unit of both socialization and production. Small peasant farmers were driven off the land or competed out of business. Cottage industry was destroyed. Ownership of the means of production became heavily concentrated in the hands of landlords and capitalists. Workers relinquished control over their labor in return for wages or salaries. Increasingly, production was carried on in large organizations in which a small management group directed the work activities of the entire labor force. The social relations of production—the authority structure, the prescribed types of behavior and response characteristic of the work place—became increasingly distinct from those of the family.

The divorce of the worker from control over production—from control over his own labor—is particularly important in understanding the role of schooling in capitalist societies. The resulting social division of labor—between controllers and controlled—is a crucial aspect of the class structure of capitalist societies, and will be seen to be an important barrier to the achievement of social-class equality in schooling.

Rapid economic change in the capitalist period led to frequent shifts of the occupational distribution of the labor force, and constant changes in the skill requirements for jobs. The productive skills of the father were no longer adequate for the needs of the son during his lifetime. Skill training within the family became increasingly inappropriate.

And the family itself was changing. Increased geographic mobility of labor and the necessity for children to work outside the family spelled the demise of the extended family and greatly weakened even the nuclear family.[4] Meanwhile, the authority of the church was questioned by the spread of secular rationalist thinking and the rise of powerful competing groups.

While undermining the main institutions of socialization, the development of the capitalist system created at the same time an environment— both social and intellectual—which would ultimately challenge the political order. Workers were thrown together in oppressive factories, and the isolation

which had helped to maintain quiescence in earlier, widely dispersed peasant populations was broken down.[5] With an increasing number of families uprooted from the land, the workers' search for a living resulted in large-scale labor migrations. Transient, even foreign, elements came to constitute a major segment of the population, and began to pose seemingly insurmountable problems of assimilation, integration, and control.[6] Inequalities of wealth became more apparent, and were less easily justified and less readily accepted. The simple legitimizing ideologies of the earlier period—the divine right of kings and the divine origin of social rank, for example —fell under the capitalist attack on the royalty and the traditional landed interests. The general broadening of the electorate—first sought by the capitalist class in the struggle against the entrenched interests of the pre-capitalist period—threatened soon to become an instrument for the growing power of the working class. Having risen to political power, the capitalist class sought a mechanism to ensure social control and political stability.[7]

An institutional crisis was at hand. The outcome, in virtually all capitalist countries, was the rise of mass education. In the United States, the many advantages of schooling as a socialization process were quickly perceived. The early proponents of the rapid expansion of schooling argued that education could perform many of the socialization functions that earlier had been centered in the family and, to a lesser extent, in the church.[8] An ideal preparation for factory work was found in the social relations of the school: specifically, in its emphasis on discipline, punctuality, acceptance of authority outside the family, and individual accountability for one's work.[9] The social relations of the school would replicate the social relations of the work place, and thus help young people adapt to the social division of labor. Schools would further lead people to accept the authority of the state and its agents—the teachers—at a young age, in part by fostering the illusion of the benevolence of the government in its relations with citizens.[10] Moreover, because schooling would ostensibly be open to all, one's position in the social division of labor could be portrayed as the result not of birth, but of one's own efforts and talents.[11] And if the children's everyday experiences with the structure of schooling were insufficient to inculcate the correct views and attitudes, the curriculum itself would be made to embody the bourgeois ideology.[12] Where pre-capitalist social institutions, particularly the church, remained strong or threatened the capitalist hegemony, schools sometimes served as a modernizing counter-institution.[13]

The movement for public elementary and secondary education in the United States originated in the nineteenth century in states dominated by the burgeoning industrial capitalist class, most notably in Massachusetts. It spread rapidly to all parts of the country except the South.[14] In Massachusetts the extension of elementary education was in large measure a response to industrialization, and to the need for social control of the Irish and other non-Yankee workers recruited to work in the mills.[15] The fact that some working people's movements had demanded free instruction should not obscure the basically coercive nature of the extension of schooling. In many parts of the country, schools were literally imposed upon the workers.[16]

The evolution of the economy in the nineteenth century gave rise to new socialization needs and continued to spur the growth of education. Agriculture continued to lose ground to manufacturing; simple manufacturing gave way to production involving complex interrelated processes; an increasing fraction of the labor force was employed in producing services rather than goods. Employers in the most rapidly growing sectors of the economy began to require more than obedience and punctuality in their workers; a change in motivational outlook was required. The new structure of production provided little built-in motivation. There were fewer jobs such as farming and piece-rate work in manufacturing in which material reward was tied directly to effort. As work roles became more complicated and interrelated, the evaluation of the individual worker's performance became increasingly difficult. Employers began to look for workers who had internalized the production-related values of the firm's managers.

The continued expansion of education was pressed by many who saw schooling as a means of producing these new forms of motivation and discipline. Others, frightened by the growing labor militancy after the Civil War, found new urgency in the social-control arguments popular among the proponents of education in the antebellum period.

A system of class stratification developed within this rapidly expanding educational system. Children of the social elite normally attended private schools. Because working-class children tended to leave school early, the class composition of the public high schools was distinctly more elite than the public primary schools.[17] And as a university education ceased to be merely training for teaching or the divinity and became important in gaining access to the pinnacles of the business world, upper-class families used their money and influence to get their children into the best universities, often at the expense of the children of less elite families.

Around the turn of the present century, large numbers of working-class and particularly immigrant children began attending high schools. At the same time, a system of class stratification developed within secondary education.[18] The older democratic ideology of the common school—that the same curriculum should be offered to all children—gave way to the 'progressive' insistence that education should be tailored to the 'needs of the child.'[19] In the interests of providing an education relevant to the later life of the students, vocational schools and tracks were developed for the children of working families. The academic curriculum was preserved for those who would later have the opportunity to make use of book learning, either in college or in white-collar employment. This and other educational reforms of the progressive education movement reflected an implicit assumption of the immutability of the class structure.

The frankness with which students were channeled into curriculum tracks, on the basis of their social-class background, raised serious doubts concerning the 'openness' of the social-class structure. The relation between social class and a child's chances of promotion or tracking assignments was disguised—though not mitigated much—by another 'progressive' reform: 'objective' educational testing. Particularly after World War I, the capitulation of the schools to business values and concepts of efficiency led to the increased use of intelligence and scholastic achievement testing as an ostensibly unbiased means of measuring the product of schooling and classifying students.[20] The complementary growth of the guidance counseling profession allowed much of the channeling to proceed from the students' own well-counseled choices, thus adding an apparent element of voluntarism to the system.

The legacy of the progressive education movement, like the earlier reforms of the mid-nineteenth century, was a strengthened system of class stratification within schooling which continues to play an important role in the reproduction and legitimation of the social division of labor.

The class stratification of education during this period had proceeded hand in hand with the stratification of the labor force. As large bureaucratic corporations and public agencies employed an increasing fraction of all workers, a complicated segmentation of the labor force evolved, reflecting the hierarchical structure of the social relations of production. A large middle group of employees developed, comprising clerical, sales, bookkeeping, and low-level supervisory workers.[21] People holding these occupations ordinarily had a modicum of control over their own work; in some cases they directed the work of others, while themselves under the direction of higher management. The social division of labor had become a finely articulated system of work relations dominated at the top by a small group with control over work processes and a high degree of personal autonomy in their work activities, and proceeding by finely differentiated stages down the chain of bureaucratic command to workers who labored more as extensions of the machinery than as autonomous human beings.

One's status, income, and personal autonomy came to depend in great measure on one's place in the work hierarchy. And in turn, positions in the social division of labor came to be associated with educational credentials reflecting the number of years of schooling and the quality of education received. The increasing importance of schooling as a mechanism for allocating children to positions in the class structure played a major part in legitimizing the structure itself.[22] But at the same time, it undermined the simple processes which in the past had preserved the position and privilege of the upper-class families from generation to generation. In short, it undermined the processes serving to reproduce the social division of labor.

In pre-capitalist societies, direct inheritance of occupational position is common. Even in the early capitalist economy, prior to the segmentation of the labor force on the basis of differential skills and education, the class structure was reproduced generation after generation simply through the inheritance of physical capital by the offspring of the capitalist class. Now that the social division of labor is differentiated by types of competence and educational credentials as well as by ownership of capital, the problem of inheritance is not nearly so simple. The crucial complication arises because education and skills are embedded in human beings; unlike physical capital, these assets cannot be passed on to one's children at death. In an advanced capitalist society in which education and skills play an important role in the hierarchy of production, then, the absence of confiscatory inheritance laws is not enough to reproduce the social division of labor from generation to generation. Skills and educational credentials must somehow be passed on within the family. It is a fundamental theme of this essay that schools play an important part in reproducing and legitimizing this modern form of class structure. (. . .)

Inequalities in schooling are not simply a matter of differences in years of schooling attained or in resources devoted to each student per year of schooling. Differences in the internal structure of schools themselves and in the content of schooling reflect the differences in the social-class compositions of the student bodies. The social relations of the educational process ordinarily mirror the social relations of the work roles into which most students are likely to move. Differences in rules, expected modes of behavior, and opportunities for choice are most glaring when we compare levels of schooling. Note the wide range of choice over curriculum, life style, and allocation of time afforded to college students, compared with the obedience and respect for authority expected in high school. Differentiation occurs also within each level of schooling. One needs only to compare the social relations of a junior college with those of an elite four-year college,[23] or those of a working-class high school with those of a wealthy suburban high school, for verification of this point.[24]

The various socialization patterns in schools attended by students of different social classes do not arise by accident. Rather, they stem from the fact that the educational objectives and expectations of both parents and teachers, and the responsiveness of students to various patterns of teaching and control, differ for students of different social classes.[25] Further, class inequalities in school socialization patterns are reinforced by the inequalities in financial resources documented above. The paucity of financial support for the education of children from working-class families not only leaves more resources to be devoted to the children of those with commanding roles in the economy; it forces upon the teachers and school administrators in the working-class schools a type of social relations which fairly closely mirrors that of the factory. Thus, financial considerations in poorly supported working-class schools militate against small intimate classes, against a multiplicity of elective courses and specialized teachers (except disciplinary personnel), and preclude the amounts of free time for the teachers and free space required for a more open, flexible educational environment. The lack of financial support all but requires that students be treated as raw materials on a production line; it places a high premium on obedience and punctuality; there are few opportunities for independent, creative work or individualized attention by teachers. The well-financed schools attended by the children of the rich can offer much greater opportunities for the development of the capacity for sustained independent work and the other characteristics required for adequate job performance in the upper levels of the occupational hierarchy.

Much of the inequality in American education exists between schools, but even within a given school different children receive different educations. Class stratification within schools is achieved through tracking, differential participation in extracurricular activities, and in the attitudes of teachers and guidance personnel who expect working-class children to do poorly, to terminate schooling early, and to end up in jobs similar to those of their parents.[26]

Not surprisingly, the results of schooling differ greatly for children of different social classes. The differing educational objectives implicit in the social relations of schools attended by children of different social classes has already been mentioned. Less important but more easily measured are differences in scholastic achievement. If we measure the output of schooling by scores on nationally standardized achievement tests, children whose parents were themselves highly educated outperform children of parents with less education by a wide margin. A recent study revealed, for example, that among white high school seniors, those whose parents were in the top education decile were on the average well over three grade levels ahead of those whose parents were in the bottom decile.[27] Although a good part of this discrepancy is the result of unequal treatment in school and unequal educational resources, much of it is related to differences in the early socialization and home environment of the children. (. . .)

The social-class inequalities in our school system and the role they play in the reproduction of the social division of labor are too evident to be denied. Defenders of the educational system are forced back on the assertion that things are getting better, that inequalities of the past were far worse. And, indeed, some of the inequalities of the past have undoubtedly been mitigated. Yet, new inequalities have apparently developed to take their place, for the available historical evidence lends little support to the idea that our schools are on the road to equality of educational opportunity. (. . .)

The argument that our 'egalitarian' education compensates for inequalities generated elsewhere in the capitalist system is so patently fallacious that few persist in maintaining it. But the discrepancy between the ideology and the reality of the US school system is far greater than would appear from a passing glance at the above data. In the first place, if education is to compensate for the social-class immobility caused by the inheritance of wealth and privilege, education must be structured so as to yield a negative correlation between social-class background of the child and the quantity and quality of his schooling. Thus the assertion that education compensates for inequalities in inherited wealth and privilege is falsified not so much by the extent of the social-class inequalities in the school system as by their very existence, or, more correctly, by the absence of compensatory inequalities.

Moreover, if we turn from the problem of intergenerational immobility to the problem of inequality of income at a given moment, a similar argument applies. In a capitalist economy, the increasing importance of schooling in the economy exercises a disequalizing tendency on the distribution of income even in the absence of social-class inequalities in quality and quantity of schooling. To see why this is so, consider a simple capitalist economy in which only two factors are used in production: uneducated and undifferentiated labor, and capital, the ownership of which is unequally distributed among the population. The only source of income inequality in this society is the unequal distribution of capital. As the labor force becomes differentiated by type of skill or schooling, inequalities in labor earnings contribute to total income inequality, augmenting the inequalities inherent in the concentration of capital. This will be the case even if education and skills are distributed randomly among the population. The disequalizing tendency will of course be intensified if the owners of capital also acquire a disproportionate amount of those types of education and training which confer access to high-paying jobs. A substantial negative correlation between the ownership of capital and the quality and quantity of schooling received would have been required merely to neutralize the disequalizing effect of the rise of schooling as an economic phenomenon. And while some research has minimized the importance of social-class biases in schooling,[28] nobody has yet suggested that class and schooling were inversely related!

Class culture and class power

The pervasive and persistent inequalities in American education would seem to refute an interpretation of education that asserts its egalitarian functions. But the facts of inequality do not by themselves suggest an alternate explanation. Indeed, they pose serious problems of interpretation. If the costs of education borne by students and their families were very high, or if nepotism were rampant, or if formal segregation of pupils by social class were practiced, or if educational decisions were made by a select few whom we might call the power elite, it would not be difficult to explain the continued inequalities in US education. The problem of interpretation, however, is to reconcile the above empirical findings with the facts of our society as we perceive them: public and virtually tuition-free education at all levels, few legal instruments for the direct implementation of class segregation, a limited role for 'contacts' or nepotism in the achievement of high status or income, a commitment (at the rhetorical level at least) to equality of educational opportunity, and a system of control of education which, if not particularly democratic, extends far beyond anything resembling a power elite. The attempt to reconcile these apparently discrepant facts leads to a consideration of the social division of labor, the associated class culture, and the exercise of class power.

I will argue that the social division of labor—based on the hierarchical structure of production—gives rise to distinct class subcultures. The values, personality traits, and expectations characteristic of each subculture are transmitted from generation to generation through class differences in family socialization and complementary differences in the type and amount of schooling ordinarily attained by children of various class positions. These class differences in schooling are maintained in large measure through the capacity of the upper class to control the basic principles of school finance, pupil evaluation, and educational objectives. This outline, and what follows, is put forward as an interpretation, consistent where testable with the available data, though lacking as yet in firm empirical support for some important links in the argument.

The social relations of production characteristic of advanced capitalist societies (and many socialist societies) are most clearly illustrated in the bureaucracy and hierarchy of the modern corporation.[29] Occupational roles in the capitalist economy may be grouped according to the degree of independence and control exercised by the person holding the job. Some evidence exists that the personality attributes associated with the adequate performance of jobs in occupational categories defined in this broad way differ considerably, some apparently requiring independence and internal discipline, and others emphasizing such traits as obedience, predictability, and willingness to subject oneself to external controls.[30]

These personality attributes are developed primarily at a young age, both in the family and, to a lesser extent, in secondary socializing institutions such as schools.[31] Because people tend to marry within their own class (in part because spouses often meet in our class-segregated schools), both parents are likely to have a similar set of these fundamental personality traits. Thus, children of parents occupying a given position in the occupational hierarchy grow up in homes where child-rearing methods and perhaps even the physical surroundings tend to develop personality characteristics appropriate to adequate job performance in the occupational roles of the parents.[32] The children of managers and professionals are taught self-reliance within a broad set of constraints;[33] the children of production-line workers are taught obedience.

Although this relation between parents' class position and child's personality attributes operates primarily in the home, it is reinforced by schools and other social institutions. Thus, to take an example introduced earlier, the authoritarian social relations of working-class high schools complement the discipline-oriented early socialization patterns experienced by working-class children. The relatively greater freedom of wealthy suburban schools extends and formalizes the early independence training characteristic of upper-class families.

Schools reinforce other aspects of family socialization as well. The aspirations and expectations of students and parents concerning both the type and the amount of schooling are strongly related to social class.[34] The expectations of teachers, guidance counselors, and school administrators ordinarily reinforce those of the students and parents. Schools often encourage students to develop aspirations and expectations typical of their social class, even if the child tends to have 'deviant' aspirations.

It is true that to some extent schools introduce common elements of socialization for all students regardless of social class. Discipline, respect for property, competition, and punctuality are part of the implicit curriculum of virtually all schools. Yet, given the existing institutional arrangements, the ability of a school to change a child's personality, values, and expectations is severely limited. The responsiveness of children to different types of schooling seems to depend importantly upon the types of personality traits, values, and expectations developed through the family. Furthermore, children spend a small amount of time in school—less than one-quarter of their waking hours over the course of a year. Thus schools are probably more effective when they attempt to complement and reinforce rather than to oppose the socialization processes of the home and neighborhood. It is not surprising, then, that social-class differences in scholastic achievement and other measures of school success are far greater than would be accounted for by differences in the measured school financial resources and other

inputs (quality and quantity of teachers, etc.) alone.[35]

In this interpretation class differences in the total effect of schooling are primarily the result of differences in what I have called class subculture. The educational system serves less to change the results of the primary socialization in the home than to ratify them and render them in adult form. The complementary relationship between family socialization and schools serves to reproduce patterns of class culture from generation to generation.

The operation of the labor market translates differences in class culture into income inequalities and occupational hierarchies. The personality traits, values, and expectations characteristic of different class cultures play a major role in determining an individual's success in gaining a high income or prestigious occupation. The apparent contribution of schooling to occupational success and higher income seems to be explained primarily by the personality characteristics of those who have higher educational attainments.[36] Although the rewards to intellectual capacities are quite limited in the labor market (except for a small number of high-level jobs), mental abilities are important in getting ahead in school. Grades, the probability of continuing to higher levels of schooling, and a host of other school success variables are positively correlated with 'objective' measures of intellectual capacities. Partly for this reason, one's experience in school reinforces the belief that promotion and rewards are distributed fairly. The close relationship between educational attainments and later occupational success thus provides a meritocratic appearance to mask the mechanisms that reproduce the class system from generation to generation.

So far, the perpetuation of inequality through the schooling system has been represented as an almost automatic, self-enforcing mechanism, operating only through the medium of class culture. An important further dimension of the interpretation is added if we note that positions of control in the productive hierarchy tend to be associated with positions of political influence. Given the disproportionate share of political power held by the upper class and their capacity to determine the accepted patterns of behavior and procedures, to define the national interest, and in general to control the ideological and institutional context in which educational decisions are made, it is not surprising to find that resources are allocated unequally among school tracks, between schools serving different classes, and between levels of schooling. The same configuration of power results in curricula, methods of instruction, and criteria of selection and promotion that confer benefits disproportionately on the children of the upper class.

It is not asserted here that the upper class controls the main decision-making bodies in education, although a good case could probably be made that this is so. The power of the upper class is hypothesized as existing in its capacity to define and maintain a set of rules of operation or decision criteria—'rules of the game'—which, though often seemingly innocuous and sometimes even egalitarian in their ostensible intent, have the effect of maintaining the unequal system.

The operation of two prominent examples of these rules of the game will serve to illustrate the point. The first important principle is that excellence in schooling should be rewarded. Given the capacity of the upper class to define excellence in terms in which upper-class children tend to excel (e.g., scholastic achievement), adherence to this principle yields inegalitarian outcomes (e.g., unequal access to higher education) while maintaining the appearance of fair treatment.[37] Thus the principle of rewarding excellence serves to legitimize the unequal consequences of schooling by associating success with competence. At the same time, the institution of objectively administered tests of performance serves to allow a limited amount of upward mobility among exceptional children of the lower class, thus providing further legitimation of the operations of the social system by giving some credence to the myth of widespread mobility.

The second example is the principle that elementary and secondary schooling should be financed in very large measure from local revenues. This principle is supported on the grounds that it is necessary to preserve political liberty. Given the degree of residential segregation by income level, the effect of this principle is to produce an unequal distribution of school resources among children of different classes. Towns with a large tax base can spend large sums for the education of their disproportionately upper-class children, without suffering a higher-than-average tax rate.[38] Because the main resource inequalities in schooling thus exist between, rather than within, school districts, and because no effective mechanism exists for redistribution of school funds among school districts, poor families lack a viable political strategy for correcting the inequality.[39]

The above rules of the game—rewarding 'excellence' and financing schools locally—illustrate the complementarity between the political and economic power of the upper class. In each case, adherence to the rule has the effect of generating unequal consequences via a mechanism that operates largely outside the political system. As long as one adheres to the 'reward excellence' principle, the responsibility for unequal results in schooling appears to lie outside the upper class, often in some fault of the poor—such as their class culture, which is viewed as lying beyond the reach of political action or criticism. Likewise, as long as the local financing of schools is maintained, the achievement of equality of resources among children of different social classes requires the class integration of school districts, an objective for which there are no effective political instruments as long as we allow a market in residential properties and an unequal distribution of income.

Thus, the consequences of an unequal distribution of political power among classes appear to complement the results of class culture in maintaining an educational system that has been capable of transmitting status from generation to generation, and capable in addition of political survival in the formally democratic and egalitarian environment of the contemporary United States.

The role of the schools in reproducing and legitimizing the social division of labor has recently been challenged by popular egalitarian movements. At the same time, the educational system is showing signs of internal structural weakness.[40] These two developments suggest that fundamental change in the schooling process may soon be possible. Analysis of both the potential and the limits of educational change will be facilitated by drawing together and extending the strands of our argument.

The limits of educational reform

If the above attempt to identify the roots of inequality in American education is convincing, it has done more than reconcile apparent discrepancies between the democratic forms and unequal content of that education. For it is precisely the sources of educational inequality which we must understand in order to develop successful political strategies in the pursuit of educational equality.

I have argued that the structure of education reflects the social relations of production. For at least the past 150 years, expansion of education and changes in the forms of schooling have been responses to needs generated by the economic system. The sources of present inequality in American education were found in the mutual reinforcement of class subcultures and social-class biases in the operations of the school system itself. The analysis strongly suggests that educational inequalities are rooted in the basic institutions of our economy. Reconsideration of some of the basic mechanisms of educational inequality lends support to this proposition. First, the principle of rewarding academic excellence in educational promotion and selection serves not only to legitimize the process by which the social division of labor is reproduced. It is also a basic part of the process that socializes young people to work for external rewards and encourages them to develop motivational structures fit for the alienating work of the capitalist economy.[41] Selecting students from the bottom or the middle of the achievement scale for promotion to higher levels of schooling would go a long way toward equalizing education, but it would also jeopardize the schools' capacity to train productive and well-adjusted workers.[42] Second, the way in which local financing of schools operates to maintain educational inequality is also rooted in the capitalist economy, in this case in the existence of an unequal distribution of income, free markets in residential property, and the narrow limits of state power. It seems unwise to emphasize this aspect of the long-run problem of equality in education, however, for the inequalities in school resources resulting from the localization of finance may not be of crucial importance in maintaining inequalities in the effects of education. Moreover, a significant undermining of the principle of local finance may already be underway in response to pressures from the poorer states and school districts.

Of greater importance in the perpetuation of educational inequality are differential class sub-cultures. These class-based differences in personality, values, and expectations, I have argued, represent an adaptation to the different requirements of adequate work performance at various levels in the hierarchical social relations of production. Class subcultures, then, stem from the everyday experiences of workers in the structure of production characteristic of capitalist societies.

It should be clear by this point that educational equality cannot be achieved through changes in the school system alone. Nonetheless, attempts at educational reform may move us closer to that objective if, in their failure, they lay bare the unequal nature of our school system and destroy the illusion of unimpeded mobility through education. Successful educational reforms—reducing racial or class dis-

parities in schooling, for example—may also serve the cause of equality of education, for it seems likely that equalizing access to schooling will challenge the system either to make good its promise of rewarding educational attainment or to find ways of coping with a mass disillusionment with the great panacea.[43]

Yet, if the record of the last 150 years of educational reforms is any guide, we should not expect radical change in education to result from the efforts of those confining their attention to the schools. The political victories of past reform movements have apparently resulted in little if any effective equalization. My interpretation of the educational consequences of class culture and class power suggests that these educational reform movements failed because they sought to eliminate educational inequalities without challenging the basic institutions of capitalism.

Efforts to equalize education through changes in government policy will at best scratch the surface of inequality. For much of the inequality in American education has its origin outside the limited sphere of state power, in the hierarchy of work relations and the associated differences in class culture. As long as jobs are defined so that some have power over many and others have power over none—as long as the social division of labor persists—educational inequality will be built into society in the United States.

Notes

1 This account draws upon two important historical studies: P. Aries, *Centuries of Childhood*, New York, Vintage, 1965; and B. Bailyn, *Education in the Forming of American Society*, University of North Carolina Press, 1960. Also illuminating are anthropological studies of education in contemporary pre-capitalist societies. See, for example, J. Kenyatta, *Facing Mount Kenya*, New York, Vintage Books, 1962, pp. 95–124. See also Edmund S. Morgan, *The Puritan Family: Religion and Domestic Relations in Seventeenth Century New England*, New York, Harper & Row, 1966.

2 Aries, *Centuries of Childhood*. In a number of places, e.g., Scotland and Massachusetts, schools stressed literacy so as to make the Bible more widely accessible. See C. Cipolla, *Literacy and Economic Development*, Baltimore, Penguin, 1969; and Morgan, *Puritan Family*, ch. 4. Morgan quotes a Massachusetts law of 1647 which provided for the establishment of reading schools because it was 'one chief project of that old deluder, Satan, to keep men from knowledge of the Scriptures.'

3 H. F. Kearney, *Scholars and Gentlemen: Universities and Society in Pre-Industrial Britain*, Faber, 1970.

4 See Bailyn, *Education in the Forming of American Society;* N. Smelser, *Social Change in the Industrial Revolution*, University of Chicago Press, 1959.

5 F. Engels and K. Marx, *The Communist Manifesto*, Allen & Unwin, 1951; K. Marx, *The 18th Brumaire of Louis Bonaparte*, New York, International Publishers, 1935.

6 See, for example, S. Thernstrom, *Poverty and Progress: Social Mobility in a 19th Century City*, Harvard University Press, 1964.

7 B. Simon, *Studies in the History of Education, 1780–1870*, vol. 1, Lawrence & Wishart, 1960.

8 Bailyn, *Education in the Forming of American Society*.

9 A manufacturer, writing to the Massachusetts State Board of Education from Lowell in 1841 commented: 'I have never considered mere knowledge . . . as the only advantage derived from a good Common School education. . . . [Workers with more education possess] a higher and better state of morals, are more orderly and respectful in their deportment, and more ready to comply with the wholesome and necessary regulations of an establishment . . . In times of agitation, on account of some change in regulations or wages, I have always looked to the most intelligent, best educated and the most moral for support. The ignorant and uneducated I have generally found the most turbulent and troublesome, acting under the impulse of excited passion and jealousy.' Quoted in Michael B. Katz, *The Irony of Early School Reform*, Harvard University Press, 1968, p. 88. See also David Isaac Bruck, 'The Schools of Lowell, 1824–1861: a Case Study in the Origins of Modern Public Education in America', senior thesis, Harvard College, Department of Social Studies, April 1971.

10 In 1846 the annual report of the Lowell, Mass., School Committee concluded that universal education was 'the surest safety against internal commotions' (*1846 School Committee Annual Report*, pp. 17–18). It seems more than coincidental that, in England, public support for elementary education—a concept which had been widely discussed and urged for at least half a century—was legislated almost immediately after the enfranchisement of the working class by the electoral

reform of 1867. See Simon, *Studies in the History of Education, 1780–1870*. Mass public education in Rhode Island came quickly on the heels of an armed insurrection and a broadening of the franchise. See F. T. Carlton, *Economic Influences upon Educational Progress in the United States, 1820–1850*, New York, Teachers College Press, 1966.

11 Describing the expansion of education in the nineteenth century, Katz concludes: 'a middle class attempt to secure advantage for their children as technological change heightened the importance of formal education assured the success and acceptance of universal elaborate graded school systems. The same result emerged from the fear of a growing, unschooled proletariat. Education substituted for deference as a source of social cement and social order in a society stratified by class rather than by rank.' (M. B. Katz, 'From voluntarism to bureaucracy in American education', *Sociology of Education*, 44, summer 1971.)

12 An American economist, writing just prior to the 'common school revival,' had this to say: 'Education universally extended throughout the community will tend to disabuse the working class of people in respect of a notion that has crept into the minds of our mechanics and is gradually prevailing, that manual labor is at present very inadequately rewarded, owing to combinations of the rich against the poor; that mere mental labor is comparatively worthless; that property or wealth ought not to be accumulated or transmitted; that to take interest on money let or profit on capital employed is unjust.... The mistaken and ignorant people who entertain these fallacies as truths will learn, when they have the opportunity of learning, that the institution of political society originated in the protection of property' (Thomas Cooper, *Elements of Political Economy*, 1828, quoted in Carlton, *Economic Influences upon Educational Progress in the United States, 1820–1850*, pp. 33–4). Political economy was made a required subject in Massachusetts high schools in 1857, along with moral science and civic polity. Cooper's advice was widely but not universally followed elsewhere. Friedrich Engels, commenting on the tardy growth of mass education in early nineteenth-century England, remarked: 'So shortsighted, so stupidly narrow-minded is the English bourgeoisie in its egotism, that it does not even take the trouble to impress upon the workers the morality of the day, which the bourgeoisie has patched together in its own interest for its own protection' (*The Condition of the Working Class in England*, Stanford University Press, 1968).

13 See Thernstrom, *Poverty and Progress*. Marx said this about mid-nineteenth-century France: 'The modern and the traditional consciousness of the French peasant contended for mastery . . . in the form of an incessant struggle between the schoolmasters and the priests' (*The 18th Brumaire of Louis Bonaparte*, p. 125).

14 Janice Weiss and I are currently studying the rapid expansion of southern elementary and secondary schooling which followed the demise of slavery and the establishment of capitalist economic institutions in the South.

15 Based on the preliminary results of a statistical analysis of education in nineteenth-century Massachusetts being conducted jointly with Alexander Field.

16 Katz, *Irony of Early School Reform* and 'From vol-untarism to bureaucracy in American education'.

17 Katz, *Irony of Early School Reform*.

18 Sol Cohen describes this process in 'The industrial education movement, 1906–1917', *American Quarterly*, 20 (1), spring 1968, 95–110. Typical of the arguments then given for vocational education is the following, by the superintendent of schools in Cleveland: 'It is obvious that the educational needs of children in a district where the streets are well paved and clean, where the homes are spacious and surrounded by lawns and trees, where the language of the child's playfellows is pure, and where life in general is permeated with the spirit and ideals of America—it is obvious that the educational needs of such a child are radically different from those of the child who lives in a foreign and tenement section' (William H. Elson and Frank P. Bachman, 'Different course for elementary school', *Educational Review*, 39, April 1910, 361–3). See also L. Cremin, *The Transformation of the School: Progressivism in American Education, 1876–1957*, New York, Knopf, 1961, ch. 2, and David Cohen and Marvin Lazerson, 'Education and the Industrial Order', 1970, duplicated.

19 The superintendent of the Boston schools summed up the change in 1908: 'Until very recently (the schools) have offered equal opportunity for all to receive *one* kind of education, but what will make them democratic is to provide opportunity for all to receive such education as will fit them *equally well* for their particular life work' (Boston, *Documents of the School Committee, 1908*, no. 7, p. 53; quoted in Cohen and Lazerson, 'Education and the Industrial Order').

20 R. Callahan, *Education and the Cult of Efficiency*, University of Chicago Press, 1962; Cohen and Lazerson, 'Education and the Industrial Order'; and Cremin, *Transformation of the School*.

21 See M. Reich, 'The Evolution of the US Labor Force', in *The Capitalist System*, ed. R. Edwards, M. Reich and T. Weisskopf, Englewood Cliffs, N.J., Prentice-Hall, 1971.

22 The role of schooling in legitimizing the class structure is spelled out in S. Bowles, 'Contradictions in US Higher Education', 1971, duplicated.

23 See J. Binstock, 'Survival in the American College Industry', unpublished PhD dissertation, Brandeis University, 1970.

24 E. Z. Friedenberg, *Coming of Age in America*, New York, Random House, 1965. It is consistent with this pattern that the play-oriented, child-centered pedagogy of the progressive movement found little acceptance outside of private schools and public schools in wealthy communities. See Cohen and Lazerson, 'Education and the Industrial Order'.

25 That working-class parents seem to favor more authoritarian educational methods is perhaps a reflection of their own work experiences which have demonstrated that submission to authority is an essential ingredient in one's ability to get and hold a steady, well-paying job.

26 See, for example, A. B. Hollingshead, *Elmtown's Youth*, New York, Wiley, 1949; W. L. Warner and P. S. Lunt, *The Social Life of a Modern Community*, Yale University Press, 1941; R. Rosenthal and L. Jacobson, *Pygmalion in the Classroom*, New York, Holt, Rinehart & Winston, 1968; and W. E. Schafer, C. Olexa and K. Polk, 'Programmed for social class:

tracking in high school', *Trans-action* 7, no. 12, October 1970, pp. 39–46.

27 Calculation based on data in James S. Coleman *et al.*, *Equality of Educational Opportunity*, vol. 2, Washington, D.C., US Office of Education, 1966, and methods described in S. Bowles, 'Schooling and Inequality from Generation to Generation', paper presented at the Far Eastern meeting of the Econometric Society, Tokyo, 1970.

28 See, for example, Robert Hauser, 'Educational stratification in the United States', *Sociological Inquiry*, 40, spring 1970, 102–29.

29 Max Weber referred to bureaucracy as the 'most rational offspring' of discipline, and remarked: 'military discipline is the ideal model for the modern capitalist factory . . .' (see 'The Meaning of Discipline', reprinted in *From Max Weber: Essays in Sociology*, ed. H. H. Gerth and C. W. Mills, Routledge & Kegan Paul, 1948, p. 261).

30 For a survey of the literature see J. P. Robinson, R. Athanasiou and K. Head, 'Measures of Occupational Attitudes and Occupational Characteristics', Survey Research Center, University of Michigan, February 1969.

31 See, for example, Benjamin Bloom, *Stability and Change in Human Characteristics*, New York, Wiley, 1964.

32 Note, for example, the class differences in child rearing with respect to the importance of obedience. See M. Kohn, 'Social class and parental values', in *The Family*, ed. R. Coser, New York, St Martin's Press, 1964; and L. Dolger and J. Ginandes, 'Children's attitudes towards disciplines as related to socio-economic status', *Journal of Experimental Education*, 15 (2), December 1946, 161–5. See also the study of differences in child-rearing practices in families headed by bureaucrats as opposed to entrepreneurs by D. Miller and G. Swanson, *The Changing American Parent*, New York, Wiley, 1958. Also, E. E. Maccoby, P. K. Gibbs *et al.*, 'Methods of child-rearing in two social classes', in *Readings in Child Development*, ed. W. E. Martin and C. B. Stendler, New York, Harcourt Brace, 1954. While the existence of class differences in child rearing is supported by most of the available data (but see H. Lewis, 'Child-rearing among low-income families', in *Poverty in America*, ed. L. Ferman *et al.*, University of Michigan Press, 1965), the stability of these differences over time has been questioned by U. Bronfenbrenner, 'Socialization and social class through time and space', in *Education and Society*, ed. W. W. Kallenbach and H. M. Hodges, Columbus, Ohio, C. E. Merrill, 1963.

33 See M. Winterbottom, 'The sources of achievement motivation in mothers' attitudes toward independence training', in *The Achievement Motive*, ed. D. C. McClelland *et al.*, New York, Appleton-Century-Crofts, 1953; and M. Kohn, 'Social class and parent-child relationships: an interpretation', *American Journal of Sociology*, 68 (4), January 1963, 471–80.

34 See, for example, S. M. Lipset and R. Bendix, *Social Mobility in Industrial Society*, University of California Press, 1959; and T. Iwand and J. Stoyle, 'Social rigidity: income and occupational choice in rural Pennsylvania', *Economic and Business Bulletin*, 22, spring-summer 1970, 25–30.

35 S. Bowles, 'Toward an educational production function', in *Education, Income and Human Capital*, ed. W. L. Hansen, New York, National Bureau of Economic Research, 1970.

36 This view is elaborated in H. Gintis, 'Education, technology, and worker productivity', *American Economic Association Proceedings*, 61 (2), May 1971, 266–79. For other studies stressing the noncognitive dimensions of the schooling experience, see T. Parsons, 'The school class as a social system: some of its functions in American society', *Harvard Educational Review*, 29 (4), Fall 1959, 297–318; and R. Dreeben, *On What Is Learned in School*, Reading, Mass., Addison–Wesley, 1968.

37 Those who would defend the 'reward excellence' principle on the grounds of efficient selection to ensure the most efficient use of educational resources might ask themselves: Why should colleges admit those with the highest college entrance examination board scores? Why not the lowest, or the middle? According to conventional standards of efficiency, the rational social objective of the college is to render the greatest *increment* in individual capacities ('value added,' to the economist), not to produce the most illustrious graduating class ('gross output'). Yet if incremental gain is the objective, it is far from obvious that choosing from the top is the best policy.

38 Some dimensions of this problem are discussed in S. Weiss, 'Existing Disparities in Public School Finance and Proposals for Reform', Research Report to the Federal Reserve Bank of Boston, no. 46, February 1970.

39 In 1969, federal funds constituted only 7 percent of the total financing of public elementary and secondary schooling. Moreover, current distribution formulas governing state and federal expenditures are only mildly egalitarian in their impact. See K. A. Simon and W. V. Grant, *Digest of Educational Statistics, 1969*, Washington, D.C., Department of Health, Education, and Welfare, 1969.

40 See S. Bowles, 'Contradictions in US. Higher Education'.

41 Gintis, 'Education, technology, and worker productivity'.

42 Consider what would happen to the internal discipline if the students' objective were to end up at the bottom of the grade distribution!

43 The failure of the educational programs of the War on Poverty to raise significantly the incomes of the poor is documented in T. I. Ribich, *Education and Poverty*, Washington, D.C., Brookings Institution, 1968. In the case of blacks, dramatic increases in the level of schooling in relation to whites have scarcely affected the incomes of blacks relative to whites. See R. Weiss, 'The effects of education on the earnings of blacks and whites', *Review of Economics and Statistics*, 52 (2), May 1970, 150–9. It is no wonder that Booker T. Washington's plea that blacks should educate themselves before demanding equality has lost most of its once widespread support.

Section II Mass schooling: its historical antecedents

4 Notes on the schooling of the English working class 1780–1850*

Richard Johnson

We may start by noting some coincidences and by providing some definitions. The period with which we are concerned saw the emergence of industrial production in its early English forms. Capitalism and even manufacture were already very old in England, but with the growth of modern industry there was much transforming work to be done. In the countryside it was necessary to remove the remaining inhibitions to a fully capitalist agriculture; in the new factory districts to create a proletariat on the basis of older forms of 'free' labour; in traditional trades to subordinate artisan production to capitalist control or transform its very base. The 'industrial revolution', understood in this way, sharpened and intensified (it did not altogether create) the main internal contradiction of the capitalist system: for capital it posed the problem of the management of working-class resistance and challenge. In particular it smashed or rendered obsolete an older system of authority relations which, following Edward Thompson, we may call 'gentry paternalism'.[1] So the English working class, in its making, posed the question of how the consent of the majority of the population was now to be won. Finally, this period also saw the origins of *mass schooling*. What follows, then, is an essay on the relations between these three processes: industrial revolution; the assertion or re-assertion of class control; the evolution of characteristically 'modern' school systems.

It is important to define *mass schooling*. What was new in England, though not in Scotland, was the birth of the ambition to get all working-class children into a school for some part of their lives. This provides one definition of the enterprise. For one key notion of the new educators was that the coverage of schools ought, eventually, to be comprehensive. They were to be, in the words of the West London Lancasterian

Association (Utilitarian pioneers of mass schooling), 'Schools for All'.[2]

Other distinctive features can be established by a brief comparison with older forms of schooling. Like capital itself and like class control, schools themselves were not new. What was novel (ambitions apart) was the form they took. We still know too little about the pre-industrial-revolution systems, but we may distinguish two kinds of institution catering for the sons and daughters of the 'populace'.[3]

The commonest form was undoubtedly the private school. This was the expression of a pecuniary arrangement between schoolmaster and parent. 'Dames' and private schoolmasters were simply people who had acquired some teachable and marketable skill, rarely more than a basic literacy, or who found in child-minding or teaching, full time or as a by-employment, some support in old age, infirmity, unemployment or other time of need.[4] Such people differed widely in their ability to teach anything of use. But it is clear that private schooling won and held the support of parents. It was remarkably persistent, expansive even, well into the nineteenth century, despite the unanimous censure of the philanthropists. Private schooling, indeed, was one of those indigenous working-class educational practices against which mass schooling was defined and which it was intended to replace.

The main difference between the two kinds of schooling—'public' and 'private'—lay in the realm of control and was also, increasingly, a matter of relative sophistication and expense. Private schools, wholly financed by parents, permitted a direct say in what was taught and how. They provided an adjunct to family and neighbourhood, existing within conditions (often brutalised) very like those of 'home'. Dame schools were really no more than a form of co-operation among women, improvised for the care of children under seven. Private schools were free from patronage and rarely carried extrinsic obligations

Source: unpublished. Dr Johnson is lecturer at the Centre for Contemporary Cultural Studies, University of Birmingham.

to go to church or chapel or dress and behave in alien ways. 'Mass schooling', by contrast, was part of a system which was 'provided'. Philanthropy viewed it as an artificial implantation within the working population, sustained and managed by 'superior influences'.[5] Mass schooling, then, was essentially a sponsored form, essentially philanthropic, essentially 'public' in that rather specialised bourgeois sense.

There were, of course, 'public' schools too in the eighteenth century. But whether we attend to town or countryside, to gentry endowments or the more collective bourgeois pattern of the urban charity school, it seems that these forms of provision were essentially *selective*. They were selective in their objects—not merely the expression of an ambition unattained. Endowments catered for groups of children deemed exceptionally unfortunate or were the expression of a gentry patronage, part of a system of sponsored social mobility, for 'poor scholars'. What was lacking was a conception of school as a massive engine of 'improvement'—for 'civilising' a class as a whole through its children. This was the distinctive feature of the new forms from the more provided types of Sunday School onwards. The attempt was made to corral all the poor children of a given neighbourhood and, in the cant phrase, 'to inure them to habits of obedience'. Other differences followed from this and from the explosive growth of population. The older forms were typically financed by perpetual endowment expressed in legal trustee-ship; the new were supported by subscriptions from a local philanthropic circle with some aid from more central agencies. The old forms were typically free and embraced a range of gratuitous benefits apart from education; the new schools, after a transitional period, typically charged fees and became more specialised institutions. In urban areas the physical size of schools and school buildings grew—witness the great single-room barracks of the monitorial phase, catering for several hundred children. In their physical proportions as well as in their clientele, nineteenth-century schools were recognisably schools for the masses.[6] These differences were signalled by all the very sharp criticisms launched by nineteenth-century reformers against the older systems: the attack on endowments as too rigid and liable to misappropriation (often a demonstrable charge); the attack on free education (or clothing, etc.) as 'empauperising'; the attack on charity schooling as teaching mere deference and not self-helping virtues; the general attack on haphazardness and lack of efficient management and oversight; above all, the attack on the failure of endowed schools to cater for the growing numbers of children.[7]

Chronologies[8]

The growth of mass schooling—crystallising in its forms but growing quantitatively too—began in the early 1780s in the shape of the Sunday School move-ment. By the mid-1840s the qualitative change was complete; the machinery and infrastructures of a system of provided mass day schooling had been laid. Growth thereafter (up to 1870 when further qualitative shifts occur in the definition of 'public') was mainly quantitative. This early growth, however, was very discontinuous and also, though this aspect cannot be covered in a mere survey, geographically very uneven.[9] The main phases may be sketched as follows.

1780—the early 1790s

The Sunday School Movement was, initially, a wide-spread philanthropic enterprise, triggered by a 'moral panic' about the juvenile crowd. The recurrent image of its propaganda was the crowds of begging, thieving, noisy, idle, playing children, pestering the citizen in the streets and threatening his property. The early movement was massively supported by a coalition representative of the dominant classes as a whole: gentry justices and clerics; millowners and merchants; methodists and scientifically-minded unitarian divines; some large landowners.[10] Sunday Schools spread rapidly, especially in the industrial north and mid-lands, the idea being disseminated by the provincial press.

It is worth adding that though the movement was the precursor of mass schooling, it came to contain, within itself, radically differing tendencies with different class bases. Sunday Schools were the least school-like of the new forms: amateur teachers, access for students of all ages, free attendance, often improvised buildings, demands on time and energy well-adapted to working-class circumstance. The forms of Sunday schooling were often appropriated by working people themselves, becoming parts of the more indigenous networks.[11] Yet where schools remained tied to the Anglican church or to the more orthodox, middle-class congregations, they are better regarded as part of the 'provided' system.

1790s–1803

This was a period of educational reaction. The educational impulses associated with gentry paternal-ism, like all its characteristic forms of control, took on a strongly coercive hue.[12] Radical bourgeois impulses, apparent within Dissent from the mid-eighteenth century, were checked. The Sunday School movement fragmented; its growth slowed.[13] The typical educational form of this phase was the 'school of industry', often a kind of workhouse for children. 'It is Schools of Industry that are wanted, to reform the manners of common people; where they are to be taught their duties everyday, and all day long.'[14]

1803–1818

This was the phase of the monitorial school—the

first form of the mass *day* school. It was advocated for its economy, for the speed with which literacy was acquired and for its ability to deal with large numbers of children at reduced *per capita* costs. The monitorial regime, as a characteristic expression of labour discipline and counter-revolution, is described in more detail below. But we should note that the 'new schools' did not spread with great rapidity. In 1818 the areas of greatest strength formed an arc of counties around London; in the industrial north, where the 'need' was often greatest, the schools remained numerically weak.[15] Here schools of the older endowed type, or mixtures of Sunday and private schooling, long remained the predominant forms, though older schools often adopted the new methods. Most large towns soon acquired a monitorial school or two in a common pattern of rivalry— Dissenting or interdenominational school first; Anglicans to follow.[16] But demographically these can have made little impact before the 1830s.

1820s

There is evidence to suggest that the rate of foundation of 'public' day schools slowed in comparison with the period up to 1818.[17] The state of public provision may have continued to deteriorate in some industrial areas. Local studies often show a hiatus in this decade.[18] Significantly, as philanthropic generosity suffered a characteristic relapse, the transition to fee-paying was accelerated.[19] Yet the 1820s was a very significant educational decade. It saw the emergence of a liberal middle-class critique of monitorialism and a cluster of educational innovations most of which concerned adults: mechanics' institutes; the promotion of popular political economy and natural science; the infant school movement. This decade was a very formative moment in the history of radical educational ideologies of both progressive bourgeoisie and insurgent working class.

1830s–1840s

Before the mid-1830s the quantitative growth of public day schooling was fluctuating and uncertain, exceptionally subject to fashion and to the general political climate.[20] But from the 1830s (and especially from 1837 to 1842) we may date a real change of gear in the whole public enterprise.[21] Quantitatively, there began a sustained growth of school places which was maintained through the 1840s and 1850s. Philanthropy now attempted, in action concerted by state and by established church, to cover the ground long left to more indigenous networks. In a complicated pattern of rivalry between dominant class fractions and their own 'educators', anticipation of the intervention of the state forced Anglicans to take the lead in school provision. By 1851 many unevennesses were beginning to be closed, especially between industrial and agricultural counties.[22]

But, as has been suggested elsewhere, the shift was also qualitative. Whereas before 1820 a conservative and sometimes reactionary educational repertoire had dominated and defined the field, after 1835 there was a late development of educational liberalism. During this period, too, the infrastructure of a school system was built: the development (through continental borrowings) of an 'educational theory'; the establishment of teacher-training; the creation (through state aid) of the profession of elementary school teaching; the growth of local ancillary associations predominantly tied to the Anglican church; the general articulation of voluntary endeavour through state and ecclesiastical apparatuses. This was associated with the elaboration of the critique of older methods and the promotion, especially through the new Education Department, of 'progressive' methods of teaching.

By 1846, then, the main lines of the English system had been established in their pre-1870 forms:
1 a 'weak' advisory state authority acting, often with some power, through financial incentives, inspection and a quite close control of teacher-training and professionalisation. These developments were consolidated in the famous *Minutes* of 1846, a set of regulations administered by the Education Department and enacted by its 'legislative' arm, the Committee of Council on Education.[23]
2 a strong, often dominant, sometimes monopolistic Anglican presence at a local level in which the Anglican clergy was the main element of local management and control.[24]
3 a characteristically decentralised pattern of provision which the state helped to finance and control but in which education, even in its 'public' forms, was seen to be indigenous to *civil society*. The direct organisers of education remained the representatives of dominant class-fractions in their own communities: clergy, gentry, manufacturers, merchants and, more marginally, tradesmen and farmers.

The economic argument and the cul de sac of 'skills'

What, then, were the links between educational expansion and industrial revolution? It must be said, in passing, that 'economic science' has been singularly unhelpful here. One recent study of *Education and the Industrial Revolution* written from the point of view of an archaic liberal economics, surveys the educational statistics (with too little scepticism), reviews the contemporary arguments (with little insight into their specific historical context) and yields the following conclusion:[25]

The main conclusion here is that despite the widespread belief to the contrary, education expanded significantly during the periods examined; and at least on a priori reasoning, there is a fair presumption that it significantly assisted economic growth throughout. There was

an Educational Revolution as well as an
Industrial Revolution; and both were interrelated.

It cannot be said that this takes us much further.
Indeed attempts to link education and industrial
revolution through some notion of the 'need' for
labour skills (for literacy or a technical know-how)
have produced, so far, mainly negative results. As
Michael Sanderson has shown for Lancashire and
others are showing for parts of the West Midlands,
the intensification of capitalist relations in industry
could have disastrous effects on literacy rates, at
least in the short run.[26] More generally it is difficult
to see how a process that often involved de-skilling
and the destruction of previously literate communities can have produced, by main economic
force, an educational revolution.[27] Much more close
work on localities and on changing occupational
patterns is needed on these themes, but the argument
looks rather unpromising at least for *this* phase of
capitalist development.

Nor does the argument fit the nature of the educational enterprise itself. Leaving literacy aside for the
moment, there is little stress, before 1850, on teaching
specific occupational skills. These seem normally to
have been learnt not in schools but in the family,
neighbourhood and through the trade itself. In
many ways the industrial revolution was parasitic on
skills indigenous to its inherited workforce. Despite
the early vogue for 'schools of industry', this device
remained a relative rarity, as training for particular
occupations was most often applied to girls (as
housewives but especially as domestic servants) and to
children who were orphaned, vagrant, 'empauperised'
or deemed potentially criminal. The well-known
exception, for adults and adolescents, is, of course,
the mechanics' institute movement. But after the
early enthusiasm, the institutes failed to attract the
'mechanics' for whom they were intended or turned
to the teaching of elementary subjects and to frankly
recreational fare.[28] They became part of the ethos
and machinery of 'rational recreation', not of technically informed labour. We might also note that the
social 'logics' of the newest forms of industry and the
schools do not coincide. Powered and mechanised
industry seems to have required the creation of skilled
elites of working men: makers and menders of
machines; supervisors of women and children. Yet
the new schools of the period were designed to capture the whole class of children most of whom were
inexorably destined for mentally undemanding labour.
It may be, of course, that schools actually operated (in
their context of gross social inequalities) to create
labour aristocracies, but they did so in defiance of the
objects of their founders, who sought to 'civilise' all
children. Educational apparatuses very commonly
work like this—'behind men's backs'. But this leaves
us without a link as expressed in human intention
and motive.

The case of literacy is more complex. The ability
to read and usually (though not always) to write was,
of course, an aim of all nineteenth-century educators.
Yet it is important to stress that literacy (which itself
is *far* from being an unproblematic concept) was
embedded in all kinds of other aims which predominated in the minds of providers. One extended
example of this must suffice. We choose the monitorial
school, harbinger of mass schooling.

Monitorial schools were intended to teach children
how to read and also, with Anglican reservations,
how to write. Enthusiasts often played a kind of stopwatch game to see how long the learning took under
the rival systems.[29] But there is a sense in which the
acquisition of skill (in its normal meaning) was a
secondary concern. As important as skill itself was
the way it was taught—what was learnt, as it were,
in the learning. Educators always stressed the 'moral'
effects inherent in the techniques. So when the
London Quaker philanthropist William Allen first
visited Joseph Lancaster's model school in 1808, it
was the orderliness of the thing that impressed him
most (and, in a Romantic age, actually moved him to
tears of joy!)[30] The first report of the Royal Lancasterian Association made the theme explicit: of
the two points of 'utility' in the system, mere literacy
was 'very inferior'. More important was 'the frame
of mind created by the discipline of education'.[31]

Monitorialists tended to speak a common language.[32] The key phrases emphasised *restraint*: 'check
upon delinquency'; 'enforcing the observance of
religious and moral principles'; 'the laws of the
school'; 'the Will of God'; 'accustom them to
obedience under controul and command'. Or *habit*:
'many beneficial habits of an indelible nature';
'steady habits of industry and integrity'; 'a right bias
to their minds'. Or *order* (the product of habit and
restraint): 'the children inured to habits of order and
subordination' and of a schoolroom, Lancaster's
statement:

On the subject of order, and the necessity of it
in all human affairs, the teacher may observe,
that order is Heaven's first law; and show the
youth under his care, that the subversion of order,
in the least degree, would produce confusion.

The analogies used to describe the working of the
school were often mechanical: 'the whole machine';
'a grand intellectual factory'. Or military: 'non-
commissioned officers selected without trouble,
and serving without pay' (Bell of his monitors),
and Lancaster again: 'the firmness, promptness and
decision attendant on military order'. The similes
employed to express the effects of education were
medical, purgative, even sanitary: 'vaccinate the
rising generation'; 'the alternative medicine'; 'as a
preventative against the poison of infidelity' and,
finally, of a school's influence on its neighbourhood:
'as a salutary stream pervades every part of the parish'.

This language expressed a socio-educational view
(and a child psychology) that was, at root, coercive.

Education was not thought of as the development of innate abilities, potentialities or skills. It was curative, regulative. Education should establish an inner restraint, a behavioural order. In some writers, especially at the Tory end of the spectrum, there was an explicit disavowal of Reason—understanding or mental ability was seen as an insufficient source of sanctions and might, besides, be dangerous in other ways. Robert Southey's thoughts about agrarian riots might equally have been applied to children: 'as for stopping them by force of reason you may as well reason with a steam-engine'.[33] The educational writings of the Rev. John Brown, an eighteenth-century antagonist of English Rousseau-ists, were much cited in these years. As Brown had put it:[34]

> 'Tis necessary, therefore, in order to form a good citizen to impress the infant with early habits; even to shackle the mind (if you so please to speak) with salutary prejudices, such as may create a conformity of thought and action with the established principles on which his native society is built.

Schooling, then, was intended to restrain, to 'shackle, minds'. It was seen to operate in several ways, but especially by implanting in the child a knowledge of divine law and of its systems of police and by forming him by the sheer habitual weight of the order of the schoolroom. So children learned to read on emphatically religious texts,[35] were required to go to church or chapel and were faced by theologically-derived sanctions as well as by more tangible punishments. This emphasis also allows us to make sense of monitorial technique itself.

As the liberals of the 1830s were to point out, it was very crude as a way of learning skills. But as a system of authority, reward and punishment it was, in its way, refined. It hinged on a kind of co-exploitation by which older children shared the authority of the single teacher and became, ideally, part of a 'machine'. In Lancaster's theory, authority ceased to have the fragility of the personal and became intrinsic to 'the system'. So children were marshalled into 'hollow squares' where, standing, they learnt their lessons (Bell) or were seated in serried ranks under their 'non-commissioned officers' (Lancaster). They moved only by command: 'sling hats'—'show slates', and spoke only in approved response. 'In my school', wrote Lancaster (with the proprietory conceit of the archetypal headmaster)—'in *my* school, talking is considered as an offence'.[36] So children were numbered and labelled and graded. They were judged by juries of peers (Bell) or entered in the Black Book. If they committed especially heinous offences (having dirty hands, reading in a sing-song voice, being 'idle'), they might become objects of Lancaster's reserve powers of ingenious and sadistic punishments. Generally, then, they were formed in obedience and discipline.

They were also kept very busy indeed. Ceaseless activity was held to be a leading benefit of the system. It replaced 'that unproductive activity called play'.[37] With its badges and prizes and 'tickets of approbation', 'orders of merit' and elaborate systems of place-taking, monitorial discipline was indeed a kind of game, though play, devised by adults, to eradicate spontaneity. If we add to this the range of religious sanctions and the many rules associated with attendance such as the prohibition of 'finery' for girls, we get some measure of the coercive intent. Monitorialism represents, on the terrain of relationships between child and adult, the more general counter-revolutionary impulse of these years.

The example is, however, historically specific, even though it may be recognised as prefiguring the essence of the mass school. Monitorialism developed at the height of the first phase of a crisis in hegemony and is perhaps the most coercive and negative moment in the whole history of schooling. It illustrates, none the less, one very important theme—that habits, attitudes, the general 'moral' orientation of the child, were of more concern than either the development of skills or the transmission of knowledge. By the 1830s educators were viewing the means of 'civilisation' differently, though it is impossible here to make the comparison in full. The approved system was less overtly coercive. The curriculum widened. Monitorialism itself was attacked. Educators stressed now the pervasive moral and personal influence of the trained missionary teacher who was seen to act, following Pestalozzi, as a kind of substitute parent.[38] The sheer cultural shock of the monitorial order was supplemented by a more subtle working upon the child's emotional economy. 'Reason' too came back into the educator's repertoire. Yet educators still sought, more than anything else, to *re*-form the child, to make a new man or woman. When liberals stressed 'useful knowledge' or even political economy, they stressed them not only for their own sakes but for the rationality they bred and for the power of such knowledge to develop intellectual and 'moral' sentiments and thus regulate the 'animal' or 'sensual' man.

So when economists or economic historians tell us that the industrial revolution 'required' new skills in the labour process, we may doubt the premise and also reply that it seems to have needed new human beings with a new, more disciplined, sociality.

Industrial capitalism and working-class resistance

In the search for more adequate explanations it is useful to turn to further statements of intention which express this time the more liberal climate of the 1830s. What was it in the working class that constituted such a problem and evoked the solution of mass schooling? One way of approaching this is to recall the familiar composite portrayals of the class found in the whole massive social problem genre of the 1830s and 1840s. Here, for example, is Sir

Thomas Wyse, leading advocate of a 'Prussian' state educational system, describing the village labourer before the education he envisages has done its work:[39]

> There are few villages in the country which do not present us specimens of the uneducated; we meet him in the gin-shop, and in the street— he is an idler, a drunkard, a quarreler—we hear of him in every riot, he is an aider and abetter in every outrage. His family are slovenly— reckless—debased—wretched. He is a quarreler because a drunkard, and he is a drunkard because he is idle. But why is he idle? Because he has never felt the value of labour—the pleasure of thinking—the joy of a good conscience . . . He has become passive . . . All his life he has been taught to spare, as much as possible, his own exertions, and to hang, beggar-like, as much as possible, on those of others.

Later Wyse describes an urban equivalent, saved this time by education, but with propensities defined negatively, so that we can see how industrial workers are, without the key solution, active, nasty and more threatening:[40]

> He will *not* be found, each Saturday night, in these dens of iniquity, with pale and haggard cheeks, applauding the licentious or infidel jest, plotting the next strike, devising some new means of intimidation or aggression against the resisting or industrious, adding to the inflammatory paragraph of the revolutionary paper, organising discontent and sedition, and, after the stale and filthy debauch of two or three successive nights, with all that is degraded and sensual, in the lowest sties of a manufacturing metropolis, returning, with sleepless eyes, on Monday morning, to his work,—the Sabbath profaned, his health gone, his week's earnings robbed from his pining family, and the seeds planted of crimes which perhaps, ere long, may consign him to the transport vessell, or the scaffold.

Not all descriptions are so hysterical—or so imaginary. But in this literature—of Blue Book, statistical inquiry or educational propaganda— village labourers do usually appear stupid, clingingly dependent and doltish on the surface, sullen and resentful underneath. Their forms of protest are, if anything, less comprehended than those of the industrial workers. Workers themselves, in their urban settings, appear alarmingly energetic, easily misled, volatile, with strong masculine passions but lacking self-control. They are as 'sensual' and as 'irrational' as village labourers but in a different way— prone to perfervid species of vice rather than the phlegmatic kinds. They are also capable of organised conspiracy on a vastly greater scale.

What is being stigmatised in all this literature is a whole way of life. If one lists those aspects of the working class that meet with censure, it is the compre- hensiveness of the indictment that is striking. The attack covers almost every aspect of belief and behaviour—all the characteristic institutions, folklore, 'common sense' and mentalities of the class, its culture (or culture*s*) in the broad anthropological meaning of the word. One reason why we are liable to miss this is that the analysis is not phrased as an analysis of culture. The defenders of industrial capitalism (or 'progress') speak the language of 'morality' instead. But we must understand 'morality' in a certain way—as the combination of culture or 'manners' plus that entirely unrelativistic ascription of guilt or blame.

It is this translation—from 'morality' to 'culture'— that allows us to penetrate the ideological con- structions around such observations and recreate the real relations. For the bourgeois observer, the problem with working people was their *obstinately ungovernable behaviour*. They refused, before his very eyes, to conform to what liberal theory and a promise of progress prescribed. They transgressed the values by which he himself sought to live his life. In their everyday behaviour, in their day-to-day attempts to live their lives under capitalism, they did indeed mount a resistance, the forms and informing values of which have been rescued, recreated and, indeed, celebrated by Edward Thompson and others.[41] Many forms of resistance were not self- consciously oppositional or only partially political. Yet when bourgeois social investigators noted resistance to work disciplines, the defence of custom- ary rights of relief, the practices of customary sports and pastimes, the equally traditional use of alcohol in sociability or need, the spending of hard-won wages on petty luxuries, the theft of property or the street life of children and adolescents, they were actually mapping a range of cultural responses that were resistant to capitalist imperatives and their corresponding values. They did not express these observations in the language of cultural analysis: they wrote instead of 'idleness', 'drunkenness', 'pauperism', 'vice', 'improvidence' and 'crime'. When they insisted, however, that such forms of behaviour were obstructive to progress or even to self-advancement within a capitalist social order, they were quite correct. It *was* necessary to cut the reproduction of the older popular culture if capitalist development in town and countryside was to be speeded and secured. Modern industry *did* need new elements in human nature, *did* require the learning of new relations. Early Victorian moralism, then, was not some gratuitous bourgeois aberration. Cultural aggression of this kind was organic to this phase of capitalist development. That is why 'class-cultural control' is a better, more explicit, expression to use than the looser term 'social control', which carries quite different meanings within different sociological traditions.[42] Even this term does not quite catch the aspect of movement: not *control* merely, but *trans- formations* were required. All the distinctive liberal social policies of this phase should be seen in this light: the creation of a new labourer by the deterrent mechanisms of the New Poor Law; the moralisation of factory children through compulsory school attendance; the continued attack on 'football' and all 'brutal sports'; the encouragement of temperance and rational recreation, etc. Education was part of this overall drive, a drive which became a partly conscious strategy in the minds of men, such as Edwin Chadwick, Dr Kay and Nassau Senior, with the percipience to see the long-term interests of capital as a whole.

We are coming close, then, to Gramsci's formulation of the problem out of a much later and very different Italian experience. Writing 'notes' on 'the educative and formative role of the State' he described the process thus:[43]

> Its aim is always that of creating new and higher types of civilisation; of adapting the 'civilisation' and the morality of the broadest popular masses to the necessities of the continuous development of the economic apparatus of production; hence of evolving even physically new types of humanity.

But there are still some important elements missing from the story. It is not clear, for instance, why bourgeois educational responses were thrust into a new mode in the 1830s, why they changed when they did, and why the growth of schooling was so discontinuous. The key to these questions lies in further aspects of class-cultural relations and also in the relative autonomies of the educational domain. Empirically it lies in the recognition of working-class *challenge* in these years; conceptually it lies in Gramsci's concepts of 'crisis in hegemony' or 'crisis of authority'.

Working-class challenge and the crisis in hegemony

Historians of education, especially in recent years, have often pointed to the relation between the 'problem of public order' and the schooling enterprise.[44] The evidence for such an association is massive, notably in the ubiquitous references to every form of working-class politics in the literature of educational propaganda. The words of a home secretary of the period, Sir James Graham, in the aftermath of the widespread northern strike movement of 1842—the 'Plug Riots'—are often quoted: 'The police and the soldiers have done their duty, the time is arrived when moral and religious instruction must go forth to reclaim the people from the errors of their ways.'[45] Historians have also noted the close coincidence in time between the peak of educational activism and the height of the Chartist movement. The period 1838 to 1843 is very properly seen as the point at which the expansion of schooling 'takes off'. It was also the period of Chartist mass activity.

More is involved here, however, than the prevention of riot or even the anticipation of insurrection

as an immediate tactical objective. Working-class radicalism did constitute a threat to the propertied classes, even momentarily and usually from limited regional bases to the security of the state.[46] But a challenge was also posed, over a longer period, to the cultural hegemony of the dominant classes. One way of viewing the social history of the whole period from the 1790s to the mid 1840s is as an extended war over the winning of consent, a prolonged crisis in hegemony, marked by partial stabilisations but also, in default of this, the repeated use of the rather underdeveloped coercive apparatuses of the state to reinforce the economic power of the gentry and industrial bourgeoisie. It was not until the 1840s, and perhaps rather late in that decade, that hegemony was re-worked in new forms.[47] Formal educational institutions and their corresponding politics have come, in a later period, to play a large part in the processes of hegemony. In this period, schooling as a public if not a state apparatus was *actually forced into existence* in England by the collapse of older systems of control.

To understand more fully how this worked we have to look, very briefly, at the educational aspects of the working-class movements of the time. As a number of studies have now shown, popular radicalism from its origins in the 1790s possessed its own educational traditions.[48] This was expressed in several ways: in criticisms of all provided forms of education including the new schools, in an alternative educational content and in the improvisation of popular educational media. The tradition was richest in prescriptions for the education of adult men and women, but radicals were concerned also with the education of children. These activities were no accidental by-product of radical activity. They were organic to the movements themselves. Chartists and Owenites in particular espoused education— 'really useful knowledge'—in much the way in which Gramsci espoused it as a latter-day 'Jacobin' and educator for Italian communism. It was tied into political strategies and infused with political meaning. Education was one potent means of revolutionising society; truly human education was an expected benefit of the achievement of social and political rights, economic justice and 'the New Moral World'.

One way of writing the educational history of this period, albeit one which neglects deeper determinations, is in terms of the shifting antagonism of 'provided education' and the counter-cultural forms. Radicalism aimed to provide substitutes to sponsored forms. Philanthropic educators sought to regulate, destroy or replace the means of cultural reproduction that existed within the working class itself and which provided networks through which radicals could work. They attacked quite directly, of course, the Unstamped Press (the main radical medium) and Chartist and Owenite schools and halls. But we will scarcely understand the attitudes of clergymen and schools inspectors to private schools and self-taught teachers and even to the working-class family itself unless we realise that these too were distrusted, partly because they might be infected by radical influences. The fear of radicalism as culture *as well as* the desire to shift older, inherited inertias lay behind the attack on parenthood and the attempt to replace it, in some of its functions, by school. It was the duality of the task—re-establishing the means of hegemony and transforming the psychological world of labour—that gave the peculiar urgency to the project. The school and schoolteacher must take the child from home and prepare it for work and loyal citizenship.

The rise of this form of educational politics can be dated with some precision. It developed in the rebound from an earlier, failed strategy characteristic of the 1820s. The break from older, more conservative forms of provided education, signalled by mechanics' institutes, the attack on endowments and the work of the Society for the Diffusion of Useful Knowledge was personified in the figure of Henry Brougham, who led each of these campaigns. The typical strategy was to appeal to the working-class adult and to forge a populist alliance against the educational patronage of the past. The people were called upon to educate themselves, with middle-class aid certainly, but in ways appropriate to a new age. Evidence of popular demand was used as a lever against educational conservatism.[49]

This picture changed after 1832 and more surely after 1836. If there was some chance of a popular liberal alliance in the 1820s, there was little in the class-conscious years that followed. The radical journalists of the Unstamped phase, Owenites and Chartists rejected the Broughamite educational innovations.[50] Liberal activists, capture having failed, ceased a direct dialogue with radical adults. Their attitudes to Chartism and Owenism were uniformly hostile—for most liberal educators 'socialism' was the terminal pathology. At the same time the education of children re-assumed its old importance. Parents were seen as a lost generation, hopelessly corrupted by a long history of educational neglect for which aristocratic misgovernment and Anglican obscurantism were largely to blame. So turning their backs on an adult population (which, in any case, rejected their most self-evident truths), they concentrated on children instead, calling on state power to aid them. In this way they set in motion a move towards state intervention, the pre-emptive strike of the Tory–Anglican coalition and the whole leap in school expansion of the late 1830s and 1840s. It was only after Chartism and its substitutional strategies faded that the popular liberal alliance on educational matters was again possible. When this matured, in the 1860s, it became an active component in the construction of popular liberalism and aided the fuller incorporation of working-class organisations. But that is a different story.

Gaps and disclaimers

It is as well to end with acknowledgments of gaps and with some denials. First, this paper is based largely on the intensive study of educational ideologies or statements of intent. Three main groups of educators have been studied: the monitorialists; radical working-class educators, especially the journalists of the radical press; the liberal 'experts' of the 1830s. An attempt has been made to penetrate ideologies through a more materialist reading of culture. Even so, we need to know much more about two crucial areas: the patterns of school foundation and the changes in the forms of capitalist production as they affected and made demands upon the culture of the workforce and the means of cultural reproduction. This involves close work on the origins, provenance and working of schools and on the precise character of the family and the labour process. Both projects point to work on particular towns, regions or occupations. We also need a more convincing chronology of public schooling which, perhaps, only fresh local research will supply, though it is my belief that the trends presented here will bear the test of elaboration, especially the basic pattern of slow start and 1830s–1840s acceleration. But we certainly need to know much more about regional variations in school provision and literacy and in their determinations.

Finally it must be stressed that we have been very little concerned with the *effects* of educational expansion. It is not to be supposed that the effects were those that were intended. There are several reasons, indeed, why the whole schooling enterprise was likely to fail or work only in rather unexpected ways. First, the desire to get children into schools competed with industrial capitalism's insatiable appetite for child labour. The desire to 'school' the English working class remained an ambition until the 1880s (and perhaps it remains an ambition now). Second, in the absence of a general legal compulsion, working people used provided schools in an instrumental manner, taking from the system what they wanted (largely the submerged element of skills) but withdrawing children from school once these skills (especially a measure of literacy) were secured. Third, there is no reason to suppose that children in the nineteenth century were any less creative in their forms of resistance within school than children are now. The monitorial system according to the gospel of Joseph Lancaster was one thing; its operation in schools of bricks and mortar with children of flesh and blood and even average ingenuity was quite another.[51] Fourth, there are general or theoretical grounds for questioning models of perfect reproduction or wholesale transformation through schooling, whether these appear as assumptions in the nineteenth-century sources (which they do) or in modern theories. It seems that schools have never acquired the autonomous power that has sometimes been envisaged for them; they are merely one of the means of cultural reproduction and have to be seen as part of a complex which includes the couplet family–school. In the period with which we are concerned it is a fair guess that family and neighbourhood and even place of work were of much greater importance than school. In any case, typically, under capitalism, schools seem to reproduce instead of the perfect worker in complete ideological subjection, much more the worker as bearer of the characteristic antagonisms of the social formation as a whole. Schools, in other words, reproduce *forms of resistance too*, however limited or 'corporate' or unselfconscious these may be.[52]

The growth of mass schooling could not, however, be without its effects. It is a matter of fine judgment whether, in the long term, these were progressive. There is, in fact, no easy escape from the dilemma which Chartists faced in the later 1840s when they turned from educational self-activity to agitate for a state educational system.

Notes

* This is a revised version of a paper first prepared for an international Round Table on 'Les Problèmes de la formation du prolétariat au temps de la première révolution industrielle' at the Centre of European Sociology in Paris. It has also been discussed with fellow members of the Centre for Contemporary Cultural Studies at Birmingham University and was given as a paper in a seminar on the history of education at the 1976 Historical Association Conference. I am grateful to all those who have commented on it in these three contexts. It is a very compressed version of the main arguments of a much longer manuscript, and apologies are made for the absence in some parts of adequate references.

1 Thompson's most compressed analysis of the eighteenth-century system is to be found in 'Patrician society, plebian culture', *Journal of Social History*, 7, 1974, pp. 382–405.

2 The title of a pamphlet by James Mill. For the history of the WLLA, the radical utilitarian wing of the monitorial movement, see Graham Wallas, *The Life of Francis Place 1771–1854*, 4th ed., London, 1925.

3 The best source for eighteenth-century developments remains M. G. Jones, *The Charity School Movement: a Study of Eighteenth-Century Puritanism in Action*, Cambridge University Press, 1938. But for rural patterns in particular see Joan Simon, 'Was there a charity school movement? The Leicestershire evidence', in Brian Simon, ed., *Education in Leicestershire 1540–1940*, Leicester University Press, 1968. There is a rather random treatment of private schools in V. E. Neuburg, *Popular Education in Eighteenth-Century England*, London, 1971, ch. 2.

4 This account of private schooling is based mainly on official or philanthropic nineteenth-century sources, notably the reports of the Manchester Statistical Society on various urban centres in the mid to late 1830s. Attempts to quantify this form of schooling are notoriously unreliable, but it was undoubtedly very extensive right up to the 1870s.

5 For an account of this cluster of attitudes see Richard Johnson, 'Educational policy and social control in early Victorian England', *Past & Present*, 49, 1970, pp. 96–119.

6 For the physical character of the new schools see Malcolm Seaborne, *The English School: its Architecture and Organization 1370–1870*, Routledge & Kegan Paul, 1971, pp. 137–53. Seaborne notes of the eighteenth century that 'the very great majority of the schools of the poor at this period were for relatively small numbers of children'.

7 The classic source for these attacks—the first time they were mounted in a consolidated way, though by no means the last—is Brougham's Select Committee On the Education of the Lower Orders in the Metropolis, 1816–18. The whole report has been reprinted by the Irish University Press in four volumes (*Education: Poorer Classes*, vols 1–4).

8 In so far as it involves quantitative assessments, this chronology is based on published local studies of educational provision (cited below where relevant) and on an analysis of the contemporary statistical series: the Parochial Returns of the Brougham Select Committee, 1818; the Lord Kerry returns for 1833 (*Parl. Papers*, vol. 43, 1835); the reports of statistical societies (especially the Manchester society) in the 1830s; the Educational Census of 1851 (*Parl. Papers*, vol. 90, 1852–3) and the statistics collected by the Newcastle Commission. For the difficulties of using these series see J. S. Hurt, 'Professor West on early nineteenth-century Education', *Econ. History Review*, 24, November 1971, and West's reply in the same number. These series will be surveyed more fully in Richard Johnson, *Education and Society 1780–1850*, Macmillan and Economic History Society, forthcoming.

9 For some of these unevennesses see W. B. Stephens, *Regional Variations in Education during the Industrial Revolution 1780–1870* (Museum of the History of Education, Leeds, 1973). Also, especially in relation to literacy, Lawrence Stone, 'Literacy and education in England 1640–1900', *Past & Present*, 42, 1969, esp. pp. 102–26. Local studies repeatedly show great variations, even from parish to parish.

10 The best account of the Sunday School movement remains A. P. Wadsworth, 'The first Manchester Sunday Schools', *Bulletin of the John Rylands Library*, 33, 1950–1, reprinted in M. W. Flinn and T. C. Smout, eds, *Essays in Social History*, Oxford University Press, 1974. The publication of T. W. Laqueur's major study is eagerly awaited.

11 So much is clear from the part played by Sunday schooling in the 'pursuits of knowledge' recorded by many working-class autobiographers of this period.

12 The best-known case of the general tendency is gentry response to the food riot. See Edward Thompson, 'The moral economy of the eighteenth-century crowd', *Past & Present*, 50, 1971.

13 e.g. Wadsworth, 'Manchester Sunday Schools', pp. 312–18 and appendix; cf. David Wardle, *Education and Society in Nineteenth-Century Nottingham*, Cambridge University Press, 1971, p. 39.

14 Clara Reeve, *Plans of Education with Remarks on the Systems of Other Writers*, London, 1792, pp. 84–5.

15 This is based on an analysis of the county breakdowns in the Brougham Parochial Returns (Digest of Parochial Returns, *Parl. Papers*, vol. 9, pt 3, 1819, p. 1171). It is possible that local agents (the Anglican clergy) under-recorded Dissenting day schools on the monitorial pattern in crowded urban districts. Even so, the geographical pattern should hold—most dissenting effort in this period continued to be expressed in Sunday schooling.

16 e.g. James Murphy, 'The rise of public elementary education in Liverpool: part I', *Trans. Hist. Soc. of Lancashire and Cheshire*, 116, 1964, pp. 186–8; Wardle, *Nottingham*, p. 46; George C. Miller, *Blackburn: the Evolution of a Cotton Town*, Blackburn, 1951, p. 178; Conrad Gill and Asa Briggs, *History of Birmingham*, Oxford University Press, 1952, vol. 1, p. 132.

17 This is suggested by a comparison of the 1818 and 1835 figures with Mann's retrospective figures of surviving foundations per decade in the 1851 census and, where foundation dates are clear, by the statistical society reports. It should be stressed that this pattern applies to 'public' schools only; aggregate figures which include private schools show a much more optimistic picture.

18 In Nottingham there were fifteen years of stagnation in provision and a decline in subscriptions to existing schools from 1811 to the late 1820s (Wardle, *Nottingham*, pp. 47–8). In Liverpool the foundation of the Corporation School (a unique experiment) was accompanied by the prostration of voluntary effort, abortive public meetings and derisory collections (Murphy, 'Liverpool: part 2', *Trans. Hist. Soc. Lancs and Cheshire*, 118, 1967, pp. 105–11). Other areas show a similar pattern, the late 1820s revival being led by the new vogue for infant schools.

19 Even Borough Road, the British and Foreign School Society's show-piece, changed to fee-paying in 1827. On the Anglican front there was also a pause in the founding of new local and diocesan associations after the initial burst of activity in 1811–12.

20 The pattern for the late 1820s and early 1830s, however, remains unclear.

21 The qualitative evidence is reviewed in Johnson, 'Educational policy and social control'.

22 Quantitative conclusions here are based mainly on a comparison between Lord Kerry's figures for 1833 and the census of 1851. All retrospective figures point to the importance of the 1830s. Local studies for Liverpool, Nottingham, Birmingham, Hull and the northern Pennines all show a surge of activity in this decade. The National Society's statistical reports for 1856 and 1866 identified the period 1837 to 1847 as one of 'extraordinary impetus' (e.g. *Statistics of Church of England Schools . . . 1866–67*, National Society, London, n.d., p. 36). Most statistical society reports tell the same story suggesting a real boom in urban areas.

23 For the character of the *Minutes* see Johnson, 'Educational policy and social control', and the standard educational histories, especially Mary Sturt, *The Education of the People*, Routledge & Kegan Paul, 1967, chs 9 and 10.

24 See, for example, the picture in Diana McClatchey, *Oxfordshire Clergy 1777–1869*, Clarendon Press, 1960, pp. 146–9.

25 E. G. West, *Education and the Industrial Revolution*, London, 1975, p. 256.

26 'Literacy and social mobility in the industrial revolution in England', *Past & Present*, 56, 1972, esp. pp. 57–89. The argument is contested and recapitulated in *Past & Present*, 64, 1974. As this debate makes clear, the later argument should be read alongside Sanderson's important earlier article, 'Social change and elementary education in industrial Lancashire 1780–1840', *Northern History*, 3, 1968. Sanderson's work generally in this area is an exemplary model for local studies. I am also grateful to Jacqueline Grayson for discussions of early results from her study of literacy in Dudley.

27 The key instances of such destruction were the weaving communities.

28 Mabel Tylecote, *The Mechanics' Institutes of Lancashire and Yorkshire before 1851*, Manchester University Press, 1957, esp. pp. 87–110. Edward Royle, 'Mechanics' institutes and the working classes 1840–1860', *Historical Journal*, 14, 1971, argues that institutes were more popular but conflates different historical phases and shows that elementary classes were the most successful aspect of the institutes.

29 This game was played repeatedly with witnesses before the Brougham Select Committee.

30 William Allen, *Life of William Allen*, London, 1846, vol. 1, p. 96.

31 Quoted in *The Philanthropist*, 1, 1811, p. 278.

32 All the phrases quoted below are from contemporary sources advocating the monitorial system. For descriptions of the two main systems by their 'inventors', see Joseph Lancaster, *Improvements in Education*, London, 1806, and Andrew Bell, *An Experiment in Education . . .*, 2nd ed., London, 1805.

33 Southey to Wynn, 23 February 1817 in J. W. Warter, ed., *Selections from the Letters of Robert Southey*, London, 1856, vol. 3.

34 John Brown, *Sermons on Various Subjects*, London, 1764, p. 8.

35 For a comparison of (rather similar) dissenting and Anglican practices see J. M. Goldstrom, *The Social Content of Education: a Study of the Working-Class School Reader in England and Ireland*, Irish University Press, 1972.

36 Lancaster, *Improvements*, p. 100.

37 William Davis, *Hints to Philanthropists*, Bath, 1821.

38 For the theme of 'parental substitution', see Johnson, 'Educational policy and social control'.

39 Thomas Wyse, *Education Reform: or, the Necessity of a National System of Education*, London, 1836, pp. 310–11.

40 ibid., p. 329.

41 The key source is of course E. P. Thompson, *The Making of the English Working Class* (Penguin Book). This work has stimulated much closer looks at working-class culture during this period in its more or less 'political' aspects.

42 I am grateful to Edward Thompson for his criticisms of the original formulation and for suggesting the term 'class control'.

43 *Selections from the Prison Notebooks of Antonio Gramsci*, ed. and trans. by Q. Hoare and G. Nowell Smith, Lawrence & Wishart, 1971, p. 242.

44 e.g. John Hurt, *Education in Evolution*, London, 1971, pp. 21–3.

45 *Hansard*, vol. 67, col. 78.

46 For one local challenge of this kind, not adequately placed, perhaps, within the context of the state nationally, see John Foster, *Class Struggle and the Industrial Revolution*, London, 1974.

47 Such shifts are difficult to date exactly. Some 'solutions' were generated in the struggles of the 1830s but only really began to have an effect in the decade that followed.

48 A number of important studies appeared in the early 1960s. They included Brian Simon, *Studies in the History of Education 1780–1870*, London, 1960; Harold Silver, *The Concept of Popular Education*, London, 1965; J. F. C. Harrison, *Learning and Living 1790–1970*, London, 1961, and Thompson, *The Making of the English Working Class*. Since then there have been many studies of Chartism, Owenism and the Unstamped Press which have stressed this theme.

49 *The* characteristic text of this period is Henry Brougham, *Practical Observations upon the Education of the People, addressed to the Working Classes and their Employers*, London, 1825, which went through many editions and helped 'launch' the mechanics' institute movement.

50 The clearest case is the Society for the Diffusion of Useful Knowledge, much lampooned in the radical press. But both infant schools and mechanics' institutes were often attacked.

51 For some interesting material on the subversion of the monitorial method see W. E. Hickson's collections of 'juvenile witness' in his anonymous 'Schools for the industrious classes', *Central Society for Education: Second Publication*, London, 1838, esp. pp. 365–7. But, unfortunately, material on this is scarce.

52 It is a valid criticism of some Marxist-structuralist accounts, notably Althusser's, that the models of reproduction employed give little place to the resistance of child (or teacher).

5 Science, nature and control: interpreting Mechanics' Institutes

Steven Shapin and Barry Barnes

(. . .) Our purpose in this paper is to show *how* the founders of British Mechanics' Institutes thought a scientific education would aid in the social control of those artisans who were their designated target. We intend to elicit from the public statements of the movement's leaders the basis and structure of their own belief that a regimen of scientific education for certain members of the working class would render them, and their class as a whole, more docile, less troublesome, and more accepting of the emerging structure of industrial society.

We cannot here hope to marshal all possible evidence establishing the credibility of the link between the Institute movement and a practical interest in social control. (. . .) Our main proposal is to develop an interpretation of *the scheme of things* in terms of which the proponents of popular education in science might plausibly believe that knowledge of a certain kind could control people. (. . .)

Included in the designation 'Mechanics' Institute' (or, less commonly, 'School of Arts') was a variety of early to mid nineteenth-century foundations, all initially created to teach aspects of the sciences to sections of the British working-classes. (. . .)

Sponsored by local coteries of utilitarians, Unitarians, philosophical radicals of various hues, and reform-minded civic leaders, Institutes had appeared in practically every sizeable British town by the 1840s. By 1851 according to one, apparently reliable, account there were over 700 'Literary and Mechanics' Institutes' in Great Britain and Ireland, with over 120,000 members.[1] This appears to mark the high point of their expansion.

(. . .) They were in general organized *by* interested members of the middle classes *for* specified sectors of the working classes. (. . .) At the local level, projectors of Mechanics' Institutes may be found among the same sorts of occupational groups as patronized the provincial scientific societies of the Midlands and North of England: physicians, surgeons and apothecaries; dissenting divines; 'enlightened' manufacturers and merchants. Having found the cultivation of science appropriate to their own situation in local society, they now found compelling arguments for the propriety and value of working-class science.

It should be emphasized that those who advocated this form of education possessed a finely graded map of society. To speak of the Mechanics' Institutes as providing science for 'the working class', as a number of their historians do, misses an important discrimination made by the actors themselves, and puts us in danger of losing much of the sense of purpose behind the entire enterprise. People in the 1820s spoke of 'the working classes' as encompassing a number of discrete sectors. Thus, when advocates of Mechanics' Institutes referred to 'artisans', or to 'operatives', or 'mechanics', they did not mean to refer to the 'working classes' as an entirety. Rather, they were pointing to occupational sub-categories which, to them, possessed 'known' attributes—economic, social, moral and intellectual. They had it in mind to provide an educational regimen for these sub-groups only, and not for 'the working classes' as a whole.[2] This precise identification of the target of the proposed educational programme is crucial to understanding why the enterprise was deemed appropriate, why some sectors of British society resisted it, and why the curriculum took the form it did. (. . .)

Practical control problems

Perhaps the strongest impression one takes away from the voluminous pamphlet literature which spewed forth with the birth of the Institute movement is of the quaintly archaic rhetorical formulations by which founders assured themselves (and their audience)

Source: forthcoming in *Social Studies of Science*, 7 (1), February 1977.

that a scientific education for the artisan and operative would result in their moral improvement. The idiom of this rhetoric of justification is of some interest.

The minds of the working classes were assumed to be occupied 'by objects of sense', so much so that 'when they seek for recreation they do it in a sensual way'.[3] Drunkenness, debauchery and promiscuity characterized workers' behaviour, according to those who advocated a remedy in scientific education. The curriculum of the Mechanics' Institutes would cope with this situation by rescuing 'them from this temptation, by providing them with pursuits above the grossness of sensuality'.

(. . .) There was assumed to be something specially effective about *scientific* education in accomplishing this job of uplift and control. 'By studying the properties of matter, and the laws of nature, it will lead them to reverence their *God*, on viewing scientifically his wonderful works', thereby rendering the working classes 'better husbands, fathers, and brothers'.[4] (. . .) Thus, a scientific education was intended to have both a general and a special uplifting and controlling outcome. In general, scientific study was to be an intellectual pastime which could be an appropriate alternative to socially undesirable activities, in particular drinking and extra-marital sex. More specifically, the study of the natural world would point out laws, relationships and the presence of design of which the worker would otherwise be unaware. And in being thus brought to perceive this rational organization of nature, he would perceive (metaphorically or directly) the rational organization of society also, in its harmonious relationship with the natural world. The effect of this perception would be to render behaviour and values more stable.

(. . .) The reason (why natural science) was thought particularly appropriate as a source of uplift, we are frequently told, lay in its objectivity and value-neutrality. (. . .) Controversial religious, political and political economy literature was almost universally banned from the Institutes' libraries.[5] In the light of the uncontrollable circulation of political and pornographic literature among the working classes at the time, the appeal of a scientific regimen to 'crowd out' bad influences was considerable. Scientific education could therefore control the working classes by substituting good currency for bad. (. . .)

This rhetoric of control reflects an authentic and deep-rooted concern.[6] The ever-pressing problem of social control had become, at the beginning of the century, particularly acute with regard to the urban working classes.[7] For industrial employers, and the bourgeoisie generally, the problem of managing the technology and economics of the industrialization process was paralleled by the equally significant problem of managing the behaviour of the labour force.[8] And, however much they made of 'laissez-faire' and the rest, the bourgeoisie were well aware that the evolution of a society which would serve their interests demanded active supervision and careful intervention.

(. . .) Educational programmes for the 'mechanic' and 'operative' were indicated by a number of inter-related control strategies elaborated from the 1820s onwards and attaining their greatest significance around 1840.[9] These, essentially 'liberalizing', strategies all attempted to build an alliance or a community of interest between the bourgeoisie and the upper section of the working classes, the labour aristocracy. In contrast to crude attempts at coercion or suppression, liberalizing strategies involved politics of 'cultural aggression' which by bribe or indoctrination would ensure that the 'natural leaders' of the working classes identified with and affiliated to those above them rather than those below. (. . .)

Mechanics, skilled operatives and artisans (i.e., the 'target' of the early Mechanics' Institutes) were, if not already an objectively defined labour aristocracy in the 1820s, well on the way to becoming one. Their political development was uncertain. They could lead the working classes in violent confrontation with the industrial system, they could lead them in drunken apathy, or they could come to set examples of acceptance and identification with the values of the industrial middle classes. In the 1820s the most politic course to take with the mechanic class was a matter of intense debate. This class, unlike the 'labouring poor', was almost totally literate.[10] *What* they read, not *whether* they should read, was already a topic of concern. Many industrial leaders feared that, in the absence of more wholesome food, the mechanic was serving himself a diet of Cobbett, Paine and pornography.[11] The mechanic was possibly already dangerously politicized. [And it is] this background of practical problems that explains the aims and curricula of the Mechanics' Institutes at their inception. (. . .)

Inputing the characteristics of the mind

In the debate over the most desirable social distribution of knowledge, actors revealed a number of organizing assumptions and theories. One of these was that there had to exist an isomorphism between the social and the intellectual, cognitive order if society was to be stable. Another was that knowledge, if it were to be successfully transmitted, must be 'appropriate' to the circumstances of its recipients.[12] It must therefore be tailored to their environment (and thus their social standing), and to their nature, or what we today would call their intellectual capacities. It is particularly interesting to examine the way in which informal theories of the mentality of the lower orders thereby came to influence proposals for curricula in the field of popular education. To do this we must first set out what these theories were.

Central to the construction of a map of the lower orders' mind was the notion of hierarchy. Both projectors and opponents of popular education accepted that there was a social hierarchy, however much they differed as to its details, future and present stability. They also both accepted that the superior sort of person was endowed with or characterized by a superior sort of knowledge, and, conversely, that the knowledge of the lower orders was in important ways defective. They shared this fundamental belief whether or not they shared a belief in the desirability or possibility of improving the minds of the lower orders through education. A number of polar oppositions were generally used to contrast thought at the base and summit of the hierarchy and to characterize the lower orders as 'stupid'. The multitude's thinking was *superficial* rather than profound; it was based upon sense data rather than abstract organizing principles, and was accordingly *sensual* not rational; it was *inconsequential*, unlike the thought of the higher orders which took proper account of the consequences of action; it was *fragmented*, and failed to perceive those necessary connections between phenomena which gave the upper classes their integrated overall understanding of society.[13]

These oppositions may all be found in the polemical literature dealing with Mechanics' Institutes and popular education in general during the early nineteenth century. The equation between the *superficiality* of the working-class mind and the defective nature of their thought is clear in 'Country Gentleman's' statement that 'The populace ever judge superficially; the probability therefore is that they are ever wrong...'[14] 'Truth', he explained, 'is said to lie at the bottom of a well, not on the surface: in other words, whatever appears only superficially right, is probably wrong.'[15] Reality, therefore, lies deep; access to it requires the going behind of appearances, whereas the imputed characteristic of the lower-class mind is precisely its entrapment in appearances. Similarly, 'Country Gentleman' was totally convinced that the lower orders' characteristic relish for 'sensual and vulgar gratifications' could never be overcome by an induced 'love of learning'.[16] Sensual gratifications were 'appropriate' to minds governed by sense, because they could not discern enduring moral verities lying deep beneath superficial sensual distortion. Even the virtues of mechanics could be turned against them with this idiom. 'It may be easily shown', claimed 'Country Gentleman',[17]

> that practice and theory seldom unite in the same individual; that the occupation of the practitioner requires all his time and thoughts to fulfil the wishes of his eye or hand: whilst the theorist reasons within himself, *and throws himself on his mind*. Theoretical excellence must have reason for its soil, which mechanics have not.

The *interior* abode of 'reason', contrasted with the *exterior* quality of sensual apprehension, therefore mapped onto the social hierarchy. The lower orders were characterized, morally and intellectually, as having little notion of things except in 'external practice'. They lacked 'that busy interior existence, which is the moral person'. They did not apprehend 'ideas of what they cannot or dare not practically realize'.[18] The daily occupations of the working classes made few, if any, demands upon the interior intellect; their minds resided in their eyes and hands, and were, therefore, susceptible of being unthinkingly routinized:[19]

> [We may] take into account of the allotment of employments to the uncultivated multitude, how much facility is acquired by habit, how much use there is of instrumental mechanism (the grand exempter from the responsibility that would lie on the mind), and how merely general and very slight an attention is exacted, in the ordinary course of some of the occupations.

As well as being shallow and sensual, the thought of the lower orders was inconsequential; it lacked purpose; it was insensitive to 'what things really mean'. 'One of the most obvious circumstances [of the 'ignorant' class]', John Foster wrote, 'is *the perfect non-existence in their minds of any notion or question what their life is for, taken as a whole*'. Their heads are full 'of trifling and corrupting ideas', but they never think: 'For what purpose am I alive? What is it that I should be? Does it signify *what* I may be?' Their thought lacks a 'general and leading purpose'.[20]

Perhaps the central opposition underlying all these various imputations is that between organized and fragmented thought. We are offered a general characterization of the thought of the lower orders as 'broken-up', marked by transient and ephemeral impressions from the sensuous world and the passions, without the integrating cement of a patterned texture of meanings, necessary connections, causal laws, and the like. The contrast between the top and the bottom of society is made in terms of the distribution of what we may loosely call two opposed epistemologies.

There is little to suggest that this imputed distribution of epistemologies was made on the basis of concrete empirical study. It is more likely that it evolved as a legitimation of the social order; it justified the division of labour in society by accounting it 'natural'. However, once established as accepted wisdom, such a theory could be used to explain working-class behaviour, and to guide initial attempts to control it.

Thus, by characterizing the thought of the lower orders as fragmented and governed by transient impressions, their perceived immorality, insolence, sensuality and political volatility could be 'explained'. As they grasped no abstract moral and intellectual principles, they were at the mercy of whatever passing desire, whim or fancy arose from within or was impressed on them from without. Since they had no stable moral and intellectual framework with which to evaluate actions, any political rabble-rouser could simply sweep them along (see n. 50 below). Bad influences simply impressed themselves upon their minds. Good influences would presumably impress themselves equally easily, but were distressingly uncommon in their environment.

For those who found the social control of the multitude problematic, this account of their mental characteristics also indicated a remedy. An educational regimen was required which took into account the nature of the minds with which it was going to deal, and which sought to instil in those minds the stable intellectual and moral patterns which it was felt they presently lacked.

The curriculum

We are now in a position to consider the curriculum which the Mechanics' Institutes were expected by their founders to sustain. Its intended nature is easily ascertained, although exactly how successfully it was embedded in teaching activity is more problematic.[21] To summarize: the curriculum was to be scientific, 'pure' rather than 'applied', factual rather than theoretical or speculative; and 'simplified' in presentation.

In the early curricula of most of the Institutes for which we have evidence, the natural sciences predominated. Although few Institutes continued to steer so close to their charted scientific course as the Edinburgh School of Arts, that enterprise was widely cited as the purest expression of the original ideas and its curriculum was copied by a number of other Institutes.[22] The plan of the School, as designed by Henry Brougham's friend Leonard Horner, was to teach chemistry and mechanical philosophy. Mathematics was soon added, but other, seemingly more 'practical', offerings like veterinary medicine were resisted by the Directors as being outwith their purpose.[23] The central position in the curriculum of physics, chemistry, mathematics, the earth and life sciences (impressionistically arranged in order of importance) characterized the great majority of Institutes in their very early years. By the late 1820s and early 1830s very many, perhaps most, had presented lecture courses on phrenology, as a science of mind and philosophical system.[24] The general tendency during the 1830s was for the proportion of courses in the natural sciences to be diluted, usually by the addition or substitution of the fine and performing arts, languages, drawing, and the like. But this shift in the content of the curriculum corresponds to a shift in the Institutes' purposes and clientele, and will not be discussed here.[25]

In itself, an elementary science-based curriculum concentrating upon the presentation and demonstration of clear-cut facts and laws may serve a variety of functions and interests. Those which are most relevant in the present instance are, however, readily discernible. Those features of knowledge which exposed its theoretical and conjectural qualities, and

hence weakened its credibility, were systematically eliminated. So were those which facilitated original speculative thinking (despite utilitarian rhetoric upon the value of the innovating mechanic). What was retained was all that might implant a subtle model of natural order in such minds as the lower orders were thought to possess.

The knowledge of nature in which the intelligentsia orientated themselves was not to be the knowledge of nature presented to the mechanics. As the Rev. Thomas Chalmers put it, by analogy with missionary work, it had been found more expedient to 'let down English knowledge and philosophy to the capacity and station of the Hindoos' than to attempt to 'raise the Hindoos to the level of English knowledge and philosophy'.[26] Brougham argued that, in teaching the 'multitude' geometry,[27]

> it is not necessary to go through the whole steps of that beautiful system, by which the most general and remote truths are connected with the few simple definitions and axioms; enough will be accomplished, if they are made to perceive the nature of geometrical investigation, and learn the leading properties of figure.

The facticity of knowledge was to be emphasized at the expense of its metaphysical and hypothetical character. Thus, an organ of the Established Church of Scotland approved of the Edinburgh School of Arts' curriculum and teaching, but condemned the idea of workers spending their time[28]

> in puzzling [their] brains in algebra . . . , or in wandering in the thorny path of metaphysics, or in the ill-macadamized roads of even physics themselves, where the lecturers . . . stand waving their rods over kittle curves and conic sections, and statements of the differential calculus, rather than in *showing by experiment how things really are in nature* . . .

The central notion, shared by very many of the projectors of Mechanics' Institutes, was precisely this: to show 'how things really are in nature', rather than to stress, or in some cases even to allude to, the provisional nature of scientific knowledge. The world of workers' science was a world of facts and laws, not a world of theories so identified. Where Brougham or Horner might orientate themselves in a body of scientific knowledge which was partly hypothetical, wholly provisional, and recognized as theoretically informed, the scientific knowledge presented to mechanics was to have none of those characteristics. It was hard, factual, solid and enduring; in no way tentative or revisable.[29]

Even mathematics was subject to audience-dependent adaptation of this sort. The Scottish educationalist and natural theologian Thomas Dick referred to the '*scientific* method of instruction generally pursued in colleges and academies', wherein the student worked through Euclid and 'the higher algebraic equations', his attention being 'chiefly directed to the *demonstration* of mathematical propositions, without being much exercized in practical calculations'. But 'a different method ought to be pursued in schools chiefly devoted to popular instruction'. Let the student concentrate upon 'practical geometry', only occasionally exhibiting some of the abstract rules, 'in so far as he is able to comprehend it'. Practical operations of geometry and their 'general utility' will enable the student in such schools to comprehend the subject more than 'were he to consider them as relating merely to *abstract truths*'.[30] Another Scottish educationalist, James Pillans, claimed that in failed popular educational establishments the prime reason for lack of success was teaching which was 'too abstruse', which contained 'too much abstraction'.[31]

The science intended for the lower orders was a highly reified body of knowledge. And, by appeal to the observable and the concrete, it affected to be indubitable. Thus, in the Edinburgh School of Arts great weight was put upon actual *demonstrations*, concrete observable illustrations of 'how things really are', which were argued to be uniquely adapted to teaching the lower-class mind. Actual things which could be seen and handled were preferred subjects of study—machines, chemical substances, geometrical diagrams; not algebraic variables and equations, metaphysical principles and unexemplified verbally expressed relationships.[32]

The immense popularity of phrenology as an element in workers' education in the 1830s is a prime example of reified knowledge as fit meat for the lower orders. In phrenology, as contrasted with academic mental science, abstract faculties become 'things', i.e. parts of the brain. An observable entity is substituted for an abstract entity. Society is reified as the outcome of the workings of parts of individuals' brains.[33]

Recalling our actors' model of the lower orders' mentality, one can recognize that this reified curriculum was intended to 'put into their heads', in the most efficient and most 'appropriate' way, an authoritative depiction of the natural world—of how nature was. All that remains is to enquire why such an insertion was attempted. What was such a representation expected to do, once it had reached its target? How could it alleviate the problems involved in the social control of the lower orders?

Certainly, part of the answer lies in treating the science of the Institutes' curriculum as a control ideology analogous to earlier variants of natural theology and political economy. Models of nature are among the universally available resources invoked to set limits on the possibilities of human action. In particular, where people refuse to recognize the inscrutable whims and fancies of God as moral constraints, the more tangible, impersonal limits allegedly inherent in the operation of the natural world are likely to be invoked instead.

Such conceptions are, of course, readily discernible at this time in 'what people actually said' about the purposes of popular education. Again, John Foster is perhaps the most interesting link between the Institute movement and popular education in general in the 1820s. In his *Essay on the Evils of Popular Ignorance* he describes the relationship between the mental characteristics of the lower orders and the problems of bringing credible sanctions to bear on their behaviour. The lower orders, we remember, are blind to abstract principles, and, therefore, the notion of God as an abstract entity has 'but slight power to restrain the inclinations to sin, or to impress the sense of guilt after it is committed'. Such a God lacks efficacy as a moral sanction 'because he is invisible'.[34] As the lower orders are, however, sensitive to the tangible and the concrete, they usually do obey limits like walls and fences. The great problem is to make them aware of, almost literally to *see*, abstract intangible limits and moral principles which 'we' recognize. Thus:[35]

as [the ignorant worker] is nearly destitute of that faculty of the soul which would perceive . . . the awful interceptive lines of that other arrangement which he is in the midst of as a subject of the laws of God, we see with what insensibility he can pass through those prohibitory significations of the Almighty will, which are to devout men as lines streaming with an infinitely more formidable than material fire.

The Church, with its abstract God, 'who is somewhere in the sky, has not, to them, the smallest force of intimidation from evil'. Now sources of moral sanctions must be developed. In the distant past of our race, Foster believes,[36]

some right injunctions of morality . . . [were] infixed in the popular mind as a matter of conscience, by the great array of things pretendedly divine and demi-divine which surrounded, and pressed closely and powerfully on, the mind of the multitude. Whereas now, when this great array is vanished, there is nothing, absolutely nothing, to enforce moral principles and rules on the ignorant portion of the people with the mighty authority of Divine sanction.

Although Foster did not fully articulate the solution, those who read his work did. The solution was in part to use a new 'divine' or 'demi-divine' nature to exert those moral sanctions required to control an unstable multitude—a 'demi-divine' nature which was, appropriately, tangible and observable.

That 'demi-divine' nature was the construction of the natural theological science of late eighteenth- and early nineteenth-century Britain. The study of nature through science revealed moral purpose and significance in the world which could be encoded as ethical principles appropriate for oneself or others. Explicitly, the study of nature was recommended to mechanics as it revealed the wisdom of God in creating things as they were. 'Knowledge', said one popular scientific lecturer, 'is virtue': 'All nature . . . offers examples innumerable of the power and wisdom with which [God] works throughout the visible world before us.'[37] Nature was God's creation; it was His visible message and the repository of His plan. Nature was therefore a good nature, and if it appeared to be evil or unjust, there was God's beneficent purpose behind what appeared to be evil, such as the existence of the social hierarchy. The moral lesson to be learnt via the inculcation of natural theological science was one of acceptance, of appreciating the systematic connections which made a seemingly unaccountable world accountable in moral terms.

Interestingly, this natural theological knowledge was much more frequently encountered in the Institutes than political economy, which drew analogous conclusions from 'the scientific study of natural laws', and which might have been expected to have greater appeal to Whigs and reformers. Political economy and its 'iron laws' were indeed frequently explicitly excluded from Institutes' curricula, whereas the natural theological flavour of many courses, particularly in physiology, phrenology and, to an extent, the earth sciences is readily apparent. The phrenologist-educationalist George Combe, for example, was a strenuous advocate of the teaching of physiology to the common people. In a pamphlet on the subject he proposed a model catechism which opened with the physiology of digestion and concluded with the following exchange:[38]

Q. If God has established all this in the framework of our bodies and the endowment of our minds, is he a clever fellow who tries to find a shorter way than by skilful and honest labour, to a supply of bread, who, for example, cheats to get it, or steals it? 'No, Sir.' . . .
Q. If, then, by working skilfully and honestly each of us in our own line, and exchanging our articles, we are all better supplied, and if God has arranged things in this manner, what kind of conduct does He prescribe to us, and approve of?

God is the ultimate source of moral suasion but now he acts through nature and natural laws. In the case above, diligent, honest and specialized labour is sanctioned by the laws of physiology, which God frames and guarantees. It is nature and the action of natural laws which exact their toll on those who violate 'natural' behaviour:[39]

The whole objects and phenomena treated of in the sciences, are the institutions of God . . . and . . . we are bound by duty to God, as well as by a regard to our own welfare, reverently and diligently to study these, and to regulate our own conduct in conformity to their modes of action.

It is not an abstract God that will strike us down if we violate a code of behaviour; it is nature. Disease, degeneration, short life, mental afflictions await us if we drink to excess, are idle or sexually promiscuous. The body exacts its revenge on those who abuse it; the workings of the body as interpreted by science:[40]

It is only by diligent study of the order of nature that we shall learn how to accommodate our conduct to the Divine laws, which regulate prosperity and adversity, health and disease, life and death, in the present state of existence.

It would, however, be misguided to treat the science of the Institutes simply and solely as a variant of natural theology, and we certainly do not advance this thesis. It was, after all, mathematics, mechanics and chemistry which initially were given pride of place in the curriculum, not physiology and phrenology. Without doubt one could draw teleological implications from mathematical and mechanical principles, but they are scarcely the most promising bases for an exercise in ideological manipulation.[41] Nor is there any but the thinnest evidence that such principles were taught other than in a reasonably straightforward, if rather didactic, way. Few of the mathematical and physical texts employed came to include the passages of moralizing and homiletic characteristic of many works in other fields, and even of some of the physical science books written for use by children.[42]

Why, then, was there such enthusiasm for the most apparently 'value-neutral' forms of science on the part of the founders and supporters of the early Institutes—people who, as we have seen, were predominantly interested in the defence of social order and stability? Why should science in general, and not just particular appropriate fields, be thought to possess a control function?[43] And why should mathematics and mechanical philosophy be set above such apparently more promising sources of control as the biological and socio-economic sciences?

In answering such questions let us recall that a number of influential advocates did indeed urge the teaching of correctly-formulated political economy, usually of the Malthusian type. Certainly, Henry Brougham did so in his *Practical Observations*.[44] And the Rev Thomas Chalmers argued at length that the Malthusian variant of political economy he favoured could be taught distinct from politics, and he encouraged its inclusion in Institutes' curricula. There was 'no likelier instrument than a judicious course of economical doctrine, for tranquilizing the popular mind'. It would be 'a sedative to all sorts of turbulence and disorder'. Moreover, it would be a splendid device for dividing the working classes: 'the infuriated operatives, instead of looking to capitalists as the cause of their distress, should look at one another'.[45] But, in practice and in many locales, the intended introduction of such subjects aroused (or was thought likely to arouse) such passions among possible patrons that the enterprise was in jeopardy. And so there are matters of local institutional politics which clearly bear upon the content of the curriculum.[46]

Another possible answer has the virtue of setting the Mechanics' Institutes and their curricula in the more general context of educational innovation. They belong toward the end of a chain of cultural innovations leading from Paley on the one hand and Adam Smith on the other, through various strands of natural theology and political economy, always to increasingly naturalistic cosmologies. It is likely that what we have before us is a series of failed experiments in the construction of ideologies, all successively rejected by the lower orders, and successively replaced by apparently more objective and naturalistic alternatives. Perhaps elite groups continually found themselves obliged to curtail and tone down what ideally they would have wished to convey to the working classes, in a vain attempt to gain credibility.

What evidence there is strongly suggests that none of these ideological manifestations successfully distracted even a small proportion of the working classes from their own spontaneous political expressions. Only in the coercive context of schools for children did blatantly teleological interpretations of nature survive for any length of time, presumably being learned by rote and happily forgotten by successive captive audiences.[47] There is nothing here to suggest that ideological manipulations *in themselves* entice people into alien cosmologies against their own interests. As Tyrrell has clearly and amusingly demonstrated, the would-be bringers of political economy enlightenment to the Scottish workers were regarded by their audience not as disinterested scholars but as 'employers' spokesmen sheltering behind a facade of religious, scientific and philanthropic notions'. One thousand Dunfermline working men subscribed to Dr Thomas Murray's political economy lectures in 1838, unfortunately for Murray as it turned out because the audience 'expected to hear the doctrines of Radicalism demonstrated'.[48]

Given previous experience with recognizably ideological formulations, it may be that the curricula of the Mechanics' Institute represent a modest, tempered and more realistic attempt at control. Their stress on mathematics and physical sciences reflects awareness that studied disinterest and apparent objectivity are essential if a suspicious audience is to be attracted and its credibility engaged;[49] this is the other side of the coin to the widespread ban upon political economy within the Institutes. And any lost opportunities for teleology and moralizing can be set against compensating advantages if only an audience of artisans can be held. By sacrificing time to mathematics and physics as 'loss-leaders', audiences for delicately-drawn implications of other sciences might be gained, and ongoing, informal contacts with the dominant sector of the lower orders established. Moreover, as we have noted already, 'value-neutral' science might crowd out even less desirable alternatives; artisans learning science are preferable to artisans plotting revolution; disinterested artisans are preferable to committed artisans. Analogously, in the world of the mind, value-neutral science 'occupies space' which the middle classes could fill with something else of their own choice. Thus, in terms of the characteristics they imputed to the minds of the lower orders, it at least is 'solid substance', producing a kind of stability and preventing that unpredictable tendency to be swept up by every kind of political stimulus characteristic of the utterly ignorant.[50]

We have obviously been treating the curriculum of the Mechanics' Institutes as a communication system, carrying messages of social control. But there are a variety of ways in which an educational situation may exert its hoped-for controlling influence, and only one of them, the content of the knowledge, is at the level of the explicit. Communication systems, and cultures generally, also carry with them a body of implicit meanings which can do important work in the social system.[51] In the present context, we should also look to the general features of scientific discourse, the parameters of a scientific cosmology and the social messages conveyed by the very institutional existence of Mechanics' Institutes as important modes of communication and possible control; in other words, to the medium as well as the message.

We should recognize that the dissemination of science expanded a communication system and medium for discourse and interaction. It constructed channels along which an indefinite number of future attempts at negotiation and control could run. It provided a framework upon which the culture of a stabilized re-integrated society might eventually be built. And if this framework appeared permanent, immutable and constraining to the lower orders, but provisional, manipulable and challenging to those above them, so much the better; straight manipulation would be a pleasant bonus, but 'rational' communication, if that was all that could be achieved, was reward enough.

As usual, our actors themselves had explored the relationship between communication and control. Foster had deplored, and identified as very dangerous, the gulf of non-communication which had arisen between the higher and lower classes of the community, between 'refinement' and 'barbarism':[52]

If so little of the sense, the information, the liberalized feeling, and the propriety of deportment, which we are to ascribe to the higher and cultivated portion, goes downward through the lower, it seems impossible but that there must be more of dissociation and repulsion between them, than of congruity and communication. But for the good of both it is exceedingly desirable that the upper and inferior orders *should* be on terms of communication . . .

and therefore that there should be a diminution of that rudeness of mind and habits which keeps them in such disconnexion and estrangement.

What was lacking was a 'medium of complacent communication', in the absence of which the lower orders were 'far removed and estranged from the more cultivated part of their fellow countrymen, and consequently from every beneficial influence under which a state of friendly contiguity, if we may so express it, would have placed them'.[53] A member of the Glasgow Mechanics' Institute praised the role of such establishments 'in removing the feeling of jealousy and distrust, which has too long obtained between the higher and wealthier orders, and those in less favoured circumstances'. The image of scientific activity as essentially harmonious and co-operative could be invoked in the cause of control:[54]

> Meeting, as both classes do, on the fair field of science, where all are as brothers, and pursuing, it may be, the same glorious objects, the wall of separation is removed for ever, and the best possible guarantee given for the inviolable maintenance of the rights of property on the one hand, and the peace and security of society on the other.

So long as significant numbers of 'mechanics' attended, the Institutes' directors rarely failed to remark on the decorous concord of classes at the lectures. How gratified the mechanics must be 'to have observed the very liberal manner in which your fellow-citizens, who occupy the higher stations of society, have come forward to assist you in obtaining that instruction which your own means alone could not command'.[55] It was a cause of immense satisfaction to directors that middle and lower classes could make common cause in the pursuit of useful knowledge. As we have shown, our informal psychological theorists believed that manipulation at the cultural level would itself produce changes in society. Perhaps, if the cosmology underlying technological processes could be implemented in the operatives' minds, there would be more ready acceptance of the industrial system and their place in it.

It remains to ask why natural science in its more 'value-neutral' manifestations was selected as the appropriate medium of communication and potential common culture. Part of the answer doubtless lies in the lack of any realistic alternative candidates. And part must lie in the previous use of scientific culture for purposes of symbolic expression by industrially-based elites.[56] But it is also possible that in some unverbalized, intuitive fashion, actors were aware of the way in which the concepts and procedures of science were particularly suited to expressing and exploring the many practical problems of organization and control they were experiencing as employers of labour and producers of commodities.

Here, indeed, we have arrived at a speculative and undocumentable hypothesis, but it is worth dwelling upon it for a brief moment before passing on. To treat matter instrumentally as the inert raw material required by a productive system organized to produce commodities requires that it be drained of moral significance and homogenized, precisely as occurs in the scientific thought of the elite. To explain and monitor systems of manufacture based upon organized sequences of single modifications of materials implies stochastically linkable, mechanistic notions of causality which are, again, characteristic of science. The control and co-ordination of complex, interdependent structures or organized productive labour is greatly facilitated in many ways by the institutionalized treatment of time as a linear continuum; many areas of science offer ideal models of such a treatment. And finally, and most importantly, modern commercial exchange and organized systematic production demand quantification and model procedures for dealing with quantified relationships, such as are again provided by the esoteric culture of natural science.

Thus, there may well have been a general, not necessarily explicit or conscious, realization that science was a particularly appropriate form of culture for general dissemination in an industrializing community. It could lay down in the mind the general form of a communication system appropriate for controlling and monitoring the current forms of production. Hence, it could help to establish the work habits required of a complexly organized workforce, where individual components had to operate within close physical and temporal margins of error, and were highly interdependent and minimally redundant.[57]

Notes

1 Sources for compiling lists of Institutes include the following: J. W. Hudson, *The History of Adult Education*, London, 1851, vol. 6, pp. 222–36 (the estimate above comes from p. vi); House of Commons, *Report from the Select Committee on Public Libraries*, 1849, especially evidence of Samuel Smiles (pp. 306–9) and J. B. Langley (pp. 310–17); T. E. Cliffe-Leslie, *An Inquiry into the Progress and Present Conditions of the Mechanics' Institutes*, Dublin, 1852; James Hole, *An Essay on the History and Management of Literary, Scientific, and Mechanics' Institutions*, London, 1853.

2 For a contemporary illustration of this, see [David Robinson], 'Brougham on the education of the people', *Blackwood's Magazine*, 17, 1825, 534–51 (538).

3 Andrew Thomson, quoted in the *Scotsman*, 8 June 1825. Dichotomies between sensual and intellectual modes of apprehension fit easily into the nomenclature of phrenology. See, for example, George Combe, *Lectures on Popular Education*, 3rd ed., Edinburgh, 1848, p. 25: 'Life with [the industrious classes] is spent

to so great an extent in labour, that their moral and intellectual powers are stinted of exercise and gratification; and hence their mental enjoyments are chiefly those afforded by the animal propensities: in other words, their existence is too little *rational*; they are organised machines more than moral, religious and intellectual beings.'

4 Steven Shapin, 'The Pottery Philosophical Society, 1819–1835: an examination of the cultural uses of provincial science', *Science Studies*, 2, 1972, 332.

5 It is interesting that workers' self-education enterprises set up in opposition to middle-class controlled Institutes often made a point of *including* novels, newspapers and political literature. See, for example, details of the Edinburgh Mechanics' Subscription Library, the *Scotsman*, 16 April 1825. Also R. G. Kirby, 'An early experiment in workers' self-education: the Manchester New Mechanics' Institution, 1829–35', in D. S. L. Cardwell, ed., *Artisan to Graduate*, Manchester University Press, 1974, pp. 87–98 (esp. pp. 92–3).

6 There was also an important *rhetoric of utility* associated with the founding of many Institutes. However, taking at face value the utilitarian justifications made for Institutes leads to serious problems of interpretation. Such an assertion may sound forced, especially to those familiar with the careers of those very few Institutes which were transformed into technical colleges later in the century, e.g., the Manchester Mechanics' Institution and the Edinburgh School of Arts. But the *initial* stress of the Institutes on 'pure' science and 'scientific principles', their *general* neglect of applied subjects and practically relevant knowledge, and their total failure to develop (or even seriously to plan for) actual technical research, does cast doubt on the extent and immediacy of genuine utilitarian concerns as motivating their foundation. Moreover, the claim that teaching *principles* created more creative and innovative employees comes oddly from those who, at the time, were obsessed with inculcating in their labour-force a rigid conformity and docile acceptance of routine. We shall see later that the Institutes' curricula included a reified, atomized, anti-theoretical version of scientific knowledge designed precisely to constrain its recipients and stultify their imagination. As for the general avoidance of clearly useful knowledge, this was probably essential at a time when employers and employees alike found it in their interests to prevent its dissemination, in order to exploit its possession by themselves.

Moreover, we now have a very detailed study of a major Mechanics' Institute in a very different social context which provides indirect support for our interpretation. Bruce Sinclair's history of the Franklin Institute (see n. 17 below) is an account of a popular scientific organization founded in Philadelphia in 1824, and largely inspired by British models. What is striking in his account is that the Franklin Institute rapidly 'makes good' the traditional utilitarian justification for scientifically educating the people. It soon is undertaking large-scale *technical* research activities which are perceived as useful by American manufacturers and politicians. There is no evidence whatsoever in Sinclair's account that problems of social control were of immediate significance to contemporary Philadelphians, or that the Institute was motivated by a desire to remedy social disorder. On the other hand, in the British urban context where social control *was* a practical problem, not one Mechanics' Institute of which we are aware undertook, in its early career, to translate its utilitarian rhetoric into applied research reality.

7 John Foster, *Class Struggle and the Industrial Revolution: Early Industrial Capitalism in Three English Towns*, Weidenfeld & Nicolson, 1974, is the best, and most provocative, recent source on this.

8 See the superb essay by Sidney Pollard, 'Factory discipline in the industrial revolution', *Economic History Review*, 2nd ser., 16, 1963–4, 254–71; also Michael Sanderson, 'Education and the factory in industrial Lancashire', ibid., 20, 1967, 266–79.

9 This thesis is advanced and established, with particular reference to Oldham, by Foster (1974).

10 Lawrence Stone, 'Literacy and education in England 1640–1900', *Past & Present*, no. 42, February 1969, 69–139 (110).

11 On this point, see Richard Johnson, 'Educational policy and social control in early Victorian England', *Past & Present*, no. 49, November 1970, 106; R. K. Webb, *The British Working Class Reader 1790–1848: Literacy and Social Tension*, Allen & Unwin, 1955; Stone, op. cit., 85–6. For a contemporary perception, see Robinson, op. cit., 542: 'the "people", when they are embarked in party-politics, will ever turn in contempt from Brougham and Place, to read Cobbett and Carlisle.'

12 Henry Brougham, *Practical Observations upon the Education of the People, addressed to the Working Classes and their Employers*, London, 1825; 13th ed, p. 9.

13 This model of thought has been widely and persistently applied. Similar characteristics have repeatedly been discerned in the thought of other races, preliterate communities, mental defectives and children. It would be interesting to explore how far recent scientific work, such as that of Jensen (*Genetics and Education*, Methuen, 1972), should be taken as a further example of this. Presumably, the model serves as a general rationalizing resource which accounts those operating on the basis of an alternative scheme of things as having *no* scheme of things, and those with alternative conventions of rationality as irrational.

14 *The Consequences of a Scientific Education to the Working Classes of this Country pointed out; and the Theories of Mr Brougham on that Subject Confuted; in a Letter to the Marquess of Lansdown. By a Country Gentleman*, London, 1826.

15 ibid., pp. 17–18.

16 ibid., p. 22. A key difference between educational reactionaries like 'Country Gentleman' and reformers like Foster and George Combe is that the one believes that the imputed mental characteristics of the lower orders are *natural* (therefore, not surmountable), while the other hold them to be induced by *society* (hence, *unnatural* and improvable by social intervention). See, for example, Combe, op. cit. He maintained that it was a violation of natural law not to exercise all the mental faculties—rational as well as animal.

17 'Country Gentleman', p. 51n; italics in text. Even in the Franklin Institute of Philadelphia, educational planners observed that 'To practical men, theoretical discussions are, in general, unintelligible' (Bruce

Sinclair, *Philadelphia's Philosopher Mechanics: a History of the Franklin Institute, 1824–1865*, Johns Hopkins University Press, 1974, p. 197).

18 John Foster, *An Essay on the Evils of Popular Ignorance: and a Discourse on the Communication of Christianity to the People of Hindoostan*, 2nd ed., London, 1821, pp. 163–4.

19 ibid., pp. 169–70.

20 ibid., pp. 133–4; italics in text. Foster (1770–1843) was a Baptist minister and essayist.

21 One great problem in writing the history of Mechanics' Institutes is that there is so little evidence as to *how* science subjects were taught in the various establishments. Even in the case of the larger Institutes, such as the Edinburgh School of Arts, only a few teaching texts survive; and there is very little anecdotal information from teachers as to their pedagogical methods and almost none whatsoever from students as to their experiences of being taught. Existing sources reveal that, with very few exceptions, the lectorial style was universal. Examination, and the awarding of diplomas, was confined to the most ambitious Institutes in the largest cities. This scarcity of evidence on pedagogy makes it impossible for us to address ourselves to the very interesting suggestions relating knowledge to control in Basil Bernstein, *Class, Codes and Control*, Routledge & Kegan Paul, 1971.

22 *Scotsman*, 1 January 1825: 'Unlike some of the mechanic institutions which have been established in other places, after the example of the *School of Arts*, but which have wandered widely from the model, the students here have their attention solely directed to those objects which will be of real practical utility to them in their trade.' The Edinburgh model was followed by the founders of the Manchester Mechanics' Institution, including the resistance to artisan-representation on the Directorate (Mabel Tylecote, *The Mechanics' Institutes of Lancashire and Yorkshire before 1851*, Manchester University Press, 1957, pp. 129–31).

23 Mathematics was soon added because it was found difficult in practice to teach physics to students with inadequate numeracy. The Directors reluctantly accepted an offer of gratis lectures on farriery and architecture, while consistently resisting the teaching of 'a great many branches of science, which would distract [the student's] attention by their multiplicity ... without increasing [the] utility [of the School]' (Leonard Horner, *Scotsman*, 2 June 1824).

24 David de Giustino, *Conquest of Mind: Phrenology and Victorian Social Thought*, Croom Helm, 1975, ch. 8; Terry Parssinen, 'Popular science and society: the phrenology movement in early Victorian Britain', *Journal of Social History*, 8, 1974, 1–20. For a phrenologically-informed programme for a Mechanics' Institute, see Sir G. S. Mackenzie, *General Observations on the Principles of Education: for the Use of Mechanics' Institutions*, Edinburgh, 1836, an address delivered to the Inverness Mechanics' Institute.

25 Edward Royle, 'Mechanics' Institutes and the working classes, 1840–1860', *Historical Journal*, 14, 1971; Tylecote, op. cit., pp. 133, 139.

26 Thomas Hanna, *Memoirs of the Life and Writings of Thomas Chalmers, D.D. LL.D.*, vol. 3, Edinburgh, 1851, p. 26; *Scotsman*, 2 June 1824; *Third Report of the Edinburgh School of Arts*, Edinburgh, 1824, pp. 4–8.

27 Brougham, op. cit., p. 9.

28 'On the general question whether the labouring classes ought to be educated, and to what extent', *Edinburgh Christian Instructor*, n.s., 2, 1833, 519–27 (519–20); italics in text.

29 Compare this with the allegedly 'metaphysical science' of the Scottish academic tradition (G. E. Davie, *The Democratic Intellect: Scotland and her Universities in the Nineteenth Century*, 2nd ed., Edinburgh University Press, 1964, ch. 8). Although the strong form of Davie's thesis remains in some doubt, there is a real contrast in the 'philosophical' character of the two forms of education.

30 Thomas Dick, *On the Mental Illumination and Moral Improvement of Mankind*, Glasgow, 1835, pp. 386–7.

31 James Pillans, *Three Lectures on the Proper Objects and Methods of Education in Reference to the Different Orders of Society ...*, Edinburgh, 1836, pp. 19–20.

32 For example, Combe on popular physiology: 'The use of function is far better understood when founded on a demonstration of the structure than when communicated merely by verbal description ...' (George Combe, *On Teaching Physiology and Its Applications in Common Schools*, Edinburgh, 1857, p. 3). The point is not that 'demonstrations' are *only* to be found in the teaching of the working classes, but that they are stressed when the students are regarded as deficient in the abstract thought required; workers were regarded as constitutively deficient.

33 Some suggestions as to the sociological basis of the two epistemologies are contained in Steven Shapin, 'Phrenological knowledge and the social structure of early nineteenth-century Edinburgh', *Annals of Science*, 32, 1975, 219–43 (235–40).

34 Foster (1821), pp. 162–3.

35 ibid., p. 157.

36 ibid., pp. 160–1; italics in text.

37 James L. Drummond, quoted in Combe, *Lectures ...*, p. 39. See also Dick on astronomy: 'It ... unfolds to our view the most striking displays of the perfections of the Deity, particularly the grandeur of his *Omnipotence*. ... In short, it prepares the mind for the employments of the future world, and demonstrates, that the Creator has it in his power to distribute endlessly diversified streams of felicity, among every order of his intelligent offspring ...' (op. cit., pp. 326, 353–5).

38 Combe, *On Teaching Physiology*, pp. 13–14. Dick (op. cit., pp. 398–9) lists the following areas where moral lessons may be derived from the teaching of physiology to the people: diet and regimen, cleanliness, modes of dress, the proper use of food and drink (especially the moral and physical evils which flow from intemperance'), 'and the evils which arise from *immoderate* exertion of the mental or corporeal powers'.

39 Combe, *Lectures ...*, p. 33; also Dick, op. cit., pp. 426–31.

40 Combe, *Lectures ...*, p. 45.

41 But see John Bird Sumner and J. T. Coleridge, 'Mechanics' Institutes and infant schools', *Quarterly Review*, 32, 1825, 414: 'A public lecturer, who is so inclined, will find no difficulty in insinuating, together with his geometry or chemistry, the elements of infidelity and sedition' [!].

42 See, for example, George Lees, *Elements of Arithmetic, Algebra, and Geometry, for the Use of the Students of the Edinburgh School of Arts*, Edinburgh, 1826. The

scarcity of surviving representatives of the genre is indicated by the bibliography of Tylecote, op. cit.

43 See the following example from the Third Report of the Haddington School of Arts, quoted in A. Tyrrell, 'Political economy, Whiggism and the education of working-class adults in Scotland 1817–40', *Scottish Historical Review*, 48, 1969, 151–65 (158): 'Our mechanics do not sufficiently know the limits of their own, nor the extent of their masters' just rights. . . . Only let the working classes be trained to discrimination, either by that general science which sharpens the faculties of all who are conversant with it; or let them be made acquainted with that particular science, part of whose object it is to elucidate the nature of the relation in which capitalists and labourers stand to each other; and we shall be as little disturbed by the spirit of combination, as by a revival of the spirit of witchcraft.'

44 pp. 5, 11.

45 'On Mechanic Schools . . .', *The Christian and Civic Economy of Large Towns*, vol. 3, Glasgow, 1826, pp. 386–92.

46 In 1882, when the physicist David Brewster attempted, for purely entrepreneurial reasons, to subvert the School of Arts, his strongest argument was the assertion that it 'had assumed a political character' (*Scotsman*, 7 September 1822). Nothing could, if proven, have been more effective in eliminating the hard-won support of Edinburgh's Tories.

47 More direct, less objective and highly anthropomorphic forms of moralizing natural science continued to be applied to children throughout the nineteenth century. The enormously popular *The Reason Why* series of Victorian science texts for children, as one example of a ubiquitous genre, topped each page with a suitably chosen Scriptural moral. This is apparent confirmation of the idea that people will resort to more indirect attempts at control only when they are obliged to by the demonstrated 'cleverness' of their hoped-for audience. See also David Layton, *Science for the People: The Origins of the School Science Curriculum in England*, Allen & Unwin, 1973, esp. chs 1, 5.

48 Tyrrell, op. cit., pp. 161, 165. The leftists in today's middle classes who fear that workers are currently deluded into acceptance of capitalism by scientist ideologies and other 'crucial' legitimations would do well to reflect on historical precedents such as this.

49 The only alternative strategy was to re-orient the curriculum directly to workers' interests and hence, *per impossibile*, against employers' interests. One variant of this strategy was in fact adopted by middle-class groups. It consisted in modifying political economy into a kind of self-help doctrine, or recipe for how to rise in the world. This could purport to offer some advantage to an *individual* worker while at the same time operating in the interest of the employer class as a whole, since its prescriptions could never bring success to workers collectively, and, if widely followed, would only set employee against employee.

50 Brougham, op. cit., p. 32: 'The more widely science is diffused, the better will the Author of all things be known, and the less will the people be "tossed to and fro by the sleight of men".'

51 Mary Douglas, *Implicit Meanings: Essays in Anthropology*, Routledge & Kegan Paul, 1975.

52 Foster (1821), pp. 200–1; italics in text.

53 ibid., pp. 202, 205.

54 David Burns, *Mechanics' Institutions: Their Objects and Tendency*, Glasgow, 1837, pp. 56–7.

55 *First Report of the Edinburgh School of Arts*, Edinburgh, 1822, p. 15.

56 See esp., Arnold Thackray, 'Natural knowledge in cultural context: the Manchester model', *American Historical Review*, 79, 1974; Shapin, op. cit.

57 This line of speculation has been pressed a considerable way by Marxists such as Needham and Hobsbawm, and more recently by Marcuse. Other scholars, however, have tried to understand the clear historical link between science and urban, commercial and industrial societies in much broader terms. As early as 1906 Veblen was accounting for the general features of modern scientific culture in terms such as these: 'In the modern culture, industry, industrial production and industrial products have progressively gained upon humanity, until these creations of mass ingenuity have latterly come to take dominant place in the cultural scheme; and it is not too much to say that they have become the chief force in shaping men's daily life, and therefore the chief factor in shaping men's habits of thought. Hence men have learned to think in the terms in which the technological processes act.' Arkwright's dream has, according to Thorstein Veblen, been fulfilled ('The place of science in modern civilization', *American Journal of Sociology*, 2, 1906, 585–609; repr. in Barry Barnes, ed., *Sociology of Science*, Penguin, 1972, pp. 321–30 (327–28)). We would not wish to take issue with those who see the connection between science and urban industrialization in the broadest terms, and we agree with Ernest Gellner that 'science is the mode of cognition of urban industrial societies' (*Thought and Change*, Weidenfeld & Nicolson, 1964, p. 72). It is worth noting, however, that mechanics avoided acquiring their 'habits of thought' at Mechanics' Institutes, and that the science they would otherwise have encountered there was hardly presented as the 'creation of man's ingenuity'.

6 The urban genesis of school bureaucracy: a transatlantic comparison

Dennis Smith

The initial concern of this paper[1] is the part played by the industrial and commercial bourgeoisie in the development of the English education system.[2] However, the analysis will not be restricted to this problem and will touch upon a number of other related areas. In the course of the paper a brief comparison will be carried out of some aspects of educational development in Birmingham, and in a number of towns in Massachusetts, USA, using data from the late nineteenth century. There are two reasons for adopting this approach. First, investigation of an English provincial city not only provides a useful check on sweeping generalisations about 'the national system' but also emphasises the importance of the structural relationship between the provinces and the metropolis, the municipalities and central government, local and national configurations of power relations. Second, a cross-societal comparison tends to throw into relief those structural characteristics which distinguish the two cases from each other as against those which are common to both. Such a comparison, it will be argued, tends to suggest that a range of structural variations is possible in processes of societal development and that such variations are strongly associated with differences in the patterns of formal education that develop.

The paper is organised in three sections. In the *first*, the account of educational developments in Massachusetts given by Michael B. Katz in a number of recent books and papers will be briefly summarised.[3] Katz emphasises the part played by the bourgeoisie in an urban power structure undergoing changes which are explained in terms of processes of industrialisation, urbanisation and bureaucratisation. Such processes were also at work, albeit in a different way, in the case of Birmingham. Some of their

manifestations will be examined in the *second* section. Particular attention will be paid to the King Edward VI Foundation in its relations with the Town Council and Birmingham School Board in the period from the 1860s to the 1890s. As in Katz's analysis, the overt 'educational issues' discussed will be the organisation of secondary education and the influence of teachers within the school system. Such a focus directs attention to relations among bourgeois, professional, gentry and aristocratic groups. The first successful independent 'working man's candidate', sponsored by Birmingham Trades Council, did not appear on the School Board until 1894. However, many of the proposals and policies to be examined betray an awareness of the potential threat of organised working-class power. In the *third* section, the similarities and differences between English and American cases will be summarised and some implications drawn out for theory and research.

I

According to Katz, the bureaucratic system of public education in Massachusetts emerged in the context of industrialisation and urbanisation. These processes weakened the social power of small-town traders, farmers and artisans and undermined the authority of old urban elites whose wealth was based on trade and commercial agriculture. The initiative was seized by new economic leaders—manufacturers, bankers, businessmen—who saw in a tax-supported education system a means to create wealth and social harmony in a thriving industrial society over which they would preside. At the summit of this new school system was the public high school, described by Katz as a 'strictly middle-class institution'.[4] As such, it was resisted by members of the genteel establishment who patronised private schools such as Lawrence Academy in Groton.[5] Its other opponents were men such as the 'fishermen, farmers, shoemakers and laborers' who

Source: article commissioned for this volume. The author is lecturer in sociology, University of Leicester.

voted for the abolition of the public high school in Beverly in 1860.[6]

The disputes in Groton and Beverly were part of a broader process. Manufacturers, bankers, professional men and many others were caught up in a series of overlapping struggles: to capture or secure the strongholds of urban society, to pacify the growing workforce upon whose labour and talents they depended, and to equip their own offspring to survive and succeed in an expanding world offering new pitfalls and opportunities. Formal education was a central arena within which these struggles were played out.

Pursuing both 'improvement' and 'economy', industrialists encouraged the development of an educational bureaucracy. This tendency was manifest in three areas: the grading of pupils and schools, the development of a more complex administrative hierarchy of professional educators, and an increase in the relative power of this hierarchy vis-à-vis the laymen whose reforming enthusiasm initially brought it into existence. Quincy and Boston provide Katz with examples.

In Quincy during the early 1870s the school committee argued that 'to have first-rate common schools, you must collect your pupils in a few centers, and then classify them as thoroughly as possible.' Thus would 'the best results . . . be obtained at the least expense'.[7] A similar rationale underlay the appointment of a full-time superintendent of schools in 1875. However, the crystallisation of a body of professional educators increasingly conscious of its own importance weakened the possibility of combining improvement with economy. In 1880, for example, the Quincy school committee decided to cut the salaries of new teachers. As a result, the superintendent left for a new job in Boston and took with him one-quarter of Quincy's teaching force.[8] The educational bureaucracy became increasingly powerful, increasingly capable of resisting the dictates of its lay masters on the elected school committees. In Boston, the committee sought to reduce the independence of the grammar school teachers by appointing six new supervisors, many of whom had very little previous experience in education. The teachers were able to mount a strong and successful campaign of resistance. The victory of the 'schoolmen', to use Katz's term, indicated that the structure of power relations had altered decisively in their favour, making lay incursions more difficult and less effective.[9]

Finally, at a more general level, Katz argues that four main models for the organization of public education were sponsored in the nineteenth-century United States.[10] The first was *paternalistic voluntarism*, whereby leading citizens used their own resources to school the poor. The second was *corporate voluntarism*, which consisted of 'the conduct of *single* institutions operated by self-perpetuating boards of trustees and financed either wholly through endowment or through a combination of endowment and tuition'.[11] Such institutions were found mainly in the secondary and higher levels of education. The third was *democratic localism*, which entailed control by the community over its own schools. The fourth was *incipient bureaucracy*, whereby control was removed from wealthy benefactors, self-perpetuating boards and community representatives. In this system, bureaucrats used the resources of the state to impose standardised structure, content and assessment within the schools. In the light of his research, Katz argues that the fourth mode became increasingly dominant. However, the institutional forms of bureaucracy incorporated some aspects of 'democratic localism' and retained the paternalism inherent in 'voluntaristic' modes of educational provision.

As in Massachusetts, many initiatives in Birmingham education were taken by industrialists. Quaker manufacturers such as the Cadbury family and the Tangye brothers did much work in adult and technical education respectively. Josiah Mason established a science college bearing his name on the basis of a fortune made in pen-nibs. The National Education League, which from 1869 to 1876 campaigned for free, compulsory, universal and nonsectarian education, included among its Birmingham leadership not only the Tangyes (engineering manufacturers) but also George Dixon (a wealthy businessman), William Kenrick (iron manufacturer), Henry Wiggin (head of a successful drapery firm), and Joseph Chamberlain who helped build up the enterprise which later became Guest, Keen and Nettlefold. Such men had aspirations for Birmingham and themselves which struck a sympathetic chord in Massachusetts. Indeed, in the words of the League's secretary, Francis Adams, its spokesmen[12]

> more often referred to the schools in Boston than those of any other city. The reason for this has been that in this city only have been found in practice three of the most essential features of the scheme advocated by the League— representative government, free admission and compulsory school attendance.

Institutions strongly reminiscent of all four of the organisational 'models' delineated by Katz could be found in late nineteenth-century Birmingham. Despite a significant amount of state support and control, the 122 schools for the poor on which Inspector Fitch reported in 1869 continued to rely on the generosity of genteel and respectable folk channelled through the voluntary societies.[13] The spirit of *paternalistic voluntarism* is nicely caught in the Honourable and Reverend Grantham Yorke's expressed intention to civilise the Birmingham youth who 'tramps or lounges along the pavement, loud in voice and truculent in manner . . . he cuts his joke aloud about the dress of the lady he passes in the street, or runs against her . . . with his burden of gun barrels.'[14]

Corporate voluntarism is manifest also: in Mason College; in Queen's College (a school of medicine and surgery); in the Birmingham and Midland Institute (founded 1854 and offering improvement and diversion to artisans and the 'middling classes', in separate departments); and in the elementary and secondary schools of the King Edward VI Foundation which furnished free education to the offspring of relatively well-off Birmingham families in artisan occupations, trade and the professions. Elements of both the spirit and the form of *democratic localism* were also strongly evident. At the Severn Street Adult School and its many branches, Quaker teachers deliberately sought to cultivate an atmosphere of openness and equality across class boundaries. They taught 427 scholars in 1850, a figure that had grown to 4,364 in 1895.[15] The clearest institutional expression of formal democratic control was the Birmingham School Board, elected by ratepayers. This was established in 1870 and remained in existence until 1903.

A major consequence of the vigorous activity of this Board, particularly after 1873, was the development of a complex educational bureaucracy. Beginning work with one clerk in 1870, by the mid-nineties the Board was running fifty-three schools whose teaching staff were under the regular supervision of eight specialist Board inspectors and four administrative departments. The Board did not use its power to appoint school managers, preferring to rely on inspectors to supervise the schools.[16] Instruction was organised in standards leading to government examinations and by 1892 two higher grade schools serving the whole city had been established. Central classes for pupil–teachers were organised in 1880, followed by a day training college in 1890. By the mid-nineties, the work of pupil–teachers, assistants and headteachers was being supplemented by a corps of specialists in science, manual instruction, singing, physical exercises, cookery and pupil–teacher training. This extensive bureaucracy was under the formal control of a Board whose seven committees (after 1880) were filled by a total of only fifteen elected members. Apart from managing its own affairs, the Board was in constant negotiation with the Education Department at Whitehall, the Science and Art Department at South Kensington, and, in Birmingham itself, the Technical School Committee, the School and Art Committee, the managers of voluntary schools and many other occupants of an increasingly dense bureaucratic jungle.

It may be suggested that Birmingham education in the 1890s resembled the Massachusetts pattern in that it was regulated through a public bureaucracy behaving in a paternalistic manner within the formal confines of local democratic control. However, such similarities coexisted with great differences both in the disposition of social relationships within the educational bureaucracy and the structures of class and political relations within which this bureaucracy was set. Evidence of the configuration exemplified in the case of Birmingham will emerge in the course of the following section.

II

Two central themes underlying Katz's work are the organisation and control of secondary education (the issue in Beverly and Groton) and the character and influence of teachers within the school system (the issue in Quincy and Boston). Similar themes underlie the brief analysis to be conducted here with respect to Birmingham. In Katz's terms, the case now to be examined could be described as a conflict between the principles of 'corporate voluntarism' and those of 'democratic localism' and 'incipient bureaucracy'. To be examined is the bitter dispute in Birmingham during the 1860s over the management and control of the endowed schools of the King Edward VI Foundation. This Foundation was a clear example of Katz's model of 'corporate voluntarism', with one minor difference. Instead of controlling a single institution, the Foundation was responsible for four elementary schools feeding into a grammar school which was divided into separate classical and English departments. The Foundation was the major provider of free, largely non-boarding elementary and secondary instruction for moderately well-to-do tradesmen and many professional and business families in Birmingham. To a great extent the dispute centred on the grammar school which was, in Katz's terms, 'operated by [a] self-perpetuating board . . . of trustees and financed through a combination of endowment and tuition'. The tuition fees were restricted mainly to a handful of boarders. When a seat on the governing board of the Foundation fell vacant, the remaining governors invited someone of their own choosing to serve.

In 1865, the Schools Inquiry Commission headed by Lord Taunton heard evidence from the headmaster of the grammar school, the school governors, the Town Council and, finally, the recently formed Free Grammar School Association. They also received a special report on the school from T. H. Green, one of the Assistant Commissioners. Nearly three decades later, in 1894, the Secondary Education Commission headed by Lord Bryce heard evidence from the Rev. A. R. Vardy, headmaster of the King Edward VI boys' high school and the Rev. E. F. M. MacCarthy, vice-chairman of Birmingham School Board. Unlike their predecessors in the 1860s who had found the Town Council and the school governors in deep conflict, the Bryce Commissioners heard a tale of harmony and co-operation between the secondary schools of the King Edward VI Foundation and the major public education authority, the School Board. However, that very year a School Board election occurred which revealed deep division within Birmingham's education bureaucracy. In the election of November 1894 the poll was decisively headed by W. Ansell, former headmaster of Norton Street Board School. He voiced the bitter complaints of board school elementary teachers about low pay and over-inspection by the School Board. In what follows, most space will be devoted to the conflict of the 1860s. Their sequel in the 1890s will be examined more briefly.

In 1865, when T. H. Green came to Birmingham to investigate the state of the King Edward VI schools, he found a 'campaign committee' already in existence. A Free Grammar School Association composed of 'leading citizens' was demanding reforms both in the curriculum and the composition of the governing body. Green described the English and classical departments of the grammar school as follows:[17]

> The best general notion can be given by saying that on the whole the classical department has set itself to teach classics, with a supplement of mathematics, and little else; that the English department sets itself to give a boy a clerk's education, with the addition of some knowledge of Latin, and (supposing him to complete the course) of English literature and history, French and German, mathematics and chemistry. [However, in his last two years at school, the boy] would have lost some of his readiness at accounts and spoilt his handwriting . . .
>
> Between the classes of boys using the two departments it is difficult to draw a more definite distinction than that the classical boys are on the whole more 'genteel' . . . The professional class . . . may be reckoned the first element in the constituency of the classical school. I do not suppose anyone belonging to it ever sent a son to the other department. . . . Anyone who distinctly meant to put his son to some business at or before the age of 16, would naturally send him to the English school, though he might take the other as an alternative. As a matter of fact, many boys do leave the classical department for business under 16, as may be seen from the returns . . . From the English school . . . almost all the boys become clerks in offices of various kinds, but the course of study in the upper classes of this department gives no special qualifications for such clerkship . . . The education *necessary* for commercial life, the school, in its English department, now adequately gives— gives, however, in its lower classes, and no better than it is given at one of the [King Edward VI] elementary schools or at a good National school. It also gives an education which qualifies, if pursued, for the highest distinctions at Oxford and Cambridge. The education, however, given in the higher classes of the English school, and to all those in the classical school, except the few who go to Oxford or Cambridge, is one having no special reference to any office or distinction to be obtained after the education itself is over.

Green acknowledged the force of the common accusation that the grammar school 'turned out a great many bad clerks for the sake of turning out a few good scholars'.[18] Much of the schooling provided was irrelevant to local vocational needs. The two principal attractions of the school to middling businessmen and the local professional circles of solicitors, ministers and medical men were its cheapness and the aura of gentility it bestowed. Significantly, the most substantial men of business did *not* patronise the school. According to Green: 'The more wealthy merchants and manufacturers, those, at least, whose wealth is of long standing, generally send their sons to boarding schools.'[19] The significance of this will be explored below.

The other major issue was the demand by the Town Council for representation on the school's board of governors. Green wrote:[20]

> the board [of governors] has fairly represented the upper or more select section of society in Birmingham, so far as this section is politically conservative and attached to the established church . . . In Birmingham, as elsewhere, there is an unfortunate, though natural tendency in the professional class, and among those commercial men whose families have been well off for one or two generations, to stand aloof from municipal affairs. The exceptions to this rule— and there are several notable exceptions—have been uniformly men of liberal politics and generally dissenters. Thus, a board composed of conservative churchmen, of good social position, has necessarily been antagonistic to the town council, and careless or contemptuous of local politics. To belong to it has been a certain social distinction. Social and municipal distinctions have not coincided, and hence the board has been an object of public animosity, irrespectively of the manner in which it has exercised its function.

The hostility between the Town Council and the board of governors must be seen as an aspect of a much broader pattern of social conflict. A preliminary idea of this broader pattern may be obtained by contrasting the membership of the school governors with the composition of the committee of the Free Grammar School Association. Contrary to what would be expected by analogy with the case of Massachusetts as described by Katz, the campaign to reform the grammar school was not dominated by businessmen. Nor was it directed against an opposition whose occupational character was fundamentally distinct. Among the eighteen governors may be found Anglican clergy,[21] doctors,[22] legal practitioners[23] and manufacturers.[24] A similar spread of occupations is represented on the Free Grammar School Association committee.[25] It is possible to identify eighteen manufacturers,[26] five merchants,[27] two well-to-do tradesmen,[28] nine members of the legal profession,[29] five other professional or semi-professional men[30] and ten clergy (of whom three were

Anglican).[31] Of the fifty-two members of the Association committee, twenty-five may be clearly identified as businessmen and twenty-four as secular and religious professionals or semi-professionals. The remaining three are difficult to identify with confidence.[32] Of the Town Council members on the committee, twelve were businessmen[33] and only three professional men.[34] However, the Town Clerk, a solicitor, was also a member of the committee. Of the two honorary secretaries, one, John Skirrow Wright, was a businessman and the other, Balthazar Foster, a doctor. C. E. Matthews, the most effective propagandist for the Association, was a prominent local solicitor.

It is tempting to argue that if occupation and source of wealth do not distinguish the two sides then religious affiliation does provide a significant criterion. In contrast to the uniform Anglicanism of the governors, the committee contained not only seven dissenting ministers but also several lay members of Quaker, Congregationalist, Baptist and other nonconformist bodies. Among them was, for example, William Middlemore, a wealthy saddler who later founded the Central Nonconformist Committee with the object of resisting educational legislation which favoured the Anglican church. However, it will be suggested that religious differences form only part, albeit an important part, of two much wider aspects of social conflict. These may be briefly stated and then illustrated in turn. First there was the resistance of *established* social groups and institutions to parvenu *outsiders* wishing to assert new-found power. Second there was the assertion of *local* interests and aspirations—expressed partly through the Town Council—against the inclinations of groups who identified with 'higher' non-local or *national* circles.

Membership of the Association manifested a variety of motivations, not simply religious ones. Among the professional members of the Free Grammar School Association committee were men such as William Harris who helped to found the Birmingham Architectural Society and was to be active in developing a new style of mass party political organisation in the wake of the 1867 Reform Act.[35] His colleagues included Balthazar Foster, a prominent member of the British Medical Association. As chairman of Birmingham and Midland Counties branch of the BMA, he was later to urge doctors to take 'their due share in the important and responsible work of local government'.[36] The businessmen included self-made men such as Arthur Albright[37] who developed the safety match and James Baldwin, the paper-manufacturer who often boasted that he had 'risen from being a working man'.[38] Professionals and businessmen such as these found that the exploitation of their wealth and expertise was hindered within a prevailing structure of political, professional and educational organisation dominated by elites who had settled into power during an earlier period. For such men,

membership of the Free Grammar School Association was one aspect of a wider social strategy which comprised on the one hand the creation of new institutions—professional associations, political party organisations, campaign committees of various kinds—and on the other hand attempts to capture and reform existing institutions, such as the King Edward VI Foundation and the Town Council. A major sphere of activity for reformers became local government. E. P. Hennock has traced the growing prestige of municipal service in Birmingham, beginning in the mid sixties, shortly after the formation of the Association.[39] Harris became a town councillor in 1865, Dr Foster in 1883. In the intervening period, many substantial businessmen and professionals in Birmingham sought and achieved office, creating a tradition of participation in local government whose high point was the mayoralty of Joseph Chamberlain between 1873 and 1876. The activities of the Free Grammar School Association must be seen in this broader context.

The distinctions between the established and the outsiders, between locals and cosmopolitans and between Anglicans and dissenters, did not always run parallel but were in many cases cross-cutting. Some indication of the range of local aspirations is conveyed in the evidence to the Schools Inquiry Commission of three members of the Association: R. W. Dale, a nonconformist minister who strongly advocated that leading local citizens should enter municipal service,[40] W. L. Sargant, a munitions manufacturer[41] and George Dixon, a merchant.[42] Since the latter two were both Anglicans from well-off families, they provide interesting instances of an emphasis on local interests and aspirations which does not stem from an experience of social exclusion on religious or other grounds. Indeed, Sargant was himself a school governor as well as an Association member.

The central theme of Dale's evidence was, as he put it, 'that among the nonconformists there are as many men competent to conduct a great educational establishment as there are among members of the Establishment in Birmingham.' He also voiced the widespread demand that Town Council nominees should be placed on the governing body. He was convinced that such nominees would be 'distinguished and effective' and that 'if the representative principle had been adopted [earlier], the strong desire on the part of the town that the mathematical element should be introduced [into the school] more freely would have been met . . . the school would not have been so exclusively classical'.[43] Sargant agreed that 'mathematics are far too much neglected' and was concerned that in Birmingham 'the education of the middle middle class is disgracefully bad'.[44] It is significant that Sargant, located in society somewhat about this 'middle middle class', sent his own offspring as fee-payers to the Edgbaston Proprietary School. The fact that the more substantial businessmen did not themselves patronise the King Edward schools in large numbers helps to explain the tenor of Dixon's evidence, which was that the funds of the Foundation should, to a much greater extent than formerly, be 'applied to the education of the children of the poorest people'. He hoped for a scheme whereby existing schools for the poor were connected with the Foundation so that 'the poorest boy in Birmingham might have the opportunity . . . if he were qualified by his industry and his talents . . . of rising from those lowest schools up to the highest'. This being so, he opposed the practice of taking boarders at the school, arguing that 'the whole of the powers of the masters should be devoted to the education of Birmingham boys, and that no part of it should be given to the instruction of boys coming from a distance.'[45]

The emphasis on local interests which all these witnesses manifested, though in different ways, stood in sharp contrast to the wishes of the headmaster of the grammar school, the Rev. Charles Evans. He wanted to take more boarders, make fee-paying general, extend the teaching of Latin into the elementary schools of the Foundation and generally free himself from 'local pressure, which may often be unwisely exerted'. He eschewed the indignity of entering the local examinations run by the universities, as Sargant had urged, and proudly claimed that 'in the classical school the routine of the education is very much the same as that adopted in the great public schools'. In general, his evidence betrayed a clear ambition to elevate his school into the higher national orbit of the public schools.[46]

On the basis of this partial analysis of the dispute over the King Edward VI schools in 1865, two tentative conclusions may be advanced. First, the most substantial body of Birmingham citizens to patronise the grammar school by sending their own children there were not businessmen but professional men—doctors, solicitors, clergy, and so on. Those business people who used the school were mainly small manufacturers and modest traders. Such men were in Birmingham society only a little above the respectable artisans, clerks and shopkeepers whose children found their way into the King Edward VI elementary schools. These in turn were separated by their respectability from the children of the 'poor' who inhabited the National schools. Professional families stood clearly above all of these groups in gentility and social influence. Their children tended to be segregated in the classical department. Second, the *most* prosperous business families and, no doubt, a number of professional families sent their children to boarding-schools out of Birmingham. At public school, such children would mix with the offspring of the gentry and aristocracy.

It may be suggested that the evidence of businessmen such as George Dixon is deeply coloured by the fact that they were speaking of the schooling not of their own children but of their future employees. The education of the poor, still very inadequate in the 1860s, was seen as a precondition of social harmony. Furthermore, they hoped that the opening up of channels of social mobility through the schools would ensure a steady flow of talents and skills which could be harnessed in the service of Birmingham industry and commerce. Since their own children were being educated in clearly superior establishments, there was little threat of serious social competition from below through the King Edward VI schools. Dixon's evidence was echoed in the opinion expressed by John Skirrow Wright, acting chairman of the Council of Birmingham's Chamber of Commerce and honorary secretary of the Free Grammar School Association.[47] He told the Schools Inquiry Commissioners of the need for 'entirely free schools for the very poorest classes [combined with] facilities for those boys who have an aptitude for learning to pass into the highest schools' of the locality.[48] The Foundation should provide such facilities and subsidise the schooling of the poor.

The grammar school was the focus of intense social pressures, caught not only between the demands of powerful 'outsiders' and a recalcitrant 'establishment' wishing to preserve its control, but also between the contrary constraints exercised by local and national configurations of power and prestige. On the one hand, the Rev. Charles Evans, the headmaster, wished to promote his school into a national sphere which comprised not only the great boarding-schools but also the ancient universities, the hierarchy of the established church, and metropolitan political and administrative circles. On the other hand, the Town Council, well represented on the Free Grammar School Association, was in the early phase of a period of expansive development which would culminate in the reforming mayoralty of Joseph Chamberlain. Its demand to be represented on the governing body of the school was an early hint of the strategy which would culminate in the great municipal exercises in 'gas and water socialism'.[49]

Further analysis of the participants to the disputes in the 1860s would no doubt reveal a complicated pattern of 'establishment' and 'outsider' relationships and a variety of local and cosmopolitan orientations among businessmen and professionals, both religious and secular. Given this complexity of constraints, alliances forged in one context might turn into enmity on other occasions. To give only the most obvious example, Dixon and Sargant, the two Anglican businessmen cited above, were to find themselves on opposite sides in the rancorous School Board debates of the early 1870s.[50]

The analysis suggested above cannot be carried out here. However, two tasks remain. First, the outcome of the dispute will be traced and its sequel in the 1890s briefly described. Second, in the final section of this paper, some general conclusions will be drawn on the basis of the comparison between the English and American examples.

Between 1865 and 1883, three schemes were proposed for the management of the Foundation, all being opposed by the Town Council. By 1894 a modified version of the third scheme had been in operation for a decade. This final compromise provided for eight Town Council nominees out of a total of twenty-one governors. In place of the King Edward VI elementary schools there were instead seven grammar schools, three for boys, four for girls. These took pupils up to the age of sixteen. There were also two high schools, one for boys and one for girls, which provided courses up to the age of nineteen. The schools became predominantly fee-paying. Transformation of the Foundation elementary schools into grammar schools was no doubt made politically easier by the creation in 1870 of a new public body, the Birmingham School Board, which had established fifty-three schools of its own by the mid-nineties. The overwhelming majority of these were non-fee-paying public elementary schools. However, as the representative of the Board told the Bryce Commission in 1894, two of these schools provided advanced training and could be thought of, to use his term, as 'board secondary schools'. One of these had been established in 1884, funded by George Dixon. As a 'seventh standard' or 'higher grade' school, it took boys from throughout the city and provided 'manual, scientific and technical education'. This school pursued in the 'public' sphere the objective of promoting low-born talent that Dixon had attempted to impose in the sphere of 'corporate voluntarism' two decades previously. The Board's representative, the Rev. E. F .M. MacCarthy, proudly claimed that 'it was the first of its kind in the country'. In 1892 the Waverley Road seventh standard school had also been opened, for boys and girls. By 1894 both schools were recognised as 'organised science schools' by the Department of Science and Art at South Kensington.[51]

The question arises, as it certainly did in the minds of the Bryce Commissioners: were the Board's seventh standard or higher grade schools in competition with the endowed secondary schools run by the King Edward VI Foundation? Was the situation in any sense equivalent to that described by Katz in Groton, Massachusetts, where the public high school established by the school committee was in open competition with a local private school, Lawrence Academy? MacCarthy told the Bryce Commissioners that the Board intended to extend their provision of higher grade schools. He was asked if he did not agree that 'the effect of that would be to expunge the endowed secondary school because it would die before the competition of the other.' He replied that they met 'different educational needs' and that there was 'no competition between the two'.[52]

There are some grounds for taking MacCarthy's reply at face value, at least as a statement of the Board's wishes. In earlier evidence, he declared that the board higher grade schools would relieve the endowed grammar schools of 'scholars with whom they could not adequately deal'. In effect, the different kinds of school would take pupils with different social backgrounds and aspirations. The endowed schools were more literary, the board schools more technical. Of the former, said MacCarthy, the high school led to Oxford and Cambridge, the grammar schools to the local Mason College or straight into commerce and the professions. The Board's higher grade schools, on the other hand, qualified their students for 'the better classes of employment with respect to the manufactures, and on the commercial side for the smaller commercial posts'. The endowed schools remained clearly dominant within the status hierarchy of local secondary education. One corollary of such a system, recognised by MacCarthy, was that those board school children who sought entry to the endowed secondary schools should be admitted only at the age of eleven or thereabouts. He told the Bryce Commission that a child who transferred at a later age would have 'a mental equipment much narrower in range than the pupils among whom he finds himself of corresponding age'. Perhaps here can be seen an early version of the practice and ideology of sponsored mobility whose later manifestations were examined by Ralph Turner.[53]

The words of MacCarthy were largely echoed by those of the Rev. A. R. Vardy, headmaster of the King Edward VI boys' high school. He also spoke of the integrated character of education in Birmingham. He eulogised the city as being 'not too large for those engaged in public work to know one another', stressing in particular that 'happily very intimate relations have for many years existed among teachers of all grades of schools'.[54] As will be seen shortly, there was unconscious irony in Vardy's last statement.

The evidence of Vardy and MacCarthy must be seen in the light of two considerations. First, MacCarthy, who had been on the School Board since 1875 and was Vice-President in 1894, was himself the headmaster of one of the King Edward VI grammar schools.[55] Second, both he and Vardy had played a major part in the creation of a corps of trained elementary school teachers in Birmingham. MacCarthy had been an honorary secretary of the Higher Education Society when it was established in the seventies. Vardy had been a founder of the Birmingham Teachers' Association in 1874. A major concern of both bodies continued to be the provision of training for the humbler men and women who would staff the Board's elementary school.[56] There is thus some evidence that the advance of public bureaucracy into a sphere previously dominated by 'corporate voluntarism' had been complemented by a kind of 'reverse colonisation' of the Board's sphere by representatives of the endowed secondary schools.

Two decades of work by MacCarthy in the sphere of teacher training culminated in the 1894 School Board election in the course of which he was roundly attacked by a candidate representing the Board school teachers, mainly in elementary schools. Ansell, the teachers' spokesman, collected more votes than the next eight candidates. Like his transatlantic colleagues in Boston and Quincy, he complained of over-inspection and low pay.[57] However, the parallel is as misleading as it was in the case of Groton mentioned above. In Boston and Quincy, teachers were defending themselves against vigorous incursions by elected representatives from other occupational spheres. In Birmingham, a leading secondary school teacher was a dominant member of the elected School Board. To a great extent the 1894 election revealed not a conflict between the 'schoolmen' and lay representatives but a division between the more genteel secondary teachers and their humbler elementary school colleagues who, it may be surmised, were expressing the resentment generated by twenty years of tutelage. In the short run, the complaints of the elementary school teachers were dealt with by a revision of pay scales (1895) and a reduction in the number of inspectors (1899). In the longer run, they were admitted into the outer rim of the charmed circle of scholarly gentility inhabited by men such as Vardy and MacCarthy. The means of doing this were the local authority grammar schools which, particularly after the issue of the Secondary School Regulations in 1904, provided a form of liberal education inspired by the example of the public schools. The grammar schools became a major avenue of teacher recruitment for the elementary schools.[58]

Such an outcome illustrates what may be a general pattern in the development of relations between the 'established' and the 'outsiders' in a number of spheres.[59] This pattern is as follows. An actual or potential challenge to a settled establishment by newly powerful, organised and self-conscious 'outsiders' is softened and dissipated by a process of osmosis or infiltration. In the course of this process, a new pattern of social allegiances is created, the most powerful members of the 'outsiders' lose their sense of exclusion, the 'established' make tactical concessions and, while altering the styles through which their authority is expressed, retain their dominance in many respects. Further research is needed to verify the occurrence of such a pattern but it is strongly suggested by a series of events discussed in this paper. Bitter hostility between the Town Council and the King Edward VI Foundation in the sixties had softened into co-operation by the nineties; the Foundation became committed to its *local* clientele, admitted town council nominees onto the governing body but retained the literary emphasis in its curriculum. The hostility of the Town Council was no doubt also muted by the fact that during the eighties and nineties the School Board provided advanced training of a kind which councillor Dixon and many of his colleagues had urged on the Foundation in the days of the Free Grammar School Association. The passage of talented and potentially troublesome working-class youths into the higher grade schools may have helped to engage their commitment to the industrial and commercial establishment which promoted their advancement. Whether or not they tended to soften some forms of class conflict within Birmingham society, the higher grade schools themselves in turn presented a potential challenge to the endowed secondary schools of the Foundation. This challenge was itself considerably weakened by the advance of powerful representatives of the Foundation onto the School Board and into the sphere of training board school teachers. However, the growing organisation and self-confidence of trained elementary school teachers expressed itself, in its turn, as a conflict between them and their more genteel and 'established' brethren in the secondary schools. Although such hostilities tended to persist, they were dampened by the increasing tendency to recruit future elementary school teachers into the local authority grammar schools whose establishment was encouraged by central government in the wake of the 1902 Act. The training given in these schools gave some guarantee of the continued dominance of that liberal culture which helped sustain the high status of schools such as those of the King Edward VI Foundation.

Two observations are prompted by the above account. First, the structure of relations between 'established' and 'outsider' groups has a complexity which cannot be reduced to simple lines of class conflict. Second, the overt manifestations of these conflicts with respect to formal education apparently tended to shift their location, particularly in the latter part of the period being examined. They moved out of the main stream of Birmingham society to appear within the ranks of the local educational bureaucracy itself and in relations between this local bureaucracy and the bureaucracy of central government. The decisive character of constraints imposed from the centre is sufficiently illustrated by the abolition of the Birmingham School Board itself in 1903.[60]

In no sense do the above remarks attempt to dissolve away power struggles between social classes, or to make them appear as bureaucratic squabbles and 'office politics'. Neither class relations nor political relations are mere epiphenomena of the other. Structures of formal schooling bear the sharp impress of both—and in their turn, through the processes of educational selection and transmission which they encompass, they make an important contribution to the development of both class and political relations. More specifically, it is apparent that many of the twists and turns examined in the above analysis require for their explanation more attention to two related processes. One of these is the development of the relationship between employers of labour and an increasingly organised workforce, which has particular relevance to the establishment of the higher grade schools. The other process, equally significant, is that whereby the potential challenge of newly powerful industrialists to the aristocracy, which continued to dominate the metropolitan circles of political power, was moderated by a massive influx of the offspring of the newly wealthy from Birmingham and elsewhere into the great public schools. Such an influx is a major instance of that process of osmosis mentioned above. In such schools, and at Oxford and Cambridge, the new recruits both adopted and adapted the styles and values of their fellows from more genteel homes. Many sons of businessmen were to find their natural sphere of activity in later life alongside their well-born colleagues, in the national and the imperial sphere. Those talents and energies which in a previous generation found their outlet in municipal government were to be devoted to the service of the 'nation' and the 'empire'.

If the 1860s and 1870s were the heyday of the 'civic gospel', the spirit of 'municipal enterprise', the 1890s and the early 1900s were to be an age of imperialism. The spirit of service to the community which nonconformist ministers such as R. W. Dale and George Dawson[61] preached to Birmingham congregations, urging them to enter the town council and take up *local* public work, was in this later period evoked by Anglican divines and Oxbridge dons training recruits for the *imperial* civil service. Significantly, the foremost prophet of this later era was the very man who investigated the King Edward VI Foundation in 1865—Thomas Hill Green.[62]

III

The first section of this paper ended with the observation that formal education in Birmingham appeared to resemble the Massachusetts pattern as described by Katz in that it was largely regulated through a public bureaucracy behaving in a paternalistic manner within the formal confines of local democratic control. As in Massachusetts also, businessmen were very active in educational reform. In the course of the second section it has become clear that the part played by businessmen and the emerging patterns of school provision were quite different in Birmingham and in Massachusetts. There was no clear evidence in Birmingham of a 'businessmen's putsch' within the sphere of education whereby local secondary schools became effectively dominated by the offspring of a business establishment which was actively hostile to the urban working class and an old mercantile and agrarian aristocracy. On the contrary, through the public schools the sons of prosperous industrialists were entering the same cosmopolitan circles as the aristocracy and gentry. Chamberlain, for example, sent his sons Austen and Neville to Rugby School. Of the local Birmingham elites, the families with the heaviest commitment to local secondary schools for their *own* children were apparently not the wealthy businessmen but secular and religious professionals. Important members of the Birmingham business community were demanding a vast extension of educational provision not for themselves but for the poor. They also sought the creation of wider opportunities for mobility through the local schools. Both these objectives were vigorously pursued by the School Board, particularly after 1873.

In the 1890s, the higher grade schools in Birmingham exemplified the strategy of the school committee in Quincy, Massachusetts, which was to 'collect your pupils in a few centers and then classify them as thoroughly as possible.' However, the outcome was not a series of common high schools but the emergence of something resembling a tripartite system of secondary schools in which pupils bound for different social destinations were effectively segregated from each other.

Finally, the major political wrangle in which teachers were involved in Birmingham appears to have denoted a split *within* the educational bureaucracy among the ranks of the 'schoolmen' rather than a conflict between professional educators and the 'laity'.

Three conclusions are suggested by the comparison between Birmingham and Massachusetts. In order of ascending generality they are as follows. First, two major structural preconditions of educational developments in Massachusetts are thrown into relief by the comparative analysis. They are the absence of a powerful aristocracy in the United States before industrialisation and the continued salience of the political structures of the major *provincial* cities in the United States in the absence of a dominant and centralised state apparatus. In both these respects the English case differs considerably. The predominance of gentry and aristocratic circles both in the counties and in the metropolis meant that not only were English industrialists liable to experience a much greater sense of 'inferiority' and 'exclusion' but also they were faced with powerful constraints in the assertion of their new influence. Furthermore, the continuing and increasing importance of the national and metropolitan power structure meant that a town like Birmingham developed in quite a different way from a town like Boston. Whereas the great American cities in Massachusetts and elsewhere continued to be enormously important not only as centres of industrial wealth but also as political stock exchanges in their own right, Birmingham became a provincial backwater.

Second, industrialising societies tend to resemble each other in that within them may be found landowners, controllers of industrial capital, wage labourers, groups with craft and professional skills, bureaucrats and so on. Furthermore, certain axes of conflict are pervasive: for example, between buyers and sellers of labour and food, between tax-payers and tax-gatherers, between bureaucrats and professionals, between tendencies towards centralisation and the maintenance or establishment of local autonomy. However, these lines of conflict may reinforce and cut across each other in different ways and the balance of advantage in each may develop in varying ways.

Considerable variation is possible in patterns of solidarity and fission both within and between groups. Structures of formal education both reflect and contribute to the establishment of such patterns.

Third, although processes such as industrialisation, urbanisation and bureaucratisation are the context in which mass systems of formal education have emerged in all societies, fundamental differences may be observed among societies not only in the sequence and rate of occurrence of such processes but also in the disposition of the social configurations within which they occur and which they in turn alter. The contrast between England and the United States may be set alongside the equal, perhaps greater, contrast between Russia and China. Empirical investigations of the structures and processes hinted at in this paper derive part of their significance, at least, from their relevance to a major and continuing theoretical challenge. This challenge is presented by the fact that different societies follow different trajectories en route from being predominantly agrarian to being urbanised and industrialised nation-states. The structure of formal education in a society is profoundly conditioned by the particular route taken. A sociological theory about the development of formal education in industrialising and industrialised societies, if it seeks to rise above abstract generalities yet move beyond the confines of a particular historical case, must find a way to cope with such variations in the trajectory of social development.[63]

Notes

1 I am grateful for comments made on previous versions of this paper by Olive Banks and members of the Sociology of Education seminar at the University of Leeds.

2 For the purposes of this paper the 'bourgeoisie' may be identified as those manufacturers, merchants, bankers and other groups whose wealth derived primarily from the productive and distributive aspects of capitalistic enterprise employing wage labour.

3 The works by Katz referred to are as follows: *The Irony of Early School Reform*, Harvard University Press, 1968 (henceforth, referred to as *Irony* . . .); 'The new departure in Quincy 1875–1881', *New England Quarterly*, 40, March 1967, pp. 3–30 (henceforth referred to as 'New departure . . .'); 'From voluntarism to bureaucracy in American education', *Sociology of Education*, 44, summer 1971, pp. 297–332 (henceforth referred to as 'Voluntarism . . .'); 'The emergence of bureaucracy in urban education: the Boston case 1850–1884', *History of Education Quarterly*, 8 (2), summer 1968, pp. 155–88, 8 (3), Fall 1968, pp. 319–57 (henceforth referred to as 'Boston . . .'); *Class, Bureaucracy, and Schools*, Praeger, 1971 (henceforth referred to as *Class* . . .).

4 *Irony* . . . , pp. 38–40.

5 op. cit., pp. 62–80.

6 op. cit., pp. 19–22.

7 'New Departure . . .', p. 12.

8 op. cit., pp. 25–6.

9 'Boston . . .', passim.

10 'Voluntarism . . .', passim.

11 op. cit., p. 310.

12 *The Free School System of the United States*, 1875, p. 256 (quoted in W. H. G. Armytage, *The American Influence on English Education*, Routledge & Kegan Paul, 1967, p. 21).

13 Return of . . . Schools for the Poorer Classes in Birmingham, 1869.

14 G. Yorke, *The School and the Workshop*, 1856, p. 11. Cited in A. F. Taylor, 'History of the Birmingham School Board 1870–1903', MA thesis, University of Birmingham, 1955, p. 20.

15 See W. White, *The Story of Severn Street and Priory First-Day Adult Schools*, 1895.

16 Taylor, op. cit., pp. 182–3, p. 114.

17 Green's Report, *Schools Inquiry Commission*, vol. 8, pp. 118–19.

18 ibid., p. 106.

19 ibid., p. 119.

20 ibid., pp. 91–2.

21 e.g. Grantham Yorke, Isaac Spooner.

22 e.g. James Johnstone, G. F. Evans, George Lloyd.

23 e.g. T. C. S. Kynnersley, G. P. Wragge.

24 e.g. J. D. Goodman, J. T. Chance, W. L. Sargant.

25 See *Schools Inquiry Commission*, vol. 4, pt 2, Appendix B.

26 A. Albright, G. Baker, J. Baldwin, W. Bartleet, W. H. Blews, R. L. Chance, J. A. Cooper, J. H. Cutler, G. Goodrick, J. Hinks, H. Manton, W. Middlemore, A. F. Osler, W. L. Sargant, G. Smith, C. Sturge, J. P. Turner, J. S. Wright.

27 G. Dixon, R. Fletcher, J. Graham, J. Poncia, J. Phillips.

28 T. Phillips, G. Turner.

29 W. Barlow, C. Bridges, J. W. Cutler, S. Evans, J. B. Hebbert, H. Luckock, C. E. Matthews, W. Morgan, H. W. Tyndall.

30 J. E. Baker (engineer), B. Foster (surgeon), W. Harris (architect and surveyor), D. Malins, jr. (accountant), S. Timmins (journalist). The terms 'professional man' and 'professional' assume the imprecise popular notion of a 'profession' rather than any of the specialised technical meanings acquired through the sociological literature. The references to 'semi-professionals' is an acknowledgment of the problem of marginality. Engineers and accountants are likely to have commanded less social authority than doctors, lawyers and ministers. On the other hand, Timmins, who was author, litterateur, journalist and magistrate, commanded considerable local prestige. At least two issues may be identified although not pursued here: first, the standing of particular *individuals* within social networks dominated by the established medical and legal professions and the most substantial businessmen; second, the long-term tendency for occupational *groups* such as engineers and accountants to improve their relative social prestige and influence.

31 S. Bache, R. W. Dale, G. Dawson, T. James, C. Clarke, C. Vince, G. B. Johnson, J. Eagles, C. Heath, S. Thornton (the last three were Anglican clergy).

32 T. Lloyd, G. Smithson, J. C. Wynn.

33 J. Baldwin, J. H. Cutler, G. Dixon, G. Goodrick, H. Manton, J. Poncia, T. Phillips, J. Phillips, G. Smith, G. Turner.

34 J. E. Baker, J. W. Cutler, W. Harris.

35 Harris practised throughout the Midlands as a quantity surveyor, and was the first in the Birmingham area to bring the qualifications of an architect to this occupation. He was the honorary secretary of the Birmingham Liberal Association from 1867 to 1870 and acquired the reputation of being the 'father' of the 'caucus', with its so-called 'vote-as-you-are-told' strategy of mobilising electoral support (*Edgbastonia*, 31, 1911, pp. 61–70).

36 This was in 1883. At the BMA conference of that year he told his colleagues: 'As a class we are too timid and too reticent: we fail to do our due share in the public work of the communities in which we live.' He suggested that the proper 'recreation' of medical men should be 'patriotic service to the community', since in 'town councils, local boards, and boards of guardians there is plenty of work for them to do useful to the community and good for the profession' (*Edgbastonia*, 4, 1884, pp. 97–100). In 1868, Foster was secretary to the Health Section of the Social Science Congress at its Birmingham meeting (*Biograph and Review*, 4, 1880, pp. 402–4). Membership of the Free Grammar School Association committee was an early instance of an interest in public affairs that was later to lead Foster to stand as a Liberal candidate for parliament.

37 Albright had begun life as a chemist's assistant and eventually went into partnership with J. E. Wilson in a firm which developed the use of amorphous phosphorus. By 1877, he was sufficiently wealthy to donate £1,000 to finance a conference of the Workmen's Peace Association protesting against the war fever directed against Russia that year. A Quaker, he was active throughout his life in movements such as the Anti-Corn Law League and the National Freedmen's Aid Union (following the American Civil War) (*Arthur Albright, Notes on his Life*, by W. King, 1901, printed for private circulation).

38 *Birmingham Journal*, 19 December 1855. Baldwin had been chairman of the Birmingham Political Council in 1848 and in the mid sixties became first president of the Midlands department of the Reform League (Victoria County History, *Warwickshire*, vol. 7, 1964, p. 305).

39 *Fit and Proper Persons: Idea and Reality in Nineteenth Century Urban Government*, Edward Arnold, 1973.

40 Dale was the minister at Carr's Lane Chapel, Birmingham. In 1863 he had told his congregation: 'it is one of the gravest facts in connection with the future social conditions of this country, that the separation seems to become wider every day between the poor and the rich . . . In our manufacturing districts, we have streets upon streets of working people, covering immense areas, in which no professional men, except the doctor and the minister of religion, are ever seen' (quoted in Hennock, op. cit., p. 102). Dale believed that 'in a country like this where the public business of the state is the private duty of every citizen, those who decline to use their political power are guilty of treachery both to God and man' (quoted in A. W. W. Dale, *Life of R. W. Dale*, 1898, p. 250).

41 The grandson of a successful manufacturer in Birmingham, Sargant was educated as a private boarder at Sutton Coldfield and spent some time at Trinity College, Cambridge. In 1870 he became chairman of the Birmingham School Board (*Edgbastonia*, 5, 1885, pp. 49–53).

42 Dixon, a town councillor for Edgbaston, was chairman of the Birmingham School Board between 1876 and 1896. He served as mayor in 1867 and became a local member of parliament in 1868.

43 *Schools Inquiry Commission*, vol. 4, pt 1, p. 968.

44 ibid., pp. 980–2.

45 ibid., pp. 986–8.

46 ibid., pp. 542, 547–8, 559.

47 Wright, a partner in a button manufacturing enterprise, lived in Handsworth near the People's Chapel which he patronised. He had extensive political influence in north Birmingham. With George Dixon, he helped Joseph Arch to found the National Labourers' Union in 1872. See Hennock, op. cit., pp. 100–3; *Biograph and Review*, 3, 1880, pp. 251–6.

48 *Schools Inquiry Commission*, vol. 4, pt 1, p. 1002.

49 In 1875 the Town Council acquired control of the Gas Light and Coke Company and the Birmingham and Staffordshire Gas Light Company. Of the nineteen company directors only one had been a councillor or alderman. In the following year, control was secured over the Birmingham Water Works Company. During the council debate on the gas companies, Chamberlain declared: 'I am inclined to increase the duties and responsibilities of the local authority, in whom I have myself so great a confidence, and I will do everything in my power to constitute these local authorities real local Parliaments, supreme in their special jurisdiction' (quoted in Hennock, op. cit., p. 120).

50 Two central issues in these disputes were religious instruction in board schools and rate subsidisation of voluntary schools.

51 *Secondary Education Commission*, vol. 3, pp. 43–61.

52 ibid., pp. 56–60.

53 ibid., p. 44; R. H. Turner, 'Sponsored and contest mobility and the school system', in E. Hopper, ed., *Readings in the Theory of Educational Systems*, Hutchinson, 1971, pp. 139–58.

54 Vol. 2, p. 202.

55 Taylor, op. cit., pp. 96–102. MacCarthy was chairman of the Education and School Management Committee from 1876 to its subdivision in February 1879. He was then chairman of the Education Committee until he became Chairman of the Board in 1896, and for a time he was also chairman of the School Management Committee, on which he always sat as a member. Taylor notes that his 'influence on the schools was . . . direct and immediate; to him the inspectors would look for instructions, and the teachers recognised him more and more as the real power on the Board' (op. cit., p. 99).

56 The Higher Education Society, founded in 1873, organised classes for elementary school teachers in arithmetic, geometry, modern languages, Latin and Greek. At their second annual general meeting, the members congratulated themselves on the enthusiasm shown by their pupils 'for an education higher and broader than that given in the Training Colleges' (Second Annual Report, 1875, p. 4). The Birmingham Teachers' Association, founded 1874, drew its membership from all kinds of local school but an examination

of its annual reports suggests that it was dominated by secondary school teachers. Vardy's role in its early days is discussed in J. H. Smith, 'Story of the first teachers' association', in Association of Church School Managers and Teachers, *Conference Guide*, 1903.

57 Taylor, op. cit., pp. 183–7, p. 248; *Birmingham Daily Post*, 13, 14, 19 November 1894.

58 See also A. Tropp, *The School Teachers*, Heinemann, 1957.

59 The following remarks do not attempt to do more than breach the issue of relations between 'established' and 'outsiders' in the context of educational development. For an important discussion, see N. Elias and J. L. Scotson, *The Established and the Outsiders*, Frank Cass, 1965.

60 Some aspects of the imposition of central authority on local bodies and the associated transmutation of many higher grade schools and pupil-teacher centres into local authority grammar schools have been analysed by E. J. R. Eaglesham and Olive Banks. E. J. R. Eaglesham, *From School Board to Local Authority*, Routledge and Kegan Paul, 1956; O. Banks, *Parity and Prestige in English Secondary Education*, Routledge and Kegan Paul, 1955.

61 As minister at the Church of the Saviour, Dawson insisted on the dignity and usefulness of municipal service. Dale, to some extent his disciple, recollected that Dawson taught his contemporaries that 'unless the best and ablest men in the community were willing to serve it, new laws could not work any great reformation and that it was the duty of those who derived their prosperity and opportunities of culture from the community to become their servants' (quoted in A. W. W. Dale, op. cit., pp. 401–2).

62 See M. Richter, *The Politics of Conscience*, Weidenfeld & Nicolson, 1964; S. Rothblatt, *The Revolution of the Dons*, Faber & Faber, 1968.

63 For a critical appraisal of a number of theoretical approaches to education systems and proposals for further theoretical development, see D. Smith, 'Selection and knowledge management in education systems', in E. Hopper, ed., *Readings in the Theory of Educational Systems*, Hutchinson, 1971, pp. 139–58; 'Power, ideology and the transmission of knowledge', in ibid., pp. 240–61; *Power Relations and Distribution Processes in Education Systems*, Open University Press, 1973; 'Codes, paradigms and folk norms: an approach to educational change with particular reference to the work of Basil Bernstein', *Sociology*, 10 (1), January 1976.

7 Open-ness and control in higher education: towards a critique of the Open University

Dave Harris and John Holmes

Introduction

Recent developments in the sociology of education have emphasised the 'new' critical awareness that educational organisations exercise considerable powers of social control in unsuspected ways. The organisation of the curriculum and of pedagogy can be seen as representing deeply held ideologies which appear to be liberating but which often serve to extend and legitimise social hierarchies, for example.[1] So far, however, most of the analysis seems to be located at the primary or secondary levels in education, and analysis of universities and colleges in these terms remains restricted to the remnants of the 'student left'.[2] We feel that university curricula and pedagogies represent excellent examples of the trends toward developing rational control over education—and that the Open University makes a particularly good case-study in that it is a modern purpose-built organisation which represents current ideologies unusually clearly.

The Open University is, moreover, Britain's largest university in terms of student numbers, and its well-publicised 'success'[3] has led to continued expansion and a spreading emulation of its organisational principles both abroad[4] and in Britain itself. Here in Britain there have been, for example, calls for 'Open Schools' and 'Open Colleges' based, to varying extents, upon the Open University. Ironically, the very difficulty of some OU courses for some students has led to a call for a kind of OU-style organisation to prepare students for the OU proper. The OU has been experimenting with younger students in the conventional eighteen to twenty-one years age-range—apparently with disappointing results so far. However, an increasing number of conventional universities and colleges are using OU materials as part of their own programmes of study.

The OU has also been in the forefront of developing a 'credit transfer' system whereby credits gained by studying approved courses can be used to gain exemption from study at other institutions. So far, the scheme has been concerned with allowing exemption for OU students who have pursued approved courses elsewhere—but there are hopes that successful completion of OU courses will enable OU students to gain exemptions elsewhere.[5] Such a scheme has been linked with the proposed Diploma in Higher Education, for example, with the OU 'topping up' DipHEs gained in other institutions, or even with an ambitious plan involving the development of the academic equivalent of a Common Market, whereby qualifications gained in European universities and colleges could be used to gain exemptions in Britain, and *vice versa*. The implications of these proposals are important—the one that concerns us primarily here involves the close integration between the OU and other educational institutions that would be produced.[6]

Recent suggestions about the directions for future developments of the OU in Britain concern the Further Education sector, which might well be reorganised around the OU.[7] In a similar way, the most strident calls for the establishment of a system of *education permanente* have emanated from the OU, and there are clear indications that this is being taken seriously as a future avenue of expansion by OU planners.[8] Such moves to expand and diversify seem to owe much to fears that the current demand for undergraduate courses from suitable groups of students might be diminishing in the near future.[9] However, these proposals also indicate the increasing acceptance of OU-style organisation as a convenient solution to the problem of providing education in an era of austerity. The arguments about the cost-effectiveness of the OU are complex,[10] but in the

Source: unpublished. Dave Harris is lecturer in sociology, College of St Mark and St John, Plymouth; John Holmes is a research associate with the National Institute of Adult Education.

current climate of reduced expenditure on education, a centralised, rationally organised teaching system with large staff-student ratios must appear to be an attractive proposition. We believe that we should take seriously the OU boast to be 'the university of the future', and in the light of these possible developments, the *educational* value of what the OU offers must be examined with the greatest care.

However, detailed criticism of the OU is particularly difficult, since it is a large, segmented and opaque organisation with a strong concern for its public image, and with a wide degree of support from a surprising range of educational thinkers and policy-makers.[11] We were able to develop a critical perspective on the OU when working in one part of the organisation at Walton Hall and we propose to offer the *beginnings* of a critique by concentrating upon some important central practices at the OU in order to try to clarify their ideological bases and their effects. We hope that those who know the OU will be able to consider the relevance of our point for themselves (especially the students who may be reading this article as part of their OU course!).

Open-ness and social mobility

The principle of open admissions can be seen as an important example of the 'progressive' thinking which dominates OU policy. Thousands of adults who had hitherto been excluded from tertiary education were to be allowed access to valuable and high-status knowledge which had always been reserved for a carefully selected elite. Further, access was to be unmediated by academics who might have censored some of the more radical aspects of such knowledge. The potentially radical implications of open admissions for some of the most deep-seated beliefs about knowledge and the organisation of university teaching were noted by several commentators.[12]

However, for many of those who supported the OU, open admissions was 'progressive' in a different sense. The OU began as an explicitly Labour Party proposal and open admission should be seen in the light of other Labour Party reforms of the educational system. The effects of pupils' 'social class' had been shown to have had an important influence upon their educational careers, as much of the classical work in the sociology of education in Britain indicates.[13] Labour Party policy can be seen in terms of attempts to remove the effects of social class as a factor in selecting candidates for particular educational careers —by widening access to elite secondary schools and by arguing for criteria of selection based upon merit rather than on social class. The culmination of this policy can be seen in the provision of comprehensive schools, where all pupils are entitled to initially attend the same school and where they have a chance to display their merit in order to pursue different careers within the one school. The socialist future educational system was to be one which corresponded

to the 'contest mobility' model rather than the 'sponsored mobility' version.[14]

Opening access to higher education is a logical extension of this policy—all adults would have an equal chance to display their merit regardless of their social origins. The old definitions of merit were not to be trusted since they had been shown to reflect irrational social prejudices—everyone was to be allowed to try afresh. Such a policy would help the nation as a whole because it would enable talented (but wrongly labelled) people to develop their interests to a new extent, and it would benefit those talented individuals in the lowest social groups most of all, thereby reducing the span of inequality. Significantly, both the national interest and the interests of 'working-class' individuals would be served by the same policy.

Although such policies are associated with the Labour Party, which, in its Fabian form, sees the path to socialism and equality in terms of rationally improving the performance of the present economic system, the origins of such policies lie in liberal thought of the early nineteenth century. The emphasis is upon individual freedoms and rights which were stressed in opposition to the social restrictions of feudalism. Individual freedoms were seen as good in themselves, as expressing some natural state of human existence in classical liberal thought, but later versions stressed the flexibility and rationality of a social organisation based on individual enterprise freed from past restrictions.[15] Liberalism began as a radical doctrine, offering freedom from the old constraints, but it quickly became seriously compromised by the development of capitalism. Classical liberalism became a mere myth, stressing freedom in a purely abstract sense and ignoring the crucial social constraints upon individual actions imposed by the developing market economy. Men became free to act only within a very limited area:[16]

[The area] within whose boundaries the sale and purchase of labor-power goes on, is in fact a very Eden of the innate rights of man. There alone rule Freedom, Equality, Property and Bentham. Freedom, because both buyer and seller of a commodity, say of labor-power, are constrained only by their own free will . . . Equality, because each enters into relations with each other, as with a simple owner of commodities, and they exchange equivalent for equivalent . . .

The reference to Bentham in the above quote is important because the Benthamite version of liberalism is central to understanding modern developments. Bentham had no time for the 'metaphysics of human rights' and for him the advantage of encouraging individual freedom was a directly rational one, since the efficiency of production was increased and the 'social good' maximised. The market ignores the social characteristics of individuals, for example, and this is clearly more efficient and personally liberating in some ways. At the same time, though, a kind of anonymous, impersonal universalism develops —*all* social and human characteristics of individuals are ignored by the market and a person's exchange-value, his abstract utility, becomes the sole basis upon which relationships are formed.[17]

Applying these analyses to the concept of open-ness, it becomes clear that open admissions offers a limited and flawed kind of freedom to individuals. People are now more free to gain access to a taken for granted social structure which limits their freedom once they are inside. As we shall see, for example, OU students are free to be exposed to a curriculum and pedagogy which exerts strong controls over their education, they are free to be assessed upon criteria which are predetermined and impersonal. Students are free to perform educational tasks in exchange for various qualifications, and just like entrepreneurs in the market they can organise their performance more or less efficiently. Above all, open admissions ensures that students will be treated in a thoroughly universal-istic and impersonal manner, that their particular social and educational circumstances will be ignored as will their particular interests, perspectives and experiences. Open admissions ensures that OU courses, like the market, are for an anonymous 'everyman'.[18]

As a final point, before we leave nineteenth century liberalism, it is interesting to note Bentham's own proposals for a rational education system. Bentham too believed that the social good was maximised when 'no scholar [was to be] considered incapable'.[19] In order to deal with a mass intake of undifferentiated scholars, the masters should devise a system of individual supervision and tight control to ensure that the most suitable kind of instruction be given.[20] At the OU, too, the educational technologists were to echo this logic, as we shall see.[21]

It can be seen, therefore, that open-ness is the culmination of a progressivism which stresses free access to an undemocratic form of social organisation, which concentrates upon individual freedom within a limited area only and which produces a profound anonymity in practice. Parallel points can be made about the kind of social mobility which the OU is supposed to promote. Social mobility based upon qualifications and merit instead of caste or class can again be seen as liberating in one sense, but once more the social mobility in question seems seriously limited. Individuals are to be made mobile and mobility takes place within given hierarchies inside an unchallenged social and economic structure. The concept of qualitative social mobility whereby individuals liberate themselves from obsolete or repressive ideas and thus come to understand and transcend their present situations is never mentioned in the discussions, for example.

The emphasis upon education as a route to social mobility is interesting in itself as a device to alleviate some of the inequalities produced by a particular economic and social system without altering that system directly. For education to function in this way, the education system has to be rationalised to fit the requirements of the economic system. The currently fashionable way to do this involves an insistence that course contents be directly 'voca-tional', of course. The OU was probably initially seen as providing courses of this type too, although for various reasons such proposals were abandoned.[22] However, the OU does meet one important 'need', since it does provide a grading service which could well act as a pseudo-rational basis for future employers to select their applicants. Actual course contents do not necessarily have to be directly 'relevant', since graded degrees can be seen as some indication of students' general worth. Finally, the kinds of skill required of students, if they are to succeed at the OU, might be precisely those skills which employers value, as we shall see.

The personal implications for the students of the way in which the OU fosters social mobility are also important. Success and eventual occupational mobil-ity is seen to occur according to rational principles involving the reliable detection of merit. The con-sequences of the inevitable failure of many OU students are obvious—as success is rationally organ-ised, so is failure, as success is individualised, so is failure. For those who are not successful, even at the OU with its apparently enormous technical expertise and commitment in catering for the unqualified and in detecting latent talent, failure must seem rational, personal and final.

Formal and hidden curricula—the rational teaching system

As we have seen, the debates about democratising education tended to centre upon the question of access. The kind of education which was to be offered was not seen as requiring any modification. The curriculum in particular was seen to be unproblem-atic, with natural 'levels' and 'subjects' as Young has pointed out.[23] Thus for Jennie Lee it followed that the Open University naturally had to have a con-ventional university curriculum if it was to maintain 'standards' and receive the support of the academic community—a university with any other kind of curriculum was almost a contradiction in terms.[24] As a result, despite some experimentation with multi-disciplinary courses or with new specialisms, the contents of courses at the OU tend to reflect the conventional views of what counts as university knowledge. The implications for open-ness and social mobility are clear—OU curricula embody many of the characteristics that seem to be connected with the failure of 'working-class' students in schools in the first place.[25] A large number of students from a range of social backgrounds were to be allowed to sample kinds of knowledge which apparently embody the values and interests and skills of a small elite.

However, even though the question of what should be taught was apparently solved by referring to the conventional answers, the issue of how the teaching should be done was a central focus for debate. The Planning Committee for the OU optimistically referred to the recent growth of a series of specialisms focusing upon curriculum design, pedagogical practices and rational evaluation schemes, which could be referred to generally as 'educational technology'. The rise of the educational technologists to the status of full members of staff at the OU is an interesting one for students of the strategies employed by occupational groups to gain status,[26] but educational technology did seem to offer considerable promise. The major problem was to design a teaching system which would solve the unique contradictions faced by the OU—between the need to maintain 'high standards' while operating with an open admissions policy, and the need to run a large-scale centralised organisation in a cost-effective way while preserving an emphasis upon the educational requirements of individual students just as in conventional universities. The actual solutions to these contradictory needs involved a series of crucial transformations, of knowledge and of the interpersonal organisation of teaching and learning, which provide a liberal appearance for what has become an advanced kind of educational bureaucracy, and the proposals and practices of the educational technologists show how these transformations took place.

The educational technologists seemed to be able to solve the problems of maintaining standards with open admissions by developing an 'individualised' teaching system. This approach was foreseen by Bentham, as we saw, and it reaches its modern peak in programmed learning techniques. The progressive connotations of such developments are clear—anyone can be taught to the highest level provided a sufficiently individualised approach is employed which lets each learner begin at a suitable level and progress at a suitable pace (both of which can be determined by the learner himself). The elitist view that only a few are capable of benefiting from a university level education is rejected.

At the same time, however, it is clear that such an approach involves a serious extension of rationalised control over the processes involved in education. The principles involve, for example, a transformation of knowledge into a set of concepts which are rationally ordered into various hierarchies (of difficulty or of abstraction, for example).[27] Individual learners are assumed to occupy individual positions on some uniform scale of ability. The contact between learners and knowledge is rationally ordered according to all kinds of technical considerations concerning 'size of step', pacing, the careful construction of chains of stimuli, and so on.[28] The processes of learning are themselves rendered in rational terms, with learners usually represented in behaviourist or mechanistic

terms.[29] The underlying view of education involves the rational ordering, presentation and exchange of information, and 'individualisation' involves just including a degree of flexibility into the processes to cater for learners with a number of personal values on some universal scales, or with a set of particular varieties of 'entry behaviours', or with personal preferences within a restricted range of 'learning styles'.

In practice at the OU full flexibility of this kind could not be developed, primarily because the cost would have been prohibitive. The courses are instead aimed to achieve an average level of difficulty, to feature a few units in a programmed format, or to incorporate a few alternative routes through the material.[30] However, the basic emphasis upon taking a rational approach to curriculum planning persists. Such an approach involves the attempt to control course development according to explicitly stated and operationalised aims, a commitment to rational evaluations of effectiveness, and so on. The educational technologists working with the academic writers on course teams began by advocating a series of specific curriculum design techniques which reflected this approach.

Initially, the courses were to be designed on the basis of using 'behavioural objectives'. The point was to pose problems of relevance throughout the course design process. The usual tendency of university lecturers to offer academic, esoteric courses based upon personal interest and unreflected criteria of relevance was to be curbed—'Irrelevant scholastic displays must be eliminated'.[31] It should be made clear that such scorn for traditional academic presentations came mostly from a desire to improve the efficiency of the teaching process, as we shall see. Academics were to bear in mind the needs of the students, to continually ask themselves what students were supposed to actually get out of the courses. In order to remove as much ambiguity and confusion as possible, student needs were to be represented as a series of desirable outcomes, ideally listed as 'behaviours' which they would achieve. 'Behaviours' were supposed to be unambiguous indicators of success compared with meaningless references to intended mental states such as understanding, as in the tradition of behaviourist psychology. Clearly, such unambiguous indicators are essential for rational control where those who receive the courses are unable to modify the courses themselves according to their own subjective knowledge of their own mental states.

In practice, the use of behavioural objectives does deny subjectivity in important ways. The complex links between thought and knowledge and action are reduced and objectified. Important educational aims like the development of personal understanding are replaced by trivial behaviours which have been pre-specified as being desirable outcomes for other people, with no alternatives permitted. Knowledge is seen as being essentially instrumental, aimed solely at producing end behaviours, just as in technical training. The idea of students being able to develop their own personal praxis as a result of the knowledge they have gained no longer features as the major point of education.

The second set of design techniques represents even more clearly this tendency to reify knowledge in an authoritarian way. The technique involves the construction of 'knowledge structures', whereby arguments are transformed into a series of concepts joined by a restricted number of logical operations. One can see some justification again in using this technique which does promise to lay bare the basic internal grammatical structure of specialisms, particularly those which involve the manipulations of symbols according to well-defined rules (as in formal logic or pure mathematics, possibly). However, the intention was to apply the technique to all specialisms —on an interesting assumption that there was some 'universal syntax' or deep structure of human thinking which 'knowledge structures' could represent.[32] Thus even the tentative, speculative and problematic interpretations of reality discussed in sociology courses could be rendered as some objective grammatical structure.

The actual processes involved in constructing such structures are interesting. It is admitted, for example, that actual ordinary-language arguments have to be interpreted and transformed, rendered in a more 'elegant' or 'sanitised' form.[33] Problems arising from multiple definitions of concepts were to be solved simply by allowing the 'numinous' academics on the course team to authorise one simple definition. Having clarified the meaning of concepts in this way, complex empirical phenomena are interpreted in terms of the concepts by using some simple authorised logical relation, as if one could simply read off reality from some set of structured concepts. After all these subjective negotiations and interpretations have taken place, the finished objectified structure could be transmitted to the students.

Since the finished structure represented the core of the argument as objectively defined by the experts, the students' role was confined to receiving the structure passively as taught. Such passivity was implied by the notions of 'completeness' and 'closure' involved in the knowledge structures project. These notions were derived from work done in the field of 'artificial intelligence', whereby computer programs have to be complete (all the concepts and operations necessary have to be fully defined) and closed (the higher order concepts and operations have to be fully entailed by the other ones). Unless these conditions are fulfilled, computers cannot be 'taught'. The same concern for completeness and closure runs throughout the proposals for course design advanced by the educational technologists.[34] The implication is that students can be taught concepts in sociology just as, for example, computers are taught to construct

arches[35]—that students have the same curious mixture of a superb capacity for pure logical operations and the profound ignorance of meanings as computers.

Both techniques can be seen as being simply neutral techniques to tighten up 'woolly thinking' and construct a more explicit pedagogy. In practice, both techniques involve attempts to control meanings of arguments—to be sure, in the interests of clarity of presentation. Knowledge structures represent the most far-reaching attempts to control meanings: the academics restrict meanings of concepts in the first place, as we saw, and anyway the concepts are organised into coherent structures which supply rigorous contextual meanings (the concept 'alienation' means only what the course author meant it to be, and only what it entails in a structure of other concepts supplied by the author). Attempts to construct courses which are simplified and *authoritative* renderings of complex arguments become *authoritarian* efforts to control meaning. In practice, students would find it extremely difficult to criticise or personalise knowledge structures, even in private, faced with such a tightly organised objectified consistent argument, with all the subjective judgments and personal choices of the academics removed from view.

Of course, there is a place in education for attempts to present a coherent and systematic argument, to demonstrate to students that, given a particular set of theoretical motives and relevances, a particular argument can be pursued to arrive at particular non-obvious conclusions and implications. In this sense, an attempt to control meanings of concepts in some way, for the purpose of argument, can be seen as legitimate and even as creative. In a similar way, a systematic attempt to introduce students into an organised set of concepts and procedures, a tradition or a paradigm[36] can also be seen as a legitimate endeavour, even if only as a first stage in an educational process. It could be argued in particular that such a highly structured approach to natural science or to mathematics is a useful, or even an essential way to proceed.

However, if education is concerned with the pursuit of personal meanings, such heavily didactic procedures can only be a part of education. Equally important is the process which permits students to relate theoretical concepts (even those of science) to their own knowledge, themes, motives and relevance systems. Such a relating involves efforts on the part of both academics and students to engage in dialogues[37] whereby 'horizons can be merged', themes enlarged in various directions, common elements of meaning in themes and horizons discovered, and so on. Dialogues of this kind seem crucial, and they flourish in situations where participants are able to communicate as equals. Such relationships are threatened where one party reserves the right to assess the contribution of the other, to claim the exclusive right to competence, knowledge, or even to abstract 'objectivity' or 'rationality'. In our view, it is crucial to recognise that all paradigms, organised perspectives and theoretical arguments involve useful, socially-supported (and in this sense non-arbitrary) *objectifications*.[38] Even science and mathematics involve such objectifications, as Young implies.[39] Knowledge structures would tend to represent arguments precisely as non-social, even non-human, reified truths, which, together with the one-way teaching system and the comprehensive assessment system, would make dialogue very difficult. In this way, this technique would have made the initiation of students into a perspective or argument an inevitably authoritarian process which was not just a part of education but was synonymous with education.

Both of these techniques reflect an underlying educational ideology, as we have suggested. This ideology assumes that education involves the accumulation of expert knowledge at the centre and its rational dispersal to ignorant students on the periphery. Paulo Freire refers to this very widespread ideology as the 'banking concept' of education— 'knowledge is a gift bestowed by those who consider themselves knowledgeable upon those whom they consider to know nothing ... the scope of action allowed to the students extends only as far as receiving, filing and storing the deposits.'[40] The educational technologists were inclined to describe the activities of the OU as 'telling',[41] but the two terms refer to the same process. Such a view of education underpins a wide range of activities at the OU including the rational organisation of course production, the evaluation exercises, and the development of the assessment system as well as the specific design techniques mentioned above. In many cases, liberal academics on the course teams perceived the authoritarian tendencies of the use of behavioural objectives or knowledge structures, and fought successful battles to bring about their abandonment—but the 'banking' ideology itself was scarcely checked by these specific reversals. All the wider activities which make up the teaching system as a whole were not modified by liberal academics—yet they can act as crucial structural and contextual determinants of the meanings of the arguments in the courses. In other words, the effects of the hidden curriculum remain, as we shall see.

The OU Vice-Chancellor saw his task as constructing a 'functional machine' which would implement the proposals of the Planning Committee.[42] Educational consultants were engaged to help in this task and they used the latest management techniques to devise an organisational structure. An important characteristic of the 'banking' concept assisted this process, since the view of education is one which permits the central elements and processes to be easily operationalised in administrative terms. In particular, knowledge can be operationalised to become the words of the experts as printed and published in course units. Once this is done, the production of knowledge as units can be organised in the same way as the production of chocolate bars— there can be a rational division of labour, for example with academics organised in course teams who will actually supply the words, printers and media specialists who will package the words attractively, and so on. The words are seen as 'containing' all the legitimate meanings that students need to know, and so despatching written materials to students is the same as communicating meanings to them. Knowledge has *literally* become a commodity at the OU, and, in the form of actual courses, it is produced, marketed and consumed like any other commodity.

This rational teaching/production system was originally devised as a means to achieve an educational end, albeit one defined in 'banking' terms, and, because of the operationalisation described above, it also happened to satisfy another important goal. It enabled the OU to demonstrate its cost-effectiveness, which was initially seen as a most effective political weapon in the struggle to become established. The 'at a distance' teaching system dealing with huge numbers of students at the same time clearly offers cost advantages compared with conventional universities. While education is thought of in 'banking' terms, the two kinds of goals can be reconciled— expert knowledge can be usefully despatched to many students instead of just the privileged few. However, any concept of education which rejected 'banking' would find the OU teaching system to be a powerful constraint—any clash between an expensive pedagogy (no matter how desirable educationally) and the present teaching system would end in defeat for the former, we believe. The teaching system which began as a tentative means to achieve an educational end has become a fixed constraint upon what can be done. Course team academics can choose to teach whatever content they wish but they are severely constrained in their choice of an educationally effective means to convey this content, unless they embrace the 'banking' view.

The assessment system plays a crucial part in determining the effectiveness of course teams too. Assessment is pervasive at the OU, largely because there needs to be large amounts of assessment if it is to act either as a diagnostic of teaching effectiveness or as a reliable discriminator of students' abilities.[43] There are serious unintended consequences of frequent assessment, however, as Becker has shown.[44] Some students begin to adopt an 'instrumental' strategy in order to meet the assessment requirements, and this can have an important effect on the ways in which these students make sense of the courses.

At the OU, little research has been done to discover whether OU students do develop such instrumental strategies. This is on the face of it rather odd since so much time and money is spent on doing research into student reactions to the courses. However, the nature of this research is important— it is undertaken with an explicitly managerial emphasis in the spirit of market research.[45] Its use of 'scientific' questionnaire techniques produces a neglect of the perspectives of students themselves in favour of simplified 'objective' data designed to assist central decision-making. As a result it produces what Gouldner calls 'a deep-going authoritarianism . . . a bureaucratic numbness'.[46] In contrast, some small-scale (and unpublished) research carried out by ourselves based on interviews with students, indicates a strong possibility that such an instrumental perspective is widespread. Some of the students we contacted based their whole approach to OU materials upon the requirements of the assignments. Whole course units, TV programmes or tutorial sessions might be omitted if they did not directly relate to an assignment, complex and open-ended arguments might be reduced to sets of 'facts' and 'recipes' which would be collected simply for assessment purposes. Personal views were rarely expressed in assignments, even where specifically requested, since such views were seen as risky in terms of ensuring good grades.

To summarise, our point is that many course team academics have resisted the more obvious devices employed by the rational curriculum planners, and have managed to include in their courses material and arguments which were not intended to be authoritarian didactic pieces of expert knowledge. Some academics do intend their students to seek personal meanings in the texts, to begin to apply the arguments to their own surroundings and so on. However, given the immovable nature of the one-way 'at a distance' teaching system, and the strong possibility of a 'hidden curriculum' fostered by the assessment system, such liberating intentions seem unlikely to be realised. The reality of the OU teaching system for students is one where large quantities of printed material arrive which express necessarily abstract and universalised arguments. No dialogue with the writers can be held concerning the personal relevance of these arguments. The only kind of communication with the central institution takes place via frequent assignments, which often call for a personal response while being graded according to impersonal 'objective' criteria.

Some students do manage to overcome this massive potential for alienation, of course.[47] Student groups, an enthusiastic regional tutor who goes beyond his official 'remedial' role, a purely fortuitous flash of insight gained from a text or a broadcast can all help students to find some personal meaning in their studies which is not merely an instrumental one. But it is clear that such meanings are peripheral, privatised, optional, even accidental in the OU system. The freedom to develop one's interests or to seek personal enlightenment operates unconstrained, but within a tiny area formed from the inevitable tiny cracks in the formal structure. Thus course team academics are allowed considerable freedom to write what they like, provided it is likely to 'sell' and provided it can be fitted into the requirements of the teaching system; students are allowed to think what they like as long as they do not expect this to affect what they are taught or how they are assessed.

Conclusions

We have tried to show how a certain kind of liberal progressiveness can fit with a certain kind of rational organisation to produce a profound extension of centralised control in higher education. In such circumstances, apparently liberating tendencies turn into their opposites; open-ness can lead to the establishment of new and more rational hierarchies, individualisation can produce a profound anonymity and alienation, liberal freedoms can exist only in so far as they can be accommodated within authoritarian structures, tentative means can become fixed ends in themselves to which the original ends have to be fitted. Such tendencies are not planned to occur by anyone necessarily, but they are common in our entire education system. They may not be permitted to run their full course, since the subdued contradictions between liberating intentions and repressive outcomes continually threaten to emerge again.

Recent developments at the OU must be seen as offering different possibilities. Within the Institute of Educational Technology, for example, there appears to have been a revived interest in 'student-initiated education' (including an interest in student 'projects'). We do not know how advanced such concerns are in terms of actual policy and organisation, but, as with existing provision for student involvement (such as summer schools and tutorials), these ideas might well have liberating consequences. On the face of it, a call for the recognition of student-initiated projects as meaningful and worth while in education seems to offer a fundamental challenge to the 'banking' concept—and it could produce a demand for a greater democratisation of the whole teaching and assessment system at the OU. While such ideas are seriously advocated and discussed, the possibility exists of a radical challenge to the present OU system being developed within the OU itself.

However, student projects could come to mean the extension of student choice to pursue optional routes through existing OU courses, to choose to receive course units in a particular order, or to apply given arguments to agreed private topics. Student projects in our experience often come to be merely the students' own attempts to approach some standard treatment of a topic as pre-defined by an academic. In such circumstances, no radical contradiction with existing practice would emerge. The OU could easily define and operationalise the concept of a 'project' in order to accommodate the proposed changes without disturbing the basic ideology of 'banking'— and we believe this is the most likely development.

Of course, though, there may still be students and staff who are able to resist the particular OU definition of the idea of student projects and discover in the term meanings and implications which contradict, and lead to criticism of, existing OU practice.[48]

However, the development of the OU so far, and its apparently widespread and uncritical popularity, shows precisely how potentially radical ideas can be managed and incorporated.

Notes

1 One can clearly see examples of such arguments in the work of the 'deschoolers', and in the works of the authors in M. F. D. Young, ed., *Knowledge and Control*, Collier-Macmillan, 1971. Perhaps the best collection of such works can be found in the Open University course, *Schooling and Society* (E202).

2 See, for example, H. Bourges, ed., *The Student Revolt*, Panther, 1968.

3 It is difficult to find articles in the British press which are even mildly critical of the Open University. Most of the major journals were apparently convinced as early as June 1973, when the first graduates appeared, that the Open University was a success.

4 Iran, Portugal, Spain, Japan, Brazil, Canada and the USA have all shown interest in developing Open Universities of their own. Iran seems to be in the lead so far as actual material commitment is concerned. Doubtless, the implications for social control of a university where the students are widely dispersed have not gone unnoticed.

5 The justification for the development of such a system— in terms of being able to respond flexibly to the 'needs' of the economy—was outlined as early as 1970 by the Open University Vice-Chancellor. See W. Perry, 'The Open University', *Proceedings of the Royal Institution of Great Britain*, 44 (203), 1970.

6 Some of the other implications involve the view that expertise gathered in various courses can somehow be added or combined. Such combination is possible only on the basis that courses are equivalent in some way— that they possess the characteristic of having taken a fixed amount of time to pursue, presumably. The close parallels with the 'banking' concept of education are evident.

7 See the discussion in *The Times Higher Educational Supplement*, 27 February 1976.

8 For example, the Open University's 'think-tank' decided in 1973 to begin to invest more money in developing 'post-experience' courses at the expense of undergraduate ones. Again, such developments were outlined even in 1970 (see W. Perry, op. cit.).

9 Thus applications from teachers seem to be declining relative to those of other groups, for example. This could be seen as being inevitable as the Open University gradually mops up the pool of talent that had been produced by unfair selection processes in the past.

10 See L. Wagner, 'The economic implications', in J. Tunstall, ed., *The Open University Opens*, Routledge & Kegan Paul, 1974.

11 Both major political parties in Britain have shown themselves willing to support the Open University (after some initial hesitation, especially from the Conservatives). A good deal of support has come from 'progressives' like Michael Young and even Paulo Freire. The staff, too, at the Open University represent a wide range of political allegiances.

12 Particularly interesting points were made, for example,

in N. Birnbaum, 'A view from New England', in Tunstall, op. cit., where strong implications were drawn of a role for the Open University in 'stripping knowledge of its bourgeois aura'.

13 We are thinking here of those works included in A. Halsey, J. Floud and C. Anderson, eds, *Education, Economy and Society*, Collier-Macmillan, 1968, for example.

14 See, for example, C. A. Crosland, *The Future of Socialism*, New York, Schocken, 1963. The terms 'sponsored' and 'contest mobility' belong, of course, to the famous article by R. Turner in Halsey *et al.*, eds, op. cit.

15 We are thinking of the liberalism of, say, Rousseau as an example of the first version, and that of Bentham as an example of the second version.

16 K. Marx, in *Capital*, vol. 1, quoted in H. Marcuse, *Reason and Revolution*, Routledge & Kegan Paul, 1973.

17 See K. Marx, 'Critique of the Gotha Programme', in K. Marx and F. Engels, *Selected Works*, vol. 2, Lawrence & Wishart.

18 Some later proposals for randomising the allocation of places to applicants (instead of using 'first come, first served' as at present) illustrate this tendency. Random allocation is seen as 'fairer', since 'first come, first served' seems to favour certain (well-organised) candidates. Yet, clearly, random allocation involves a *complete* anonymity for the applicants.

19 J. Bentham in *Chrestomathia*, quoted in J. Bowring, ed., *The Works of Jeremy Bentham*, vol. 8, New York, Russell & Russell, 1962 (reprint of 1838–48 edition).

20 Bentham advocated the use of a certain 'Bell's Instructional System', which offered a number of suggestions for keeping the attention of the pupils, many of which resembled Bentham's own proposals for the design of a centrally supervised penitentiary!

21 In practice, an individualised teaching system was prohibitively expensive, as we shall see. As a result, possibly, some senior educational technologists were prepared to help to devise an elaborate selection scheme which would have had the effect of excluding or deterring the unqualified from gaining access after all! Such a selection scheme was never used—largely because the unqualified did not apply in large numbers after all. The educational technologists presumably felt that without the power to 'individualise' the teaching system, some power to control the range of individuals entering the system was the only alternative.

22 Harold Wilson's original intention seemed to have involved using the Open University to train the technologists needed to boost Britain through the famed 'white hot heat of the technological revolution' in the 1960s—according to J. Pratt's article, 'Open, University!', *Higher Education Review* 3 (2), 1971. Jennie Lee apparently played a large part in getting this early orientation abandoned, according to B. MacArthur,

'An interim history of the Open University', in Tunstall, op. cit.

23 M. F. D. Young, 'An approach to the study of curricula as socially organised knowledge', in *Knowledge and Control*.

24 See B. MacArthur (op. cit.) and the speeches by J. Lee at the 1973 Open University degree ceremony (reported in *Open University Gazette*, 2 (5), December 1973): 'Our Open University is going from strength to strength. And why . . . ? Because we refused to compromise at all in its standards of scholarship.' Or, later: 'It is *not* a working class university. It was never *intended* to be a working class university. It was planned as a *university*. It is the *Open* University.'

25 OU curricula certainly seem to be as abstract, literary and individually assessable as those criticised by M. F. D. Young (op. cit.), for example.

26 Educational technology had always been relegated to a rather minor place in universities, as R. Hooper's article in Hooper, ed., *The Curriculum: Context, Design and Development* (Oliver & Boyd, 1971) makes clear. The continuing struggle to appear to be 'useful' is a dominant feature of life inside the Open University's Institute of Educational Technology, and an important effect of such insecurity has been to encourage the development of an uncritical, pragmatic, 'problem-solving' perspective.

27 A good review of such principles can be found in Leslie J. Brigg's *The Sequencing of Instructions According to Hierarchies of Competence*, American Institute for Research monograph no. 3, 1968.

28 A particularly systematic account of the working out of a detailed theory of instruction, based on behaviourist principles, is given in Thomas F. Gilbert, *Mathetics: an Explicit Theory for the Design of Teaching Programmes*, RECALL supplement 1, London, Longmac, 1969.

29 An influential mechanistic view of learning as 'information processing' of a particular kind runs throughout the work of G. Pask (see n. 33) and is reflected in the Open University course unit he wrote (unit 9 of E283).

30 The Open University Science Foundation Course (S100) featured the use of 'black pages' in the course units which represented more complex optional routes for the well qualified to pursue, for example.

31 B. N. Lewis, 'Course production at the Open University. II: activities and activity networks, *British Journal of Educational Technology*, 2 (2), May 1971.

32 Such an assumption was expressed most clearly in a draft for G. Pask's Open University OU unit (see n. 29), and in various seminars conducted by Professor Pask at the Open University.

33 G. Pask, 'Uncertainty Regulation in Learning Applied to Procedures for Teaching Concepts of Probability' (monograph available from Systems Research Ltd, 2 Richmond Hill, Richmond, Surrey). Printed in January 1972, the monograph represents the most fully developed 'knowledge structure' we have seen.

34 See, for example, the series of articles with the general title 'Course production at the Open University', *British Journal of Educational Technology*, from 1971 to 1973.

35 The example given refers to the work undertaken by a team of computer specialists who were concerned to see if a machine could be taught to 'see and learn visual concepts'. This and other examples of the sorts of work seen as relevant to the development of 'knowledge structures' are well described in two papers by M. Macdonald-Ross of the Open University's Institute of Educational Technology: 'Behavioural Objectives and the Structure of Knowledge' (presented to the APLET Conference 1972), and 'The Problem of Representing Knowledge' (presented to the Structural Learning Conference, Philadelphia, 1972). Both papers are available from M. Macdonald-Ross at the Open University.

36 We are using the term as in T. Kuhn, *The Structure of Scientific Revolutions*, University of Chicago Press, London, 1969.

37 We are conscious that we cannot devote sufficient space to the discussion of the central concept of dialogue in this article. We believe that useful discussions of the concept appear in P. Freire, *Pedagogy of the Oppressed*, Penguin, 1972. The phenomenological terms referred to in this paragraph ('themes', 'horizons' and so on) are discussed in A. Schutz, *Phenomenology of the Social World*, Heinemann, 1972, and in A. Schutz and T. Luckmann, *Structures of the Life World*, Heinemann, 1974. See also the section on Gaudamer in R. E. Palmer, *Hermeneutics*, Northwestern University Press, 1969.

38 We are using the terms 'objectifications' and 'reifications' as in the article by P. Berger and S. Pullberg, 'Reification and the sociological critique of consciousness', *History and Theory*, 4, 1965.

39 M. F. D. Young, *Studies in Science Education*, 1 (1), January 1974.

40 op. cit.

41 See B. N. Lewis and J. Cook, 'Toward a theory of telling', *International Journal of Man-Machine Studies*, 1, 1969, 129–76. Despite its obscurity, this article seemed to have a wide influence on the educational technologists at the Open University. The paper itself points out the complexities in communicating—even in communicating simple shouts of warning—but the educational technologists tended to believe that all these difficulties of interpretation could be overcome by good course design. The main role of the Open University was seen as involving one-way transmission of information of this kind—and one educational technologist even suggested that subjects that could not be 'told' should not be included in the Open University curriculum.

42 W. Perry, 'The Open University'.

43 Both the diagnostic and the discriminatory functions of assessment were present from the beginning—but in a fascinating series of developments designed initially simply to improve the assessment scheme, the discriminatory function became dominant. See D. Harris, 'Educational technology at the Open University: a short history of achievement and cancellation', *British Journal of Educational Technology*, 7 (1), 1976, 43–53, for a brief discussion of this transformation.

44 H. Becker, B. Geer, and E. C. Hughes, *Making the Grade: the Academic Side of College Life*, New York, Wiley, 1968.

45 See N. E. McIntosh, 'The Use of Survey Research in the Planning of Higher Education' (paper presented to an ESOMAR Conference, Budapest, 1973, and published in the Conference Proceedings).

46 A. Gouldner, *The Coming Crisis in Western Sociology*, Heinemann, 1972.

47 One student in our small sample claimed to have been so inspired by reading Goffman that he began to see his marriage in a new light—and eventually became separated from his wife! There are also students who refer to the 'joy of at least thinking and talking away some of the fuzzy nonsenses of my life . . . when I go home [from tutorials] almost every time I feel excited and stimulated. By the time I get home I want to do somersaults and things'. It is interesting to note that the tutor who collected these comments (and reported them at a Conference on Correspondence Tuition at Maryland College, Woburn, June 1973) advocates a greater decentralisation of the Open University system, and even a system which might encourage 'major divergence from the course where there is a really good case' if such joyful moments are to be sustained.

48 Similar alternatives arise over the inclusion of this article in a book which is to be a part of the Open University course E202. Our intention is to provide some basis for what we hope will be a widespread discussion of the Open University which will include participation by students and staff at the Open University itself. There are possibilities for these discussions—although we must recognise that they are limited, as we have suggested. By using the Open University's own facilities for disseminating our arguments, we may be helping to encourage a profound, but liberating, discussion of a wide range of Open University practices. On the other hand, however, our efforts could be incorporated, as others' have been, in a spirit of 'repressive tolerance', by becoming subject to the very constraints and controls we ourselves have uncovered. Our arguments in this article could be rendered ineffective as critique while adding to the liberal appearance of Open University materials. We can only hope that the incorporation will not be a total one—but all those who contribute to Open University courses must be aware of the risks!

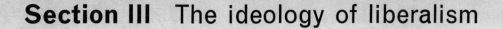

Section III The ideology of liberalism

8 Liberalism and the quest for orderly change
Clarence J. Karier

As conflict in American culture increases and the idea of revolution is no longer dismissed as some absurd anarchist dream but increasingly entertained by men of more moderate persuasion, more and more voices can be heard echoing a common warning. The warning is this: The new left must either temper its attacks on the military, corporate, and educational establishment in this country, or we will all suffer the wrath of a fascist nightmare. Put in these terms the new left is made responsible for the coming American fascism. The usual analysis proceeds with the notion that the attack on the liberal center from both the right and left weakens and eventually destroys democratic institutions. The process begins with the left questioning the mythologies that sustain bourgeois society thus threatening the security of those in power and ends with a repressive fascist order. In this sense, the more the left agitates, the more the fascist right can be expected to grow. There are few political and social analysts in this country who seriously doubt the possibility that given an open confrontation the fascist would win. Virtually every observer seems to predict that a socialism of the right not the left would emerge. It is interesting that in times of severe crisis, most liberals can be relied upon to move to the right rather than to the left of the political spectrum.

There are, of course, a number of problems with the above analysis. It is clear that this analysis is created by liberals who see themselves as the guardian of a kind of middle-class democracy who abhor conflict and violence and who take pride in endorsing reasoned intelligent change. Espousing the moderate humanitarian virtues of the enlightenment, these liberals see themselves as victims of extremist thought and action on both the left and right. Such an analysis, in effect, justifies the liberal's capitulation to fascist power. It was, after all, the agitation of the left that forced the liberals to support the fascist solution for law and order in the streets and the universities. Thus, the liberals are quick to point out that the responsibility for the destruction of democratic institutions lies with their intemperate brothers on the left and not with any failure or perhaps fatal flaw in liberal philosophy. Although such an analysis is heavy on justification, it is relatively light on explanation. It does not, for example, explain how, despite the strong pragmatic liberal influence in American social, political, economic, and educational institutions for the past half century, the problems of race, poverty, and militarism have been exacerbated rather than alleviated. Such an analysis, furthermore, does not help us to understand just why it is that when the chips are down liberals can be expected to move to support a fascist order rather than an equalitarian revolution.

Without suggesting a scapegoat view of the past, it might be fruitful to reexamine critically some of the key tenets of the twentieth-century liberal's faith. A more critical view of that faith might reveal some of its major sources of weakness as well as a more realistic assessment of its strengths. Such an analysis might also shed some light on current problems. If, for example, we had fully appreciated the liberal's commitment to expert knowledge over populist opinion or his desire for unity, order, and universalism over respect for idiosyncratic needs of individuals and groups, we might have more realistically anticipated or at least understood his stand on such confrontations as Ocean Hill-Brownsville.

The roots of the current crisis in American culture lie deeply imbedded in both the social and intellectual history of the last one hundred years. In a very real sense the crisis is a result of both the success and the failure of the enlightenment philosophy of progress.

Source: *History of Education Quarterly*, 12, spring 1972, pp. 57–67, 71–80; also appeared in C. J. Karier, P. Violas and J. Spring, eds, *Roots of Crisis...*, Rand McNally, 1973, pp. 84–107.

The collective side of that philosophy with its scientifically organized technology and computer-managed bureaucracy has become a reality; on the other side, however, individual freedom, dignity, and well-being have not fared so well. Caught up in collective institutional progress, the individual has become a means rather than an end to social order. Both the philosopher of nineteenth-century classical liberalism, John Stuart Mill, and the philosopher of twentieth-century liberalism, John Dewey, were centrally concerned with this issue. Both agreed, in principle, that the enlightened society must strive to achieve the greater happiness of the greater number.[1] They disagreed, however, on how this was to be achieved. While Mill maintained a mistrust of state power and discussed freedom in terms of freedom from government interference, the new liberals reversed this process and saw individual freedom tied to a positive use of state power. In this context positive liberalism means more than just the opposite of negative liberalism. The use of unchecked state power to control the future through shaping the thought, action, and character of its citizens could ultimately lead to a totalitarian polity. The basic assumptions of many who espoused the philosophy of positive liberalism were succinctly put by Isaiah Berlin in his *Four Essays on Liberty* when he said:[2]

First, that all men have one true purpose, and one only, that of rational self-direction; second, that the ends of all rational beings must of necessity fit into a single universal, harmonious pattern, which some men may be able to discern more clearly than others; third, that all conflict, and consequently all tragedy, is due solely to the clash of reason with the irrational or the insufficiently rational—the immature and undeveloped elements in life—whether individual or communal, and that such clashes are, in principle, avoidable, and for wholly rational beings impossible; finally, that when all men have been made rational, they will obey the rational laws of their own natures, which are one and the same in them all, and so be at once wholly law-abiding and wholly free.

To be sure, not all positive liberals held all these assumptions. They were, however, implicit in the thought and action of most.

Whether it was the negative freedom of Mill or the positive freedom of Dewey, each, in his own way, became a philosophic justification for the dominant economic organization of the period. By the time John Dewey assumed the role of philosophic leader in America, the laissez-faire idea, which characterized much of the nineteenth-century economic rhetoric, was beginning to be replaced by the theme of a managed corporate economy, more characteristic of the twentieth century. As capital began to be organized at the end of the century in new and unique ways, the corporate state of the twentieth century was born.[3] Classical liberalism with its philosophic justification of a competitive economy, private property, individualism, and freedom from state interference gave way to the new liberalism that espoused controlled economy, state planning, group thought, and managed change.

Behind this ideological change from a laissez-faire liberalism to a state welfare liberalism existed social, political, and economic conflict of a violent nature. Violence was not new to frontier-minded America, nor was it new to the immigrant worker desperately trying to survive in a competitive industrial society. What was new, however, was the emergence of the corporate mass technological society, and with it the rise of a middle-class liberalism that eschewed violence, conflict, and rugged individualism. The new liberals criticized the ends (private profit), but not the means (scientifically organized technology) of the emerging corporate society. They repeatedly expressed their faith in the rational knowledge of the expert and rejected the irrationalism of the masses. Fearing the potential for violence and chaos implicit in the uncontrolled immigrant masses of our urban ghettoes, the new liberal turned increasingly toward the development of nonviolent but coercive means of social control.

The new liberals directed the nation's social thought and action toward an acceptance of a compulsory state in which the individual would be 'scientifically' shaped and controlled so as to fulfill the nation's destiny.[4] Such a compulsory state would as easily require compulsory schooling as military service. Rejecting both the classical liberal's rhetoric concerning individual autonomy as well as his 'robber baron' practices, many new liberals turned to some form of state socialism. In the process, they turned to the social science expert for knowledge that would control and shape that state. The rhetoric of the new liberalism, whether in politics or education, reflected a key concern for more effective and efficient means of social control in order to eliminate conflict and to establish the harmonious organic community. Some of these men looked to a highly romanticized version of the nineteenth-century American village as a source of community. Others opted for a future in which scientific intelligence might rule out bloody conflicts and overt coercion as a means of social control. The new 'science' of psychology applied to the schooling of the masses could be used to prevent revolution by committing the children of the disinherited to the larger more universal social order through a process of internalizing the shared goals and ideals of the controlling middle class.

The immigrant was often viewed as a threat to social order. By 1900 America was a land of strangers. Approximately half of the population was foreign born or children of foreign born. The real threat came when the flow of immigration abruptly shifted from northern Europe to southern Europe.[5] By the closing decades of the nineteenth century, the northern

European immigrant was viewed by the white Anglo-Saxon Protestant community as relatively safe; while the southern Europeans were viewed as an acute threat to the mores of America. The stranger in the land had to be Americanized so as to protect the 'American way.'

Traditional Protestant theology offered little solace to those who felt the dangers to social order. After Darwin and the higher criticism of the Bible, little intellectual vitality remained to support the credibility of theological, doctrinal disputes. What remained, however, was the moral capital of a pious Protestant past and a missionary zeal to convert the heathen in our own midst. Missionary work needed to be done, not only in Africa and the Far East, but in Hell's Kitchen in New York City and on Halsted Street in Chicago. The new immigrants had to be made safe for the streets of New York and Chicago, so that a better, more efficient American might emerge. The Social Gospel, whether preached by Walter Rauchenbusch in Hell's Kitchen or by Jane Addams at Hull House, had a similar ring. The immigrant had to be educated for his own 'good' and that 'good' was defined by the mores of the new liberal.

The religion of the settlement houses and the urban ministries reflected the collapse of theological Protestantism and the rise of a secularized socially conscious Protestant Christianity made relevant to a rising middle class. Those men and women, reared in the earlier faith, and who, in the twilight of their youth, found themselves searching for more creditable meaning to their lives, usually turned to a secularized Protestant moral value system as the basis for their new progressive, reformist faith. Jane Addams, speaking before the Ethical Culture Society's summer session at Plymouth, Massachusetts,[6] proclaimed that the settlement house movement embodied the true spirit of Christ in the world. Similarly, John Dewey expressed his belief that the teacher in his concern for the 'formation of the *proper* social life,' and the 'maintenance of *proper* social order,' and the 'securing of the *right* social growth: is the prophet of the true God and the usherer in of the true kingdom of God.'[7] Both were translating their personal values into a new religion of humanity. Most spokesmen for progressive education in America were fundamentally moralists, working in the interest of the hegemony of an emerging middle class. To Dewey, as to many that followed him, science and technology were the new theology. All was tied to a quest for 'The Great Community' where men would ultimately learn, as Dewey put it, to 'use their scientific knowledge to control their social relations.'

Political progressivism was bent, not on the destruction of capitalism, but rather on rationalizing and stabilizing the system. Stability, predictability, and security were the expected consequences of a controlled rational process of social change.[8] Federal control and regulation of labor, management, and the consumer market became the trademark of the political progressive movement. Through the efforts of such liberals as Jane Addams, John R. Commons, Charles W. Eliot, Samuel Gompers, and others in the National Civic Federation, labor, management, and government were brought into a cooperative relationship.[9] The triumph of political progressivism meant the rise of the new managerial class to positions of power in the newer reform-type city governments, as well as in the growing bureaucratic structures in both the state and federal systems.[10] By World War I, the corporate state emerged embodying many of the values of both the political and educational progressives.[11] World War I brought political and educational progressives even closer together in common cause. Although most twentieth-century liberals believed that one could best serve the interest of the individual through involvement in a larger corporate society,[12] it is not at all clear that liberal thought and action have always served the interest of the individual in any sense other than that which happened to coincide with the needs of the corporate society. John Dewey set the problem for the twentieth-century liberal fairly succinctly when, in discussing 'What America Will Fight For,' he said:[13]

> Politics means getting certain things done. Some body of persons, elected or self-constituted, take charge, deciding and executing. In the degree in which a society is democratic this governing group has to get the assent and support of large masses of people. In the degree in which the things to be done run counter to the inertia, bias and apparent interests of the masses, certain devices of manipulation have to be resorted to. The political psychology of the older school, that of Bentham and Mill, taught that in a democratic state the governing body would never want to do anything except what was in the interests of the governed. But experience has shown that this view was over-naive. Practical political psychology consists largely in the technique of the expert manipulation of men in masses for ends not clearly seen by them, but which they are led to believe are of great importance for them.

Rejecting this 'practical political psychology' as both inefficient and ineffective in achieving broader social aims Dewey went on to call for a more 'business-like psychology' that would consist of 'intelligent perception of ends . . . and effective selection and orderly arrangement of means for their execution.' In this way the road could be kept open for the possibilities of 'world organization and the beginnings of a public control which crosses nationalistic boundaries and interests.' In the closing days of the war, Dewey pointed with pride to the intelligent mobilization and management of the nation in crisis. He then looked to the future with hope that the same intelligence might be applied in developing a 'New Social Science' which would help shape the new order in the future along similar lines.[14]

The major impetus of progressive reform, whether political or educational, was to make the system work efficiently and effectively and to do so by using the compulsory power of the political state to achieve that end. The thrust of progressive reform was indeed, conservative.[15] In this way, many socialists were also, in effect, conservative. They were conservative in their quest for efficiency, orderly change, and in their desire to maintain the system. For example, John Dewey in his *Confidential Report* to the War Department during World War I was centrally concerned with the manipulation of Polish affairs so that we would not lose our cheap labor supply after the war through emigration. As Dewey said:[16]

> The great industrial importance of Polish labor in this country must be borne in mind and the fact that there will be a shortage of labor after the war and that there is already a movement under foot (which should be carefully looked into) to stimulate the return of Poles and others of foreign birth in Southeastern Europe to their native lands after the war. With the sharp commercial competition that will necessarily take place after the war, any tendencies which on the one hand de-Americanize and on the other hand strengthen the allegiance of those of foreign birth to the United States deserve careful attention.

Although Dewey considered himself a socialist, these were not the concerns of a radical socialist but rather one of a management welfare state socialist interested in the development and maintenance of the system. To be sure, Dewey's values did not coincide with the values exhibited by the National Association of Manufacturers, which represented the smaller entrepreneurs, but the thrust of his values with respect to order, conflict, and social change was not far from that of the National Civic Federation which supported progressive social legislation in the interest of the new emerging corporate society.[17] John Dewey was committed to the economic growth and progress of that society, even though such progress might require manipulation of Polish workers. From this perspective, one can also account for his intense dislike and distrust of Papal Catholics as opposed to Protestant Catholics, as well as his condescending attitude toward ethnic differences, which appear throughout the report. Ethnic and religious differences were viewed as a threat to the survival of the society and had to be overcome through assimilation.[18] Dewey, as well as other liberal reformers, was committed to flexible, experimentally managed, orderly social change, which included a high degree of manipulation. (. . .)

Although liberals are not fascists or communists, their quest for orderly change within a managed society led some of them at times to become enthusiastic about certain characteristics of emerging totalitarian societies. Just as Dewey became en-

thusiastic about the role the Soviet schools were playing in the creation of a new Soviet Union, so, too, other liberals were impressed with Italian corporate fascism as a grand experiment in social engineering. Herbert Croly, for example, warned critics of fascism to 'beware of outlawing a political experiment which aroused in a whole nation an increased moral energy and dignified its activities by subordinating them to a deeply felt common purpose.'[19] Italian fascism was warmly received among such well-known American liberals as Charles Beard, Horace Kallen, Herbert Croly, and Lincoln Steffens (1926–1930). This reception was prompted by more than a simple desire to have 'the trains run on time.' While Beard was impressed with the flexibility of the fascist state and its freedom from 'consistent scheme,' others were more impressed with the ability of that state to act decisively by subordinating outworn 'principles to method' and law to order. For many, corporate fascism seemed to satisfy the need of the corporate society for unity, order, efficiency, collective meaning, social engineering, and experimentation as well as freedom from the older rationalistic liberal philosophies that tended to value individual liberty over state authority. It was not until the early 1930s that these liberals began to see the consequences of the fascist experiment in terms of political refugees. At that point, they reversed their opinion about fascism. Historically, we have tended to treat this sympathetic treatment of fascism by pragmatic liberals as an 'accidental flirtation,'[20] or perhaps an aberration in which normally rational men got carried away with the zeitgeist of the time. If we had critically analyzed pragmatic liberal thought within the context of the corporate state, we might have understood the fascist flirtation as a logical and reasonable extrapolation of certain characteristics of liberal thought. If we considered the liberal's need for social experiment and reconciliation of opposites, we might further have understood why Charles A. Beard looked upon Benito Mussolini's fascist Italy as working out 'new democratic direction,' and why he might conclude that:[21]

> Beyond question an amazing experiment is being made here, an experiment in reconciling individualism and socialism, politics and technology. It would be a mistake to allow feelings aroused by contemplating the harsh deeds and extravagant assertions that have accompanied the fascist process (as all other immense historical changes) to obscure the potentialities and the lessons of the adventure— no, not adventure, but destiny riding without saddle and bridle across the historical peninsula that bridges the world of antiquity and our modern world.

The role of the liberal within American society was essentially that of the knowledgeable expert dedicated to the survival of the system through growth. The liberal educational reformer, just as the liberal political reformer was, in effect, a flexible conservative. To be sure, Dewey sharply disagreed with the mechanistic conservatism of men like David Snedden, Edward L. Thorndike, and Charles A. Prosser. His own commitment, however, to flexible experimental change would contribute to the survival of the system. In this sense Dewey's experimentation in education as well as most of twentieth-century progressive education can be viewed as conservative. (. . .)

Dewey had long ago rejected the classical conception of individualism and its political corollary of a free marketplace of conflicting ideas. The traditional notion of democracy, dependent on conflict of parties and public discussion, according to Dewey, had passed. In *Liberalism and Social Action*, Dewey talked of the collapse of both the capitalistic system and laissez-faire democracy. Neither had much in common with scientific method. He said:[22]

> The idea that the conflict of parties will, by means of public discussion, bring out necessary public truths is a kind of political watered-down version of the Hegelian dialectic, with its synthesis arrived at by a union of antithetical conceptions. The method has nothing in common with the procedure of organized cooperative inquiry which has won the triumphs of science in the field of physical nature.

Rejecting confrontation politics, Dewey turned to science and what he termed a method of intelligence. The solution was to be found in the new *scientific* socialism, not in a democratic socialism (democratic in the older sense of the term). The new theology, for Dewey, had become science and technology. In a way, it had become a creator of new values and ends. As he put it, 'Take science (including its application to the machine) for what it is, and we shall begin to envisage it as a potential creator of new values and ends.'[23]

Just as the older theology called for a new Adam, so too, Dewey's unbounded faith in science and technology led him to call for a new man.[24] Such a man must work well within the corporate system where, almost in Orwellian fashion, positive freedom would mean control. Freedom for Dewey meant rational control over future possibilities, as he put it, 'Control is the crux of our freedom.'[25] This kind of freedom over future possibilities would be maximized when the 'great society' would become the 'great community.' Only thus, would a true public exercising a maximum degree of freedom and control come into being. Such a public would assert its 'general will' in Rousseauian fashion where 'force is not eliminated but is transformed in use and direction by ideas and sentiments made possible by means of symbols.'[26] Ideas, sentiments, and words become the force vehicles of social control in Dewey's great community.[27] One side of his search for the great com-

munity had its precursors in Rousseau, Emerson, Royce, and Walt Whitman; while another side was rooted in Lester Frank Ward, Albion Small, and Herbert Croly. As Dewey put it, 'Democracy will come into its own, for democracy is a name for a life of free and enriching communion. It had its seer in Walt Whitman. It will have its consummation when free social inquiry is indissolubly wedded to the art of full and moving communication.'[28] The age-old problem of educating the man or the citizen would be resolved when the great society became the great community, and the new man, indeed the one-dimensional man, would become a living reality. This new community was one in which men would 'systematically use scientific procedures for the control of human relationships and the direction of the social effects of our vast technological machinery.'[29] The solution to social conflict, for Dewey, remained the intelligent use of education for social control. The direction that such control should take, he believed, could be determined by scientific method.

Dewey's benign faith in the scientific method and technology remained undaunted. Perennially optimistic, he believed there was a way of humanizing American social institutions, be they industrial or educational. He saw the possibility in the progress of science and technology toward what he called a 'humane age.' The experimental method, he believed, was 'the foe of every belief that permits habit and wont to dominate invention and discovery, and ready-made system to override verifiable fact.'[30] With a somewhat romantic view of the scientific community in mind, he went on to suggest that not only are science and technology revolutionizing our society, but that science carries with it the germ of a more open society. He said:[31]

> No scientific inquirer can keep what he finds to himself or turn it to merely private account without losing his scientific standing. Everything discovered belongs to the community of workers. Every new idea and theory has to be submitted to this community for confirmation and test. There is an expanding community of cooperative effort and of truth . . . Suppose that what now happens in limited circles were extended and generalized.

The problem, here, is that although theoretical science may be open-ended, technology concerned with serving particular social institutions may not be so dedicated to truth or an open community of discourse. On the contrary, a social institution dedicated to survival may find it expedient to sacrifice truth.[32] The new liberalism of Dewey and others failed at this critical juncture. Perhaps in some ideal world where all men were governed by 'rational self-direction,' Dewey's idea of science might be applicable. In the world of twentieth-century power politics, however, most scientists and technologists became hired men of the industrial militarized society. It is significant that neither Dewey nor the many educators who followed him preaching the gospel of science in education paid much attention to the social environment in which modern science and technology were born and bred, i.e., Prussian Germany. Instead, the rhetoric of American educators abounds with the association of freedom and democracy with scientific method and technology.[33] Dewey made a significant contribution to this mythology. Repeatedly, he treated technology as either a positive or a neutral tool and seldom ever seemed to sense or show serious concern with the negative and limiting consequences of the technological system itself.[34] More fundamental, however, he failed to realize that neither democracy nor individual freedom had any necessary inherent connection with science and technology. It could, however, have a very intimate connection with his passion for unity, order, and systematic, rational change, as well as his high regard for the knowledgeable expert. These were all characteristic of his new liberal ideology. These constructs, moreover, remained fairly constant from his Chicago Laboratory School days until late in life when he favorably reviewed Karl Mannheim's book, *Man and Society* (1940), in which Mannheim called for elites to plan the new social order.[35] Dewey's faith in science, knowledgeable elites, and scientific social planning remained firm. By 1943, R. Bruce Raup, George E. Axtelle, Kenneth D. Benne, and B. Othanel Smith published *The Improvement of Practical Intelligence* that attempted to create a method of social dialogue through which collective planning might occur. Dewey's response to this work was that he believed it to be too subjectivistic and that, furthermore, values for social planning could be arrived at through an objective science. Two decades later, Daniel Bell, following in the footsteps of John Dewey, published *The End of Ideology*, in which he asserted that the new social order will be planned by an ideology-free social scientist, charting the course of a future civilization.

Just a century after Comte had prophesized the emergence of a positive objective science of man and values, liberals such as Dewey and Bell heralded the development of an objective science of human values.[36] Bell had correctly surmised that this was, indeed, the end of ideology. It was also the culmination of one of the most significant ideologies in the first half of the twentieth century—liberalism itself. If human values could be objectively determined and predictably controlled by the social science expert using systems analysis in the cybernated world of the future, then little need existed for that once burning faith which called for rational progressive change. To be sure, the 'games' that engaged the 'think tank' experts seemed a pallid substitute for the philosophic discourse in which the liberals had engaged for the past century; nevertheless, they were still a logical extension of liberal thought and action. Just as many nineteenth-century liberals found themselves justifying 'robber

baron' capitalism, so too, many twentieth-century liberals found themselves justifying the military industrial establishment. This, however, could be expected. The twentieth-century liberal was in many ways the articulate spokesman for that managerial middle class that actively participated in the creation of the militarized society in the post-World War II period.

Perhaps, if we had fully appreciated the liberal's commitment to the survival of the system through evolutionary, orderly change, we might have understood why so many were impressed with early fascist and Soviet experiments in human engineering. It might also have been easier to understand why the 'liberal'-dominated Committee for Cultural Freedom (1939) opted for McCarthy-like solutions to the problems of communist teachers in the schools fully a decade ahead of the McCarthy era.[37] Nor would it seem unusual that Sidney Hook would be one of the founders of the American Committee for Cultural Freedom (1951), an offspring of the CIA-supported Congress for Cultural Freedom.[38] Finally, if we had an accurate historical analysis of the role the liberal has played in the development and maintenance of the corporate state, we would not have been so repeatedly surprised along the road from Berkeley to Attica to find a liberal mind behind the hand on the policeman's club or trigger.

In education, the liberal supported the creation of a mass system of schooling dedicated to filling the need of society for a citizen capable of adjusting to the necessities of an industrial system. Such a society required citizens who respected the authority of the knowledgeable expert and who believed the mythologies that sustained bourgeois culture. Despite the equalitarian rhetoric, educational liberals most often, in practice, supported an education directed from the top down. In this respect, they repeatedly stood for the professionalization of the expert-teacher and the use of improved technique to enlighten the ignorant masses. 'Enlightenment,' for most, implied education for social control.

With Dewey and other liberals, words such as freedom, democracy, and individualism took on new and different meanings. The philosophy of John Dewey and most liberals who attacked the ancient dualisms could readily lead to a one-dimensional view of reality where opposites appeared blurred. Freedom, for example, became control. Dewey's conception of *Democracy and Education* bypassed the politically potent power questions and instead moved toward a cultural participatory perspective that assumed an increasing acceptance on the part of the masses of the scientific method as the 'key to social betterment.' Cultural participation, however, was no substitute for political and economic power. In spite of the fact that Dewey in *Liberalism and Social Action* called for a greater militancy, the behavior of liberals in the past decades has been best characterized as acquiescence in the face of political, economic, and military power. Perhaps Isaiah Berlin put his finger on the problem when he suggested that 'virtue is not knowledge, nor freedom identical with either.'[39] Liberals tended to confuse all three. They sought social change without conflict and violence by placing their faith in science and technology as a 'creator of human values' and turned to a mass system of education that would impart those values to the children of the immigrant. In the process, education of the individual was sacrificed for the greater need for social control and security. As a consequence, large numbers of people were ultimately not educated to be critical individual citizens, but trained to seek security and comfort in the symbols and mythologies manipulated by Madison Avenue social science experts. Political office came to be as saleable as soap and the people the pawns of 'expert policy decision makers.' In this way, neither science nor technology was effectively employed to enhance democracy (rule by the people) but rather became an effective tool of the powerful in controlling the social system. Perhaps the liberal faith in science and technology is not an adequate substitute for a philosophy of man.

During times of crisis this weakness in the liberal ideology is exposed. Whether it was Dewey calling for a more effective manipulation of the Polish immigrant during World War I or it was President Johnson manipulating public opinion so as to escalate the Vietnam war, liberals in crisis usually directly or indirectly supported the existing power structure. They were, in fact, *Servants of Power*.[40] If, indeed, the unfortunate time shall come when the left confronts the right in open confrontation, little doubt should remain where many liberals will stand.

Notes

1 See Robert Paul Wolff, *The Poverty of Liberalism*, Boston, 1968, p. 31.

2 London, 1969, p. 154.

3 For example, Charles Forcey in *The Crossroads of Liberalism*, New York, 1961, p. xiv, points out that, 'In 1897 the total capitalization of all corporations individually valued at a million dollars or more came to only 170 millions. Three years later the same figure for total capitalization stood at five billions, and in 1904 at over twenty billions.' For the conservative effect of liberal reform see Gabriel Kolko, *The Triumph of Conservatism: A Reinterpretation of American History 1900–1916*, New York, 1963, and James Weinstein, *The Corporate Ideal in the Liberal State 1900–1918*, Boston, 1968.

4 See Herbert Croly, *The Promise of American Life*, New York, 1963.

5 For example, during the following decades, the percent of the total immigrant population that came from southern Europe increased as follows: 1881–1891—18.3%; 1891–1901—51.9%; 1901–1910—70.8%. See Samuel Eliot Morison and Henry Steele Commager, *The Growth of the American Republic*, New York, 1956, vol. 2, p. 177.

6 See Jane Addams, *Twenty Years at Hull House*, New York, 1935, pp. 113–27.

7 Martin S. Dworkin, *Dewey on Education*, New York, 1959, p. 32. Italics mine.

8 See Kolko, *The Triumph of Conservatism*.

9 See Weinstein, *The Corporate Ideal*.

10 See Samuel P. Hayes, 'The politics of reform in municipal government in the progressive era', *Pacific Northwest Quarterly*, October 1964, pp. 157–69; reprinted in A. B. Callon, Jr, ed., *American Urban History*, New York, 1969.

11 For the relationship between the schools and the political reformist groups, see Joel Spring, 'Education and the Corporate State', doctoral dissertation, University of Wisconsin, 1969.

12 See John Dewey, *Individualism Old and New*, New York, 1930.

13 *The New Republic*, 18 August 1917.

14 See John Dewey, 'A new social science', *The New Republic*, 14, no. 79, 6 April 1918.

15 See Kolko, *The Triumph of Conservatism*.

16 'Conditions among the Poles in the United States', *Confidential Report*, Washington, DC, 1918, p. 73.

17 See Weinstein, *The Corporate Ideal*.

18 In the *Confidential Report* to the Military Intelligence Bureau of the War Department, Dewey was highly critical of those Poles who maintained strong loyalties to the Papacy. This report grew out of his seminar that he held in the Polish ghetto of Philadelphia. As Dewey saw it, the object of the seminar was to 'ascertain forces and conditions which operate against the development of a free and democratic life among the members of this group, to discover the influences which kept them under external oppression and control,' and to further develop a workable plan based on practical knowledge 'to eliminate forces alien to democratic internationalism and to promote American ideals in accordance with the principles announced by President Wilson in his various public communications' (*Confidential Report*, p. 2). Brand Blanshard, a student in that seminar, has reported that during this time Dewey viewed the Poles as a 'cyst' on the American community. For this documentation and for a further elaboration of Dewey's seminar, see Walter Feinberg, 'Progressive Educators and Social Planning', unpublished paper, Champaign, Ill., September 1971.

19 'An apology for fascism', *New Republic*, 49, 12 January 1929, pp. 207–9.

20 For example, see John P. Diggins, 'Flirtation with fascism: American pragmatic liberals and Mussolini's Italy', *American Historical Review*, 71 (2), January 1966, pp. 487–506. Although Diggins does an excellent review of the literature of the period, he fails to seriously consider the possibilities that there may be significant characteristics of liberal thought that can lead one to enthusiastically support a fascist regime.

21 'Making the fascist state', *The New Republic*, 57, 23 January 1929, p. 278.

22 New York, 1935, p. 71.

23 *Individualism Old and New*, pp. 160–1.

24 ibid.
25 *Human Nature and Conduct*, New York, 1922, p. 311.
26 John Dewey, *The Public and Its Problems*, New York, 1927, p. 153.
27 ibid., p. 153.
28 ibid., p. 184.
29 Quoted in Nelson Blake, *A History of American Life and Thought*, New York, 1963, p. 408.
30 Dewey, *Individualism Old and New*, p. 145.
31 ibid.
32 This may account in part for the fact that the Nazi movement received stronger support from those who worked in the applied sciences and more resistance from those who worked in the theoretical sciences. The conservative characteristics of technologists may be as much a function of the role they play in serving the interests of the established institutions as it is their own social-class origins or personal idiosyncrasies.
33 The term 'science' in American educational rhetoric has been one of the more controlling, yet unexplored, myths in American twentieth-century education.
34 See, for example, Jacques Ellul, *The Technological Society*, New York, 1964.
35 See John Dewey, 'The techniques of reconstruction', *Saturday Review*, 22, no. 19, August 1940, p. 10. It is significant that Karl Popper and others consider Mannheim an enemy of the open society. For these and other insights I am indebted to the research of Joseph Hamilton, University of Illinois.
36 See John Dewey, *Theory of Valuation*, in Otto Neurath, ed., *The International Encyclopaedia of Unified Sciences*, 1 and 2, Chicago, 1939.
37 See Paul Violas, 'Fear and constraints in academic freedom of public school teachers, 1930–1960', *Educational Theory*, 21 (1), winter 1971, pp. 70–81.
38 See Christopher Lasch, 'The cultural cold war: a short history of the congress for cultural freedom', an essay in Barton J. Bernstein, ed., *Towards A New Past*, New York, 1968, pp. 322–59.
39 *Four Essays on Liberty*, p. 154.
40 See Loren Baritz, *The Servants of Power*, New York, 1960.

9 Fabian criminology

Ian Taylor, Paul Walton and Jock Young

In a pointed description of the components of Britain's national culture, Perry Anderson (1968, p. 4) has argued that:

> Britain, the most conservative major society in Europe, has a culture in its own image: mediocre and inert. . . . It is a culture of which the Left has been a passive spectator, and at times a deluded accomplice. Twentieth century culture was by and large made against it. Yet the Left has never questioned this 'national' inheritance which is one of the most enduring bonds of its own subordination.

The social-democratic tradition in Britain was a direct production of such an empiricist culture. In the same way as the British bourgeoisie never accomplished a total transformation of an aristocratic society and never recast that society in its own image, so working-class politics in Britain has been endowed with a myopia which could rarely conceive of the total reformation of a class society. Working-class politics has consistently taken the form, from the Chartists to the modern-day Labour Party, of a piecemeal though highly detailed reformism.

The apotheosis of this reformism ideologically was Fabianism, a Fabianism that has been characterized by Nairn (1964, p. 45) as

> a derived Utilitarianism, the timid and dreary species of bourgeois rationalism embraced by the British middle-class during the Industrial Revolution. In it, bourgeois rationalism became socialist rationalism chiefly through the substitution of the State for the magic forces of the *laissez-faire* capitalist market: the former was seen as bringing about 'the greatest happiness of the greatest number' almost as automatically as the latter had been.

Source: *Critical Criminology*, Routledge & Kegan Paul, 1974, pp. 9–14.

The irony of the social-democratic 'opposition' to the laissez-faire philosophy of English utilitarianism was that, instead of attempting to deny the status of utility as the arbiter of social merit, it merely set about the task of rationalizing it. The central contradiction of utilitarianism stems from its emphasis on the importance of reward through merit and effort, and its status as a social philosophy erected in defence of property alongside the continuing inheritance of the means to achieve success in a propertied society. Gouldner (1970, p. 324) puts this well:

> Men who attempt to live by the [meritocratic] value system are demoralized not simply by their *own* lack of means and their own *failures*, but also by witnessing that others may *succeed* even though they lacked the valued qualities.

Fabianism attempts the impossible: it tries to create a truly meritocratic society without transforming the property relationships which work continuously to obstruct such a competitive egalitarianism. So, the British Labour Party's commitments have very largely been to a 'bread-and-butter' politics, spread over with a welfare reformism; and its aspirations have extended little further than the limitation of material poverty, help for the sick, ill and infirm, and, ultimately, the establishment of a healthy meritocracy. This political package is the direct legacy of the Labour Party's origins in Fabianism, buttressed by its religious affiliation to Methodism.

Fabian 'utilitarianism' differed from its bourgeois variant in pointing to the absence of equal opportunity in the wider society. The Fabian project can indeed be seen as the creation of such equal opportunity, via the gradual erosion of the most severe examples of material inequality, in order that a genuinely utilitarian society, based on a universally-appropriate social contract, could be created. The thrust of Labour Party policies in government, and its various manifestoes, is concerned not with a critique of capitalism as a mode of social and industrial organization, but with the inequality of access to participate in such a society (or, alternatively, with the way in which improper control of such a society could enable some to 'get-rich-quick' and others not).

Nowhere is the utilitarian edge to Labour Party thinking so apparent as in its commitment to welfare, *and* in the limits to that commitment. In the period after the Second World War, the Labour government, engaged on behalf of 'the nation as a whole' in what it termed the task of 'social reconstruction', gathered into itself an army of specialist and expert middle-class constituencies—most notably, architects and town planners, academics and teachers, and, most significantly for criminal and civil legislation, the bulk of the British social-worker population. The concern was to win sections of the middle class to the struggle against those personal, social, environmental, educational and even spatial deprivations which helped to disqualify vast sections of the (working-class) population from meaningful participation in the newly-reconstructing society, a society in which the opportunities (to be unequal) would be more equally distributed. If ever the Labour Party had been a defender of class interests as such, this particular role was translated into one of *social* defence, whereby class interests were now seen to involve its incorporation and the imposition on the class of 'universal' (i.e. system) values. The institutional changes to be encouraged were those that would attack deprivation (better industrial relations as a way to fairer distribution of wealth) and those that would encourage the creation of balance and equilibrium in the conduct of social life (mixing of the social classes in newly-planned housing estates). The end-result would be a society based not upon the inequalities of inherited (or other unearnt) wealth, but on merit—success and social mobility would become a matter of personal effort and initiative in a society of equals.

At the back of such policies lie ideological assumptions that can be traced not only to the Fabian translation of utilitarianism, but also to the legacy of Methodism in the early history of the Labour movement. For Methodism (unlike Anglicanism, with its tolerance of inequality and power, a religion that was later to be pilloried by Aneurin Bevan as 'the Conservative Party at prayer') is nothing if not a theology of conformity and unity. Hence, Methodism has often been used as an ideology to castigate and segregate off members of local communities who persist in deviant or militant activities when others have desisted. The role of Methodism during the 1926 General Strike illustrates the ways in which theology can be used to encourage a community to struggle, but also the ways in which it can unite the 'conformists' against, for example, those 'deviant' miners' lodges that refused to surrender so easily. It is the double-edged nature of Methodism as the working-man's Protestant Ethic

that helps us to understand the apparently contradictory thrust in the Labour Party's welfare programmes—the commitment to welfare, in the shape, ultimately, of the Welfare State itself; and the commitment to punitiveness towards those 'deviants' identified or construed as unwilling to recognize, or unwilling to participate in, a utilitarian and reconstructing society.

The contradictions are worth emphasis, for it is against such an ideological mix that any serious critique, founded upon a socialist defence of diversity, would have to proceed.

It is possible to argue, contrary to popular impression, that the Labour Party has had more impact on the systems of social control (the prison system, the probation service, the courts, etc.) and on the systems of social welfare than the Conservative Party (for all that the Conservative Party contains so many senior judges and members of the legal profession and for all that that Party is renowned for its perennial debates on the 'crime-wave'). Certainly, it was a Labour government that introduced the militaristic detention centres into Britain in 1948, with the object of administering a 'short, sharp shock' to recalcitrant youth. It was a Labour government in 1966 which appointed and approved the Mountbatten Enquiry into Security in Prisons, an enquiry whose report set back liberal hopes of 'individualization of treatment', in prisons, on parole, and on liberalization of imprisonment generally for years. And, finally, it was a Labour government which, in 1969, five years after the publication of the Party's study group document *Crime—A Challenge to Us All*, legislated, in the Children and Young Persons Act, for a vast increase in the power of social workers to control the disposition of 'troublesome youth' and for the establishment of the benevolent but paternal community homes as substitute family settings for children from 'poor' or 'undesirable' homes.[1]

The influence of the Labour Party in social control is perfectly explicable in terms of its ideological grounding in Fabian and Methodist doctrine. The *primary* concern of Labourism was, and is, to attack deprivation: and it is significant to note the ways in which this insistence has paved the way for alliances to be struck not only with 'sociological' criminologists (in the 1950s, with criminologists like Howard Jones and John Barron Mays, whose works were concerned with the role of 'social' and 'environmental' factors in the creation of criminality, i.e. material inequality), but also with the psychological and social-work professions. The centrality of the family as an agency of socialization (preparing the child for meritorious labour) in large part explains the openness of Labour Party thinkers and policy-makers, on the one hand, to psychiatrists like John Bowlby, who would reduce criminality specifically to a personality disturbance produced by 'maternal deprivation', and, on the other, to more explicitly Freudian and psychoanalytically-oriented casework theorists who would concentrate on the variety of psychic repressions that disable the 'problem' client from 'normal' social participation. The contrast between social-democratic criminology as such and criminology as a whole is best seen in terms of the types of theory *which are omitted*. The aim of Fabianism was to create a meritocratic society and to help (through social-work agencies) those whose home life disabled them from participating in the meritocratic struggle. Thus, social democrats can embrace both opportunity theory on the one hand, and psychoanalytical theory on the other. But, inevitably, as the Labour Party was unsuccessful in ushering in a full-blown meritocratic social structure, the emphasis in the (expanded) social-work profession came increasingly to fall on personality theories. Indeed, given the failure of the Fabian project, theories stressing maladjustment were vitally necessary. But it is important to observe that the initial Fabian emphasis on the environmental causes of crime would lead them to eschew psychological theories stressing the genetic basis of crime, or the conservative theories (of classicism) based on the notion of a widespread *wickedness* (Man's fall from Grace). If environment was the prime factor, and Fabian attempts to change this environment unsuccessful in practice, then the environmental factors of broken home, maternal deprivation or 'bad' area had to assume a primacy in social-democratic criminology.[2]

The numerical ascendancy of the social-work profession during the 1960s (paralleled in Scandinavia with its similar heritage in social democracy, (cf. Stang Dahl, 1971) is explicable in terms of the need to control (and individualize) the emerging social problems of unemployment, racial tension, industrial and social discontent[3] (as well as to contain those members of society designated off in institutions as 'useless'), but its real social *influence* is to be explained in terms of the appropriateness of social-work 'wisdoms' as statements about the disabling deprivations standing in the way of a fair, contractually-based, society.

Labourism, however, cannot conceive of the possibility of meaningful dissent or refusal. The only 'alternative reality' allowed is that of power and privilege, and it is from that reality that all Conservative or other opposition must flow. Deviants of any other kind are necessarily either undersocialized (socially, psychiatrically or otherwise) or corrupted (by lack of religion, or by ideologies alien and inappropriate to an equalizing and improving society). Hence, punishment for repentance is *the* social democratic second-line of social defence: it is the proclamation of the general interest against sectarian or individual recalcitrance. Thieves and hooligans harm not only the conduct of a conforming social life, but threaten also the meaningfulness—and hence the existence—of welfare programmes. The collapse of the welfare programmes would, of course, entail the collapse of the Labour Party's social and political

ideology as such—it would signal a collapse of the Fabian vision of a society of equals before the Conservative vision of a society dominated by those born to rule, necessarily holding the rest of an unworthy population in check via its system of schooling, individual punishment, social segregation and institutionalization.

Sceptical deviancy theory can be understood, against this background, as a *cri de coeur* on behalf of the victims not only of an inert and conservative judicial system, but also the victims of social-welfare control. Indeed, as both Gouldner (1968) and Young (1970) from slightly different viewpoints have shown, the critical edge of sceptical deviancy theory in the USA (and also in Britain) was very largely directed at the 'mopping-up' agencies—identifying the ways in which social-work treatment, however much it might be described as being in the client's own interest, could often result in spirals of spurious labelling, further deviant commitment and, finally, the irreversible channelling of individuals into careers in prison, in mental hospitals or on skid-row.

Placing the activities of social-welfare agencies in political and ideological context, however, it is easy to see that the everyday decisions of workers in those agencies flow not from an ill-formed understanding of 'deviant' 'maladjustment' but from a clearly formulated, Fabian-conformist, and essentially *liberal* ideology. The key words of social-work training reflect that overarching ideology without ambiguity— the encouragement 'to adjust', 'to encourage good citizenship', 'to mature'—and, indeed, to accept the good offices of the 'helping agencies' themselves.

The logic of the political ideologies surrounding the discussion of crime is now rendered more clear. Orthodox criminology can be seen as an attempt to correct and control the worst excesses of a punitive and repressive Conservative judicial system, via an appeal to the amelioration of the environment or the building of a social-work and helping profession. Sceptical deviancy theory, in its turn, can be viewed as an attempt to highlight some of the excesses of a social-control system that substitutes 'care' for 'punishment'—and tends, in the process, to withdraw those rights (for example, of due process) that Conservatives in the judiciary had paternalistically protected. But sceptical deviancy theory, unlike social democratic criminology before it, has no coherent alternatives (other than those of an abstracted and individualistic idealism) and no organized constituency (like social work or the Labour Party itself). It is exhausted except as a form of moral gesture.

The rise of Fabian criminology is to be related to the post-war development of the Welfare State and the rapid expansion of a non-commercial, middle-class constituency of social workers, teachers, and experts: 'The Welfare State becomes the agency through which the "useless" are made useful or, at least, kept out of the way' (Gouldner, 1970, p. 82). The rewards of the Welfare State for its practising professional persons are apparent, both in Britain and in the USA. Thus (Gouldner, 1970, p. 81):[4]

> The type and level of activity of the Welfare State, and of investment in it often bears little demonstrable connection with the effectiveness of its programs. What frequently determines the adoption of a specific welfare program is not merely the visibility of a critical problem, not only a humane concern for suffering, not only a prudent political preparation for the next election. What is also of particular importance is that the adopted solution entails a public expenditure that will be disbursed, through the purchase of goods or the payment of salaries, among those who are *not* on welfare. It is this that enables the Welfare State to attract and retain a constituency among middle class and professional groups.

Notes

1 For examinations of the increasing influence of social-work lobbies on juvenile legislation, see Platt (1969) and Lemert (1970) on the USA, Stang Dahl (1971) on Norway, and Bottoms (1971) on England and Wales.
2 The parallels here between the failure and transformation of Fabianism and the metamorphosis of the Kennedy–Johnson Mobilization for Youth programme in America in the 1960s are not accidental. Mobilization for Youth initially involved a commitment to the social-democratic 'opportunity-structure' theory developed by Richard Cloward and Lloyd Ohlin (1960). Over time, the project came up against a variety of vested interests which resolutely opposed the creation of new opportunities for deprived youth; and the resort of the project leadership, in such circumstances, was to move over to theories of personality maladjustment (which had the important quality of being inoffensive to middle-class conceptions of the causes of delinquency). For an exposition and critique of the Mobilization for Youth project, see Frances Fox Piven's 'Federal intervention in the cities: the new urban programs as a political strategy', in Smigel (1971, pp. 591–608).
3 The individualizing of social problems ('public issues') into private problems in social work was first highlighted by C. Wright Mills (1943).
4 For a trenchant analysis of such a process, see James A. Jones's 'Federal efforts to solve social problems', in Smigel (1971, pp. 547–90).

References

Anderson, Perry (1968), 'Components of the national culture', *New Left Review*, 50, July–August, 3–57.

Bottoms, A. E. (1971), 'On the decriminalisation of the English juvenile court', paper delivered to the First Anglo-Scandinavian Seminar in Criminology, Borkesjø, Norway; extended version appearing in Roger Hood, ed., *Festschrift for Sir Leon Radzinowicz*, Heinemann, 1974.

Cloward, Richard and Ohlin, Lloyd (1960), *Delinquency and Opportunity: A Theory of Delinquent Gangs*, New York, Free Press.

Gouldner, Alvin W. (1968), 'The sociologist as partisan: sociology and the welfare state', *American Sociologist*, 3, May, pp. 103–16; reprinted in J. D. Douglas, ed., *The Relevance of Sociology*, New York, Appleton-Century-Crofts, 1970.

Gouldner, Alvin W. (1970), *The Coming Crisis of Western Sociology*, New York, Basic Books; also London, Heinemann, 1971.

Lemert, Edwin M. (1970), *Social Action and Legal Change: Revolution within the Juvenile Court*, Chicago, Aldine.

Mills, C. Wright (1943), 'The professional ideology of social pathologists', *American Journal of Sociology*, 49 (2), pp. 165–80.

Nairn, Tom (1964), 'The anatomy of the Labour Party', *New Left Review*, 27, September–October, pp. 38–65.

Platt, Anthony M. (1969), *The Child Savers: The Invention of Delinquency*, University of Chicago Press.

Smigel, Edwin O., ed. (1971), *Handbook on the Study of Social Problems*, Chicago, Rand McNally.

Stang Dahl, Tove (1971), 'The emergence of the Norwegian child welfare laws', paper presented to 1st Anglo-Scandinavian Research Seminar in Criminology, Borkesjø, Norway; revised, extended version forthcoming from Martin Robertson, London.

Young, Jock (1970), 'The zookeepers of deviancy', *Catalyst*, 5, pp. 38–46.

10 The trap of environmentalism

Stanley Aronowitz

Liberal humanists (those who oppose inequality but refuse to locate its sources in the social structure) are mobilizing their intellectual and political forces to combat what *Social Policy* has characterized as the 'new assault on equality.' This assault has taken many forms and seems to emanate from several directions. The most discussed, the attempt by Arthur Jensen and Richard Herrnstein[1] to revive the idea that a close correlation exists between heredity and intelligence, and that Blacks are demonstrably inferior to whites when measured by IQ tests, has drawn the fire of all those deeply committed to racial equality. But the critics of genetic explanations have sought to make their case in environmental terms. Whatever may be the cultural or genetic inheritance of any group, liberal humanists seem to have no choice but to focus on the environment. For example, they point out that it is impossible to measure intelligence objectively. 'There are no tests of native intelligence. In fact, the concept of native intelligence is essentially meaningless.'[2] All the IQ test measures is the probable performance of children in schools as presently constructed. Or they contend that schools presume a certain cultural orientation by students and have developed norms that accord with this orientation. There are no tests that measure the capacity of Black children to survive in the everyday life of the ghetto, they point out. The intelligence needed to live in a way radically different from the dominant American culture is of no concern to the dominant society. (On the other hand, the few attempts to devise 'culture-free' tests are simply not as effective in predicting school achievement.)

The problem with the environmentalist rebuttal to genetic determinism is, however, that they are fighting on their so-called enemy's terrain. Despite their serious differences with those identified as conservatives, the liberal critics who assert their adherence to

equality are constrained by their own acceptance of the prevailing social division of labor—and the role of IQ measures, public schools, and merit within it. Too often they share the conservative belief that incremental changes can remedy the illnesses of society and only differ with them about the pace and extent of these changes. But even when this is not the case, the liberal egalitarians' environmentalist defense against the kind of genetic assertions presented by Arthur Jensen continually concedes the upper hand to the opposition. The fact is that genetic theories of the performance of groups in society carry with them the force of real social arrangements.

The very category of measurable intelligence itself implies a social order that requires it. We need to alter the presuppositions and change the fulcrum of debate when we are talking seriously about modifying and eradicating socially bred inequities. Environmentalists are diverted by a false dichotomy. To be sure, there are both environmental and innate aspects to the development of any aspect of human activity. (The person is not merely the sum of social forces that shape him or her.) But the defensive polarity of environmentalism diverts our attention from the ways children of different classes, races, and sexes are taught and from the introjection of socially determined attitudes of inferiority among those who can expect to remain powerless, propertyless, and oppressed all of their lives. This internalization of failure is not groundless.

In addition to considering intelligence as a factor in learning, we have to consider what is to be learned, by whom, and for what purpose. If the object of education is to provide a labor force for the existing social structure with its hierarchical division of social labor, then there is good reason to expect Black children and working-class children to fail. Economic and social power in the United States and all advanced industrial countries is built on a pyramidal configuration. There is no room at the top. The mobility

Source: *Social Policy*, September/October 1972, pp. 34, 36–8.

achieved by working-class people through education is normally confined to movement from unskilled to skilled manual labor, and to the expanding number of niches in industries and occupations where the manipulation of symbols rather than things constitutes the substance of work.

The IQ test, around which so much of the equality debate rages, was devised as a screening process to assist schools and industry to rationalize the prevailing social divisions of labor on a scientific basis and to determine which children shall occupy the various economic niches within the social order. The test made its appearance a few years before World War I, when the United States was beginning to exhibit the same economic stagnation and rigidity of class structure as its European counterparts. The importance of the IQ was that it reinforced the myth of a meritocracy, the only viable ideology for a society that teaches its children that there are no classes and proclaims adherence to the doctrine of equality. The individual's failure to rise is attributed to his or her inability or unwillingness to seize the unlimited opportunities available to the energetic, intelligent, or talented.

The IQ test symbolizes America's interpretation of equality to mean equality of opportunity. Emphasis on equality of opportunity has meant trying to make it possible for the poor to become less poor by encouraging them to overcome the environmental pressures on them. In this context environmentalists implicitly assume the standards set by the standardized IQ measure—namely, access to a job as reward, not access to a more powerful participation in determining how the pie is to be divided. By assuming this objective uncritically, the environmentalist legitimized the view that poor people—and Black poor people in particular—have capitulated to negative environmental conditions. This left two options: help them or give up on them. They had to earn their rights by proving themselves in the existing mainstream. The obligation of the mainstream was to try to make this possible. In effect, then, the environmentalist position tended to confirm the system, calling for its expansion to include more people who earned their place by the merit teased out of them; it failed to question the normative basis of a system with relative future, and absolute future, built into it. It said that the system (by its favorite measures) was selecting out too many people for its own good. The environmentalists did not say opportunity should be an outgrowth of inalienable human rights, instead of an anvil to which more people must be led and tested on.

The development of the IQ test coincided with the effort to make compulsory public education responsive to the tremendous advances of technology accompanying the industrial revolution in late nineteenth-century American capitalism. Free public education was a way to deal with the superfluity of child labor as well as the demands of the new techniques being introduced in American industry. The public schools became a vast container for children who were no longer needed in the factories and a mechanism for socializing appropriate industrial employee behavior. Despite the humanistic purposes of many educators, the schools served the need of the economic order for a labor force preselected according to criteria that place responsibility on the individual to perform in conformity with standards of behavior and intelligence determined from above.

And what of those standards? Instead of the critical thinking and personal autonomy with which the rhetoric of schooling has been padded, intelligence tests have been a perfect instrument for the selection of people possessing characteristics best suited to conformity in bureaucratically organized systems. As Erich Fromm so effectively put it, intelligence tests measure 'not so much the capacity for reason and understanding as the capacity for quick mental adaptation to a given situation: "mental adjustment tests" would be the adequate name for them.'[3] The items used on the tests do not require any intrinsic interest or curiosity on the subject's part. On the contrary, if a person became too interested in any one item, too much time might be spent on it, possibly leading to unconventional responses that might be marked wrong. The test does not call for interest in the specific questions as such, but rather an overall competitive motivation to do well. (But the intelligence of certain people may not really be tapped unless they are deeply involved in the specific problem on which they are working.)

Indeed, a good case could be made that IQ tests really inversely measure authentic problem-solving intelligence and reason; that doing well on these tests implies a trained incapacity to think in depth, to think innovatively, to be creative.

Meanwhile, the possibility of upward mobility for all Americans has remained a powerful ideology—for liberals, conservatives, as well as for the victims of this society for whom the promises perenially prove false. The fight for civil rights was a fight for the access other minority groups appeared to have achieved. This program, like the myths underpinning it, seemed viable as long as the economy was expanding, especially in those sectors requiring new workers, such as the public sector. And even then not all places were equal. But in the late 1960s it became evident to many Black militants that the political economy was only admitting Blacks into the working class; genuine mobility seemed a long way off. At the same time second-generation white workers began to perceive that their fate was circumscribed by conditions of birth. That is, young workers were sharing the fate of their fathers, with the notable exception that, while their fathers were employed largely in manual occupations, many of the youth were being squeezed by a tight white or gray collar.

The liberals are in a quandary because they have accepted the equation of equality with equality of opportunity; they, and the upwardly mobile masses of less fortunate Americans who hoped with them, confused access to jobs with access to power. Therefore, when the social and occupational structure provides little room for movement, there is only frustration. One clear possible direction is to abandon the superficial concepts of the environment inherited from the nineteenth century. The social environment is, first, the class structure within which the production of goods and services takes place. Second, it is the hierarchically arranged strata within the class structure that perpetuate and reinforce doctrines of inequality. By accepting the prevailing social divisions of labor—that is, the distinctions based on mental and physical labor, seniority, presumed skill levels, and credentials—liberals cannot combat distinctions based on race and sex, which are functions of the larger social structure. Women may enter the professions or Blacks may find their way into managerial posts within the public sector, but these token advances accorded to 'meritorious' members of the sex or race have nothing to do with real political or social power; nor do they alter materially the inequality of the larger system. The only way to advance the reality of equality is to examine the way in which the social system is organized, to develop a critique of the concept of authority and hierarchically determined role differences, distinguishing between the divisions necessitated by technological criteria and those determined by bureaucratic and authoritarian criteria.

The distribution of power in America remains unaltered despite 'equality of opportunity.' The concentration and centralization of capital has increased the power a few large corporate groups exert over American society. The intermeshing of corporate leadership and the government has become more complete in the past thirty years, owing to the necessity for large-scale government intervention in the economy in order to maintain a modicum of economic stability. The government's power, but not its autonomy, has been enlarged as a result of its new functions. It has been colonized by the corporations, who choose periodically to surrender their autonomy to the government when there are differences between them, as long as they are certain that the state represents their general interests. We are witnessing an erosion of pluralistic political ideology. The difference between the national state and other crucial institutions of social cohesion is diminishing. Trade unions, educational institutions, health institutions, and local governments are all dependent on the coordinating apparatus of the state for their sustenance. Moreover, the slowing down of economic growth constitutes a barrier to the perpetuation of the doctrine of merit, according to which all groups have equal access to occupational mobility through education. The manifest surplus of highly credentialed workers has created new tasks for corporate-minded theorists.

If all this is true then the concept of equality must come under attack from all sides: from the frustrated, from the disappointed, and from those for whom it has been a useful but insincere persuasion. The recourse to theories of genetic determinism makes perfect sense unless a new theory arises that discounts the illusory classlessness of this society and the supposed leveling function of the schools. The present impact of Jensen and Herrnstein (scientists provided similar studies in the 1940s and 1950s) must be interpreted in the context of shrinking employment opportunities and the strength of the hierarchical organization and division of labor in this society. Furthermore, the present resurgence of discussion about IQ tests must also be seen within the context of other arguments for genetic determinism. Arguments for a genetically determined IQ stem from the same sources as arguments for the 'instinctual' basis of aggression, for the chromosomal basis of criminality, or for the physiological and biochemical basis for differences between men and women in their ability to 'bond' and form political association.[4] We are witnessing the resurgence of dormant aspects of a conventional wisdom geared to competitive scarcity in response to strains and stresses of a system characterized by these terms. Recall what Marx said in *The German Ideology*: 'The ruling ideas are nothing more than the ideal expression of the dominant natural relationships, the dominant material relationships grasped as ideas.' The same holds true today, both as analysis and as a focus for action.

Notes

1 Arthur R. Jensen, 'How much can we boost IQ and scholastic achievement?', *Harvard Educational Review*, 39, winter 1969, 1–123; Richard Herrnstein, 'IQ', *Atlantic Monthly*, 228 (3), September 1971.

2 'Education, ethnicity, genetics and intelligence', *IRCD Bulletin*, 5 (4), 1969. Publication of the ERIC Information Retrieval Center on the Disadvantaged.

3 Erich Fromm, *Man for Himself*, Routledge & Kegan Paul, 1971, p. 75.

4 Konrad Lorenz, *On Aggression*, Methuen, 1966; Robert Ardrey, *African Genesis*, Collins, 1961. Ardrey's later books also uphold this view, although in increasingly modified form. See also Lionel Tiger, *Men in Groups*, Nelson, 1970.

11 The politics of reading and writing

George Martell

(. . .) [This article] begins by outlining three major developments in the expansion of the Canadian school system of the 60s which took place as a reflection of certain basic corporate needs: (1) the development of schools as a major market for both old and new educational technology and capital goods, (2) the shift in the social control aspect of the schools towards the more general and growing practice of what is called 'state therapy', (3) the creation of a highly centralized bureaucratic structure in education required to facilitate the first two developments. Then [it] goes on to argue that what's happening in the 70s, with the recent decline of the school system as a major market for the corporations, is the push to refine the new 'therapeutic' social control dimension in education, which includes an even more highly centralized bureaucratic structure, integrating the schools more thoroughly into the provinces' health and welfare apparatus.

One of the first major results of these developments has been an increased squeeze on funds for education. (. . .)

A second major result has been a substantial shift in the nature of the real curriculum in the schools towards overt social therapy or what is called 'socialization', directed primarily to the personnel requirements of the large corporations. The effects of this socialization process are seen most clearly in the fact that working class kids don't read and write as well as middle class kids and in the streaming which is permitted by these differing skill levels. (. . .)

. . . In Ontario the most consistent and the most influential ideological statement tying together these various 'therapeutic' approaches has been *Living and Learning* or the Hall-Dennis Report.[1]

Written by powerful insiders[2] defending a school system they were in the process of building, the report met with remarkable political success, particularly

Source: *This Magazine*, 8 (2), 1974, pp. 12–15.

among the rising new leadership in Canadian educational administration. Even though its language is now more than a little uncool, its basic intellectual framework has been and continues to be repeated with minor variations in countless Departmental and Board statements on education right across the country.[3]

Attention should be paid.

For Hall-Dennis, men and women and children live mostly outside history, inside society maybe, but untouched by it in any fundamental way. We live as individuals. We have no fates. There is no central human nature shaped by work, by loves, by families, by neighbours, and no one therefore has to deal with their destiny—fight it or accept it, or both. All of us, and especially the young, are almost infinitely malleable, blank slates for the loving educator:[4]

> The underlying aim of education is to further man's unending search for truth. Once he possesses the means to truth, all else is within his grasp. Wisdom and understanding, sensitivity, compassion and responsibility, as well as intellectual honesty and personal integrity, will be his guides in adolescence and his companions in maturity. . . . This is the key to open all doors. It is the instrument which will break the shackles of ignorance, of doubt, of frustration; that will take all who respond to its call out of their poverty, their slums, and their despair.

There is nothing our children cannot have:[5]

> They must be made to feel that the world is waiting for their sunrise, and that their education heralds the rebirth of an 'Age of Wonder'. Then surely, the children of tomorrow will be more flexible, more adventurous, more daring and courageous than we are. Each will have learned, with Don Quixote, in *Man of La Mancha*: To dream the impossible dream . . .

It is only a matter of getting rid of the 'lock-step structure of past times' to enable the child to 'progress from year to year without the hazards and frustrations of failure'. With 'feasible requirements', good guidance and assessment procedures, plus lots of flexibility, 'going to school will be a pleasant growing experience, and as [the child] enters and passes through adolescence he will do so without any sudden or traumatic change and without a sense of alienation from society.'[6]

Just as there are no necessary traumas at school, so equally there is no inherent oppression at the workplace following school. Respect and appreciation of other individuals are all we need to fix things up. There is, in other words, no real class system:[7]

By recognizing the dignity of work at all levels, and respecting all people who carry out this work, be it physical or intellectual, by realizing the necessity of diversified occupations, we must build a genuine acceptance and appreciation of the various training centres at the secondary and post secondary levels which complement the education and training offered at the traditional universities. Moreover, respect for every child, and the adult he is to become—respect for his mind, his feelings, his idiosyncrasies, his special interests, his right to be himself—is an essential component in helping a child see himself as master rather than as slave of the electronic colossus.

Finally, not only do children remain fundamentally untouched by social class, but their growing-up takes place outside the history of their own people. Nothing of substance is passed down from generation to generation. Each child starts fresh:[8]

Learning by its very nature is a personal matter. There is virtually a metabolism of learning which is as unique to the individual as the metabolism of digestion. Parents and teachers may create conditions for learning, and may provide stimulating experiences with learning in mind, but the actual learning experience is intimate and subjective, for each human being reaches out to the world in his own idiosyncratic way. . . . The road to learning takes personal effort, and no human being can jump hurdles for another.

In the end, what we are left with from Hall-Dennis is the idea of a society where people experience neither collective roots nor class oppression, and where individuals can only look forward to more 'freedom' for personal growth, with no connection to any larger social purpose. Quoting Heraclitus, the Report 'realizes' all that's certain is change: 'Life is perpetual motion, and repose is death'.

What's important to stress here is that these basic ideas of Hall-Dennis are not unique to it, but are fundamental to the larger ideology of the State under modern capitalism, what is often called the ideology of corporate liberalism.

This ideology underlies and supports the second major task the state performs for its ruling class: insuring future profits by maintaining the long term stability of the class system—the task of social control.

The form of this control, however, as it is presented here, and its covering ideology are fairly recent.

The essence of the approach is contained in what might be termed a policy of 'state therapy', in which the velvet glove of the government psychologist and social worker provides a cover for the older iron fist of the police and the army.

At its centre lies the ideas you find in Hall-Dennis: that this is a society without classes, without inherent conflict of interest between the ruled and the rulers, a society in which individual growth can flourish, provided there is sufficient 'communication' between the corporations, the government, and the people. The solution to any problem lies in our capacity to talk about it, openly and warmly. For each of us, personal happiness lies just around the corner. And it's up to each of us, as individuals, to make that potential happiness come true, with a little help from our 'shrink' or our 'worker'.

This position, I might add, is not limited to the 'social engineers' of the state system. It is equally important for those promoting 'industrial democracy' in the factories and the 'good life' on TV, the latter understanding that if you can't talk about your problems, you will at least hope to buy something for them.

The Hall-Dennis ideology in practice: socialization for capitalist production

Here's a question we are often faced with: 'Isn't this process, which I'm calling 'social control', really necessary to society's survival? Don't people have to learn to get along with each other? Is there, for example, really all that much wrong with the Hall-Dennis Report? At worst, isn't it just motherhood, banal but unobjectionable?'

The answer is no. Like the ideology of motherhood, Hall-Dennis may be banal, but there are lots of objections to it, not the least of which is that it's a lie.

The first part of the lie, as I've implied above, is that it covers things up. Underneath the social philosophy of a 'pleasant growing experience' lies the oppression of the society: its poverty, the nature of its work, and the forces undercutting its sense of community and destroying its natural environment. Covered too is the knowledge of who profits by this oppression and the struggle that has taken place, and must continue to take place, to resist it.

The second part of the lie is found in what Hall-Dennis and Co. actually promote:

The 'socialization' process they recommend has, in practice, nothing to do with 'individual growth' (always an impossibility outside a collective purpose and way of life). It is never 'pleasant'. It is always oppressive. At best, it's the 'novocaine' (to borrow Malcolm X's phrase) that lets you 'suffer peacefully' for a while. But the pain always returns.

This process of socialization has finally a much more substantial role than simply helping to provide a comfy mystification of the social repression kids will have to face once they leave school. Primarily, I want to argue, it's to fit the kids into the various levels of the job hierarchy (or class system) of modern capitalism, where they must work under conditions of deepening alienation.

From this perspective the shift in emphasis during the 60s towards overt 'socialization' should be seen as part of the process by which the schools are catching up (as all cultural institutions must do) with the changing personnel requirements of the economy, now dominated almost entirely by large American corporations.

Businessmen increasingly need people who can accept working within a finely graduated bureaucratic order, in which they are no more than machines —persons stripped of decision-making power, both in the process of determining the purpose of their work or the way it will be carried out. More unskilled and semi-skilled workers must accept permanent unemployment and dead-end service jobs. More skilled workers must accept industrial jobs where few skills are required. And more and more the children of the middle class must look to jobs either in the middle management of American branch plants and service industries or in the middle level of government bureaucracies—administrators and social workers of various types. (The public schools, I should add, have not yet concerned themselves much with the education of the children of the ruling class, although some of these children are now showing up in public classrooms.)

How, then, do our schools prepare kids to fit in at these various levels of working class and middle class employment?

It's a very complex process, and I can hardly do it justice here. All I can offer is a very short outline.

Primarily, it seems to me, the job is done by setting up a social system within the schools, in which the social relationships the kids will, day in and day out, experience as the norm are the same as they will later experience in factories and offices.

This transplanted social system in the schools is there when the kids arrive. In order to survive in it, the kids have to fit in (and are fitted in) to that level of the system for which their already developed public character has prepared them. That is, by the time they reach school, they already have a way of living within the society as they experience it, and that way of living or behaving—including forms of resistance, acquiescence, and local community life— is appropriate to a certain stream or grouping within the school system. Since their public character is of somewhat the same sort as that which has permitted

their parents and neighbours to survive at *their* levels of the social system—determined by their role in the economy—what the schools are basically doing is *reinforcing* the already existing class structure we see operating in factories and offices. Furthermore, as Sam Bowles and Herb Gintis argue, the official thrust of the school system is to *promote* acquiescence to this class structure, whatever the feelings of kids and teachers:

> the social relations of schooling are structured similarly to the social relations of production in several essential respects. The school is a bureaucratic order with hierarchical authority, rule orientation, stratification by 'ability' (streaming) as well as by age (grades), role differentiation by sex (physical education, home economics, etc.), and a system of external incentives (marks, promise of promotion and threat of failure) much like pay and status in the sphere of work.

Bowles and Gintis go on to make the point that the public character reinforced at various levels of the school system (what they call 'personality traits') differs 'according to the work role' required of various kinds of employees:[9]

> those at the base of the hierarchy requiring a heavy emphasis on obedience and rules and those at the top, where the discretionary scope is considerable, requiring a greater ability to make decisions on the basis of well-internalized norms. . . . Note the wide range of choice over curriculum, life style, and allocation of time offered to college students, compared with the obedience and respect for authority expected in high school. Differentiation occurs also within each level of schooling. One needs only to compare the social relations of a junior college with those of an elite four year college, or those of a working class high school with those of a wealthy suburban high school, for verification on this point.

The politics of reading and writing

The clearest end-product of the differing socialization process applied to working class and middle class kids in school is found in their differing abilities to read and write, as measured both by standardized reading tests and traditional classroom assignments. As you move down the socio-economic class scale, kids read and write less and less well.[10]

The importance of this matching of school literacy and social class can be seen in the fact that the ability to read and write serves as the primary means by which children are streamed. IQ tests simply reinforce the judgement of the reading tests, although as the Gates–MacGinitie Reading Tests rightly 'assume', 'the circumstances that contribute to high or low IQ scores in school population are also the main factors contributing to high or low reading scores'.[11]

The question is, how does this socialization process —the experiencing of a capitalist social hierarchy— which I've described above, result in a situation where the class order is accurately reflected in the reading scores?

Let me take the answer from two perspectives:

First, the social relationships of a class system, by their very nature, must resist any language that seriously threatens them. Such language in schools is thus neither encouraged nor permitted, and if it occurs anyway, it must be punished. The only honest writing we see among children in school, *that has any official backing*, comes in the first three or four grades, in which the child has a very small world of family and friends and immediate neighbours. In these grades, realities can be stated with no explanations attached. However, as kids get older and explanations become necessary, the honesty must stop; it threatens the social order, both inside and outside the school. (This is not to say that honest teachers don't make an attempt at such explanations, only that without political support, they inevitably fail.)

In order for kids to move beyond these early words of childhood into explanation, it becomes necessary, particularly for working class kids, for them to define their class enemies and to understand their friends, both in terms of their present oppression and their future resistance to it. This must include finding a place for themselves inside a larger movement of working class people. Words unconnected to these realities make no sense. They are just words, suitable for the static, one-dimensional world of reading tests, IQ tests, true and false tests and multiple choice tests. Empty of meaning.

As these useful words are buried, working class kids are increasingly alienated from the language of the school. Furthermore, the more oppressed a kid is (the further down the class scale he is), the *more* alienated he will become from a language that doesn't recognize or try to do anything about his oppression, and the worse he will do at handling it. Thus we get the remarkably close correlation we do between socio-economic class standing and the reading scores.[12]

What's happening, in other words is that the kids from working class backgrounds are being made 'dumb', a significantly double-edged word, meaning both someone without use of words and someone who's unintelligent. What's being created, to use Paolo Freire's phrase, is a 'culture of silence', the silence deepening with the depth of the oppression.

To turn now to the second perspective on this process of making working class kids 'dumb': what are the words available *now* to these kids in school? What fills the 'silence'?

The answer, increasingly common to both administrators and critics, is that the language used in schools, as well as the curriculum built on it, is that of the 'middle class'. Learning to be 'middle class' is the top level of the curriculum, the 'path to mobility'; it's the standard all kids are judged against, passed and failed on. Here, for example is the statement of the Special Education bureaucrats at the Toronto Board explaining why 'when children . . . appear to be "smart" in their own small community [they] fail to achieve in school':[13]

> One of the primary reasons appears to be that, while the curriculum offered in the school system is designed to develop in each child his maximum potential, this is his potential as it relates to his ability to succeed in the essentially middle class world of higher education, business and industry. The charge is frequently made that this curriculum is not relevant to the child's own community and in a very broad sense this is true. Of course, efforts are made to relate the curriculum to the community in which the school is located, but if the objectives sought by parents are to equip the child with the skills to be a 'success' in the world of today and tomorrow, and if this word 'success' is equated with having a good job which produces an income which will allow this person to live at the material standards of the middle-class, then it follows that this person must meet the middle class criteria established by society for entry to this income level.

What are these 'middle class criteria'? What is it, to put the question another way, that our ruling class asks of the middle class, to whom it pays wages? Two things mostly, and they're thoroughly inter-related: first, to help make state and corporate bureaucracies run smoothly, and second, to obscure the oppression of the working class by the ruling class. And for both these tasks a certain language is required, which, again, everybody calls 'middle class' language. It is the crucial 'skill' required for 'success'.

The nature of this language corresponds to the work of its users, a class 'in the middle', ironing out bureaucratic wrinkles and laundering unpleasant realities.

It's the language of Hall-Dennis, the language of euphemism—of small problems and comfortable solutions applied to big problems and hard solutions. It's language that has only words for the middle ground, of toothless reform: That lets you divide history between neurotic revolutionaries and encrusted reactionaries as a defense for the 'reasonable' people in the middle who won. Or lets you analyse a strike 'taking both sides into account', the boss offering $2.00 an hour, the union demanding $3.00, and then permits you to come up with the 'reasonable' solution of $2.50 an hour. It's language that does *not* tell the reality of bringing up a family on that amount.

The further down a child is on the class scale, the less appropriate is this middle class language to him, the more it obscures his reality, the less he is capable of learning it, the worse he does on the reading scores.

This language, of course, isn't any 'truer' for middle class kids. But it does get them a job, and it's much easier for them to learn, being the language of the home. (. . .)

Notes

1 See W. G. Fleming, *Education: Ontario's Preoccupation*, University of Toronto Press, 1972, pp. 30–1.
2 See W. G. Fleming, *Ontario's Educative Society*, vol. 3, University of Toronto Press, p. 556.
3 The latest in this long line of official documents is Alberta's Worth Report, *A Choice of Futures*. Despite its much cooler tone, its hip, almost mechanical style, the ideological framework it presents is almost identical to that of Hall-Dennis. Only the innocence is missing, a circumstance one might also have gathered from a recent piece of advice 'Wally' Worth passed on to a convention of Saskatchewan teachers in February of this year. 'Teach', he cautioned them, 'so the hammer marks don't show.'
4 *Living and Learning*, Newton Publishing, Toronto, 1968, p. 9.
5 ibid., p. 47.
6 ibid., p. 15.
7 ibid., p. 56.
8 ibid., p. 63.
9 See Sam Bowles and Herbert Gintis, 'IQ in the US class structure', *Social Policy*, Nov./Dec. 1972 and Jan./Feb. 1973, pp. 19, 20, 21, 22, of the combined manuscripts.
10 See Table 17, City of Toronto Board of Education, *Research Report* no. 108, p. 17.
11 *Technical Manual, Gates–MacGinitie Reading Tests*, Teachers College Press, Teachers College, Columbia University, New York, p. 2. The Gates–MacGinitie series is probably the most popular of all the reading tests used in Canada.
12 See n. 10.
13 City of Toronto Board of Education, *Special Education Report*, 1970, p. 9.

12 The school as a conservative force: scholastic and cultural inequalities*

Pierre Bourdieu

It is probably cultural inertia which still makes us see education in terms of the ideology of the school as a liberating force ('l'école libératrice') and as a means of increasing social mobility, even when the indications tend to be that it is in fact one of the most effective means of perpetuating the existing social pattern, as it both provides an apparent justification for social inequalities and gives recognition to the cultural heritage, that is, to a *social* gift treated as a *natural* one.

As processes of elimination occur throughout the whole of the period spent in education, we can quite justifiably note the effects they have at the highest levels of the system. The chances of entering higher education are dependent on direct or indirect selection varying in severity with subjects of different social classes throughout their school lives. The son of a manager is eighty times as likely to get to university as the son of an agricultural worker, forty times as likely as the son of a factory worker and twice as likely as even the son of a man employed in a lower-salaried staff grade.[1] It is striking that the higher the level of the institution of learning, the more aristocratic its intake. The sons of members of managerial grades and of the liberal professions account for 57 per cent of students at the Polytechnique, 54 per cent of those at the École Normale Supérieure (noted for its 'democratic' intake), 47 per cent of those at the École Normale and 44 per cent of those at the Institut d'Études Politiques.

However, simply stating the fact of educational inequality is not enough. We need a description of the objective processes which continually exclude children from the least privileged social classes. Indeed, it seems that a sociological explanation can account for the unequal achievement usually imputed to unequal ability. For the most part, the effects of cultural privilege are only observed in their crudest forms—a good word put in, the right contacts, help with studies, extra teaching, information on the educational system and job outlets. In fact, each family transmits to its children, indirectly rather than directly, a certain *cultural capital* and a certain *ethos*. The latter is a system of implicit and deeply interiorized values which, among other things, helps to define attitudes towards the cultural capital and educational institutions. The cultural heritage, which differs from both points of view according to social class, is the cause of the initial inequality of children when faced with examinations and tests, and hence of unequal achievement.

Choice of options

The attitudes of the members of the various social classes, both parents and children, and in particular their attitudes towards school, the culture of the school and the type of future the various types of studies lead to, are largely an expression of the system of explicit or implied values which they have as a result of belonging to a given social class. The fact that different social classes send, despite equal attainment, a different proportion of their children to *lycées* is often explained by such vague terms as 'parental choice'. It is doubtful whether one can meaningfully use such expressions except metaphorically, as surveys have shown that 'in general there is a massive correlation between parental choice and options taken'—in other words, parental choice is in most cases determined by real possibilities.[2] In fact, everything happens as if parental attitudes towards their children's education—as shown in the choice of sending them either to a secondary school or leaving them in the upper classes of an elementary school, and of sending them to a *lycée* (and thus accepting the prospect of prolonged studies, at least, to the *baccalauréat*) or to a *collège d'enseignement général* (and thus accepting a shorter

Source: J. Eggleston, ed., *Contemporary Research in the Sociology of Education*, Methuen, 1974, pp. 32–46.

period of education, until the *brevat*, for example)—were primarily the interiorization of the fate objectively allotted (and statistically quantifiable) as a whole to the social category to which they belong. They are constantly reminded of their fate by a direct or indirect intuitive grasp of the statistics of the failures or partial successes of children of the same kind, and also less directly, by the evaluation of the elementary school teacher who, in his role as a counsellor, consciously or unconsciously takes into account the social origin of his pupils and thus, unwittingly and involuntarily, counterbalances the over-theoretical nature of a forecast based purely on performance. If members of the lower middle and working classes take reality as being equivalent to their wishes, it is because, in this area as elsewhere, aspirations and demands are defined in both form and content by objective conditions which exclude the possibility of hoping for the unobtainable. When they say, for example, that classical studies in a *lycée* are not for them, they are saying much more than that they cannot afford them. The formula, which is an expression of internalized necessity, is, we might say, in the imperative indicative as it expresses both an impossibility and a taboo.

The same objective conditions as those which determine parental attitudes and dominate the major choices in the school career of the child also govern the children's attitude to the same choices and, consequently, their whole attitude towards school, to such an extent that parents, to explain their decision not to let the child go to secondary school, can offer as a close runner-up to the cost of study the child's wish to leave school. But, at a deeper level, as the reasonable wish to get on through education will not materialize as long as the real chances of success are slim, and although working class people may well be unaware of their children's 2 in 100 chance of getting to university, their behaviour is based on an empirical evaluation of the real hopes common to all individuals in their social group. Thus it is understandable that the lower middle class—a transitional class—lays more emphasis on educational values as the school offers them reasonable chances of achieving all they want by mixing the values of social success and cultural prestige. In comparison with working-class children, who are doubly disadvantaged as regards facilities for assimilating culture and the propensity to acquire it, middle-class children receive from their parents not only encouragement and exhortation with regard to their school work but also an ethos of 'getting on' in society and an ambition to do the same at and by means of school, which enables their keen desire for the possession of culture to compensate for cultural poverty. It also seems that the same self-denying ethos of social mobility which gives rise to the prevalence of small families in certain sections of the lower middle classes also underlies their attitude towards the school.[3]

In the most fertile social groups, such as agricultural workers, farmers and factory workers, the chances of going into the *sixième* decrease clearly and regularly as a further unit is added to the family, but they fall drastically for less fertile groups such as artisans, small tradesmen, clerks and lower-salaried personnel, in families of four and five children (or more)—i.e., in families distinguished from others in the group by their high fertility—so that instead of seeing in the number of children the causal explanation of the sharp drop in the percentage of children attending school, we should perhaps suppose that the desire to limit the number of births and to give the children a secondary education are a sign, in groups where *both* these traits are noted, of the same inclination to make sacrifices.[4]

In general, children and their families make their own choices by reference to the constraints which determine them. Even when the choices seem to them to follow simply from taste or vocational sense, they nevertheless indicate the roundabout effects of objective conditions. In other words, the structure of the objective chances of social mobility and, more precisely, of the chances of a social mobility by means of education conditions attitudes to school (and it is precisely these attitudes which are most important in defining the chances of access to education, of accepting the values or norms of the school and of succeeding within the framework and thus rising in society) through subjective hopes (shared by all individuals defined by the same objective future, and reinforced by the group's pressure for conformity), which are no more than objective chances intuitively perceived and gradually internalized.[5]

A description of the logic of the process of internalization, at the end of which objective chances have become subjective hopes or lack of hope, would seem necessary. Can that fundamental dimension of class ethos, the attitude to the objective future, be in fact anything but the internalization of the objective future course of events which is gradually brought home to and imposed on every member of a given class by means of the experience of successes and failures? Psychologists have observed that the level of aspiration of individuals is essentially determined by reference to the probability (judged intuitively by means of previous successes or failures) of achieving the desired goal.

'A successful individual', writes Lewin, 'typically sets his next goal somewhat, but not too much, above his last achievement. In this way he steadily raises his level of aspiration . . . The unsuccessful individual on the other hand, tends to show one of two reactions: he sets his goal very low, frequently below his past achievement . . . or he sets his goal far above his ability.'[6] It is quite clear that a circular process occurs: 'If the standards of a group are low an individual will slacken his efforts and set his goals far below those he could reach. He will, on the other hand, raise his goals if the group standards are raised.'[7] If we also accept that 'both the ideals and the action of an individual depend on the group to which he belongs and upon the goals and expectation of that group',[8] it can be seen that the influence of peer groups— which is always relatively homogeneous from the point of view of social origin as, for example, the number of children going to *collèges d'enseignement général*, *collèges d'enseignement technique* and *lycées* (and, within these, their spread through the various types of education offered by each) is very much a function of the social class of the children—reinforces, among the least privileged children, the influence of the family milieu and the general social environment, which tend to discourage ambitions seen as excessive and always somewhat suspect in that they imply rejection of the individual's social origins. Thus, everything conspires to bring back those who, as we say, 'have no future' to 'reasonable' hopes (or 'realistic' ones, as Lewin calls them) and in fact, in many cases, to make them give up hope.

The cultural capital and the ethos, as they take shape, combine to determine behaviour in school and the attitude to school which make up the differential principle of elimination operating for children of different social classes. Although success at school, directly linked to the cultural capital transmitted by the family milieu, plays a part in the choice of options taken up, it seems that the major determinant of study is the family attitude to the school which is itself, as we have seen, a function of the objective hopes of success at school which define each social category. M. Paul Clerc has shown that, although both scholastic attainment and the rate of entry into the *lycée* depend closely on social class, the overall inequality in the rate of entry to the *lycée* depends more on the inequality in the proportion of those of equal attainment who enter the *lycée* rather than on inequality of attainment itself.[9]

That means in fact that the handicaps are *cumulative*, as children from the lower and middle classes who overall achieve a lower success rate must be more successful for their family and their teachers to consider encouraging further study. The same method of double selection also comes into operation with the age criterion: children from peasant and working-class homes, usually older than children from more privileged homes, are more severely eliminated, at an equal age, than children from the latter. In short, the general principle which leads to the excessive elimination of working- and middle-class children can be expressed thus: the children of these classes, who because of a lack of cultural capital have less chance than others of exceptional success, are nevertheless expected to achieve exceptional success to reach secondary education. But the process of double selection becomes increasingly important as one rises to the higher levels of secondary establishments and ascends the socially selective hierarchy of subject departments within them. There, once again, given equal achievement, the children of privileged classes go more often than others both to the *lycée*,

and the classics side of the *lycée*, the children of underprivileged strata mostly having to pay for their entry to the *lycée* by relegation to a *collège d'enseignement général*, while the children of well-to-do classes, who are not clever enough to go to a *lycée*, can find a suitable alternative in a private school.

It will be seen that here too advantages and disadvantages are cumulative, because the initial choices (of school and subject department) determine the school future irreversibly. Indeed, one survey has shown that results obtained by arts students over a series of exercises aimed at measuring the comprehension and manipulation of language and in particular of the language of education were directly related to the type of secondary establishment attended and to knowledge of Greek and Latin. Choices made when entering the *lycée* thus close the options once and for all so that the child's part of the cultural heritage is determined by his previous school career. In fact, such choices, which are a commitment of a whole future, are taken with reference to varying images of that future. 31 per cent of the parents of children at *lycées* want their children to go on to higher education, 27 per cent to the *baccalauréat*, only a tiny proportion of them wanting the children to proceed to a technical diploma (4 per cent) or to BEPC (2 per cent): 27 per cent of parents of children at *collèges d'enseignement général* on the other hand want to see them obtain a technical or professional diploma, 15 per cent the BEPC, 14 per cent the *baccalauréat*, and 7 per cent want them to go on to higher education.[10]

Thus, overall statistics which show an increase in the percentage of children attending secondary school hide the fact that lower class children are obliged to pay for access to this form of education by means of a considerable diminution in the area of their choices for the future.

The systematic figures which still separate, at the end of their school career, students from different social milieux owe both their form and their nature to the fact that the selection that they have undergone is not equally severe for all, and that *social* advantages or disadvantages have gradually been transformed into *educational* advantages and disadvantages as a result of premature choices which, directly linked with social origin, have duplicated and reinforced their influence. Although the school's compensating action in subjects directly taught explains at least to some extent the fact that the advantage of upper-class students is increasingly obvious as the areas of culture directly taught and completely controlled by the school are left behind, only the effect of compensation combined with over-selection can explain the fact that for a behavioural skill such as the scholastic use of scholastic language, the differences tend to lessen to an overwhelming extent and even to be inverted, since highly selected students from the lower classes obtain results equivalent to those of the higher social classes who have been less rigorously selected and better than those of the middle classes, who are also penalized by the linguistic atmosphere of their families, but are also less rigorously selected.[11]

Similarly, all the characteristics of a school career, in terms of schools attended or subjects taken, are indices of the direct influence of the family milieu, which they reflect within the logic of the scholastic system proper. For example, if greater mastery of language is always encountered, in our present state of pedagogical traditions and techniques among arts students who have studied classical languages, this is because pursuit of a classical education is the medium through which other influences are exerted and expressed, such as parental information on subjects of study and careers, success in the first stages of a school career, or the advantage conferred by entry into those classes in which the system recognizes its élite.

In seeking to grasp the logic by which the transformation of the social heritage into a scholastic heritage operates in different class situations, one would observe that the choice of subjects or school and the results obtained in the first year of secondary education (which themselves are linked to these choices) condition the use which children from different milieux can make of their heritage, be it positive or negative. It would no doubt be imprudent to claim to be able to isolate, in the system of relations we call school careers, determining factors and, *a fortiori*, a single predominant factor. But, if success at the highest level of a school career is still very closely connected to the very earliest stages of that career, it is also true that very early choices have a great effect on the chances of getting into a given branch of higher education and succeeding in it. In short, crucial decisions have been taken at a very early stage.

The functioning of the school and its role as a socially conservative force

It will be easy—perhaps too easy—to accept what has been said so far. To stop there, however, would mean not questioning the responsibility of the school in the perpetuation of social inequalities. If that question is seldom raised, it is because the Jacobin ideology which inspires most of the criticism levelled at the university system does not really take inequality with regard to the school system into account, because of its attachment to a formal definition of educational equity. If, however, one takes socially conditioned inequalities with regard to schools and education seriously, one is obliged to conclude that the *formal* equity, which the whole education system is subject to, is in reality unjust and that in any society which claims to have democratic ideals it protects privileges themselves rather than their open transmission.

In fact, to penalize the underprivileged and favour the most privileged, the school has only to neglect, in its teaching methods and techniques and its criteria when making academic judgements, to take into account the cultural inequalities between children of different social classes. In other words, by treating all pupils, however unequal they may be in reality, as equal in rights and duties, the educational system is led to give its *de facto* sanction to initial cultural inequalities. The formal equality which governs pedagogical practice is in fact a cloak for and a justification of indifference to the real inequalities with regard to the body of knowledge taught or rather demanded. Thus, for example, the 'pedagogy' used in secondary or higher education is, objectively, an 'arousing pedagogy', in Weber's words, aimed at stimulating the 'gifts' hidden in certain exceptional individuals by means of certain incantatory techniques, such as the verbal skills and powers of the teacher. As opposed to a rational and really universal pedagogy, which would take nothing for granted initially, would not count as acquired what some, and only some, of the pupils in question had inherited, would do all things for all and would be organized with the explicit aim of providing all with the means of *acquiring* that which, although apparently a natural gift, is only *given* to the children of the educated classes, our own pedagogical tradition is in fact, despite external appearances of irreproachable equality and universality, only there for the benefit of pupils who are in the *particular position* of possessing a cultural heritage conforming to that demanded by the school. Not only does it exclude any questions as to the most effective methods of transmitting to all the knowledge and the know-how which it demands of all and which different social classes transmit very unequally; it also tends to disparage as 'elementary' (with undertones of 'vulgar') and paradoxically, as 'pedantic', pedagogical methods with such aims. It is not by chance that higher elementary education, when it was in competition with the *lycée* in its traditional form, unsettled working class pupils less and attracted the scorn of the élite precisely because it *was* more explicitly and technically methodical. We have here two concepts of culture and of the techniques of transmitting it which, in the form of corporate interests, are still visible in the clash between teachers emerging from the elementary schools and those following the more traditional route through the secondary system.[12] We should also have to examine the role played for teachers by the pious horror of cramming for examinations as opposed to 'general education'. Cramming is not an absolute evil when it consists simply of realizing that pupils are being prepared for an examination and of making them aware of this. The disparagement of examination techniques is merely the corollary of the exaltation of intellectual prowess which is structurally akin to the values of culturally privileged groups. Those who have by right the necessary *manner* are always likely to dismiss as laborious and laboriously acquired values which are only of any worth when they are innate.

Teachers are the products of a system whose aim is to transmit an aristocratic culture, and are likely to adopt its values with greater ardour in proportion to the degree to which they owe it their own academic and social success. How indeed could they avoid unconsciously bringing into play the values of the milieu from which they come, or to which they now belong, when teaching and assessing their pupils? Thus, in higher education, the working- or lower-middle-class student will be judged according to the scale of values of the educated classes which many teachers owe to their social origin and which they willingly adopt, particularly, perhaps, when their membership of the élite dates from their entry into the teaching profession. As soon as the lower-middle-class ethos is judged from the point of view of the ethos of the élite, and measured against the dilettantism of the well-born and well-educated man, the scale of values is reversed and, by means of a change of sign, application becomes pedantry and a respect for hard work grinding, limited pettiness, with the implication that it is intended to compensate for a lack of natural talents. On the other hand, of course, the dilettantism of students from privileged social classes, which is apparent in many aspects of their behaviour and in the very style of their relationship with a culture which they never owe exclusively to school, corresponds to what—often unconsciously—is expected of them by their teachers and even more by the objective and explicit demands of the school. Even minor signs of social status such as 'correct' dress and bearing and the style of speech and accent are minor class signs and—again most often without their knowledge—help to shape the judgement of their teacher.[13] The teacher who, while appearing to make judgments on 'innate gifts', is in fact measuring reference to the ethos of the cultivated élite conduct based on a self-sacrificing ethos of hard and painstaking work is setting one type of relationship to culture against another, and all children are born into one or the other. The culture of the élite is so near to that of the school that children from the lower middle class (and *a fortiori* from the agricultural and industrial working class) can acquire only with great effort something which is *given* to the children of the cultivated classes—style, taste, wit—in short, those attitudes and aptitudes which seem natural in members of the cultivated classes and naturally expected of them precisely because (in the ethnological sense) they are the *culture* of that class. Children from the lower middle classes, as they receive nothing from their family of any use to them in their academic activities except a sort of undefined enthusiasm to acquire culture, are obliged to expect and receive everything from school, even if it means accepting the school's criticism of them as 'plodders'.

What the education system both hands on and demands is an aristocratic culture and, above all, an aristocratic relationship with it.[14] This is particularly clear in the relationship of teachers to language.

Moving to and fro between charismatic use of the word as a lofty incantation whose function is to create in the pupil a suitable receptivity to grace, and a traditional use of university language as the consecrated vehicle of a consecrated culture, teachers assume that they already share a common language and set of values with their pupils, but this is only so when the system is dealing with its own heirs. By acting as if the language of teaching, full of allusions and shared understanding, was 'natural' for 'intelligent' and 'gifted' pupils, teachers need not trouble to make any technical checks on their handling of language and the students' understanding of it, and can also see as strictly fair academic judgements which in fact perpetuate cultural privilege. As language is the most important part of the cultural heritage because, as syntax, it provides a system of transposable mental postures which themselves completely reflect and dominate the whole of experience, and as the gap between university language and that spoken in fact by the different social classes varies greatly, it is impossible to have pupils with equal rights and duties towards university language and use of language without being obliged to hold the gift responsible for a number of inequalities which are primarily social. Apart from a lexis and a syntax, each individual inherits from his milieu a certain attitude towards words and their use which prepares him, to a greater or lesser extent, for the scholastic games which are still to some extent, in the French tradition of literary studies, games with words. This relationship with words, whether reverent or emancipated, assumed or familiar, thrifty or extravagant, is never more obvious than in oral examinations, and teachers consciously or unconsciously distinguish between 'natural' ease of expression composed of fluency and elegant lack of constraint, and 'forced' ease, common among lower middle and working class students, which reflects the effort to conform, at the price of not getting quite the right note, to the norms of university discourse, indicating some anxiety to impress, and too evidently an attempt to create the right impression to be free of all taint of self-seeking vulgarity. In short, the teachers' *certitudo sui*, which is never more clearly seen than in the high eloquence of a lecture, is based on class ethnocentrism which authorizes both a given usage of academic language and a certain attitude to the use which students make of language in general and of academic language in particular.

Thus, implicit in these relationships with language, there can be seen the whole significance allotted by the educated classes to learned culture and the institution responsible for transmitting it—the latent functions which they give to educational institutions, i.e. the task of organizing the cult of a culture which can be offered to all because in fact it is reserved for the members of the class whose culture it is, the hierarchy of intellectual values which gives the impressive manipulators of words and ideas a higher rank than the humble servants of techniques, and the inner logic of a system whose *objective* function is to *preserve* the values which are the basis of the social order. More deeply, it is because traditional education is objectively addressed to those who have obtained from their social milieu the linguistic and cultural capital that it *objectively* demands that it cannot openly declare its demands and feel itself obliged to give everyone the means of meeting them. Like common law, the university tradition merely specified infringements and punishments without ever openly stating the principles underlying them. Thus, to take examinations as an example, it is quite clear that the more vaguely what they ask for is defined, whether it be a question of knowledge or of presentation, and the less specific the criteria adopted by the examiners, the more they favour the privileged. Thus, the nearer written examinations come to the more traditional kind of 'literary' exercise, the more they favour the exhibition of imponderable qualities in style, syntax of ideas or knowledge marshalled, the *dissertatio de omni re scribili* which dominates the great *concours* in literary subjects (and still plays an important part in scientific ones), the more clearly they divide candidates of differing social classes. In the same way, the 'inheritors' are more favoured in oral examinations than in written ones, particularly when the oral becomes *explicitly* the test of distinguished and cultivated manners which it always *implicitly* is.[15] It is quite clear that such a system can only work perfectly as long as it can recruit and select students capable of satisfying its objective demands, that is as long as it can be directed towards individuals possessing a cultural capital (and able to make it pay off) which it presupposes and endorses without openly demanding it or transmitting it methodically. The only test to which it can really be put is not, it is clear, that of numbers, but that of the *quality* of students. 'Mass education', about which we talk so much nowadays, is the opposite of both education reserved for a small number of inheritors of the culture demanded by the school and of education reserved for any small number of students of any *kind whatever*.

In fact, the system can take in an increasingly large number of pupils, as happened during the first half of this century, without having to change profoundly, provided that the newcomers are also in possession of the socially acquired aptitudes which the school traditionally demands.

On the other hand, it is bound to experience crises (which it will describe as 'a lowering of standards') when it takes in an increasingly large number of pupils who have not acquired the same mastery as their predecessors of the cultural heritage of their social class (as happens when there is a continuous increase in the percentage of children undergoing secondary and higher education from the classes which have traditionally enjoyed it, if there is a similar drop in the rate of selection) or who, coming from culturally underprivileged classes, have no cultural

heritage. A number of changes now taking place within the education system can be ascribed to determining factors which can properly be described as *morphological*. It is therefore clear that they affect nothing essential, and that there is very little question, either in programmes of reform or in the demands of teachers and students, of anything affecting specifically the traditional system of education or its working. It is true that enlarging the social basis of recruitment to the *sixiéme* would no doubt be a decisive test entailing very probably major changes in the functioning of the system in its most specific form, if the segregation of children according to the hierarchy of types of schools and 'sides' (ranging from the *collèges d'enseignement général* or the *collèges d'enseignement technique* to the classical 'sides' of the *lycées*) did not afford the system a protection tailored to its own inner logic, in that lower-class children, who do not bring to their school work either the keenness to learn of lower middle class children or the cultural capital of upper-class children, take refuge in a kind of negative withdrawal which upsets teachers, and is expressed in forms of disorder previously unknown. It is of course obvious that in such cases it is enough to let matters take their own course to bring crude social handicaps into play and for everything to return to normal. To meet this challenge in a really effective way, the education system should have at its disposal the means to carry out systematic and widespread educational priority programmes of the kind that it can dispense with as long as it is aimed at children from the privileged classes.[16]

It would therefore be ingenuous to expect that, from the very way of working of a system which itself defines its methods of recruitment by imposing demands which are all the more effective for being implicit, there should arise the contradictions capable of determining a basic change in the logic of its own working and of preventing the institution responsible for the conservation and transmission of culture from carrying out its task of social conservation. By giving individuals educational aspirations strictly tailored to their position in the social hierarchy, and by operating a selection procedure which, although apparently formally equitable, endorses real inequalities, schools help both to perpetuate and legitimize inequalities. By awarding allegedly impartial qualifications (which are also largely accepted as such) for socially conditioned aptitudes which it treats as unequal 'gifts', it transforms *de facto* inequalities into *de jure* ones and *economic and social* differences into *distinctions of quality*, and legitimates the transmission of the cultural heritage. In doing so, it is performing a confidence trick. Apart from enabling the élite to justify being what it is, the *ideology of giftedness*, the cornerstone of the whole educational and social system, helps to enclose the underprivileged classes in the roles which society has given them by making them see as natural inability things which are only a result of an inferior social status, and by persuading them that they owe their social fate (which is increasingly tied to their educational fate as society becomes more rationalized) to their individual nature and their lack of gifts. The exceptional success of those few individuals who escape the collective fate of their class apparently justifies educational selection and gives credence to the myth of the school as a liberating force among those who have been eliminated, by giving the impression that success is exclusively a matter of gifts and work. Finally those whom the system has 'liberated'—teachers in elementary, secondary and higher education—put their faith in *l'école libératrice* at the service of the school which is in truth a conservative force which owes part of its power of conservation to that myth. Thus by its own logic the educational system can help to perpetuate cultural privileges without those who are privileged having to use it. By giving cultural inequalities an endorsement which formally at least is in keeping with democratic ideals, it provides the best justification for these inequalities.

At the end of *The Republic* Plato describes how souls about to start another life had to make their own choice of lots among patterns of lives, all possible animal and human lives, and how, once the choice was made, they had to drink the water of the River of Forgetfulness before returning to earth. The theodicy Plato's myth assumes devolves, in our societies, on university and school examiners. But we can quote Plato further:[17]

> Then a prophet first marshalled them in order, and then taking lots and patterns of lives from the lap of Lachesis, mounted upon a high pulpit and spoke: 'The word of the daughter of Necessity, maid Lachesis. Souls of a day, here beginneth another circle that bears the mortal race to death. The angel will not cast lots for you, but you shall choose your angel. Let him whose lot falls first have first choice of a life to which he shall be bound by Necessity . . . The

responsibility is on him that chooseth. There is none on God.'

In order to change fate into the choice of freedom, the school, the prophet of Necessity, need only succeed in convincing individuals to rely on its judgement and persuading them that they themselves have chosen the fate that was already reserved for them. From that point there is no questioning the divinity of society. We could consider Plato's myth of the initial choice of lots with that proposed by Campanella in *La Città del Sole*: to set up immediately a situation of perfect mobility and to ensure the complete independence of the position of fathers and sons, one thing only is necessary—the separation of children from their parents at birth.[18]

Statisticians are in fact implicitly invoking the myth of perfect mobility when they refer the empirically observed situation to a situation of total independence between the social position of inheritors and that of parents. We should no doubt allow a critical role to this myth and the clues it enables us to create, as they help to expose the gap between democratic ideals and social reality. But even the most cursory examination would make it clear that considering these abstractions presupposes ignorance of the social costs and of the conditions in which a high degree of mobility would be possible.[19]

But is not the best way of judging to what extent the reality of a 'democratic' society conforms to its ideals to measure chances of entering the institutionalized instruments of social elevation and cultural salvation open to individuals of different social classes?[20] If so we are then led to the conclusion that a society which allows the most privileged social classes to monopolize educational institutions— which, as Max Weber would say, hold a monopoly of the manipulation of cultural goods and the institutional signs of cultural salvation—is rigid in the extreme.

Notes

* Reprinted from Pierre Bourdieu, 'L'École conservatrice', *Revue française de sociologie*, 7, 1966, pp. 225–6, 330–42, 346–7; translation by J. C. Whitehouse.
1 Cf. P. Bourdieu and J. C. Passeron, *Les Héritiers*, Éditions de Minuit, 1964, pp. 14–21.
2 Correlation frequently occurs between the wishes expressed by parents with children finishing the *cours moyen*, opinions given later on the choice of a particular school, and the real choice. 'By no means all parents want their children to go to a lycée . . . Only 30 per cent of parents with children in *collèges d'enseignement général* or *fin d'études* say yes, whatever the previous achievement of the child may have been', P. Clerc, 'La famille et l'orientation scolaire au niveau de la sixième. Enquête de juin 1963 dans l'agglomération Parisienne', *Population*, 4, August–September 1964, pp. 635–6.
3 Cf. P. Bourdieu and A. Darbel, 'La fin d'un malthusi-

anisme', in Darras, *Le Partage des bénéfices*, Éditions de Minuit, 1966.
4 Analysing the differential influence (exerted by the dimension of the family in various milieux) on the access to secondary education, A. Girard and H. Bastide write, 'Although two-thirds of the children of officeworkers and skilled craftsmen and traders go into the *lycées*, the proportion is highest in the smallest families (i.e. of one or two children). With these groups, however, children from large families (i.e. of four or more) do not enter the *lycée* in greater numbers than those of families of factory workers having only one or two brothers and sisters', A. Girard and H. Bastide, 'La stratification sociale et la démocratisation de l'enseignement', *Population*, July–September 1963, p. 458.
5 There is a presupposition in this system of explanation by means of the common perception of objective and

collective chances that the advantages or disadvantages perceived are the functional equivalent of the advantages or disadvantages really experienced or objectively verified in that they influence behaviour in the same way. This does not imply that we underestimate the importance of objective chances. In fact, every scientific observation, in very different social and cultural situations, has tended to show that there is a close correlation between *subjective hopes* and *objective chances*, the latter tending to effectively modify attitudes and behaviour by working through the former (cf. P. Bourdieu, *Travail et travailleurs en Algérie*, Mouton, 1962, pt 2, pp. 36–8; Richard A. Cloward and Lloyd E. Ohlin, *Delinquency and Opportunity: a theory of delinquent gangs*, Routledge & Kegan Paul, 1961; Clarence Schrag, 'Delinquency and opportunity: analysis of a theory', *Sociology and Social Research*, 46, January 1962, pp. 167–75.

6 Kurt Lewin, 'Time, perspective and morale', in *Resolving Social Conflicts*, New York, Harper, 1948, p. 113.

7 ibid., p. 115.

8 ibid., p. 115.

9 P. Clerc, op.cit., p. 646.

10 It is probably by reference to a *social definition* of a reasonably obtainable diploma that individual career projects and hence attitudes to school are determined. This social definition clearly varies from class to class: while, for many of the lower strata of the middle class, the *baccalauréat* still appears to be seen as the normal end of studies—as a result of cultural inertia and lack of information but also probably because office workers and the lower grades of supervisory personnel are more likely than others to experience the effectiveness of this barrier to promotion—it still appears more to the upper reaches of the middle classes and to the upper classes as a sort of entrance examination to higher education. This image of the scholastic career perhaps explains why a particularly large proportion of the sons of office workers and lower grades of salaried staff do not go on to study after the *baccalauréat*.

11 Cf. P. Bourdieu, J. C. Passeron and M. de Saint-Martin, op. cit. In order to have a complete measurement of the effect of the linguistic capital, it would be necessary to find out, by means of experimental studies similar to those carried out by Bernstein, whether there are any significant links between the syntax of the spoken language (e.g. its complexity) and success in fields other than that of literary studies (where the link has been shown)—for example, in mathematics.

12 See V. Isambert-Jamati, 'La rigidité d'une institution: structure scolaire et systèmes de valeur', *Revue française de sociologie*, 7, 1966, p. 306.

13 Similarly elementary school teachers, who have fully absorbed the values of the middle classes from which they increasingly come, always take into account the *ethical colouring* of conduct and attitudes towards teachers and disciplines when making judgments on their pupils.

14 At the heart of the most traditional definition of culture there lies no doubt the distinction between the contents of the culture (in the subjective sense of an interiorized objective culture) or, perhaps, *knowledge*, and the characteristic means of possessing that knowledge, which gives it its whole meaning and value. What the child received from an educated milieu is not only a *culture* (in the objective sense), but also a certain *style* of relationship to that culture, which derives precisely from *the manner of acquiring it*. An individual's relationship with cultural works (and the mode of all his cultural experiences) is thus more or less easy, brilliant, natural, difficult, arduous, dramatic or tense according to the conditions in which he acquired his culture, the osmosis of childhood in a family providing good conditions for an experience of familiarity (which is the source of the illusion of charisma) which schooling can never completely provide. It can be seen that by stressing the relationship with culture and setting great value on the most aristocratic style of relationship (ease, brilliance) schools favour the most privileged children.

15 The resistance of teachers to *docimology* and their even greater resistance to any attempt to rationalize testing (one has only to think of the indignant protests at the use of closed questionnaires) is unconsciously based on the same aristocratic ethos as the rejection of all pedagogical science, even though a 'democratic' excuse for it is found in the ritual denunciation of the danger of technocracy.

16 Can the pressure of economic demand impose decisive changes? It is possible to imagine industrialized societies managing to meet the need for trained personnel without any major widening of the basis of recruitment from secondary, and more particularly from higher education. If we use only criteria of cost, or rather, of formal rationality, it is perhaps preferable to recruit—in the face of all the claims of educational equality—from those classes whose social culture is the nearest to educational culture, and thus dispense with the need for any educational priority programme.

17 Plato, *The Republic*, Book 10, 617, Dent, Everyman, 1942, p. 322.

18 Cf. Marie Skodak, 'Children in foster homes. A study of mental development', *Studies in Child Welfare*, University of Iowa Studies, 16 (1), January 1939, pp. 1–56; B. Wellmar, 'The fickle IQ', *Sigma XI Quarterly*, 28 (2), 1940, pp. 52–60.

19 Apart from the difficulty of obtaining a precise assessment of mobility, and the discussions on the point in the careers of father and son which should be taken to obtain a relevant comparison, mention should be made of the fact that, as Bendix and Lipset have pointed out, 'perfect mobility' (in the sense of completely equal chances of mobility), and 'maximum mobility' are not necessarily linked, and that a distinction should be made between forced and intentional 'rigidity' or 'mobility'.

20 We should also take into account the differential chances of social elevation given identical use of institutional means. We know that, at an equivalent level of instruction, individuals from different social classes reach varying levels in the social hierarchy.

Section IV Science, psychology and social control

13 The politics of neurobiology: biologism in the service of the state*

Steven Rose and Hilary Rose

Biologism is the attempt to locate the cause of the existing structure of human society, and of the relationships of individuals within it, in the biological character of the human animal. For biologism, all the richness of human experience and the varying historical forms of human relationships merely represent the product of underlying biological structures; human societies are governed by the same laws as ape societies, the way that an individual responds to his or her environment is determined by the innate properties of the DNA molecules to be found in brain or germ cells. In a word, the human condition is reduced to mere biology, which in its turn is no more than a special case of the laws of chemistry and hence of physics.

As a theoretical model, biologism is thus a form of that reductionism which is the dominant paradigm of contemporary western science. As a philosophy, reductionism's premises are that

(a) Sciences are arranged in a hierarchical order, varying from high level disciplines such as economics and sociology to lower level ones, such as biology, chemistry and, at the base, particle physics; and

(b) that events in high-level sciences can be reduced on the basis of a one-for-one correspondence to events and hence laws appropriate to the lower-level science; ultimately, therefore, that physical laws can be derived which will subsume and explain sociology.

To appreciate the significance of reductionism as a philosophy, it is necessary also to recognise that reductionism as an experimental approach has been at the heart of the scientific method ever since the emergence of modern physics with Galileo and Newton. As an experimental method, reductionism is merely a procedure for explaining the properties of simplified, model systems, of holding all parameters except one constant, and varying that systematically. This makes the experimental problems under study more approachable; it has been the key to the success of the 'biological revolution' over the past two decades, and as a tool it is unchallenged. Problems arise only when the tool is elevated into a philosophical principle, so that it is ignored that, for a complete explanation of an event or a process, it must be taken out of the vacuum into which reductionism plunges it and replaced in the bustle of the real world with which it is, in actuality, in constant interaction.[1]

At one level, it is the very success of reductionism as a tool in the biological revolution, in the unravelling of the genetic code and exploring the chemistry of the cell, which has led to the ready way in which its philosophical premises too have become accepted. Thus we find molecular biologists such as Jacques Monod, author of *Chance and Necessity*, arguing that in the long run all of biology, and hence all 'higher' sciences, are to be derived from a study of the properties of the macromolecules of which the cell is composed (such as DNA) and their interactions, and may be best understood by studying the chemistry and organisation of the intestinal bacteria *Escherichia coli* or—even more reduced—a bacteriophage, the virus which preys upon it.

Exposing reductionist ideology has become more complicated in that the modes of thinking of reductionism have become so dominant in recent years that they have come to constitute what may almost be described as an ideology of science itself, which claims that reductionism has universalistic importance, superseding all other forms of knowledge. The ideology of reductionism is thus positivist. But it also has ethical overtones, claiming that the scientific rationality it represents provides rules for the proper conduct of human society. The only true

Source: forthcoming in H. and S. Rose, eds, *The Political Economy of Science: Ideology in the Natural Sciences*, Macmillan.

goal for humanity becomes, in this view, the systematic incorporation of all aspects of human existence into a framework provided by 'the laws of physics'; the rationality and objectivity of reductionism replace all else; they provide their own guide to human progress. Science, a social product, becomes both the goal and the method for all society.

The opposition to reductionism comes primarily from dialectical materialism, which argues that, while events at any given hierarchical level represented by the different sciences must correspond to events at higher or lower levels, they cannot be reduced, by the application of causal laws or relations, to lower ones; biology cannot be invoked to explain away sociology; instead there will be a dialectical interaction between them. Thus, despite the vicissitudes of Marxism in the Soviet Union, there has been a constant attempt to maintain a non-reductionist science, which has been particularly successful in the case of neurobiology.

But why is all this not merely a superstructural squabble about epistemology, without real relevance for serious political struggle or major ideological thrust? The answer to this lies in the present situation of capitalism—the particular strengths and weaknesses which have made it both necessary and possible to recruit biologistic biology as the generator of ideologies and technologies in its struggle for survival. To follow this we must look at the present role of biology and biologism.

So far as technologies are concerned, the major role of the new biology (outside of agriculture and some areas of medicine) is firmly locked into the processes of social control. The new needs which have generated the technologies and their attendant ideologies can be located in the changing nature of imperialist struggle abroad and class struggle at home. The characteristic mode of warfare of the latter half of the twentieth century has been anti-imperialist, guerilla struggle. Such struggles of national liberation essentially involve a people at war against an army (the change is symbolised by the statistic that in the First World War, 90 per cent of the deaths were of soldiers; in the Indochina war of the 1960s and 1970s, at least 90 per cent of the deaths have been of civilians). In such struggles the highly mechanised imperialist army, equipped with devices generated by its physicists and engineers, has been outmanoeuvred by the guerillas, the fish in their pond of peasants, What is more, such struggles are no longer confined to the Third World countries, but take place within the metropolitan countries themselves; in Britain and the United States, urban guerrilla war has become a characteristic feature of the landscape.

Physics has its contribution to such struggles in the form of fragmentation weapons, night-vision detectors, electronic sensors and computers, but biological methods become of increasing importance; the chemical crop destruction campaign in Vietnam was an example, and at home, where property is sacrosanct and large-scale damage unacceptable, the pressure to develop methods for people-control and manipulation, both on a general, population basis and aimed at specific individuals, has become very strong. The emergence of these technologies is heavily dependent upon the area of interface between biology, the social sciences and the so-called behavioural sciences—the field best known as 'neurobiology', which has generated, and is generating, developments based on the extensive use of drugs on a population basis, behaviour modification techniques and the—widely resisted—use of psychosurgery and brain and behaviour modification by electrical brain stimulation.

At the same time, the second, directly ideological, role of biologism as a legitimator of the social order has shown a massive resurgence. This is not the first time that biologism has played such a role. In the nineteenth century, bourgeois theorists adapted evolutionary ideas to legitimise the capitalist mode of production and its consequent social relations as corresponding to the inevitable workings-out of the 'iron laws of biology'. Both class structure at home and imperialist expansion abroad were justified under the name of Social Darwinism. In the present period of social crisis, where the more traditional legitimating ideologies of capitalism have been exposed and weakened, if not destroyed, the importance of biologism is again 'proving' that capitalism and imperialism derive from 'man's innate aggressiveness'; that all human experience can be subsumed into categories of stimulus and response, reward and punishment, and that individuals' success or failure in a competitive society, their capacity to revolt against the state, is a result of a flaw in their chemistry or brain structure. This 'proof' both justifies the oppression and, by opposing their struggles with scientific rationality, devalues, divides and demoralises the oppressed. It is this ideological role, as much as its attendant technologies, which forms the present-day importance of biologism not merely at the superstructural level but in every present dimension of struggle.

In order to combat both the technologies and the ideology of biological reductionism, we have to examine its claims. In doing so, we must recognise that ideology, posing as science, itself creates paradigmatic frameworks within which endless apparently 'objective' research is done and learned journals and popular books produced. Particular technologies of oppression—whether of behaviour modification through conditioning, the apparatus of psychometrics or chemical brain manipulation—are frequently derived from a strange bastardisation of science and pseudo-science; their rationale is established within what is apparently a scientific, but in reality an ideological framework. As a result, particular technologies often appear merely as abuses of an otherwise value-free science, or are regarded as symbols of the inevitably oppressive role of a scientific rationality from which the only escape is retreat into irrationality.

Marxist analysis rejects both these partial accounts; we must instead link the technologies directly with the ideology which sponsors them, and show their coherence and social function. By analysing both ideologies and technologies as the products of a re-emergent biologism we do not mean to imply that the technologies do not 'work'—drugs or psychosurgery will indeed 'pacify' individuals, even if they do so by reducing them to cabbages. This is the peculiar force of biologism; that ideology, occupying the terrain of the natural sciences, may indeed generate effective oppressive technologies. What we are concerned with is to show the underlying ideological coherence of the many forms of biologism which now compete with biology within the area of neurobiology. To do this, in the following sections, we describe several different forms which biologism takes, and the attendant technologies which flow from them. For analysis, we separate the forms into varying types of reductionism, from molecular and genetic reductionism, through evolutionary reductionism to behaviourism. One whole area, that of scientific racism [warrants separate treatment and is not dealt with in this article].

Molecular reductionism

Molecular reductionism can be seen at its sharpest in the explanation of madness. What is the cause of schizophrenia? Is it to be seen—as the school of 'orthomolecular psychiatry' would argue—in the absence of certain key chemicals in the brain, or in the presence of abnormal metabolites due to genetic disorders? If so, treatment is to be found by dietary modification or the development of drugs which antagonise in some way the abnormal metabolites. Following the lead of such individuals as H. Osmond and J. R. Smythies,[2] this school argues strongly that there is an organic, brain-located *cause* for the individual's response. This belief has a long history, for at all stages in the development of biochemistry the fashionable molecule of the moment has tended to be implicated as the cause of schizophrenia, from the amino acid glutamate in the 1950s, through an abnormality of energy metabolism in the 1960s to today's attention to the problem of the sugar galactose in the diet. Whatever the proximate biochemical cause, there is on this thesis an underlying genetic defect, a *propensity to be* schizophrenic. Although the original idea of the 'illness' as due to a defect in a single gene is now relatively disfavoured by comparison with more complex multiple gene effects, over the last decades all the classical apparatus of the clinical biochemists, in their search for bizarre substances indicative of abnormality in schizophrenic brain, blood, urine or sweat, and of the human population geneticists with their hunt for identical and non-identical twins and heritability estimates,

have been employed, with singularly little success, to track down the offending chemical.[3]

The ideological components within the reductionist paradigm are apparent; the inborn view of schizophrenia at once refuses to admit criticism of social structures, such as the family[4] and alienated work forms, whilst at the same time encouraging a manipulative view of treatment. This is even more apparent when we look at the respective analyses, biochemical or social, as applied to the affective disorders such as depression. Those who argue a biochemical cause of depression, such as the psychiatrist W. Sargant,[5] look for treatment by way of anti-depressant drugs; treatment is effective if it adjusts the depressed individual (typically a woman post-natally or around menopause) back into an acceptable social role, such as that of the good housewife and mother. The stability and appropriateness of the social order is taken as a natural given in this situation, and the job of the psychopharmacologist and clinician is to chemically fit people to it; it is not surprising to learn that 50 million patients were given chlorpromazine within the first decade of its use, or that 12 million barbiturate and 16 million tranquilliser prescriptions are issued a year in Britain. Note that we do not argue that the drugs themselves do not 'work' in the sense that they affect an individual's responses and performance, often, though not always, in the predicted and hoped for (by the clinician) direction. However, even here there are some difficulties, because one consequence of the reductionist mode of thought is that drugs are supposed to have a single site of action; effects other than those sought for are seen as 'side-effects' to be eliminated. The complexity of drug-behaviour interactions, which has been so revealingly brought out even in the context of an apparently much less controversial agent, L-dopa, in the treatment of an apparently straightforward motor disorder, Parkinsonism, tends to be dismissed by the reductionists.

But this is only a relatively marginal point; the crucial issue is that the ideology which reflects itself in a reductionist model of the cause of schizophrenia and depression, and upon which is based a vast research and development programme at all levels, from the universities to the drug houses, also finds expression in an output at the social level, which essentially regards individuals as objects, to be manipulated into required social patterns. Compare the average clinical research paper's description of the behaviour of patients exposed to given agents with the multi-levelled account of the patients to whom the doctor Oliver Sacks gave L-dopa in his book *Awakenings*.[6] For each of his twenty patients Sacks provides an account of the workings of L-dopa, in terms of both minutely observed behaviour associated with different levels and occasions of giving the drug, and also of the personal histories and present relationships of the patients. Throughout there is a constant emphasis on the integration of all the effects of the drug into the complex individual situation. Sacks's model is clearly a dialectical one; truly scientific rather than ideological.

The search for a biological rationale for problems of the social order has reached new heights in recent years with the development of a new clinical concept, that of 'minimal brain dysfunction' (MBD), which, an almost unrecognised category a few years back, was recently warranted a full symposium of the New York Academy of Sciences.[7] Minimal brain dysfunction is essentially a behaviour-defined syndrome; that is the concept of brain dysfunction is invoked to explain a particular pattern of socially disapproved behaviour, although no brain abnormality can in fact be detected by physiological techniques. In general, minimal brain dysfunction is supposed to be a disease of childhood, and has derived from an extension of the concept of 'hyperkinesis', a disease state believed to characterise an overactive child. In Britain, there are estimated to be a few hundred children categorised as hyperkinetic. A large proportion of these are institutionalised; they are described as being unable to sit still without forcible restraint. In the United States the diagnosis of hyperkinesis has become much broader, to cover a very large group of children who show 'behaviour problems' at school, being poor learners, inattentive in class, and disrespectful of authority. Among the diagnostic signs for minimal brain dysfunction are, according to Wender, being 'aggressive socially . . . playing with younger children, and, if a boy, with girls'. For all these patterns of behaviour, treatment with amphetamine or its congener, Ritalin, is proposed. Indeed, Wender waxes euphoric about the effects of Ritalin treatment, going so far as to claim that minimal brain dysfunction children may be regarded as suffering from 'hypoamphetaminosis'. Under the drug, 'children often begin to talk about and behave in a manner consistent with their parents' formerly unheeded "oughts" and "shoulds".' One bright eight-year old referred to d-amphetamines as his 'magic pills which make me into a good boy and make everybody like me'. The child turns from a 'whirling dervish' into being 'quiet, compliant', and with an 'improved class behaviour, group participation and attitudes to authority' under medication. What is more, Ritalin is cheaper than 'expensive, non-organic therapies'.[8]

Small wonder that Ritalin is now prescribed, at a daily dose of 5–40 milligrams, and, on the basis of school reports, to 250,000 American schoolchildren daily. Here indeed is a conspicuous success for a reductionist research and development programme that discards alternative explanation for a child's inattentiveness in class or poor attitude to authority; not even other biological factors which may have apparently similar consequences, such as nutrition, are considered, still less that inattentiveness in class may reflect poor teaching or an irrelevant educational programme, or that disrespect for authority may represent a more socially appropriate response to oppression than does subservience.

Biochemistry is not the only brain discipline whose reductionism has both ideological and direct social significance. Physiology and anatomy have shown similar tendencies. Over recent years it has become increasingly apparent that electrical activity in the cells of particular brain regions is associated with specific behaviour patterns, so that, for instance, when certain nerve cells in the hypothalamus, a region deep in the interior of the brain, are electrically stimulated by implanted electrodes in the cat or rat, then, depending on the particular cells stimulated, the animal shows hunger, thirst, satiety, anger, fear, sexual arousal or pleasure. Surgical removal of these regions is associated with the reciprocal behavioural effect to that of cellular stimulation. The reductionist interpretation of these experiments is that the firing of particular cells in the hypothalamus *causes* anger, sexual arousal, and so on, and, as with the biochemists, the social technologies which have emerged, notably in the hands of J. M. R. Delgado in the United States and in Spain,[9] have been human experimentation in which schizophrenics and 'low IQ' patients have had electrodes permanently implanted in the hypothalamus, remotely radio controlled by the doctor/experimenter. Passing current through the electrodes is associated with sharp mood changes in the patients. Once again, the patient's anger, arousal and so on are seen as a consequence of the functioning of particular brain cells; the cells can be manipulated and so the patient can be manipulated, irrespective of the external circumstances which might be expected to affect the individual's mood. According to Delgado, implanted electrode studies and their utilisation in practice can be expected to develop substantially in the next few years.

Still more revealing is the recent growth in popularity of techniques for the removal or destruction of particular brain regions—psychosurgery as it is called—in the United States, and also in Britain, Japan and other countries.[10] The advocates of these techniques argue that particular behavioural patterns are associated with malfunction or hyperfunction of particular brain regions, so that the appropriate medical strategy is the removal of these regions, a surgical approach which is a modification of the old pre-frontal lobotomy popular for use with schizophrenics in the early 1950s, but more recently a relatively declining treatment. Psychosurgical operations have recently been rapidly increasing in number in Britain and the United States.

Increased knowledge of the hypothalamic centres and related regions of the limbic system (a part of the brain associated with fear, anger and similar emotional responses) has led to a considerable ramification of these techniques. Surgical removal of such brain regions has been both proposed and practised to deal with individuals suffering from 'behaviour problems' without any obvious 'organic' brain dysfunction.

Such psychosurgery is intended as a pacifier, producing better-adjusted individuals, easier to maintain in institutions or at home. In the United States the commonest groups of patients are claimed to be working-class blacks and women. A book by two psychosurgeons, Vernon Mark and Frank Ervin,[11] has drawn on the circumstances of the revolt in American cities to query whether there may not be brain abnormalities present in ghetto militants, to be cured by surgery. Their estimates argue that between 5 and 10 per cent of Americans might be candidates for such treatment.

Nor is this discussion purely theoretical; psychosurgical research has been supported by law-enforcement agencies in the United States. While in a recent Detroit court case, proposed brain surgery on a prisoner was ruled illegal despite his consent, the number of operations conducted apparently continues to increase. An indication of the candidates for such operations is provided by an exchange of correspondence between the Director of Corrections, Human Relations Agency, Sacramento (what need for a Ministry of Love?), and the Director of Hospitals and Clinics, University of California Medical Center, in 1971.[12] The Director asks for a clinical investigation of selected prison inmates 'who have shown aggressive, destructive behavior, possibly as a result of severe neurological disease' to conduct 'surgical and diagnostic procedures... to locate centers in the brain which may have been previously damaged and which could serve as the focus for episodes of violent behavior', for subsequent surgical removal.

An accompanying letter describes a possible candidate for such treatment, whose infractions while in prison include problems of 'respect towards officials', 'refusal to work' and 'militancy'; he had to be transferred prisons because of 'his sophistication... he had to be warned several times... to cease his practising and teaching Karate and judo. He was transferred... for increasing militancy, leadership ability and outspoken hatred for the white society... he was identified as one of several leaders in the work strike of April 1971... Also evident at approximately the same time was an avalanche of revolutionary reading material.' To which request, the Director of Hospitals and Clinics replies, agreeing to provide the treatment, including electrode implantation, 'on a regular cost basis. At the present time this would amount to approximately $1,000 per patient for a seven day stay.'

Clearly such cases are those to whom the label 'these animals are dangerous; when attacked they bite' might well be attached. Once again, the reductionist slogan is the reverse of that painted on the Oxford college wall: 'Do not adjust your mind; there is a fault in reality.'

In such examples of molecular reductionism we see an amalgam of all those features of the ideological penetration of science discussed above. The research paradigms not merely dictate the experimental operations conducted, such as the search for abnormal metabolites or particular 'centres' in the brain, but have an ideological significance which lies both in determining scientific directions and in providing a powerful scientific rationale for particular social interests. But, not only do these paradigms provide ideological support for the existing social order (it is your brain that is at fault if you are disaffected), they also provide a set of social technologies which help to maintain precisely the same social order.

Genetic determinism

Genetic determinism represents a particular paradigm within the broad framework of molecular reductionism. Its research programme is based upon the premise that all human behavioural characters can be analysed as representing the algebraic sum of two components; a contribution from genetics and a contribution from the environment, with a further separable balancing item for interaction included. From this premise follows the belief that experiments can be devised to answer the question: 'How much does environment, and how much does heredity, contribute to differences in behaviour between individuals or between populations'. Note that such a question, with its implicit claim that behavioural characters can be teased apart and reduced into elemental components which summate, is itself archetypally reductionist.

While genetic analysis of particular behaviour traits has been attempted with non-human animals, it is with humans that most of the work is concerned. Heritability studies have been performed on traits such as schizophrenia and other mental disorders and there have been attempts to explore the genetic basis of criminality (for instance the attention paid to the proposed relationships between a particular genetic defect found in certain males, the XYY chromosomal abnormality, and a propensity to violent crime). This relationship was first canvassed some years ago in Britain, and had apparently fallen into disfavour,[13] but has recently emerged again as the subject of a vigorous research programme in Boston, Massachusetts, in which the parents of male children, screened and found to have the abnormal chromosome, are told at the child's birth that he may grow up abnormally![14]

However, not only has there been a debate concerning the existence of genes for criminality; there has also been a re-emergence of the claim that there are genes for low IQ. [The IQ racket] is *the* outstanding example of biologism [and] must be seen as a key element within the general picture of a neurobiology penetrated by ideology.

Evolutionary reductionism

Among the several reductionist strands present within genetic determinism, some perhaps belong more properly to that paradigm group we have classed as 'evolutionary reductionism'. The most clear cut and prominent examples of this paradigm are provided by certain tendencies within ethology, the study of the behaviour and social relations of animals studied as far as possible in a natural environment and unrestricted by laboratory conditions. The development of ethology, evolving as it did in reaction to the sterility of much laboratory psychology (see below) has certainly provided a new approach to an understanding both of patterns of behaviour and of relationships between individuals of a species, which has enriched the understanding of the complexities of social behaviour. However, it has also manifest within it some very obvious and vulgarly ideological reductionist models, typified by, for instance, Desmond Morris's *The Naked Ape*,[15] in which he argues that human conduct is most fruitfully interpreted, predicted and controlled in the light of studies of other primates. While Morris's more extreme books, or for that matter Robert Ardrey's *The Territorial Imperative*[16]—which makes claims for the innate aggressiveness of human beings and their urge to possess 'territory'—are by and large deplored by professional ethologists as being oriented towards the lay rather than the professional audience, they are none the less influential in determining research both within ethology and in neighbouring areas, and they have generated hosts of anthropological and sociological camp-followers who busy themselves in demonstrating how today's managerial capitalist society is the direct biological (inevitable) descendant from humanity's hunting past and non-human ancestry.[17] What is particularly apparent in these publicist accounts of ethology is the clarity with which they articulate some of the central dogmas of ethological authority. Thus the innate aggressiveness of humans is claimed directly by experimentalists like Konrad Lorenz[18] and I. Eibl-Eibesfeldt,[19] while Ardrey's exposition of territoriality in man derives sustenance from research studies on territoriality in red grouse on Scottish moors, extrapolated to the human world.[20]

Reductionist paradigms, in which a mode of operation becomes elevated by some invisible hand into a principle, is like goal displacement in organisations; a kind of explanation displacement occurs so that research which may provide an elegant account of certain aspects of animal behaviour is displaced into a total account of the whole human condition. Scarcely surprisingly, if humans are interpreted as ill-suppressed bundles of aggressive instincts, the formulation for social policy relates to control rather than liberation. Thus an ethologically-based legitimation for conserving the social order is provided by the dominance hierarchy ('pecking order') studies; stratification is not associated with specific societies and cultures, but reflects a genetically laid-down necessity. The limitations of this particular type of ethological approach have been criticised by, for

instance, Patrick Bateson,[21] who has pointed out that not only do studies of pecking orders and dominance hierarchies relate merely to particular species examined under particular conditions, but in addition, even within a group, the pecking order itself is not rigidly ordained but relates rather precisely to a particular type of experimental situation; in other situations, quite different orders may obtain, so that different hierarchies may be apparent between, for example, eating activities and sexual activities.

Reductionist analyses of hierarchies, even in non-human species, must be replaced by dialectical ones which take into account the environmental circumstances of individuals and their past experience. But a reductionist ethology is one which, by definition, appropriates a set of linear and pared down analyses of particular situations, and therefore is far more prone to extract out from the richness of the experimental data the simplistic and linear concept of a pecking order or a dominance hierarchy. In so far as the social and political beliefs of such ethologists are apparent from their writings, there are few areas of contemporary neurobiology in which ideology stands out so sharply as in the work of ethologists such as Konrad Lorenz, in his time a paid-up member of the Nazi Party, now a Nobel Laureate and author of his own tract for the times on human survival, *Civilized Man's Eight Deadly Sins* (sic).

In this respect, reductionist ethology in the 1960s and 1970s has played, and is playing, the same role that Darwinism in the form of Social Darwinism played in the nineteenth century.[22] Then, Victorian capitalism was interpreted as obeying the iron laws of biology; the struggle for existence and the survival of the fittest demanded a *laissez-faire* economy at home and legitimated imperialism and colonialism abroad. Today, managerial capitalism, bureacracies and social stratification, and social conflict of all types from football hooliganism through class war to struggles of national liberation and wars between national states, are seen as the inevitable result of human evolution from the primate. Such explanations ignore the entirely new dimensions to human behaviour generated by the human capacity for communication, social existence and, above all, production. Economic and sociological accounts of conflict or social structures thus become diminished to the working out of the evolutionary imperative.

Behaviour reductionism

Our final example is drawn from a powerful school of psychology: that known as 'behaviourism'; here, the framework into which all human behaviour is to be reduced is that of reward and punishment, the so-called 'contingencies of reinforcement'. Behaviourist theory is one which is simultaneously extremely environmentalist and highly reductionist. It takes almost as a tenet of faith that all aspects of animal or human behaviour can be, and are, shaped by means of particular combinations of rewarding or aversive stimuli. At the same time, however, it claims to be able to reduce all aspects of human activity to a system of 'emitted behaviours'. What is important to behaviourism is what is measurable; events which occur within the brain and which are unobservable (intervening variables) are of little importance. The animal model for human behaviour favoured by the behaviourist is that of a rat or pigeon in a box provided with a lever it can press for reinforcement; indeed the key behaviourist concept is that of 'reward'. This approach to human behaviour is a classic category reductionism, where all aspects of human activity, from the writing of an academic paper, through the factory production line to altruistic self-sacrifice in war or struggle, are defined as behaviours emitted in mechanistic response to past patterns of reinforcement for the individual. The behaviourist school is sharply distinguished from other psychological paradigms, publishing its own journals and regarding as its mentor B. F. Skinner, and it is therefore interesting to examine the behaviourist position on human behaviour as evinced by his book *Beyond Freedom and Dignity*,[23] in which he argues that all human activity is embraced within his concepts. This type of reductionism is at its worst when Skinner considers the relationship of culture to individuals, serving to control and manipulate them. He cannot see that the contradictions between individuals are themselves a part of and contained within the overall structure of society, that it is not culture as a reified abstract which controls individuals, but that culture is a product of competitive classes and groups within society. Parents and teachers manipulate and control children, as Skinner points out; but it is ignored that these parents and teachers have themselves in their turn been manipulated and controlled.

Because of this, despite Skinner's emphasis on the possibility of designing a culture, there is an ahistoric, static quality about his concept of society. Nowhere does he present a vision of a future culture: instead he emphasises the 'ethical neutrality' of his techniques, applicable presumably equally to fascism, liberal democracy or socialism. Simultaneously he makes the strange error of claiming that 'no theory changes what it is a theory about'. Yet the remarkable thing about humans and their society is that they *are* changed by theories, precisely because theories modify consciousness. In fact, because Skinner's ahistoric concept carries conviction only within the atmosphere engendered by a society of the sort Marcuse characterised as one of repressive tolerance, Skinner's position is irreconcilably conservative, and its emphasis on reward as the unifying concept for describing human behaviour is deeply ideological.

Combating biologism

Throughout this account of reductionism in neurobiology, we have attempted to show both that reductionism is more than merely 'bad science', in the Anglo-Saxon sense of being poor theory or ill-conceived experiments, but that it is bad science *because* it is ideological; that is, its research programme and organising paradigms are permeated with those 'ruling ideas' which express class interest, and that the technologies that they generate are essentially defensive of that class interest, serving to protect it both physically, by manipulating and pacifying would-be protesters, and ideologically, by providing an apparent biological justification for the social order.

How can biologism be combated? There are those, particularly within the alternative culture, who respond to its oppression by turning away in distaste not only from the technologies but also from the 'science' they see as generating them. In disgust with the inhumanity of science, the young Bohemian strata turn again towards the irrational as an explanation for human suffering and joy. As the risk of fascism grows in Europe, the support of a seemingly innocent irrationalism unwittingly increases the dangers. As M. Horkheimer wrote during a previous wave of irrationalism, 'the philosophical dismissal of science is a comfort in private life, in society a lie'.[24]

The point is that, despite the loss of the terrain held by science to ideology, particularly in the crucial area of neurobiology, to abandon science along with scientism is a sure road to defeat, a way to ensure the strengthening of the very system which generates biologism. Nor is it enough merely to 'expose ideology' in the shelter of 'anti-bourgeois research' or cultured lectures to student audiences. Instead, the way forward must lie in linking the superstructural struggle with that in the work-place, the home and the streets. Powerful movements of resistance have sprung up and are growing against biologism's brutal pessimism. Campaigns of parents and schoolchildren have developed in Britain against, for instance, ESN-labelling, particularly of black children, and against Ritalin in the United States. The developing American prisoners' movement has used both agitational and legal forms of struggle against psychosurgery and the massive behaviour modification programmes which form part of the US 'law enforcement' strategy. The campaigns against racism in Britain and the United States have not been confined either to factory struggles or academic disputations of 'hereditarians versus environmentalists' but have identified scientific racism as one of the main enemies to be fought at all levels. The point is that such struggles, if they are to succeed, cannot ignore theory in the development of practice.

Notes

* An earlier version of this paper was published as Hilary Rose and Steven Rose, 'Do not adjust your mind, there is a fault in reality: ideology in the neurobiological sciences', in Richard Whitley, ed., *Social Processes of Scientific Development*, Routledge & Kegan Paul, 1974, pp. 148–71.

1 S. Rose, *The Conscious Brain*, Weidenfeld & Nicolson, 1973.

2 'Schizophrenia: a new approach', *Journal of Mental Science*, 98, 1952, pp. 309–15.

3 L. L. Iversen and S. P. R. Rose, *Biochemistry and Mental Disorder*, London, Biochemical Society, 1974.

4 However, a causal theory of madness which locates the problem exclusively within the family (as did R. D. Laing and A. Esterson in *Sanity, Madness and the Family*, Penguin, 1970), while opening the way to criticism of one particular oppressive social structure, limits itself by excluding both other social forms and human biology itself from theoretical consideration.

5 *The Unquiet Mind*, Heinemann, 1967.

6 *Awakenings*, Duckworth, 1973; Penguin, 1976.

7 F. F. de la Cruz, B. H. Fox and R. H. Roberts, 'Minimal brain dysfunction', *Annals of the New York Academy of Science*, 205, 1973 (entire volume).

8 P. H. Wender, *Minimal Brain Dysfunction in Children*, New York, Wiley, 1971. In Britain, amphetamine prescription is generally discouraged by the BMA. Connoisseurs of British children's comics will also note the strong resemblance of Wender's disapproved-of hyperkinetic child to the weekly *Beano* hero Billy Whizz.

9 *Physical Control of the Mind: Towards a Psychocivilized Society*, New York, Harper & Row, 1971.

10 P. R. Breggin, *U.S. Congressional Record (H.R.)*, 118 (26), Washington, 1972.

11 *Violence and the Brain*, New York, Harper & Row, 1970.

12 E. M. Opton, documents circulated at winter conference on Brain Research, Vail, Colorado, 1973.

13 L. S. Penrose, in W. Fuller, ed., *The Social Impact of Modern Biology*, Routledge & Kegan Paul, 1971.

14 J. Beckwith and J. King, 'The XYY syndrome: a dangerous myth', *New Scientist*, 64 (923), 14 November 1974, pp. 474–6. This programme was curtailed in 1975 following strong political action by the Boston Science for the People group.

15 Cape, 1973.

16 New York, Dell, 1971; Collins, 1967.

17 See for example L. Tiger and R. Fox, *The Imperial Animal*, Secker & Warburg, 1972.

18 *Civilized Man's Eight Deadly Sins*, Methuen, 1974.

19 *Ethology, the Biology of Behavior*, New York, Holt, Rinehart & Winston, 1970.

20 V. C. Wynne-Edwards, *Animal Dispersion in Relation to Social Behaviour*, Oliver & Boyd, 1962.

21 P. P. G. Bateson, *Are Hierarchies Necessary?*, London, Brain Research Association, 1974.

22 R. Hofstadter, *Social Darwinism in American Thought*, Boston, Beacon Press, 1955.

23 Cape, 1972.

24 *The Eclipse of Reason*, Columbia University Press, 1947.

14 Testing for order and control in the corporate liberal state*

Clarence J. Karier

In 1897, the total capitalization of all corporations, individually valued at a million dollars or more, came to only 170 million. Just three years later, the same figure for total capitalization stood at five billion, and in 1904 at over twenty billion.[1] With this rapid consolidation of corporate capital, there emerged mass production industries with their own needs for standardized producers and consumers.[2] During this same time the last great wave of immigrants flooded into the burgeoning urban centers, manning the rapidly expanding mass production industries. The complex problems which resulted from urbanization, industrialization and immigration were eventually faced by large corporate interests following the lead of Germany in utilizing the state to ameliorate social, economic and political problems. Unlike Germany, however, American social-service institutions at the city, state and federal level were not as responsive to efficient management. Neither the populist nor the immigrant in the urban ghetto was easily managed.[3] The thrust of progressive reformers, working at the city, state and eventually national level, was to reorganize a pluralistic America for efficient, orderly production and consumption of goods and services.

The corporate liberal state which thus emerged during the progressive era[4] has withstood the varied tests and challenges of two world wars, the Great Depression and the Cold War. Each decade of the century brought new and unexpected problems which, in turn, helped shape the direction and growth of that state. While the Depression served to stimulate the growth of corporate-state power along the lines of welfare capitalism, the effect of the Cold War has been to stimulate the growth of that same power along the lines of a military capitalism. In spite of the massive growth and significant changes in direction

that have occurred, there still remain certain characteristics of that state which appear fairly constant. One such characteristic is the cooperative working relationship between big labor unions, corporate wealth and government which had its origin in the National Civic Federation, founded in 1900.

To most members of the National Civic Federation representing labor, government and corporate wealth, the nineteenth century notion of laissez-faire capitalism was a self-destructive concept which had to be replaced by a more comprehensive view of enlightened self-interest. Such a view clearly recognized that if large corporate interests were to survive and effectively prosper in the twentieth century, a cooperative alliance with labor, government and corporate wealth was necessary for the efficient development of both production and consumption of goods and services. Although cut-throat competition had proven to be destructive for large corporate interests, and therefore those interests had taken effective political action by 1918 to protect their own vital concerns, most small entrepreneurs continued to express the rhetoric and live the actuality of laissez-faire capitalism to their own demise well into the twentieth century. In general, the larger corporations took the more enlightened view that ultimately their own best interests were served through a regulatory system which eliminated conflict and stabilized the economic-social system. George W. Perkins of International Harvester put it best when, in arguing for industrial compensation for laborers, he said that cooperation in business 'is taking and should take the place of ruthless competition . . . and that if this new order of things is better for capital and better for the consumer, then in order to succeed permanently it must demonstrate that it is better for the laborer.'[5] While the old liberalism justified individualism and cut-throat competition, the new corporate liberalism which emerged in the thinking of such men as Herbert Croly, Edward Ross, John R. Commons and others

Source: *Educational Theory*, 22 (2), 1972, pp. 154–70, 172–6, 178–80; also appeared in C. J. Karier, P. Violas and J. Spring, eds, *Roots of Crisis* . . . , Rand McNally, 1973, pp. 108–37.

would protect the basic structure of wealth and power in the 'new order' by increasing the standard of living for a larger middle class. Herbert Croly expressed these sentiments well when he suggested that progressive democracy was 'designed to serve as a counter poise to the threat of working class revolution'.[6]

The corporate liberal state which emerged by World War I included an array of bureaucratic regulatory agencies which cooperatively worked with business and labor to achieve that optimal balance of interests for all concerned. The logical thrust of corporate industry, as well as the progressive liberals who tended to dominate the new social sciences, was toward the development of a new scientific management in order to socially engineer for control and order.[7]

Whether it was John R. Commons, Edward A. Ross and Richard T. Ely at the University of Wisconsin; or Samuel Gompers and Andrew Carnegie in the National Civic Federation; or perhaps Jane Addams and Walter Rauschenbusch in the settlements of Chicago and New York, all thought and worked toward a larger, more orderly corporate state, utilizing knowledgeable experts to ameliorate the many varied problems of that state. On the one hand, old public institutions had to be reorganized to increase the effectiveness of administrative and bureaucratic functions at each level of government.[8] On the other hand, in the private sector relatively new organizations were created which effectively channeled corporate wealth toward the support of liberal progressive reform. Philanthropic foundations became a major stimulus for political as well as educational reform. For example, many of the major municipal research bureaus whose urban studies provided the evidence that led to progressive reform of city governments (which indirectly but effectively disenfranchised many immigrant groups) were originally funded by large foundations and later taken over by the city councils.[9] The practice of foundations initiating various kinds of activity and then allowing the public sector to assume control became a common practice of the major foundations dealing with policy formation in America. The profound influence of foundations issues from their ability to flexibly employ large blocks of wealth for research, initiate new activities and facilitate existing programs.[10] As Fred M. Hechinger aptly put it:[11]

> The ideal foundation-sponsored enterprise is one that blazes a new trail, thrives for a while on sponsored dollars, gathers momentum, and is quickly taken over as a permanent program by the local school board, the state education authority, or a university's own budget.

The emergence of foundations to a key role in the policy formation of the corporate liberal state reflected a development of virtually a fourth branch of government which effectively represented the interest of corporate wealth in America. That interest, however, was usually broadly interpreted to include financial support for projects which varied in range all the way from hospital development to research on urban slums. The breadth of support reflected the liberal influence in the dissemination of foundation wealth in attempting to maintain a flexible growing society. One does not need to conjure up a conspiracy theory of history to recognize that the foundations did not consciously, over any extended period of time, support that which threatened to destroy the basic framework of the corporate liberal state. Looking back over the support policy of the foundations in the twentieth century, one can conclude that for the most part, the philosophy behind the policy makers for the foundations appears to have been that of a liberal pragmatist who appreciated the need for survival.

To be sure, America has had a long history of philanthropy; however, the development and creation of large corporate foundations was very much a twentieth century phenomenon. Foundations of varied sorts grew rapidly in numbers from 21 in 1900, to a total of 4,685 in 1959.[12] To the chagrin of many congressmen and taxpayers, the tax-exempt foundations in the United States also grew from 12,295 at the close of 1952 to 42,124 by the end of 1960.[13] From the very beginning of the century, the new philanthropic endeavors of corporate wealth were directed at influencing the course of educational policy. John D. Rockefeller's General Education Board, which received its national charter in 1903, greatly influenced and shaped educational policy for Black America in the South, while the Carnegie Institute of Washington (1904) and the Carnegie Foundation for the Advancement of Teaching (1906) came to play a major role in shaping educational policy in both the South and the North. By 1912, however, John D. Rockefeller and Andrew Carnegie faced an increasingly hostile Congress at the national level and sympathetic Legislative support at the state level. Thus, the incorporation of philanthropic foundations proceeded along lines of least resistance, i.e., at the state rather than the national level. By 1913, a concerned 62nd Congress directed the Industrial Relations Commission to investigate the role of foundations. Charles W. Eliot testified as to the noble purposes and activities of all foundations. As he said:[14]

> I have never known a charitable or educational corporation to do anything which threatened the welfare or the liberties of the American people. I have had no observation of any such corporation—of any such attempts. And I have, on the other hand, seen a great deal of the activity and intelligent promotion of the public welfare by such corporations. There is in them, so far as my experience teaches me, not only no menace, but a very great hope for the Republic.

Nevertheless, after a year of testimony, the majority of the Commission concluded that, 'The domination of men in whose hands the final control of a large part of American industry rests is not limited to their employees, but is being rapidly extended to control the education and social service of the nation.'[15] They went on to point out that the policies of the foundations would inevitably be those of the corporations which sponsored them. While some members of the Commission called for the confiscation of the foundations, liberals such as John R. Commons and Florence Harriman cautioned against such precipitous action. Even though the findings of the commission cut very close to the heart of the problem of power in the corporate liberal state, the commission's findings were ignored as the attention of the Congress and the nation shifted to the war that was developing in Europe.

America's entry into the war brought to a head certain trends which were evolving within the progressive era. Radical populists and socialists were jailed in the name of national unity and a native American Left was demoralized, while the larger corporations found more profitable ways to work with government and a large cadre of social science experts tried out their newfound techniques for the management of the new corporate state. John Dewey, for example, saw in the war the great possibility for 'intelligent administration'[16] based eventually on a solid social science. The corporate liberal state emerged from the war stronger than ever. Progressive liberal reform did not come to an end with the war but rather became institutionalized. Henceforth, most social change would be institutionally controlled and the interest of government, corporate wealth and labor more securely managed. The state which thus emerged included a mass system of public schools which served the manpower needs of that state. One of the more important ways that system served the needs of the state was through the process of rationalizing and standardizing manpower for both production and consumption of goods and services.

For many 'professional educators,' the school as a trainer of producers and consumers necessarily led to a view of the school as a business model or factory.[17] Ellwood P. Cubberley spoke for many professional educators in the twentieth century when he said:[18]

Every manufacturing establishment that turns out a standard product or a series of products of any kind maintains a force of efficiency experts to study methods of procedure and to measure and test the output of its works. Such men ultimately bring the manufacturing establishment large returns, by introducing improvements in processes and procedure, and in training the workmen to produce larger and better output. Our schools are, in a sense, factories in which the raw products (children) are to be shaped and fashioned into products to meet the various demands of life. The specifications for manufacturing come from the demands of twentieth-century civilization, and it is the business of the school to build its pupils according to the specifications laid down. This demands good tools, specialized machinery, continuous measurement of production to see if it is according to specifications, the elimination of waste in manufacture, and a large variety in the output.

The testing movement, financed by corporate foundations helped meet the need for 'continuous measurement' and 'accountability.' It also served as a vital part of the hand which helped fashion the peculiar meritocracy within that state.

Although the testing movement is often viewed as getting under way with the mass testing of 1.7 million men for classification in the armed forces in World War I, the roots of the American testing movement lie deeply imbedded in the American progressive temper which combined its belief in progress, its racial attitudes and its faith in the scientific expert working through the state authority to ameliorate and control the evolutionary progress of the race. While America has had a long history of eugenics advocates, some of the key leaders of the testing movement were the strongest advocates for eugenics control. In the twentieth century the two movements often came together in the same people under the name of 'scientific' testing and for one cause or the other received foundation support.

One such leader of the Eugenics Movement in America was Charles Benedict Davenport who, having seriously studied Galton and Pearson, sought to persuade the new Carnegie Institution of Washington to support a biological experiment station with himself as director. In 1904, he became director of such a station at Cold Spring Harbor on Long Island. As his interest in experiments in animal breeding began to wane, he used his influence as secretary of 'the Committee on Eugenics of the American Breeders Association' to interest others in the study of human heredity. Supported by the donations of Mrs E. H. Harriman, Davenport founded the Eugenics Record Office in 1910, and by 1918, the Carnegie Institution of Washington assumed control. The work of the Record Office was facilitated by the work of committees on: 'Inheritance of Mental Traits' which included Robert M. Yerkes and Edward L. Thorndike; 'Committee on Heredity of Deaf-mutism' with Alexander Graham Bell; 'Committee on Sterilization' with H. H. Laughlin and the 'Committee on the Heredity of the Feeble Minded' which included, among others, H. H. Goddard.

These committees took the lead in identifying those who carried defective germ-plasm and disseminating the propaganda which became necessary to pass sterilization laws. For example, it was Laughlin's

'Committee to Study and Report on the Best Practical Means of Cutting off the Defective Germ Plasm in the American Population,' which reported that 'society must look upon germ-plasm as belonging to society and not solely to the individual who carries it.'[19] Laughlin found that approximately 10 per cent of the American population carried bad seed and called for sterilization as a solution. More precisely he defined these people as 'feebleminded, insane, criminalistic (including the delinquent and wayward), epileptic, inebriate, diseased, blind, deaf, deformed and dependent (including orphans, ne'er-do-wells, the homeless tramps and paupers).'[20] Social character, from murder to prostitution, was associated with intelligence and the nature of one's germ-plasm. The first sterilization law was passed in Indiana in 1907, followed in quick succession by 15 other states. In Wisconsin, such progressives as Edward A. Ross and Charles R. Van Hise, president of the University of Wisconsin, took strong public stands supporting the passage of sterilization laws. America pioneered in the sterilization of mental and social defectives twenty years ahead of other nations.

Between 1907 and 1928, 21 states practiced eugenical sterilization involving over 8,500 people. California under the influence of the Human Betterment Foundation which counted Lewis B. Terman and David Star Jordan as its leading members accounted for 6,200 sterilizations. California's sterilization law was based on race purity as well as criminology. Those who were 'morally and sexually depraved' could be sterilized. Throughout the sterilization movement in America ran a *zeitgeist* reflecting the temper of pious reformers calling for clean living, temperance, fresh air schools as well as sterilization (see Figure 14.1). The use of sterilization for punishment reached the point where laws were introduced which called for sterilization for chicken stealing, car theft, as well as prostitution.[21]

H. H. Goddard, fresh from G. Stanley Hall's seminars at Clark University, translated the Binet-Simon scale (1908) using the test to identify feebleminded at the training school at Vineland, New Jersey. Various scales and tests which were freely used and patterned after the original scale were later proven to lack reliability to the extent that, according to some testers, upward of half the population was feebleminded. From the Binet scale, Goddard went on to publish *The Kallikak Family*, which showed the family history of Martin Kallikak as having sired both a good and bad side to his family tree. The bad side, which began with his involvement with a feebleminded girl, contributed such 'social pests' as 'paupers, criminals, prostitutes and drunkards.' Goddard's next book, *Feeble-mindedness: its Causes and Consequences*, gave further 'scientific' justification

---

The Race Betterment Movement Aims

To Create a New and Superior Race thru EUTHENICS, or Personal and Public Hygiene and EUGENICS, or Race Hygeine.

A thoroughgoing application of PUBLIC AND PERSONAL HYGIENE will save our nation annually:

1,000,000 premature deaths.
2,000,000 lives rendered perpetually useless by sickness.
200,000 infant lives (two-thirds of the baby crop).

The science of EUGENICS intelligently and universally applied would in a few centuries practically

WIPE OUT

Idiocy Insanity Imbecility Epilepsy

and a score of other hereditary disorders, and create a race of HUMAN THOROUGHBREDS such as the world has never seen.

Methods of Race Betterment

Simple and Natural Habits of Life.

Out-of-Door Life Day and Night, Fresh-Air Schools, Playgrounds, Out-of-Door Gymnasiums, etc.

Total Abstinence from the Use of Alcohol and Other Drugs.

Eugenic Marriages.

Medical Certificates before Marriage.

Health Inspection of Schools.

Periodical Medical Examinations.

Vigorous Campaign of Education in Health and Eugenics.

Eugenic Registry.

Sterilization or Isolation of Defectives.

Evidences of Race Degeneracy

Increase of Degenerative Diseases . . .
{ Cancer
Insanity
Diseases of Heart and Blood Vessels
Diseases of Kidneys
Most Chronic Diseases
Diabetes }

Increase of Defectives
{ Idiots
Imbeciles
Morons
Criminals
Inebriates
Paupers }

Diminishing Individual Longevity

Diminished Birth Rate

Disappearance, Complete or Partial, of Various Bodily Organs . . . .
{ According to Wiedersheim there are more than two hundred such changes in the structures of the body. }

Figure 14.1

MARTIN KALLIKAK

He dallied with
a feeble-minded
tavern girl

He married a
worthy Quakeress

She bore a son
known as ' Old Horror'
who had ten children

She bore
seven upright
worthy children

From ' Old Horror's '
ten children came hundreds
of the lowest types of
human beings

From these seven worthy
children came hundreds
of the highest types
of human beings

Figure 14.2 The influence
of heredity is illustrated
by the 'good' and the
'bad' Kallikaks (from
Henry E. Garrett, *General
Psychology*, New York,
American Book Co., 1955,
p. 65; also in 2nd ed.,
1961, p. 56)

to the notion of the relationship between feeble-mindedness and moral character.

Interestingly enough, the liberal tradition in America from Jefferson on usually assumed a positive relationship between 'talent and virtue.' It was then not surprising to find people assuming that anyone with less talent will have less virtue. This relationship was assumed in the passage of most sterilization laws. Society would rid itself of not only the genetic defective, but more importantly, the socially undesirable. Laughlin, Goddard, Terman and Thorndike all made similar assumptions. Terman argued that the feebleminded were incapable of moral judgements and, therefore, could only be viewed as potential criminals. He said:[22]

all feeble-minded are at least potential criminals. That every feeble-minded woman is a potential prostitute would hardly be disputed by anyone. Moral judgment, like business judgment, social judgment or any other kind of higher thought process, is a function of intelligence.

The same thinking which guided Terman to find a lower morality among those of lesser intelligence had its mirror image in the work of Edward L. Thorndike, who found a higher morality among those with greater intelligence. Thorndike was convinced that, 'To him that hath a superior intellect is given also on the average a superior character.'[23] The sterilization solution to moral behavior problems and the improvement of intelligence continued to be advocated by Thorndike, as well as by his pupils. By 1940, in his last major work, he concluded that:[24]

> By selective breeding supported by a suitable environment we can have a world in which all men will equal the top ten per cent of present men. One sure service of the *able* and *good* is to beget and rear offspring. One sure service (about the only one) which the inferior and vicious can perform is to prevent their genes from survival.

The association of inferior with vicious and intelligence with goodness continued to appear in the psychology textbooks. Henry E. Garrett, a former student and fellow colleague with whom Thorndike was associated, who won a 'reputation for eminence,'[25] continued to project the story of Martin Kallikak in terms of goods and bads in his textbook on *General Psychology* as late as 1955. Just in case someone might miss the point, the children of the feebleminded tavern girl were pictured as having horns, while the 'highest types of human beings,' were portrayed as solid Puritan types (see Figure 14.2).[26]

This view of the Kallikaks was no accident. As chairman of Columbia's department of psychology for sixteen years and as past president of the American Psychological Association, as well as a member of the National Research Council, Garrett was in sympathy with Thorndike's views on the place of the 'inferior and vicious' in American life. By 1966, as a Professor Emeritus from Columbia, in the midst of the civil rights movement, he produced a series of pamphlets which drew out what he believed to be the implications of sixty years of testing in America. Sponsored by the Patrick Henry Press, over 500,000 copies of his pamphlets were distributed free of charge to American teachers. In *How Classroom Desegregation Will Work*; *Children Black and White*; and especially in *Breeding Down*, Garrett justified American racism on 'scientific' grounds. Going back to Davenport and the Eugenics Record Office as well as Terman's work and others, Garrett argued:[27]

> You can no more mix the two races and maintain the standards of White civilization than you can add 80 (the average IQ of Negroes) and 100 (average IQ of Whites), divide by two and get 100. What you would get would be a race of 90s, and it is that 10 per cent differential that spells the difference between a spire and a mud hut; 10 per cent—or less—is the margin of

civilization's 'profit'; it is the difference between a cultured society and savagery.

> Therefore, it follows, if miscegenation would be bad for White people, it would be bad for Negroes as well. For, if leadership is destroyed, all is destroyed

He went on to point out that the Black man is at least 200,000 years behind the White and that intermarriage, as well as desegregation would destroy what genetic lead the White man had achieved through 'hard won struggle' and 'fortitudinous evolution.' The state, he argued, 'can and should prohibit miscegenation, just as they ban marriage of the feeble-minded, the insane and various undesirables. Just as they outlaw incest.'[28]

The style and content of Garrett's arguments were but echoes of similar arguments developed earlier by Davenport, Laughlin, Terman, Brigham, Yerkes, and Thorndike. For example, C. C. Brigham spoke of the superior Nordic draftees of World War I and seriously worried about inferior germ-plasm of the Alpine, Mediterranean and Negro races in *A Study of American Intelligence*.[29] What disturbed Brigham as well as the US Congress was, of course, the fact that 70 per cent of the total immigration in the early 1920s was coming from Alpine and Mediterranean racial stock. H. H. Laughlin of the Carnegie Foundation of Washington provided the scientific evidence to the Congress in his report, 'An Analysis of America's Melting Pot.' Using information from the army tests and from his Eugenics Record Office dealing with the insane and feeble-minded, Laughlin built a case that the new immigrant from Southern Europe was of inferior racial stock by virtue of the numbers that appeared as wards of the state.[30]

Supported by the Commonwealth Fund, Lewis M. Terman reported similar evidence from his study. Addressing the National Education Association at Oakland, California on July 2 1923, he expressed concern about the fecundity of the superior races. As he put it:[31]

> The racial stocks most prolific of gifted children are those from northern and western Europe, and the Jewish. The least prolific are the Mediterranean races, the Mexicans and the Negroes. The fecundity of the family stocks from which our gifted children come appears to be definitely on the wane . . . It has been figured that if the present differential birth rate continues, 1,000 Harvard graduates will at the end of 200 years have but 50 descendants, while in the same period 1,000 South Italians will have multiplied to 100,000.

It was this kind of 'scientific' data derived from the testing and Eugenics Movement which entered into the dialogue which led to the restrictive immigration quota of 1924, that clearly discriminated against southern Europeans.

After World War I America had moved toward a more restrictive immigration policy. While small manufacturers, represented by the National Association of Manufacturers and Chamber of Commerce, tended to favor a sliding-door policy which would open according to the labor needs of the small manufacturers, most larger manufacturers and labor unions, represented by the National Civic Federation, favored restricting immigration. Perhaps the motivation was best stated by Edward A. Filene, a pioneer in employee management, of Boston, when he said:[32]

Employers do not need an increased labor supply, since increased use of labor-saving machinery and elimination of waste in production and distribution will for many years reduce costs more rapidly than wages increase, and so prevent undue domination of labor.

The Carnegie money that Laughlin used in his campaign for greater restrictions was ultimately money well spent in the interest of the larger manufacturer. Nevertheless, the rhetoric of the times and of the testers was, perhaps, best put when President Coolidge proclaimed, 'America must be kept American.'

The nativism, racism, elitism and social class bias which were so much a part of the testing and Eugenics Movement in America were, in a broader sense, part of that *zeitgeist* which was America. This was the land of the Ku Klux Klan, the red scare, the Sacco-Vanzetti and Scopes trials as well as the land of real opportunity for millions of immigrants. It was this kind of contradictory base in which the corporate liberal state took firm root, building a kind of meritocracy that even Plato could not have envisioned. Just as Plato ascribed certain virtues to certain occupational classes, so too, Lewis Terman assigned numbers which stood for virtue to certain occupational classes. It was clear to Terman that America was the land of opportunity, where the best excelled, and the inferior found themselves on the lower rungs of the occupational order. Designing the Stanford-Binet intelligence test, Terman developed questions which were based on presumed progressive difficulty in performing tasks which he believed were necessary for achievement in ascending the hierarchical occupational structure. He then proceeded to find that according to the results of his tests the intelligence of different occupational classes fits his ascending hierarchy. It was little wonder that IQ reflected social class bias. It was, in fact, based on the social class order. Terman believed that, for the most part, people were at that level because of heredity and not social environment. He said:[33]

Preliminary investigations indicate that an IQ below 70 rarely permits anything better than unskilled labor; that the range from 70 to 80 is preeminently that of semi-skilled labor, from 80 to 100 that of the skilled or ordinary clerical labor, from 100 to 110 or 115 that of the semi-professional pursuits; and that above all these are the grades of intelligence which permit one to enter the professions or the larger fields of business. Intelligence tests can tell us whether a child's native brightness corresponds more nearly to the median of (1) the professional classes, (2) those in the semi-professional pursuits, (3) ordinary skilled workers, (4) semi-skilled workers, or (5) unskilled laborers. This information will be of great value in planning the education of a particular child and also in planning the differentiated curriculum here recommended.

Plato had three classes and Terman had five; both maintained the 'myth of the metals' and both advocated a differentiated curriculum to meet the needs of the individuals involved. Terman so completely accepted the assumption of the social class meritocracy and the tests which were based on that meritocracy that he never seemed to even wonder why, in his own study of the gifted: 'The professional and semi-professional classes together account for more than 80 per cent. The unskilled labor classes furnish but a paltry 1 per cent or 2 per cent.'[34]

Social class was not the only problem with the tests. Whether one reads Terman's Stanford-Binet or his Group Test of Mental Ability or the Stanford Achievement Tests, the army tests, or the National Intelligence Tests,[35] certain characteristics emerge. They all reflect the euphemisms, the homilies and the morals which were, indeed, the stock and trade of *Poor Richard's Almanac*, Noah Webster's Blueback *Speller*, as well as *McGuffey's Readers*. The child who grew up in a home and attended a school where these things were in common usage stood in distinct advantage to the newly arrived immigrant child. At a time when over half the children in American schools were either immigrants or children of immigrants, this movement represented discrimination in a massive way.

By 1922, Walter Lippman, in a series of six articles for *The New Republic* questioned whether intelligence is fixed by heredity and whether the tests actually measure intelligence.[36] While Lippman challenged the validity of the test, he did not attack the presumption of meritocracy itself. Although Lippman seemed to get the best of the argument, Terman fell back to the high ground of the condescending professional expert who saw little need to debate proven 'scientific' principles.[37]

Conscious of the social implications of their work, Goddard, Terman and Thorndike viewed themselves as great benefactors of society. The concern for social order and rule by the intelligent elite was ever present in their writings. Goddard put it bluntly when he argued that, 'The disturbing fear is that the masses—the seventy or even eighty-six million—will take matters into their own hands.'[38] The 'four million' of 'superior intelligence' must direct the masses. Throughout the literature of this period the fear of the masses appears as a constant theme. Under such circumstances one could hardly turn to the masses for an enlightened solution. The assumed role of the 'professional' scientific expert was to lead the masses out of the irrational morass of ignorance. The definition of democracy had changed. It no longer meant rule by the people, but rather rule by the intelligent. As Thorndike put it, 'The argument for democracy is not that it gives power to men without distinction, but that it gives greater freedom for ability and character to attain power.'[39]

Luckily, mankind's wealth-power-ability and character were positively correlated. This, indeed, was not only Plato's ideal, but the testers' view of the meritocracy which they in fact were fashioning. Late in life, Thorndike reflected on these concerns and said:[40]

> It is the great good fortune of mankind that there is a substantial positive correlation between intelligence and morality, including good will toward one's fellows. Consequently our superiors in ability are on the average our benefactors, and it is often safer to trust our interests to them than to ourselves. No group of men can be expected to act one hundred per cent in the interest of mankind, but this group of the ablest men will come nearest to the ideal.

To be sure, there have been and still are inequities between men of intelligence and of wealth, Thorndike argued, but through the 'beneficence of such men as Carnegie and Rockefeller,' this discrepancy had been somewhat overcome.[41]

Although Thorndike was directly involved in the Army classification testing during World War I and the creation of the National Intelligence Test after the war, all of which skyrocketed the testing movement in American schools, perhaps his most profound influence on American schools came through his work in organizing the classroom curriculum. His name appears on approximately 50 books and 450 monographs and articles, including the much used Thorndike *Dictionary*. He wrote many of the textbooks, tests, achievement scales and teachers' manuals. In short, he told the school teachers what to teach and how to teach it, and in turn, how to evaluate it. Much of his work was, indeed, made possible through the beneficence of Carnegie. The Carnegie Foundation from 1922 to 1938 had made grants supporting his work totaling approximately $325,000.[42] It was men like Thorndike, Terman and Goddard, supported by corporate wealth,[43] who successfully persuaded teachers, administrators and lay school boards to classify and standardize the school's curriculum with a differentiated track system based on ability and values of the corporate liberal society. The structure of that society was

based, then, on an assumed meritocracy, a meritocracy of White middle class, management-oriented professionals.

The test discriminated against members of the lower class—Southern Europeans and Blacks—indirectly by what they seemed to leave out, but more directly by what they included; for example: On a Stanford-Binet (1960 revision), a six-year-old child is asked the question, 'Which is prettier?'[44] and must select the Nordic Anglo Saxon type to be correct. If, however, the child is perhaps a Mexican American or of Southern European descent, has looked at himself in a mirror and has a reasonably healthy respect for himself, he will pick the wrong answer. Worse yet is the child who recognizes what a 'repressive society' calls the 'right' answer and has been socialized enough to sacrifice himself for a higher score (see Figure 14.3). The same is true in the case of the Black six-year-old (see Figure 14.4). Neither

Figure 14.3 Stanford-Binet Intelligence Scale, 1960 (L-M IV-6, 1 card C)

Figure 14.4 Stanford-Binet Intelligence Scale, 1960 (L-M IV-6, 1 card A)

Blacks nor Southern Europeans were beautiful according to the authors of the Stanford-Binet, but then, there was no beauty in these people when Goddard, Laughlin, Terman,[45] Thorndike and Garrett called for the sterilization of the 'socially inadequate,' the discriminatory closing of immigration, the tracking organization of the American school, or for that matter, defined their place in the meritocracy.

The test, then, discriminated in content against particular groups in the very questions that were used as well as the questions that were not used with respect to particular minority experiences. While some educational psychologists sought to eliminate bias from the content of the test, as well as introduce a broader cultural basis for the test, others sought the impossible: a culturally free IQ test. Still other educational psychologists, hard pressed to define intelligence, fell back to the assertion that it was simply that which the tests measured. Although many gave up their concern about intelligence, others argued that the various intelligence tests were achievement tests which could also be good predictors of success within both the corporate society and the bureaucratic school system which served that society. At this point, the testers had come full circle ending up where Terman started.

Terman's tests were based on an occupational hierarchy which was, in fact, the social class system of the corporate liberal state which was then emerging. The many varied tests, all the way from IQ to personality and scholastic achievement, periodically brought up-to-date, would serve a vital part in rationalizing the social class system. The tests also created the illusion of objectivity which on the one side served the needs of the 'professional' educators to be 'scientific,' and on the other side served the need of the system for a myth which could convince the lower classes that their station in life was part of the natural order of things. For many, the myth had apparently worked. In 1965, the Russell Sage Foundation issued a report entitled, *Experiences and Attitudes of American Adults Concerning Standardized Intelligence Tests*.[46] Some of the major findings of that report indicated that the effects of the tests on social classes were 'strong and consistent' and that while 'the upper class respondent is more likely to favor the use of tests than the lower class respondent,' the 'lower class respondent is more likely to see intelligence tests measuring inborn intelligence.'[47]

The lower class American adult was, indeed, a product of fifty years of testing. He had been channeled through an intricate bureaucratic educational system which, in the name of meeting his individual needs, classified and tracked him into an occupation appropriate to his socio-economic class status. The tragic character of this phenomenon was not only that the lower class learned to believe in the system, but worse, through internalizing that set of beliefs, made it work. It worked because the lowered self-image which the school and society reinforced[48] on the lower class child did result in lower achievement. A normal child objectified as subnormal and treated by the teacher and the school as subnormal will almost surely behave as a subnormal child. Likewise, the lower class child who is taught in many ways to doubt his own intelligence can be expected to exhibit a lower achievement level than those children who are

repeatedly reminded that they are made of superior clay,[49] and therefore, are of superior worth.

Intelligence and achievement tests used throughout American society are a vital part of the infrastructure which serves to stabilize and order the values of that society.[50] Arthur R. Jensen put it well when he said: 'Had the first IQ tests been devised in a hunting culture, "general intelligence" might well have turned out to involve visual acuity and running speed, rather than vocabulary and symbol manipulation.'[51] Jensen, as Terman and others, argued that:[52]

> what we now 'mean' by intelligence is something like the probability of acceptable performance (given the opportunity) in occupations varying in social status.
>
> So we see that the prestige hierarchy of occupations is a reliable objective reality in our society. To this should be added the fact that there is undoubtedly some relationship between the levels of the hierarchy and the occupations' intrinsic desirability, or gratification to the individual engaged in them. Even if all occupations paid alike and received equal respect and acclaim, some occupations would still be viewed as more desirable than others, which would make for competition, selection, and again, a kind of prestige hierarchy.

The hierarchy, Jensen argued, was inevitable because, 'Most persons would agree that painting pictures is more satisfying than painting barns, and conducting a symphony orchestra is more exciting than directing traffic.'[53] While the hierarchy was culturally determined, it is clear that certain values which Jensen preferred appeared to him more intrinsic than others. Nevertheless, he admitted that, 'We have to face it: the assortment of persons into occupational roles simply is not "fair" in any absolute sense. The best we can hope for is that true merit, given equality of opportunity, acts as the basis for the natural assorting process.'[54] Herein lies the crucial weakness of the argument. Given the current racist, economic, and socially elitist society where wealth, power and educational privilege are so unevenly distributed, what does it mean, then, to assume 'equality of opportunity' and 'hope' that 'true merit' will somehow result from a 'natural assorting process'?

Jensen, like Thorndike and Terman before him, assumed an ideal liberal community where 'equality of opportunity' balanced with lively competition produced a social system where 'true' merit was rewarded. Although the 'Jefferson-Conant' ideal of the good community is in itself questionable, the problem was compounded when the ideal society was confused with the real society. In spite of Terman, Thorndike and Jensen's idealized assumptions about 'equal opportunity' and 'natural assorting process,' all based their objective data on the real world of economic and social privilege. With highly questionable sociological data they proceeded to even more questionable biological conclusions. The leap from sociology to genetics was an act of faith.

Most testers refused to admit the possibility that they were, perhaps, servants of privilege, power and status, and preferred instead to believe and 'hope' that what they were measuring was, in fact, true 'merit.' This was also an act of faith, a faith based on the belief that somehow the 'prestige hierarchy of occupations' and the people in it who provided the objective standard upon which the tests were based, were there not because of privilege, wealth, power status and violence, but because of superior talent and virtue. This was a fundamental axiom in the liberal's faith in the meritocracy which emerged in twentieth century American education.

Throughout this century, within this liberal faith, there emerged a series of doctrinal disputes engaging the attention of millions of people. The nature-nurture argument was one such continuous dispute from Galton to Jensen. The course of this dispute reflected little more than increasing refinement o'' statistical techniques and accumulation of data on both sides of the issue. Given the extent of unprovable propositions on both sides of the issue, one finds the choice between heredity or environment more a matter of faith than hard evidence. In many respects, the nature-nurture argument is a misleading issue. One can accept a strong hereditarian position and still advocate political, economic and social equality just as one might accept a strong environmentalist position and still argue for political, economic and social inequality. There is in fact no inherent logic either in the mind of man or in the universe which predetermines that differences in intellectual ability necessarily should mean differences in social power. Why for example should one more favorably be rewarded because, through no effort of his own, he happened to inherit a superior intelligence or because he happened to be born into a superior social environment. Repeatedly, from Terman to Herrnstein, psychologists have attempted to link ability to the meritocracy without questioning the values inherent in the meritocratic principle itself.[55]

Most psychologists did not take their position to its logical conclusion, for to do so would be to question not only the ideal assumption upon which the meritocracy rests (such as equal opportunity and the inherent value of competition), but to further question the hierarchy of values which undergird the work of the professional knowledgeable expert in the liberal society. The professional expert, with his esoteric knowledge, is a vital element in both the creation and maintenance of the corporate merit-ocracy. His economic and political self interest as well as his very survival is at stake. Thus, it is under-standable that so few in the professional middle class are disturbed by the presumed meritocracy, or are seriously inclined to question it. Those who have done well by the system can hardly be expected to be its best critics. To be sure, some are willing to

suggest that we ought to look at the social system from the bottom up, and out of humanitarian motives, or perhaps survival motives, allow more opportunity for those who have been cut out of the system, but few are willing to doubt critically the validity, if not the equity, of the system itself. (. . .)

Virtually all educational debate seemed to end with that criteria. The need to classify and standardize an entire nation so as to efficiently maximize productivity had become a reality by 1970.[56] There were problems, however, in both the way in which people were tested and classified and the way in which this classification system was used to restrict employment opportunities within the corporate liberal state. As various institutions within that state increasingly used tests and educational requirements more as a vehicle for keeping people out of specific occupations rather than a test of actual job performance, the credentialing system became strained and inflated to the point where employers could discriminate against minority groups with relative ease.[57] By 1971, the United States Supreme Court struck down the personnel policies of Duke Power Company's Dan River power station which required a high school diploma or acceptable performance on two standardized tests. The company had difficulty showing any clear relationship between these educational requirements and actual job performance. Even though this decision sent a cold chill through those private companies who serviced the 55 million dollar educational testing business, the court did not attack the testing procedure but merely the test's relationships to actual job performance. The court declared that the employer who uses personnel tests must show a 'manifest relationship' of such tests to the 'employment in question.' Tests, then, were used to discriminate against children in their schools and against adults in their occupations. While some might see in these events minor problems in Condorcet's dream of progress, others saw it as an Orwellian nightmare of 'double think.' Perhaps they were the same.

By 1965, the Carnegie Foundation under the leadership of Francis Keppel, John Gardner and James B. Conant initiated the development of a national testing program called, 'A National Assessment of Educational Progress.' Reminiscent of Ellwood Cubberley's concern for 'continuous measurement of production,' Conant's national assessment filled the current efficiency need for 'accountability.' Somewhat akin to the school's surveys of the earlier efficiency movement which concentrated on local educational production, national assessment would give indications of regional productivity. While the earlier movement was characterized by the stopwatch and the efficiency expert, the new movement was characterized by the computer and the system's analyzer. Employing the same statistical sampling techniques used to measure industrial productivity, some system analyzers suggested that eventually a 'growth' national product index could be developed to measure the progress of American schools. National Assessment was advocated by Conant, in part at least because of the difficulty he had in obtaining hard data when he did the earlier reports on the *American High School, Junior High School* and *Teacher Education.* This concern, coupled with his interest in the development of a commission which would serve as a vehicle to shape national educational policy led him to propose, while financially supported by the Carnegie and Danforth Foundations, the development of the 'Compact of the States.'[58] The 'Compact' provided the 'quasi-public' vehicles through which national testing proceeded without too much public interference. Reflecting back over his many and varied educational accomplishments, Conant in *My Several Lives* counted the 'Compact' as his 'greatest' achievement.

On the surface it might appear that American education is locally controlled by elected boards and that at the national level a power vacuum exists due to the reluctance of the American people to create a national system of education. This, however, is misleading. There does exist within the corporate liberal state quasi-public bureaucracy of boards, compacts, councils and commissions which serve to shape policy by giving and withholding both public and private funds at key points in the system. The American Council on Education is one such agency through which hundreds of philanthropic foundations, private businesses and public colleges and universities work in establishing nation-wide educational policy.[59] In many ways, the Council has acted as both a meeting ground for what appear disparate interests, but also a conduit for channeling funds into selected areas of higher education, and thereby effectively shaping practice as well as policy.

While World War I provided the national stimulus for the testing movement, foundations like the Carnegie Foundation for the Advancement of Teaching, the Common Wealth Fund, the Graduate Records Office of the Carnegie Foundation and others, provided the funds which sustained and propelled the movement, it was World War II which demonstrated the usefulness of systems analysis and the efficient need for systematic overall manpower planning[60] and the crucial need for a centralized testing service.

In 1946–7, the American Council on Education received a report from the Carnegie Foundation for the Advancement of Teaching recommending the consolidation of a number of testing units which had developed over the years such as the College Entrance Examination Board and the Graduate Records Office.[61] Under a self-perpetuating board of trustees which included people drawn from the American Council on Education, the foundations, public and private colleges as well as business and government, the Educational Testing Service was born with a grant from the Carnegie Foundation. The rapid growth of ETS is reflected in its operating budget. Operational expenses for ETS increased from approximately two million dollars in 1947 to twenty-nine million seven hundred thousand dollars by 1969.[62] By 1969, ETS, a private non-profit organization, provided the tests taken by millions of Americans which determined their eligibility, all the way from the service academies to the Peace Corps, colleges and universities, as well as the professions.[63] The doorway to virtually every profession in the corporate liberal state came under the influence and control of the new organization. It is interesting, but not unusual, that such power would be exercised by private rather than public boards. This is one of the key characteristics of this state.

That fourth branch of government which was born in the progressive era, representing liberal corporate interests, i.e. foundations, has flexibly and effectively served to maintain the interests of corporate wealth through the support and maintenance of the liberal state. Through the varied shifting support policy of the foundations in the twentieth century, one need not conjure up a conspiracy theory in order to perceive some rather consistent practices which emerge. The key is enlightened self-interest. The foundation trustees and executives were intelligent men who recognized their own interests in what they viewed as a progressively developing society. It was in the interest of what they perceived as racial progress that the Carnegie Foundation of Washington supported the Laughlin studies used to close immigration, and in the interest of educational progress that they supported the testing movement after the war and the standardization of American education along the values laid down by Thorndike. Whether it was Terman calling for special education for the gifted, or Conant founding the Educational Testing Service, all served to classify, standardize and rationalize human beings to serve the productive interests of a society essentially controlled by wealth, privilege and status.

The tests, whether measuring intelligence or achievement, as well as the meritocracy itself, served to so mask power as to effectively immobilize any real revolutionary opposition. If a man truly believes that he has a marginal standard of living because he is inferior, he is less likely to take violent measures against that social system than if he believes his condition a product of social privilege. In the nineteenth century, Daniel Webster said that 'Public education is a wise and liberal system of police, by which property, and life, and the peace of society are secured.' In the twentieth century, a similar condition prevails. In this sense, the foundations' deep involvement in educational policy whether it was the Ford Foundation in educational television or the Carnegie Foundation in testing or the Rockefeller Foundation in Black education, all had an interest in an effective, efficiently managed system. The foundations' management of educational policy in the twentieth century has been clearly at the cutting edge of every educational reform from the 'Carnegie Unit' to the 'open classroom.'

Even the rhetoric which engages the professional educators seems fairly well managed. Throughout the last four decades, the pendulum of educational rhetoric has swung from the child-centered discussion of the thirties to the society-determined needs of the fifties, then again, to the child-centered needs of the seventies. In the thirties, the Carnegie Foundation supported the Progressive Education Association with over four million dollars, while in the fifties, James Conant's study of American schools was supported by Carnegie as was the project which culminated in Charles Silberman's *Crisis in the Classroom* in the 1970s. It is interesting to note that during periods of labor surplus, our educational rhetoric tends to be child-centered, while in periods of shortage, the rhetoric shifts to society-oriented needs. This may be the propelling factor. It is interesting, however, that when the rhetoric becomes so heated that people can be heard suggesting that we do away with the system or radically change it, the Carnegie Foundation supported James Conant, who, in effect, said the system was basically sound but then co-opted the rhetoric of the attackers to recommend limited change. It was, after all, the survival of the system which Conant had in mind when he spoke of social dynamite in the ghettoes. By the 1970s, when most manpower projections clearly indicated surplus of labor for the next decade, the educational reform rhetoric shifted from training scientists and engineers to open classrooms. Again, critics could be heard suggesting that the system be radically altered if not abolished, and once again, the Carnegie Foundation supported a study by Silberman which, in effect, said that the system was basically sound but needed some reforming. Once again, the rhetoric of the attackers was coopted for limited change. While the Carnegie Foundation obviously does not control the pendulum, they have played a major role in managing the rhetoric at critical points when the system is in acute danger.[64] It is this function as governor of the educational machinery which prevents destructive unmanaged revolution that foundations have performed so well. One, then, is left to ponder the question of whether Charles W. Eliot was right when testifying before Congress (1913) that he had 'never known a charitable or educational corporation to do anything which threatened the welfare or the liberties of the American people.' Or was the majority of that committee which heard his testimony perhaps more correct when they concluded that the policies of the foundations would inevitably be those of the corporations which sponsored them, and that 'The domination of men in whose hands the final control of a large part of American industry rests is not limited to their employees, but is being extended to control the education and social services of the nation.'

Notes

* For much of the research in this essay I am indebted to the research assistance of Russell Marks at the University of Illinois. For calling my attention to the material used in this article which reflects the racial bias of the currently used Stanford-Binet test, I am also indebted to La Monte Wyche.

1 Charles Forcey, *The Crossroads of Liberalism*, Oxford University Press, 1961, p. xiv.

2 Robert H. Wiebe, *The Search for Order*, New York, Hill & Wang, 1967.

3 See Norman Pollack, *The Populist Response to Industrial America*, New York, W. W. Norton, 1962. Also see William Appleman Williams, *The Roots of the Modern American Empire*, New York, Random House, 1969.

4 See James Weinstein, *The Corporate Ideal in the Liberal State*, Boston, Beacon Press, 1968. Also see Gabriel Kolko, *The Triumph of Conservatism: A Reinterpretation of American History 1900–1916*, New York, Free Press, 1963.

5 As quoted in Weinstein, op.cit., p. 45.

6 ibid., p. xi.

7 See Loren Baritz, *The Servants of Power*, New York, Wiley, 1960.

8 Increased efficiency in city, state and federal government often meant a corresponding decrease in political influence on the part of the poor and the disinherited. See Samuel P. Hayes, 'The politics of reform in municipal government in the progressive era', in Alexander B. Callon, Jr, ed., *American Urban History*, New York, Oxford University Press, 1969.

9 See Norman N. Gill, *Municipal Research Bureaus*, Washington, DC, American Council on Public Affairs, 1944, pp. 15–17.

10 See David W. Eakins, 'The Development of Corporate Liberal Policy Research in the United States, 1885–1965', unpublished PhD dissertation, University of Wisconsin, 1966. Also see James Weinstein, *The Corporate Ideal in the Liberal State 1900–1918*, Boston, Beacon Press, 1968.

11 Warren Weaver, *U.S. Philanthropic Foundations*, New York, Harper & Row, 1967, p. 245.

12 John Lankford, *Congress and the Foundations in the Twentieth Century*, Wisconsin State University—River Falls, 1964, pp. 6, 92.

13 ibid., p. 92.

14 As quoted in ibid., p. 29.

15 As quoted in ibid., p. 31.

16 See 'A new social science', *The New Republic*, 14, no. 79, 6 April 1918.

17 For a discussion of the efficiency movement in business and industry, see Samuel Haber, *Efficiency and Uplift: Scientific Management in the Progressive Era 1890–1920*, University of Chicago Press, 1964. For a similar discussion in education, see Raymond Callahan, *Education and the Cult of Efficiency*, University of Chicago Press, 1962.

18 *Public School Administration*, Boston, Houghton Mifflin, 1916, p. 338.

19 As quoted in Mark H. Haller, *Eugenics*, Rutgers University Press, 1963, p. 133.

20 ibid., p. 133.

21 State authority is still being used to sterilize people. On 4 March 1971 a bill was introduced into the Illinois Legislature which required sterilization of a mother who had two or more children while on welfare roles before that mother could draw further support. The argument, however, is no longer based on racial purity or punishment, but rather more on the economic burden to society. While the constitutionality of pauper sterilization might be questionable, the right of the state to sterilize for eugenics purposes was settled in the Buck v. Bell case when Justice Holmes argued: 'The principle that sustains compulsory vaccination is broad enough to cover the cutting of the Fallopian tubes . . . three generations of imbeciles are enough,' as quoted in Haller, *Eugenics*, p. 129.

22 *The Measurement of Intelligence*, Boston, Houghton Mifflin, 1916, p. 11.

23 'Intelligence and its uses', *Harper's*, vol. 140, January 1920, p. 233.

24 *Human Nature and the Social Order*, New York, Macmillan 1940, p. 957. Italics added.

25 Geraldine Joncich, *The Sane Positivist*, Wesleyan University Press, 1968, p. 443.

26 See Russell Marks' paper delivered at the AERA, spring 1971, 'Testing for Social Control'.

27 *Breeding Down* (pamphlet), Richmond, Patrick Henry Press, undated, p. 10.

28 ibid., p. 17

29 Princeton University Press, 1923, pp. 159, 207, 210. It should be noted that in the decade of the 1930s, however, Brigham went through considerable effort to refute his former work.

30 See US Congress, House Committee on Immigration and Naturalization, *Europe as an Emigrant-Exporting Continent and the United States as an Immigrant-Receiving Nation*, by H. H. Laughlin, 68th Congress, 1st Session, 8 March 1924, p. 1311.

31 'The conservation of talent', *School and Society*, 19 (483), 29 March 1924, p. 363.

32 As quoted by Robert DeC. Ward, 'Our new immigration policy', *Foreign Affairs*, September 1924, p. 104.

33 *Intelligence Tests and School Reorganization*, New York, World Book Co., 1923, pp. 27–28.

34 'The conservation of talent', p. 363.

35 The National Intelligence Test interestingly enough was standardized on army officers and used in the school after World War I.

36 'A future for the tests', *The New Republic*, 29 November 1922. Also see 'The mental age of Americans', 25 October 1922; 'The mystery of the "A Men"', 1 November 1922; 'The reliability of intelligence tests', 8 November 1922; 'The abuse of tests', 15 November 1922; 'Tests of hereditary intelligence', 22 November 1922.

37 See Lewis M. Terman, 'The great conspiracy', *The New Republic*, 27 December 1922, p. 117.

38 H. H. Goddard, *Human Efficiency and Levels of Intelligence*, Princeton University Press, 1920, p. 97. It is interesting to note that the total population of the United States in 1920 was 105.7 million.

39 'Intelligence and its uses', p. 235.

40 'How may we improve the selection, training and life work of leaders?', *Addresses Delivered Before the 5th Conference on Educational Policies*, New York Teachers College, Columbia University Press, 1939, p. 32.

41 ibid., p. 31.

42 US House, *Special Committee to Investigate Tax Exempt Foundations Summary of Activities*, 9 June 1954, p. 20.

43 It should be noted here that up to 1954, the Carnegie Foundation, alone, had invested $6,424,000 in testing (ibid., p. 78).

44 It should be noted here that this is the latest revision of the Stanford-Binet Intelligence Test.

45 Of this group, only Terman wavered from the original position. When he wrote his autobiography in 1932 he had stated his belief, 'That the major differences between children of high and low IQ and the major differences in the intelligence test-scores of certain races, as Negroes and whites will never be fully accounted for on the environmental hypothesis.' By 1951, he penciled in around that statement, 'I am less sure of this now,' and in 1955, again another note said, 'I'm still less sure.' See Ernest R. Hilgard, 'Lewis Madison Terman', *American Journal of Psychology*, 1957.

46 Orville G. Brim, John Neulinger and David C. Glass, Technical Report no. 1 on the Social Consequences of Testing, *Experiences and Attitudes of American Adults Concerning Standardized Intelligence Tests*, New York, Russell Sage Foundation, 1965.

47 ibid., p. 89.

48 ibid. One of the findings was that a member of the lower class 'estimates his intelligence as inferior to others.'

49 For an analysis of the way the idea of self-fulfilling prophecy works, see R. Rosenthal and L. Jacobson, 'Self-fulfilling prophecies in the classroom: teachers' expectations as unintended determinants of pupils' intellectual competence', in M. Deutsch, I. Katz and A. R. Jensen, eds, *Social Class, Race and Psychological Development*, Holt, Rinehart & Winston, 1968.

50 For an analysis of the role of psychologists in business, see Loren Baritz, *The Servants of Power*.

51 'How much can we boost IQ and scholastic achievement?', *Harvard Educational Review*, 39 (1), winter 1969, p. 14.

52 ibid., pp. 14–15.

53 ibid., p. 15.

54 ibid.

55 For these particular ideas on the implications of the nature-nurture controversy I am indebted to Russell Marks. For Herrnstein's association of meritocracy and IQ see Richard Herrnstein, 'IQ', *Atlantic Monthly*, 228 (3), September 1971. See also Alexander Alland, Jr, *Human Diversity*, Columbia University Press, 1971, pp. 177–207.

56 See Harold C. Hand, 'The camel's nose', and Ralph W. Tyler, 'Assessing the progress of education', *Phi Delta Kappan*, September 1965, pp. 8–18.

57 For the questionable relationship between education and actual job performance, see Ivar E. Berg, *Education and Jobs: the Great Training Robbery*, New York, Praeger, 1970.

58 See *Shaping Educational Policy*, New York, McGraw-Hill, 1964. The financial report of the 'Compact' as of May 1966 showed Carnegie and Danforth contributed $300,000 of a $318,000 budget. See Frederick Raubinger and Harold C. Hand, 'It is later than you think', unpublished manuscript, 1967, p. 29.

59 For the membership in that council, see *A Brief*

Statement of the History and Activities of the American Council on Education (1918–59), Washington, DC. There is some similarity between the kind of make-up and function of the American Council and the earlier National Civic Federation which also served disparate interests, and at the same time, worked for the common good of the liberal state.

60 It should be noted that it was Conant's concern for manpower planning which led him to recommend the G.I. Bill. One of the arguments used to support the G.I. Bill legislation was that it would effectively check severe unemployment in the immediate post-war period.

61 For the connection, I am indebted to Professor Fred Raubinger.

62 See *ETS Developments*, 17 (4), May 1970, p. 2.

63 The kinds of tests used: 'The Preliminary Scholastic Aptitude Test, the Advanced Placement Examinations, the College Placement Tests, the College-Level Examination Program, and the Comparative Guidance and Placement Program—the last for two-year colleges.'

ETS also administers other admissions tests: the Graduate Record Examinations for admission to graduate study; more specialized tests for admission to Architectural Schools and to the Colleges of Pediatry; and now a test for admission to grades 7 through 11 of independent secondary schools. As one staff member remarked, 'We have a test for admission to everything except heaven!'

Achievement tests. In addition to the achievement tests of the College Board, there are the numerous Cooperative Tests (which now extended even to a Preschool Inventory); the Undergraduate Program (replacing the Graduate Record Examinations as formerly used by colleges for testing undergraduates); and the Graduate School Foreign Language Testing Program (to satisfy the language requirement for advanced degrees).

In a special category is the Test of English as a Foreign Language to measure the English proficiency of foreign students, government trainees, and others who apply for education in an English-speaking country.

Professional examinations. Among the many professional examinations offered by ETS are the National Teacher Examinations, the National Council of Architectural Registration Boards Examinations, the Chartered Life Underwriter Examinations, the American Board of Obstetrics and Gynecology Examination, and Examinations in Speech Pathology and Audiology. Perhaps the stiffest of all examinations offered by ETS is called the Written Examination for Appointment as Foreign Service Officer (for Department of State and US Information Agency assignments), from *ETS Developments*, 17 (4), May 1970, p. 2.

64 This seems to occur more as a condition of who the foundations support rather than any overt attempt to control the rhetoric directly.

15 Class structure and the concept of intelligence

Paul Henderson

Discussions on the subject of intelligence have tended to focus on the ways in which an individual *acquires* a given *level* or *amount* of intelligence. As such, these discussions seek to explain differences in the level of intelligence between individuals and the aetiology of these differences in the individuals concerned. Symptomatic of this situation is the heredity and/or environment controversy that has been waged during the last half century. The three main contributions to this controversy have been from those who believe that intelligence is mainly acquired through inheritance, those who believe that it is mainly acquired through learning, and those who believe that the relative contributions of these two factors cannot be assessed; intelligence being acquired through an interaction between physical structures and environment.

Superficially, these approaches differ widely, and such differences are compounded by the fact that each view tends to be associated with a different political position.[1] These differences, sharp as they may appear, nevertheless share a common frame of reference. Under the domination of this framework, focus is directed to the acquisition of intelligence, rather than towards the social basis of the concept of intelligence and the functions performed by this concept in a class society. That is to say, our questions are guided by the 'heredity-environment' controversy (i.e. the 'acquisitional' approach) in preference to questions relating to the way in which intelligence, as defined, is a crucial determinant of social status, the reasons why it developed in this way, and the relationship between the concept of intelligence and changes in the class structure of industrial society. Viewed from this perspective, the whole 'acquisitional' paradigm is thrown into question.

Central to the paradigm is a conceptualisation of the abilities of men that reduces behaviour patterns to a series of abstracted characteristics that individuals 'hold' or do not 'hold'.[2] Thus intelligence comes to be treated as a quantity within an individual, rather than as a pattern of behaviour—intelligent behaviour—carried out in relation to others, and meeting a specific response from these others.[3]

Conceptualisation in this latter form allows us to ask a different range of questions from those asked within the framework of the 'environment-heredity' debate. The central issue, rather than being concerned with the way in which an individual becomes intelligent in greater or lesser degree, comes to focus on the way in which intelligent behaviour is defined, made relevant, evaluated and rewarded within a specific social context, and with explanations of this situation. For this reason, we need primarily to direct our attention to the social basis of our conceptions of intelligence and the social functions performed by these conceptions.

The neglect of the implications of such a viewpoint is surprising in view of the importance of the concept of intelligence held in western industrial society. The level of intelligence as such, abstracted from behaviour, is commonly suggested as the *explanation* for differences of status between people and, used in this same sense, the concept of intelligence is unknown in non-industrial society. On a more practical level, the career of a child in school—and subsequently—is most likely to be determined by the 'level' of intelligence attributed to him by his teachers, whether this 'level' is determined by formal or informal means.

As well as the importance of 'intelligence' in determining and justifying the life-chances of individuals in our society, we should also note the reluctance on the part of those using the term to put forward any acceptable definition for it. The definition most commonly given is that intelligence is 'that which intelligence tests measure' which is in no

Source: unpublished. Paul Henderson is lecturer in sociology, University of Leicester.

sense a definition in the scientific sense of the word, as writers like Simon have pointed out.[4]

Finally, 'intelligence', used in both its measured and less formal sense, has acted as a highly efficient discriminator between children on the grounds of social class. The question as to whether the working-class child is *inherently* less intelligent than the middle-class child is not relevant to the present argument; the fact is, assessment of the intelligence of children by teachers or by intelligence tests has tended to divide the children into groupings differentiated by social class.

Given these three facts, namely, the importance of our conceptions of intelligence, the lack of any acceptable definition of the term, and the efficiency of the assessment of intelligence in discriminating between classes,[5] we should expect a plethora of research writings on the epistemological basis of this concept, and the way in which this is related to the structure of society. Sociologists especially, whose work is based on the assumption of a relationship between social structure and the knowledge generated by this social structure, should be at the forefront of such a discussion, attempting to show the social genesis of the idea of intelligence, and the functions performed by the idea in our society. Unfortunately, where sociologists *have* entered into discussions on 'intelligence', it has usually been to show that the 'hereditarians' are 'wrong' and that 'social environment' has more of an effect on the 'level' of intelligence than was previously believed.[6]

Thus, the sociologists' contribution to this discussion has allowed the basic assumptions underlying the individualised, 'quantity' model of intelligence to stand unquestioned, as also stand the ruling definitions of intelligence and the use of the concept of 'intelligence' to legitimate the division of schoolchildren and adults into different 'streams' and occupational categories each of which is differentiated from the other in terms of social status. The foundations on which the whole edifice rests are accepted without doubt.[7]

In a similar way, I would argue, sociologists have tended to accept an existing frame of reference and have tended to focus on the way in which a child 'acquires' a given level of intelligence without calling into question either the social bases of dominant conceptions of intelligence or traditionally assumed uses of the concept of intelligence. The raising of either or both of these questions would involve challenges—the former to the definitions of intelligence supplied by psychologists and educationists, the latter to the view that the division of labour in industrial society calls for people of differing intelligence to take on the occupations requiring more and less intelligence, and that the 'needs' of industrial society for 'intelligent' people leads the society to reward such people with high status.[8]

The failure of sociologists to question this model— in fact, their very willingness to work within it[9]—is

seen by Esland as deriving from the 'dominance of structural functionalist explanations in the sociology of education'.[10] Similarly, the dominance of the 'psychometric' model[11] in education is suggested as being 'fostered by the search of psychologists for a professional identity',[12] and the genesis of the pedagogy, it is claimed, 'has close affinities with the empiricist tradition of the nineteenth century . . . and also social Darwinism.'[13] My own feeling is that this situation finds its source, not in the power of 'structural-functional' sociologists or psychologists to influence social thought and behaviour, nor in the ideas of 'nineteenth-century empiricists' and 'social Darwinists', but in concrete social situations, and, in particular, in features of the class structure of our society, and in changes in this class structure. For this reason, I feel that it may be more fruitful for our purposes to treat the *conception* of intelligence, and the 'image' of man embodied in the 'psychometric' model of education, as an ideology, which is derived from specific social conditions, and serves specific social functions in terms of the class structure, rather than from the ideas held by any group or groups within society.[14]

Setting out from the proposition that intelligence is no more and no less than one form of behaviour among others—intelligent behaviour—we can ask three main questions. The first of these relates to the field of activities in which intelligent behaviour is of most relevance, the second to the positive response elicited within our society to behaviour adjudged 'intelligent' and the third to the criteria of intelligent behaviour and the means by which these criteria are arrived at.

In order to understand the way in which intelligent behaviour came to have relevance for a fairly specific range of activities, it is necessary for us to examine briefly the history of mental testing. One of the earliest writers to suggest the idea that mental abilities could be tested was Francis Galton, whose best-known work, *Hereditary Genius*, was first published in 1867[15] but who was a prolific writer and researcher on this topic in the last half of the nineteenth century generally. Galton felt that 'genius', 'mediocrity', 'imbecility', and various categories between, were analogous in their statistical distribution throughout the population to certain physical characteristics of that population.[16]

The relationship he posited between physical characteristics and 'mental capacity' led him to believe that knowledge of the former would lead to knowledge of the latter. In accordance with this belief, he devised a number of tests, some of which were crude attempts to relate such features as circumference and capacity of the head to 'mental capacity', others which were more sophisticated, and included attempts to measure sensory capacities—the ability of a subject to discriminate between colours, or between smells and so on—and that subject's 'mental' capacity. As Frank S. Freeman says:[17]

Apparently Galton assumed that the simpler measurable sensory capacities would show a significant correlation with intelligence, and that if these simpler sensory measures were obtained they would afford a means of judging or predicting an individual's intellectual capacity.

Although Galton was an early investigator of the possibilities of mental testing, he was by no means alone in the field. Between 1860 and 1900 research on mental testing was being carried out in Britain, the USA, France and Germany. Most of the measurement involved mainly sensory and reflex activity. Towards 1900 the tests were becoming more complex and sophisticated, but there was little change in perspective.[18] Thus while Galton in Britain and Cattell in the United States were concerned with the sensory capacities, Muensterberg in Germany tested the ability to read aloud rapidly, giving rapidly the colours of named objects, rapidly naming and classifying animals, plants and minerals. Muensterberg also used tests of addition, memory and spatial judgment.

However, it appears that around 1900 there was a movement away from such implied definitions of 'mental capacity'. There were two reasons for this, the first being that the different sensory capacities were found to have only a low correlation one with another and the second—of more direct relevance for my argument—that the measurement of these capacities showed only a low correlation with school teachers' estimates of the mental capacities of their pupils.

It is thus open to us to ask why assessments of intelligence came to have relevance mainly within the educational system, or put in another way, why were tests of sensory ability abandoned in favour of tests that correlated more highly with teachers' estimates of children?

After 1900, testing came to be focused far more on intellectual activities as such, with particular reference to *academic* abilities. The work in Britain of Charles Spearman was directed exclusively towards this end, as was that of Cyril Burt, who in 1913 became the country's first psychologist appointed to a local authority with special reference to educational matters. To understand why the focus of testing changed in this way, an examination of changes in the social structure of Britain during the last half of the nineteenth century is necessary. Although I cannot, within the confines of this paper, deal with this issue exhaustively, I may be able to suggest the direction an enquiry may take.

Over the period 1851 to 1911, while the population of Great Britain increased from 9.4 to 18.2 millions, the number of workers employed in the primary sectors of industry (agriculture, forestry, hunting and fishing) declined from 2.1 to 1.4 millions.[19] This represented a proportionate decline from 22.2 to 7.8 per cent of the total labour force. This decline was countered by an increase mainly in the tertiary sector (public and private services, commerce, transport and communications, entertainments) from 2.7 to 8.3 millions which, proportionally, meant an increase from 29 per cent of the occupied labour force to 45.4 per cent.[20] The secondary sector (mining and quarrying, manufacture, building and construction, public utilities) increased in terms of absolute numbers—from 4.6 to 8.5 millions, but showed little proportional change, from 48.8 to 46.8 per cent.[21]

As well as this change, which implied a considerable degree of social mobility, there was a sharp increase in urbanisation and concomitant rural depopulation, combined with the development of large industrial concerns and the spread of bureaucratisation.

These four changes—in social mobility, geographical mobility, urbanisation and bureaucratisation—had, I suggest, serious implications for the social position of the established professional and upper middle classes. They faced competition from those recently risen 'from the ranks', as it were, in a number of ways. Their status position was becoming weakened; this was reflected in rapid infiltration of their living areas, the narrowing margin between their standards of consumption and the standards of others,[22] and the increasing difficulty, for the lower echelons of this group, of using personal influence to obtain a living of the sort to which they were accustomed.

Furthermore, changes over a longer period but of a similar order to those above were changing the bases of legitimation of this group of their high status position. The dictum, 'The rich man in his castle, the poor man at his gate, He made them high and lowly, He ordered their estate', which implied that one class was *innately* predisposed to rule and the other to be ruled, could not easily be maintained in the face of increasing social mobility out of the 'ruled' class, and into that of the 'rulers'. People from lowly social origins who had so far been seen as, and who saw themselves as, innately unsuited for higher status positions, were finding themselves in these positions, carrying out the work quite as adequately as their 'betters' had done.[23]

There is evidence to support the thesis that the increasing pressure for educational qualifications is also derived from such changes in the social structure. Commonly, this pressure is explained by the 'need' of an industrialising society to have a more intelligent workforce, with an education commensurate with the higher level of skills demanded by this society. This may be accurate on one level of analysis; however, when we examine the nature of the pressure for educational qualifications, it appears that support for this change came, not from those most successful in the upper middle class, but from those least successful; that is those who were most vulnerable to the changes mentioned above. Unpublished work on the medical profession, referring mainly to the earlier part of the century but still relevant to my case, seems to bear the contention out[24] that it was marginal members of the medical profession—rather than those more successful and secure—who sought to impose a policy of compulsory registration and educational qualifications for members. Certainly, with respect to the architectural profession, Barrington Kaye has noted that those members of the profession most active in calling for compulsory registration and educational qualifications in architecture, were looked on with scorn by those most powerful in the profession, and were classed as 'mediocrities'.[25]

Generalising from knowledge of the professions, I would like to suggest that similar 'mechanisms' may have been involved in the later part of the nineteenth century, given such changes in the social structure as I have mentioned above. That is to say, that pressure for educational qualifications came about less as a response to a 'need' for more skills, but rather to control social mobility into the middle classes, and to ensure that those who were already favourably placed with respect to educational opportunity—the children of middle-class parents—would be equally well placed with respect to occupational opportunities.[26] It is for this reason, I suggest, that education became a crucial 'arena' in this period, for 'contests' between middle- and working-class children over the opportunities and facilities offered for social mobility.

These changes in occupational structure resulting in rapid upward social mobility are to me a crucial issue underlying changes in the educational system and the development of the idea of measurable intelligence at the end of the nineteenth century and the beginning of the twentieth century. Right through until the 1920s, there was continuing pressure on educational resources, and it was in the 1920s that intelligence testing began to be used on a large scale to divide children from junior schools into those who would attend the grammar schools and those who would find themselves remaining at the elementary schools.

By 1926 the division of secondary education into 'academic' and 'vocational' sectors was well advanced. Intelligence testing was by this time in use and the concepts necessary for such testing to be carried out were well established and it is not necessary to examine the educational system in any depth. It is worth noting, however, that intelligence testing, which was brought into large-scale usage just after the First World War, developed in a context of greatly increased pressure on educational resources, and a growing influx of working-class pupils into the grammar schools.[27]

It is possible to suggest, then, that over this period the educational system became the principal 'arena' in which the 'contests' between the middle and working class were fought over access to positions of high status in the wider society. I should also like to suggest that the IQ test constituted a powerful weapon for use in this contest, and that the concept of

'intelligence' used in a general sense came to constitute an ideological justification for the existing stratification system. This contention cannot be maintained without an examination of two of the claims put forward by those concerned with the 'measurement' of intelligence. These are, in the first place, that tests and less formal assessments of intelligence measure characteristics that are randomly distributed in our society and that are amenable to 'objective' measurement, and, second, that they have predictive validity; that is, that the tests are so highly correlated with future educational and job performance that they are useful for the categorisation of pupils or employees.

Taking the first point, it is apparent that we are dealing with questions relating to the definition of intelligence, and again the work of Francis Galton is of relevance.

In *Hereditary Genius*, Galton examined the statistical interrelationship between certain 'eminent' men and the eminence, or otherwise, of certain of their family members. He found that, of his sample of 'eminent' men, 31 per cent had eminent fathers, 48 per cent had eminent sons, and 41 per cent had eminent brothers.[28] These proportions were far higher than would be expected in any random sample of the whole population. From these findings, Galton concluded that the 'genius' shown by these men was largely inherited. Galton has been criticised for ignoring the possible effects of environmental similarities in the background of these men, but this is of no relevance for my present argument.

My interest lies more in the criteria of 'eminence' used by Galton. On examination, it appears that Galton's sample of 997 eminent men was drawn wholly from the established upper- and upper-middle-class strata and paid no heed to the 'captains of industry and commerce' who had, for the most part, no 'background' in the established upper and upper middle class.[29] Thus it can be seen that 'eminence', for Galton, was eminence only within a certain specific range of activities—Galton, himself the nephew of Charles Darwin and of definite upper-middle-class background, was faithfully reproducing the judgments and estimations of *his own stratum* as to what constituted *true eminence*.

A similar comment can be made on the work of Charles Spearman, a British psychologist who, in 1904, set out his ideas in an article in the *American Journal of Psychology* entitled ' "General intelligence": objectively determined and measured'.[30] Spearman maintained that, if various tests were administered to a group of people, different degrees of correspondence between performances on each test would be obtained. For instance, there may be a high degree of correspondence between performances in geometrical tests and tests of spatial perception, and a low degree of correspondence between performances in tests of musical ability and tests of weight discrimination.

Spearman maintained that there was some degree of correlation between all of the test results; this indicated to him that, underlying these different 'abilities', there was a general factor which would affect performance in all tests, but would be more prominent in some correlations than others. Thus, those tests for which the results showed high correlations (e.g. geometry and spatial perception) would be more heavily 'g' saturated than others which did not show high correlations (e.g. musical ability and weight discrimination).[31]

It was suggested, then, that the 'g' factor underlay all mental operations, to a greater or lesser extent, and that if this general factor could be ascertained, it would approximate to 'true' intelligence. Thus attention came to be focused on the determination of this 'true' intelligence and, to this end, tests showing a high 'g' saturation were seen as more valuable indications of intelligence than those which had only a low 'g' saturation. The determination (and the existence) of 'g' clearly depended heavily upon the range of abilities selected by the tester; in this respect, it is instructive to examine the way in which Spearman isolated his 'g' factor.[32]

Although Spearman later modified his ideas, in this earlier paper there is much that has been retained in the methodology of psychometrics, and that for this reason is of relevance for my present argument. Spearman isolated four main kinds of 'intelligence' which, when correlated with each other, would show a clear statistical relationship. The four 'kinds of intelligence' he utilised were: 'present efficiency', 'native capacity', the 'general impression produced upon other people', and 'common sense'.

By 'present efficiency', Spearman referred to 'the ordinary classification according to school order' in 'such matters as Latin, Greek, Mathematics, etc.'.[33]

'Native capacity' was arrived at by taking the difference between each boy's rank in school and his rank in age, and the third category, the 'general impression produced upon other people', was obtained by asking the teacher of a class who was the brightest pupil, who was the next brightest, and so on.

The fourth and last sort of 'intelligence' noted by Spearman was that of 'common sense'. This ranking was produced by asking the oldest child in the class to rank his or her schoolfellows on the basis of 'sharpness and common sense out of school'.[34] She seemed, said Spearman, 'to have no great difficulty in forming her judgments concerning the others, having indeed, known them all her life'.[35] As a check on the reliability of this ranking, a similar list was obtained from the Rector's wife, who had always lived in the village. She was, however, Spearman notes regretfully, unable to judge all the children, as some she did not know.

Spearman's work, at this stage, did not involve separate tests, but correlations of the assessment of teachers. It is important to note, however, the way in which the ranking of children by their teachers is used by Spearman as basic data. Intelligence tests, right up to the present day, are checked by this means among others. As Freeman notes, in his textbook on mental testing, common criteria of validity of tests are: 'scholastic marks, teachers' judgments of individuals' abilities, cumulative scholastic averages over a period of years'.[36] The reasons for using these as criteria are[37]

(1) that scholastic records are evidence of mental ability even though influenced by factors other than intellectual ability; (2) that teachers are in a position to evaluate individual ability with some validity, because they observe their pupils over a long period and are able to make inter-pupil comparisons . . .

Thus, if the embryo test, when applied to a sample of children, does not result in a similar ranking to that supplied by the teacher, the test is changed until similar rankings *are* produced.[38]

It could then be fairly suggested that use of teachers' assessments of a child in the testing of intelligence tests are subject to the same objections that we may wish to make of Galton's study of 'eminent' men. This is, namely, that the behavioural characteristics deemed 'worthy' are based wholly on the assessments of one particular stratum of society, and refer to behaviours seen as 'worthy' in their eyes only.[39] This sort of behaviour I shall suggest later is that in which members of this stratum are most likely to excel, due to their social location and their favourable access to certain scarce resources.

Many other criticisms can be made of the theoretical basis of intelligence testing. These are not directly relevant to the present argument, although it may be noted in passing that the strength of the criticisms made by such writers as B. Simon[40] are so telling that they serve to reinforce the point that defences of the whole edifice are conducted more from an ideological than a scientific standpoint.

Two points can here be made. In the first place, I am suggesting not that intelligence testing and assessment had the effect of halting social mobility from the working class into the middle class. The demands of the occupational structure would have made this impossible in any case. What I am suggesting is that the putting into practice of the conception of intelligence acted to *control* social mobility in such a way that only those acceptable to the middle class would become mobile. Second, I am suggesting that the use of teachers in the evaluating of intelligence ensured that this situation would prevail. That is to say, only the child who was seen by the teachers as conforming to their image of the good child would find himself in this position. My argument is that this evaluation was not made on the basis of criteria external to the class structure; on the contrary, at all points the class structure acted as a touchstone for the evaluation.

The further argument is that relating to the 'predictive' value of intelligence tests. It is often stated that assessments of intelligence are so highly correlated with future performance that this fact is their major justification.[41] However, much research now indicates that the high correlations are in fact spurious in that the observed relationship between high performance in intelligence tests and future high academic performance may in fact constitute a 'self-fulfilling prophecy'.[42]

Such findings as there are seem to indicate the weakness of the claim that intelligence tests and assessments are justified in terms of their results. The 'predictive validity' of such assessments may be related more to the fact that, on categorisation, the children are placed in different streams (or even different schools) which reinforce the position of the child, both in his or her own estimation, and in that of the teachers of that child. Such an argument would apply, of course, with reference both to intelligence tests and to less formal means of assessment.

Thus far, I have suggested that:

(1) The conception of intelligence adhered to in a society, both in its measured and less formal sense, acts as a mechanism of control over social mobility and as a legitimator of the allocation of high status positions.

(2) The definitions of intelligence in a society are drawn not from 'core values' of the society as a whole, but from the perspective of the dominant stratum in a society. That these definitions may be accepted by other strata does not necessarily imply the legitimacy (in a scientific sense) of the definitions, but is more related to the power of the dominant stratum in terms of the control of knowledge.

(3) Such definitions tend to be based, not on any objective criteria of intelligence (in the sense of any absolute value to a society of 'intelligent' as against 'non-intelligent' people), but on the view of the dominant stratum as to what constitutes 'worthwhile' behaviour, and on some aptitudes rather than others.

I shall now attempt to link these suggestions together, to propose that, for these conceptions of intelligence to be effective as an ideology, the definitions of intelligence as put forward by the dominant stratum must be definitions that result in this stratum maintaining their hegemony over social mobility. To this end, I shall suggest that definitions of intelligence arise from the power of certain sections of the middle class to define as worthy of high esteem (i.e. to define as 'intelligent') those skills that they themselves hold in comparison with the skills held by others. It must be emphasised that I am not suggesting that intelligent behaviour does not exist, only that particular behaviour patterns are chosen as being manifestations of 'intelligence', while others are ignored.

In more detail, I am suggesting that, over the period of its existence, the middle class has developed certain behaviour patterns in contradistinction to those patterns developed by the working class. Changes in the social structure outlined above necessitated certain defensive measures to be undertaken, and the ideological form taken by these measures resulted in our present-day conception of intelligence. That is, the behaviour patterns characteristic of the middle-class life situation came to be defined as 'intelligent', and were used as the basis for our assessment, both formal and informal, of intelligence.

This view of intelligence is opposed to those which hold that assessments of intelligence constitute some kind of objective, supra-class 'yardstick' which is competed for by all, with the middle class having better chances in this competition because of their superior power over the distribution of resources, their genetic make-up, etc. These are the various forms taken by the 'heredity-environment' controversy. It seems as absurd to me to propose this latter argument as it would be to say that 'whiteness of skin' is something that both white and black people compete for in order to get better jobs, houses, and so on. The fact is that 'whiteness of skin' is something white people *have*, and this fact is used to guarantee the exclusivity of their jobs, houses and general life chances. The dominant group have, in fact, the power to define certain characteristics, which they already have (i.e. 'white skin' or 'intelligence' as they define it), as necessary criteria for entry to their social position. It becomes from this point of view irrelevant to ask whether this black skin or intelligence is genetically acquired or learned—the important and central questions lie elsewhere.

This is not, then, an argument that maintains that the middle class, on account of their advantageous position in terms of scarce resources (better schools, possibility for study, language codes, for instance), have an advantage over the working class in the acquisition of intelligence, a further scarce resource. Such a viewpoint would imply that intelligence has concrete properties, and that it can be objectively measured, outside of its class context. Rather, my view is that definitions of intelligence are, as it were, 'tailor made' in that they correspond closely with ways of thought that are *already* existent in the middle class, due to the patterns of social relationships in which members of this class find themselves. (. . .)

Again, it can be seen that definitions of intelligence are congruent with behaviour patterns arising within the middle class, and modes of thought that are more likely to be found in the middle than the working class. The intelligent person, as defined, must be able to describe events in such a way that they can be abstracted from their immediate context, and made comprehensible to the outside observer.

The importance of the foregoing discussion lies in the insistence that differences in the distribution of intelligence are related less to the advantageous position of the middle class in terms of the *acquisition* of intelligence (conceived of as an absolute, material quality) and more to the *power* of the middle class in *establishing the actual definitions* of intelligence. Put briefly, these definitions derive from this class, and to a large extent refer to abilities which they already possess by virtue of the social situation in which they have, both historically and in the present day, found themselves.[43]

The distinction between the conceptualisation of intelligence as something one acquires (by virtue of environmental features, or through the genes), and intelligence as a 'label' applied to the behavioural characteristics found in members of a dominant class, is of the utmost importance and, in posing the problem in terms of the latter conceptualisation, we are lifted out of the heredity-environment controversy, which becomes no longer of relevance.

This perspective in turn raises further questions about the ideology of intelligence as a mechanism of control over social mobility and the social conditions under which this situation arose. Some of these questions have been raised in this paper in a tentative way, although I feel that a more exhaustive investigation is necessary.

I shall now sketch briefly some of the main issues. I have attempted to show that those approaches to the discussion of intelligence which set out to examine the acquisition of intelligence operate within a paradigm which can itself be questioned. Fundamental to this is the inability of such contributions to consider the social basis of the concept of intelligence held within our society.

If we treat intelligence in terms of its more usual definitions (the capacity for abstract thought, the awareness of relationships of cause and effect, and so on), my question is not so much concerned with the ways in which people acquire these capacities; i.e., whether they 'inherit' or 'learn' them, but with why these capacities are evaluated in a positive way in our society, and why command of them is necessary for social mobility.

The standard answer to this question is to say that intelligence is a necessary skill in our society and, for this reason, it is 'rewarded' by the conferring of prestige on the intelligent person.[44] This argument, which carried conviction at first glance, nevertheless has certain weaknesses.[45] My main comment is that the argument, by stating that some skills are more necessary than others, does violence to the concept of society as being made up of interdependent parts. As is evident, power workers, miners and dockers, in spite of their relatively low-status rankings, are not without importance in our society!

The answer to this comment would, without doubt, be in terms of the 'scarcity value' of those people with higher status. That is, while there are many people in our society who are able to become, say, dockers (in terms of the skills involved), there are far fewer who are able to become, say, doctors. For this reason, doctors are in a better position to place a high value on their services. However, the key word in this statement is the word 'able' and here, it seems to me, we have two broad choices. We can say either that this ability is derived from an inherited disposition to these particular skills, or that it stems from the power position of groups within our society to restrict entry to their positions, and thus to make or keep their ability 'scarce'. I have chosen the latter position.

From this point of view, I have suggested in this paper that one way in which abilities are kept scarce is by the conception of intelligence, as it is used in our society. This conception, I have suggested, is ideological. Certainly differences of intelligence, as measured by standard criteria, exist; the ideological nature of this conception rests more in the nature of the criteria used, the range of behaviours seen as appropriate for the application of the criteria, and the claims made for the conceptions of intelligence in assessing the worth of a given person.

My argument is that because of their dominance in the class structure, the middle class are able to *select* and *define* those behavioural characteristics which are to be considered 'intelligent'. Furthermore, that the characteristics selected and defined are those characteristics that they themselves are most likely to be in command of, which arise from their location in the class structure and the way of life which stems from this location. Finally, with respect to the view held that assessments of intelligence measure some kind of absolute quality, the worth of a person to society, I have suggested that assessments of intelligence measure no such thing, but are instead a mechanism by which control over social mobility is maintained: a mechanism finding its source in a situation in which such control was becoming weakened.[46]

Thus, I would suggest that it may be fruitful to invert an established proposition. This proposition, stated broadly, maintains that certain people in our society, because they are intelligent, come to find themselves in privileged positions. It seems to me that it is possible to say that it is due to their privileged position that people are intelligent.

Clearly, my argument goes much further than an assertion that, because some people are advantageously placed with respect to certain scarce resources, they are therefore able to ensure that their children become intelligent. This may well be so, but it in no way throws open to question the existing definitions of intelligence, and the functions they serve. This viewpoint alone returns us to the 'heredity-environment' controversy; intelligence assessment is seen as some kind of objective yardstick, outside the class structure, and the principal problem becomes how this intelligence is acquired.

My suggestion that the middle class in our society are able to select the criteria by which to judge intelligence, and that they do this 'in their own image' as it were, does not imply any conscious manipulation, or 'plot', on the part of the middle class. Any group in relation of dominance to another will tend to set up entrance requirements that are in close ccrrespondence with their own standards of acceptability. An exclusive golf club, for instance, if threatened by an 'invasion' by a group whose members are considered to be inferior to the club members, will set up rules in order to protect their exclusivity. If well-intentioned reformers succeed in forcing the club to amend its rules, other mechanisms of control will tend to take the place of these rules.[47]

This is why I feel it necessary to stress that our focus now should be on the conceptions of intelligence held in our society, and the relationship between these conceptions and the nature of the class structure. Attempts to show that intelligence is 'learned' rather than 'inherited' and that assessments of intelligence are 'unfair' and should be modified have the effect, I suggest, of confusing the central issues involved. The 'unfairness' of intelligence relates, not to some arbitrary failings of intelligence-testers or assessors, but to the fact that there are a limited number of occupations of high status in our society.

The concept of intelligence thus becomes a protective mechanism which legitimates and perpetuates the social position of these occupations as dominant, and it is in this sense that the term 'ideology' was used at the beginning of this paper. This ideology is derived directly from the class structure and, unless and until changes are made in this structure, such 'unfairnesses' as there are will remain.

For this reason, it is important that we examine the *social* basis of the concept of intelligence, rather than restricting the examination to questions finding their source in the 'heredity-environment' controversy and the 'acquisitional' contributions to our knowledge of this phenomenon. These approaches tend to obfuscate the central issues involved, by their focus on the individual's acquisition of intelligence, without any examination of what is meant by the term 'intelligence'. This reductionist tendency is likely to lead social research into a cul-de-sac. As I see it, the central issues are concerned with the nature of the class structure and the forms of knowledge generated in support of it. It is with this problem that this paper has been concerned.

Notes

1 As Stephen Wiseman has pointed out: 'The witchdoctor, the prince-bishop, the baron, the emperor have all proclaimed the power of inborn factors—the reformer, the republican, the radical, the revolutionary have emphasised the equality of man and the potentiality of education, training and a favourable environment. It is therefore, a social and political question first, and an educational question second' (*Education and Environment*, Manchester University Press, 1964, p. 30).

2 This viewpoint has been called the 'phlogiston' approach to intelligence by Geoffrey M. Esland. '[The teachers'] taken for granted, natural world has contained assumptions about the existence of a substance called "intelligence", which, like "phlogiston", is "given off" when certain stimuli are applied to the child' ('Teaching and learning as the organisation of knowledge', in Michael F. D. Young, ed., *Knowledge and Control: New Directions in the Sociology of Education*, Collier-Macmillan, 1971, pp. 70–115 (pp. 71–2)).

3 Such a formulation has the advantage of avoiding the dangers of physiological reductionism. For example, it has often been said that as eye colouring, which is inherited, is distributed in different proportions, the same could be true of 'intelligence'. Thus A. Jensen has argued that 'nearly every anatomical, physiological, and biochemical system shows racial differences. Why should the brain (i.e. intelligence) be an exception?' (quoted in H. J. Eysenck, *Race, Intelligence and Education*, Temple Smith, 1971, p. 20). This form of physiological reductionism—treating physical *brain* as synonymous with *behaviour*—has no scientific validity, the only examples of such a relationship being those in which gross brain damage has occurred. If we treat intelligence as a form of behaviour, which is after all

the only way in which we can recognise it, such correlations become difficult to maintain.

4 B. Simon, *Intelligence, Psychology and Education: a Marxist Critique*, Lawrence & Wishart, 1971, or *Intelligence Testing and the Comprehensive School*, Lawrence & Wishart, 1953.

5 It is interesting to note in this connection that the United States Supreme Court has recently declared intelligence testing to constitute a 'discriminatory action' (Griggs *v.* Duke Power Co., 8 March 1971). It was said that 'The Supreme Court has decided that employers who rely on basic intelligence and aptitude tests in hiring and promoting are guilty of discrimination' (*Career Development*, 1 (3), June 1971).

6 cf. A. H. Halsey, 'Genetics, social structure and intelligence', *British Journal of Sociology*, 9 (1), 1958, pp. 15–28.

7 As Esland has pointed out, in the context of the sociology of education, sociologists have tended to focus on the *role* of the teacher and the way in which knowledge is *transmitted*, rather than on questions relating to the *content* of that knowledge: 'the practical activity of teaching and its supporting rationales ... are hardly represented in sociological theory. The existential matrix of intentions, cognition and the knowledge on which they are founded, and the situational variants of these are ignored or subsumed under "beliefs" or "values" which are then taken as given' (op. cit., pp. 71–2).

8 Undoubtedly, with the division of labour, diverse skills are called for—the question is, why should the possession of some skills demand higher status than others or, put in a different way, why should the terms 'bright' and 'dull' imply, in the one case, praise, and in the other, condemnation? Clearly, society does not 'need' doctors any more than it 'needs' labourers.

We cannot understand the difference in status between these two without making some reference to the relative dispositions in the power held by each of these groups.

9 As Esland says, 'a good deal of "sociological" research has been encapsulated within its orbit. In the drive to taxonomize the influences which impede "learning", various social contingencies have been labelled as being capable of retarding the development of "achievement motivation", or ₗlinguistic/cognitive/affective potential—or even of annihilating them' (ibid., p. 90).

10 ibid., p. 71.

11 In which the child is seen as a passive object, a deficit system, whose progress is determined by the unfolding of certain innate 'abilities' which have a certain ceiling, and which cannot be exceeded. As Esland notes, the teacher's function is to select and monitor the progress of the child by 'objective' measures such as IQ tests. Cf. Esland, op. cit., p. 89.

12 ibid., p. 90.

13 ibid.

14 Esland himself notes the possible social basis of this ideology, when he remarks that ' "Intelligence", in the form of IQ ... [is] ... an immense legitimation for power distribution in society' (p. 90). However, not only does he neglect to follow this statement through in any way, he also implies, throughout his essay, that education can be treated as a 'closed system' having no relationship with the wider society—that the ideologies so fruitfully isolated, exposed and described by him, can be affected by changes in the curriculum, and different methods of training for teachers. In fact, as the persistence of 'streaming' within comprehensive schooling demonstrates, this is not so. The relationship, within industrial society, between education and social mobility is such that any division, conceptual or otherwise, between the school and the class structure will tend to distort the nature of the phenomena with which we deal, and lead to the very 'reifications' that Esland rightly finds so disturbing.

Furthermore, the problem of 'intelligence' has wider sociological ramifications, taking it outside the scope of 'classroom' interest. The fact that the 'heredity-environment' controversy, in spite of its spuriousness as a scientific controversy, has deep rooted political connotations and arouses violent antagonisms, should alert us to its importance in this respect. Stephen Wiseman, ed., *Intelligence and Ability*, Penguin Modern Psychology, 1967, especially Introduction. Also, and connected with this, a frequent explanation of our stratification system is in terms of the allocations of differential 'intelligence' and this makes the whole topic of importance for our understanding of the theory of social class. For these reasons, I feel it justified to claim that, although the problem of 'intelligence' takes on its most explicit form within education, that is by no means any justification for treating it as an 'educational' problem.

15 London, Macmillan.

16 'If we had measurements [of stature] of the adult males in the British Isles', he said, 'we should find those measurements to range in close accordance with the law of deviation from an average ... now if this be the case with stature, then it will be true as regards every other *physical* feature—as circumference of head, size of brain, weight of grey matter, number of brain fibres, etc.; and thence, by a step on which no physiologist will hesitate, as regards mental capacity' (*Hereditary Genius*, ch. 3, emphasis added).

17 *Theory and Practice of Psychological Testing*, New York, Holt, Rinehart & Winston, 1960, p. 96.

18 ibid., pp. 97–8.

19 C. Clark, Conditions of Economic Progress, *United Nations Report on the World Social Situation*, 1957.

20 ibid.

21 ibid.

22 Cf. J. A. Banks, *Prosperity and Parenthood*, Routledge & Kegan Paul, 1954.

23 Such a change as this clearly has implications for the 'heredity-environment' controversy. It could be suggested, in fact, that the basis for this problematic lies in such social changes as the ones mentioned above.

24 I. Waddington.

25 Barrington Kaye, *The Development of the Architectural Profession in Britain*, Allen & Unwin, 1960.

26 I am aware that, in the upper stratum of the middle class, qualifications may have been demanded as an offensive measure against the patronage system operated by the upper class. This is not incompatible with my present thesis, although it is not of direct relevance.

27 See G. Bernbaum, *Social Change and the Schools, 1918–1944*, Routledge & Kegan Paul, 1967, for a well-documented account of these changes.

28 P. G. Vernon, *Intelligence and Attainment Tests*, University of London Press, 1960, p. 139; Robert Thomson, *The Pelican History of Psychology*, Penguin, 1968, pp. 106–8.

29 In this respect, it is most interesting to compare Francis Galton's sample with that of Samuel Smiles, whose book *Self Help: the Art of Achievement Illustrated by Accounts of the Lives of Great Men*, was published in 1859. Most of Smiles's 'great men' find their origins in the lower class.

30 *American Journal of Psychology*, 115, 1904, pp. 201–92.

31 It would be interesting to examine some differences between British and American psychologists in their theories of intelligence. Unfortunately this cannot be done within the scope of this paper.

32 I am aware that this brief account does little justice to the richness of Spearman's work, especially in respect to the relationship he postulated between the 'g' factor and abilities in each respective ability (the specific, or 's' factor). Descriptions of Spearman's work that are more elaborated can be found in most histories of psychology (e.g. Thomson, op. cit., pp. 186–9) and a description in depth is not relevant to my present point.

33 *American Journal of Psychology*, 115, 1904, pp. 201–92.

34 ibid.

35 ibid.

36 Freeman, op. cit., pp. 27–8.

37 ibid.

38 The 'image' of the teacher implied by such procedures is one that fits in a hand-in-glove way with what has been referred to above as the 'psychometric' model of the teaching situation. The teacher is assumed to be somehow 'outside' society and social pressures in his or her assessment of the child; also, there can be no question, in this model, of the *relationship* between the social class of the teacher and that of the pupil affecting the 'intelligence' of the child. Such a viewpoint can only be maintained whilst it is accepted that

'intelligence' is *something that can be isolated* from other characteristics of the child; it is not seen as a behavioural characteristic, acted out in relationship with others, but an 'amount' that the child holds in greater or lesser degrees.

The 'intelligent' child, I have suggested, may tend to have other characteristics that should not be considered apart from the ascribed 'intelligence'. These other characteristics may lead to a high evaluation of the child in the eyes of the teacher, which in turn may lead to the child being placed in a high ranking position in his or her school class. Assuming that the evaluations of teachers tend to be, in many respects, patterned evaluations, the use of school class rankings in the initial formulation and validation of intelligence tests (and less formal assessments of 'intelligence') may thus attain, not greater objectivity, but an ossification and systematisation of the values of school teachers. That is to say, intelligence tests may measure not something called 'intelligence', but a whole cluster of behavioural characteristics that could loosely be called 'traits that fit the teachers' model of the "ideal" child'.

39 This is not to say that the development of intelligence testing did not remove much of the arbitrariness of the previous system of selection. In effect, the personalised relationship between teacher and pupils observable before 1900 gave way to a more bureaucratic system of assessment, in which power was taken from the teachers, and placed more in the hands of educational psychologists. In this respect, it was undoubtedly easier for a working class child who was 'intelligent' to gain a scholarship than under the former system. The essential feature however, is that *control* over who was to gain a place in the grammar school stayed firmly in the hands of the middle class.

40 op. cit., 1953, cf. 1971.

41 Cf. 'What do intelligence tests really measure', H. J. Eysenck, *Uses and Abuses of Psychology*, Penguin, 1953, ch. 1.

42 See, for instance, the short summary in Esland, op. cit., p. 91, and Rosenthal and Jacobson, 'Teachers' expectations', in Liam Hudson, ed., *The Ecology of Human Intelligence*, Penguin Modern Sociology Readings, 1970, pp. 177–81.

43 A criticism that I would make of Bernstein's work, for instance, is that while providing a fruitful and stimulating insight as to the way in which each class is differentially placed with regard to the acquisition of intelligence as measured by intelligence tests, Bernstein fails to follow this through in any way. Bernstein speaks of the 'social structure', but, on examination, it appears that he is talking of the structure of social relationships *within* each class. It seems to me that when we speak of 'social structure' we should be speaking of, among other things, the relationship *between* classes, in order that we understand why it is that the definitions of intelligence are heavily weighted in favour of the middle class.

44 Cf. the debate over the 'functional' theory of social stratification put forward by Davis and Moore in their article, 'Some principles of stratification', *American Journal of Sociology*, 10 (2), 1945, pp. 242–9.

45 Many of which were put forward by Tumin in his rejoinder to the Davis and Moore article (ibid.). See 'Some principles of stratification: a critical analysis', ibid., 18 (4), 1953.

46 Of course, it may be that this 'control function' also corresponds to the 'needs' of society—the two are not necessarily incompatible—in a particular historical period, but this is another question altogether.

47 Thus it seems ludicrous to me for liberal reformers to suggest that tests of intelligence are 'unfair' and that more 'culture fair' items should be included. At best, such measures can ensure that only a few of those previously excluded will 'pass' into the dominant group, and at worst, alternative means of exclusion will develop. This is precisely what has happened with respect to comprehensive education, in which field we have seen the continuing stress on streamed classes, and the area-specific nature of these institutions.

16 The psychology of child psychology

David Ingleby

When St John the Divine writes, 'I was in the Spirit on the Lord's day', he seems to be letting us know that 'being in the Spirit' was a necessary condition for having the revelation he proceeds to unfold. In this paper I want to suggest that (although we are not told this, but have to find out for ourselves) the revelations of child psychology also require that one be in a certain spirit before they become convincing; that they are as much products of the mentality which is brought to bear on the evidence as of the evidence itself.

The mentality we are talking about is not, as in St John's case, a transitory state of the individual: it is the shared corpus of concepts, attitudes and methods of inquiry into which the 'fully trained' psychologist has been initiated. (...) I shall try first of all to elucidate this mentality, and then to demonstrate that it can only be understood in terms of its place in (to borrow Laing's useful definition) 'the *political* order ... the ways persons exercise control and power over one another' (Laing, 1967, p. 107).

In other words, I want to consider this mentality not just as a set of ideas viewed apart, but as an ideology; the essential difference being that an ideological critique takes into account the interests which a particular mentality is defending. As Mannheim states:

> The concept 'ideology' reflects the one discovery which emerged from political conflict, namely, that ruling groups can in their thinking become so intensively interest-bound to a situation that they are simply no longer able to see certain facts which would undermine their sense of domination. There is implicit in the word 'ideology' the

insight that in certain situations the collective unconscious of certain groups obscures the real condition of society both to itself and to others and thereby stabilises it. (1936, p. 36)

The 'psychology of child psychology' I am thus trying to sketch is an exercise quite different in spirit from child psychology itself; I shall be attempting to practise the kind of psychology which that profession does not apply, in order to show why it does not apply it. For—with a few deviant exceptions (e.g. Reich or Laing)—child psychology has not looked at its subject-matter in the light of the political system in which it is found: the political order is usually seen as a source of extraneous variance which must be partialled out of the data to make them truly 'psychological'. If this is how psychology is to be defined, indeed, then the present essay is not psychology at all: but its purpose is to demonstrate that the 'facts' produced by any psychology which attempts to ignore the political context of what it observes will be about as useful as, say, an analysis of a violin concerto which ignores what the orchestra is playing.

In an earlier paper (Ingleby, 1970) I collected some examples of the way in which the approach which has come to be regarded as 'scientific' psychology seemed to be shot through with ideological biases. In the light of these biases I went on to contend that the 'scientific' label is a device for throwing us, ideologically speaking, off the scent: for that which is 'scientific', by definition, does not depend for its authority on the political loyalties implicit in it. My contention was that the social function which determines the spirit of inquiry in psychology—whatever convictions psychologists may have about it—is the maintenance of the *status quo*: psychology borrows habits of thought from natural science and applies them to the human sphere in a manner which is logically quite inappropriate, but politically highly

Source: M. P. M. Richards, ed., *The Integration of a Child into a Social World*, Cambridge University Press, 1974, pp. 295–9, 303–8.

functional. This activity was referred to as 'reification', defined as 'the misrepresentation of praxis as process'—'praxis' being the type of activity which characterises an agent, and has to be understood as projects or communications having meanings, and 'process' being the activity of things, which does not harbour meanings in the same sense, but can be completely understood in terms of its antecedent causes (the traditional scientific paradigm of explanation). The effect of the many reifications that occur in psychology is to dehumanise the individual in the same way that the political system dehumanises him, i.e. to represent as impersonal, thing-like processes those aspects of people which the political order itself needs to remove from their agency; either to eliminate them, as in the case of 'deviant' behaviour (and other attempts men make to build their own order of values and perceptions), or—by abolishing the very distinction between people and things—to facilitate the use of people as if they were things. Where reification assists in the elimination of deviance, it is also accompanied by a 'normative' component (for instance, in the 'disease model' of abnormal experience or behaviour): the logic of 'correct/incorrect' functioning is superimposed on the dimension 'socially desirable/undesirable', via the use of metaphorical dichotomies like sickness/health, disordered/well-ordered, adjusted/maladjusted, adaptive/maladaptive, and so on.

Thus, in the earlier paper, the ideological content of psychology was located in a single general concept—reification—instances of which were described in theories of intelligence, personality and learning, and in psychiatry. The issues have been greatly clarified for us since then by Harré and Secord's (1972) analysis of the 'paradigm shift' which they claim to detect in the social sciences; their 'old' and 'new' paradigms overlap to a large extent with my 'process/praxis' distinction, though—in line with the current paradigm of 'philosophy of science' itself—they do not dwell on the political significance of these modes of explanation. In this essay I wish to return to the same theme, by showing how child psychology has wished out of existence the all-important political context of childhood, and how it is obliged to do this by virtue of the social function of the 'people professions' to which it belongs.

To summarise, then: I start from the belief that practically every act in relation to a child, from the moment of his birth and even before, reflects constraints dictated by that child's place in the political system. (From this point of view, we might say that the whole field of child development ought properly to be regarded as the study of socialisation.) In psychology, however, this determination is not simply ignored, but the evidence about it is suppressed by the very methodology of the profession (. . .)

Now the most effective means which psychologists have devised for keeping the political context of childhood out of the picture was the creation of that venerable distinction between 'socialisation' and the rest of development, and the relegation of ideology to the waste-paper basket of 'cultural variables', which are supposed to enter only into the learning of explicit moral principles, allegiances, and social concepts. Having thus disposed of political factors, psychologists have moved increasingly towards areas where these influences are regarded as minimal, and towards a methodology which does not cater for them. The hope appears to be that if child development is studied sufficiently early on and in a sufficiently 'biological' way—which means, in the main, using concepts and observational methods borrowed from the study of animals, whose politics are less of a problem—if this is done, a picture of the process can be built up which will hold good regardless of the structure of the society in which the child develops. (. . .)

We shall see later, in fact, how usable conclusions may be drawn from such research only by the addition of unstated and untested assumptions. The political system is inextricably present in the most basic aspects of childrearing and in the process of conception and gestation as well: its influence is manifest in the whole environment in which the child undergoes the first stages of his life.

This is true, first, in a practical and material sense. For example, the extent to which a mother can *afford* to meet her child's demands—how much food and attention she can give and when, how much crying she can permit or tolerate—must be strongly influenced by her position in the system of production and consumption; so that even the simplest 'time-and-motion study' approach is portraying the results of a given political system. Here, in fact, it might make sense to 'partial out social class' in order to study the effects of such environmental variables in their own right. On a different level of analysis, however, the influence of the child's environment cannot be disentangled from the socioeconomic determinants of that environment. I am referring to the moulding of a child's mentality which starts with the first interactions, and which is all the more potent for being unconscious as well as unspoken: that is, the formation of his ideas about his own needs and propensities, and the response to them that can be expected from the world around him—about what he may take, own, reject, give, do or say; all of which boil down to expectations derived from early experience. These ideas are not so much expounded in the process of socialisation as embodied and enacted in it.

Psychology does not, in fact, provide us with a very adequate way of describing and measuring what I have called here the child's 'mentality': the topic spreads out untidily under several headings—concept formation, construct theory, motivation, language learning, attachment theory, object relations, psychodynamics. However vague it seems one must remain about its definition, this seems to me no drawback in asserting that it must be to a large extent a product of the political system—the totality of power relations— that the child grows up in. This, of course, is a truism in Marx (cf. 1910, p. 119: 'The same men who establish social relations conformably with their material productivity, produce also the principles, the ideas, the categories, conformably with their social relations'): but its application within the field of child psychology has been not only neglected, but quite strongly resisted.

Thus, the aim of studying the child as if he and his family were living on a desert island is a futile one: they aren't—and even if they were, they would probably still behave as though they weren't. From the start, the responses which the child receives to his demands and activities are shaped by the fact that both his 'input' and his 'output' are destined for the slots which the social system will provide for them. In the type of society most psychology is written about, these slots will be highly specific ones, requiring the individual to adapt his demands obediently to market conditions (cf. Jules Henry's (1966) 'virtuoso consumer'), and to tailor his creative capacities to labour conditions, since—to the system that sustains him—his physical energy, sensory-motor skills, and imagination (should he be privileged enough to retain any) are all essentially *commodities*. Precisely how the prevailing relations of production and consumption will impinge on him will vary greatly with his class position, but it is those relations which are the most important factors in determining the mould in which 'socialisation' casts him. (. . .)

The reluctance of child psychologists to think too hard about these questions is well demonstrated in the notion that the 'rules, proscriptions, values and modes of behaviour' which a child must acquire to become 'social' are those which his *parents* require him to absorb. In the sense that parents may have wishes for the child that reflect their identification with interest-groups outside the family, this is partly true: but on the obvious interpretation, this notion seems a straightforward reversion to the 'desert island' school of socialisation. It turns a blind eye to the fact that parents are not simply acting in their own interests, or even in those of the child, in bringing him up: they are first and foremost *representatives* of a particular sector of a particular political system, and —ultimately—it is in the cause of the perpetuation of that system that efforts will be directed. This oversight achieves an important misrepresentation of the nature of parental authority. (. . .)

Both the psychologist's and the parent's pretence that primary socialisation serves only the interests of the primary group provides a vital line of defence for the interests it really serves. To modify the infant's propensities in such a way as to make coexistence with him possible will surely be agreed by everyone to be not only necessary but in the child's own interests. Hence—since no genuine conflict of interests exists—there can be no argument about whose side to take: we are all on the same side. Such a picture

can only obscure the true reasons for 'failures of socialisation'. If the parents fail to produce a child adapted and reconciled to his allotted place in society, then on this model something is wrong with either the child or his parents (cf. the 'breakdown of family life' which is sometimes blamed for black unrest): for Science has shown that under normal conditions of family rearing, people will grow up adapted. It does not take much thought to see that what is masquerading here as a biological discovery is, in fact, nothing but a political preference for the *status quo*. In reality, children may also fail to acquire the 'right' values because they recognise the conflict between them and their actual interests, or because the parents do not fulfil their parental function (political rather than biological) and impose them. There are plenty of circumstances in which a family that produced, say, draft-evaders or transgressors of the law of property would not be in any sense biologically malfunctioning.

Faced with such an argument, the psychologist is likely to admit that the ethic into which a child is socialised does, after all, contain certain norms which subsume even the interests of the family to the smooth running of society as a whole. It is traditional to assume, at this point, that stating the need for some kind of 'social contract' sanctions whatever notion of 'social' or 'anti-social' behaviour is current in the situation being observed. It is not the purpose of this article to dispute whether some rule-based social structure—i.e. a political order—is necessary: but the argument that *some* version of the 'reality principle' must be instilled into a child cannot be used to justify the imposition of whichever happens to be around at the time. Such a presumption can only be based on the belief that the prevailing political system is the only possible or desirable one: an illusion which psychologists are not alone in holding.

Yet mere ethnocentricity is too simple an explanation of why psychologists present a view of socialisation which serves to protect the *status quo*. Their involvement with the power-structure within which they work has to be understood via a more careful examination of the exact role which they play in that structure: for this mentality does not arise in ivory towers. (Neither, one might add, does the so-called 'ivory-tower' mentality itself.) When we explore the channels through which psychological knowledge is made effective, we find first that those responsible for implementing it belong to what we might call the 'people professions'—those whose province is the regulation of human behaviour and the removal of 'social problems': that is, psychiatry, social work, the educational, penal and welfare systems. (I have deliberately avoided the widely used term 'helping professions' because I want to emphasise what the latter have in common with behaviour-regulating institutions such as the prison system, which nobody— as yet—speaks of as 'helping'.)

Now it is not within my competence or this paper's scope to offer a thorough analysis of the way these institutions work, but for the purposes of my argument several key features of them may be singled out; the point I want to make being that it is implicit in their role in the social system that their energies will be devoted to adapting men to that system, instead of helping to adapt the system to human needs. It is the job itself, rather than the people who do it or the theories they inherit, that is by nature conservative.

First, the 'people professions' are almost entirely financed and administered by public authorities. This is an inevitable—and in one obvious way, desirable—feature of a welfare system; but it does seem to have led to the consequence that the people the professions in practice cater to—who, incidentally, also represent for the most part the economically least privileged sector of society—have no say in the way they are organised, no access to their secrets, and no right to dispute their advice.

Secondly, their manner of functioning is primarily by way of 'confiscating' problems: either by institutionalising problem individuals, or by defining their difficulties in a specialised language which purports to remove them from the layman's province—for instance, the jargon of clinical psychiatry, psychodynamics, or educational psychology. (Thus, there is more than a grain of truth in the vulgar criticism that psychology says what everybody knows in a language nobody understands.) This, again, stems from the concept of 'welfare services' as a system set up *alongside* existing society, rather than part of it, whose task is to repair the damage done to human beings by the way of life the social system entails for them: its function thus being inevitably corrective, rather than preventive.

Thirdly, in consequence of this, the social expertise of the people professions must stop short abruptly at a certain level of the power structure; and the contradictions which these limits give rise to are responsible for much of the anguish among workers in these professions—whether they realise it or not. (See, e.g. Cannan, 1972.) The closer one works to the client, the more conspicuous the contradictions become. Consider, for example, the paradox of social workers and therapists who use 'object relations theory' to help their clients—an elaborate language for dealing with, among other things, the problems of having, getting, and giving, and the distinction between 'using' others as objects and relating to them as people. Their task is to raise their clients' consciousness of these issues, but somehow to stop short of the level where questions would start to arise about the same issues in relation to the larger structures of society. It is healthy for members of a family to become conscious of their envy, to resist being used, and so on—as long as they do it in the privacy of their own home; but what if they extend the process to their landlords, employers and rulers? One may make the same point by noting that the

problems of having, getting, giving, and 'using' people are precisely what Marx wrote about (i.e. property, consumption, production and alienated labour); but no social worker is likely to be initiated into the analysis he offered.

In a sense, then (not a very nice one), the people professions treat their clients as if they were children, with very limited rights to knowledge about, and responsibility for, their own situations; but, of course, they are not children, and this state of affairs is not adequately explained by the nature of their problems. A certain degree of authority is proper to anyone in an advisory role, but the 'people professions' operate with a variety of paternalism that is quite incompatible with their claim to be 'helping people to lead better lives', and betrays the fact that their real duties lie altogether elsewhere. If such were really their aim, then we should expect their voice to be the most insistent in articulating and attacking the ways in which the political system itself systematically limits the quality of their clients' lives: moreover, it would be the latter to whom they would divulge their analyses of the situation, not to the others in authority over them. In practice, they apply their energies to ways of dealing with problems that offer the minimum disruption to the existing order—on peril of their jobs. For if the human wreckage produced by the way society is organised can be discreetly removed, processed, and returned in re-usable form by these social garbage-workers, then not only will the service avoid producing disruption itself: it will prevent the disturbance which might result if the evidence of the political system's failure to meet human needs were left in our midst.

These, then, are the trades to which psychology purveys the commodity of its knowledge, and to whose functions it thereby allies itself; just as the child's mentality is tailored to the social functions he will perform, so is that of the child psychologist. It is by virtue of the need to maintain the myth that the prevailing order is the only possible or desirable one that statements such as Ainsworth's 'the child is born social' gain approval: Reich, Laing, Henry, Sartre, or Marcuse can only offer the type of knowledge for which psychology—quite literally—has no use.

Here, then, we arrive back at the central theme of this paper: that how people are trained to act and think—whether they are children, parents, researchers, or practitioners with people—has to be understood in terms of their position in the political order: we cannot pretend any longer that it isn't there. Both science and the people professions still confuse themselves and the rest of society with a Victorian image of magnanimous neutrality—one which might, indeed, have had some relevance in the days when science was still within the technical and intellectual means of curious gentlefolk, and charitable activities were an individualistic free-for-all. Now, however, these activities have become industries, and those who staff these industries are a new proletariat, who (like the rest) must submit to being used in order to stay alive. We must therefore be extremely careful not to set up these mental and emotional workers as 'enemies of the people', as much so-called radical criticism tends to do: in reality, the scientist, psychiatrist or social worker (like the teacher, the policeman, or the parent) is as exploited as those whose exploitation he facilitates, as brainwashed as those he brainwashes. What species of prostitute is more pitiable than the person whose most highly developed thoughts and feelings are bought and put to uses he has no inkling of?

Finally, if it is true that the mentality informing most psychological research is inherently conservative, our most urgent task is to find a framework within which psychologists could work who do not share the conviction that the existing political order is the only possible or desirable one. My belief here is that a sufficiently thorough analysis of the existing framework will supply all the keys to the construction of a new one.

Following a line of thought suggested by Gabel (1970), we may consider the problem as analogous to the psychotherapy of psychoses. The analogy runs as follows: Ideologies are epistemological structures whose intrinsic rigidities preclude the perception of certain areas of reality which must be concealed for the security of the existing power-structure; in the same way, it has been argued by those who have studied psychosis in its familial context, that psychotic thought-patterns represent attempts to embrace reality without betraying the power-structure of the relationships an individual is entangled in. (Mme Mannoni's therapy, in these terms, consists in telling her patients the truths which the family finds unspeakable, in order that their experience may make sense again.) The limits a psychologist unwittingly imposes on his own awareness, by assimilating the 'spirit' of the profession, correspond to the paranoid individual's defences against reality-testing: any evidence which might threaten the overall picture is either systematically ignored or turned into evidence confirming it. And this is not to protect the psychologist's (or paranoiac's) own interests, but the interests of those who rely on his unawareness to maintain their own positions. Anyone who sets out to do therapy on such thought-structures must do so primarily by analysing their inherent contradictions. We must work in the same way as the therapist, who, for example, demonstrates to a person that their difficulty in finding a 'lovable' person to live with stems from their deeper need for the presence of an 'unlovable' person by contrast with whom *they* can feel lovable. The people professions have difficulty in 'helping people to lead better lives', and the human sciences in understanding man in his social matrix: both must be helped to see, for a start, the extent to which their role in society requires them to fail at these very tasks.

If, then, the object is to produce a psychology which is genuinely open to reality testing (which is, after all, what a 'scientific' psychology would be), what has to be done is to restore an open-mindedness to psychology which will allow the situations it studies to impress their own logic on the observer—rather than imposing on these situations the fetishised concepts which survived the test of ideological acceptability. This does not imply a return to some naïve theory of 'direct' perception, but ceasing to delimit in advance the concepts which will best serve to grasp a situation, and replacing the closed 'shop-talk' of psychologists with an open language that will admit all perceptions. This goal would seem to correspond to the phenomenologists' 'return to the things themselves' (see Merleau-Ponty, 1962): but if our earlier analysis is correct, this kind of objectivity cannot be achieved by intellectual thoroughness alone, but by withdrawal of one's allegiance to the interest groups defended by the existing framework. 'Divergent thinking' is not enough: in the human sciences, phenomenology is inescapably a political activity, in that it must involve the undermining of a major system of power and control—that is, intellectual orthodoxy.

In other words, the relationship of psychology to the 'people professions', and of these professions to the existing order, must change. I have tried to show that membership of the élite to which most of my readers will belong confers many powers, but entails—indeed, is conditional on—a systematic attenuation and distortion of one's awareness. To set right that 'false consciousness', it is not enough simply to set off in pursuit of a wider range of viewpoints—as if, by some ingenious system of mirrors, one could see what the world would look like from a different position in the political order: one doesn't escape so easily from the bemusement of one's own mentality, from the habits of thought and perception laid down during the many years spent socialising into a class and a profession. The only way is to analyse just what this mentality is: and the shortest route to an understanding of it, as I have tried to show, is by discovering the power-structure it props up.

References

Cannan, C. (1972), 'Social workers: training and professionalism', in T. Pateman, ed., *Counter Course*, Penguin.

Gabel, J. (1970), *Sociologie de l'aliénation*, Paris, Presses Universitaires de France.

Harré, R. and Secord, P. F. (1972), *The Explanation of Social Behaviour*, Oxford, Blackwell.

Henry, J. (1966), *Culture against Man*, Tavistock.

Ingleby, J. D. (1970), 'Ideology and the human sciences', *Human Context*, 2, 159–80; reprinted in T. Pateman, ed., *Counter Course*.

Laing, R. D. (1967), *The Politics of Experience*, Penguin.

Mannheim, K. (1936) *Ideology and Utopia*, Routledge & Kegan Paul.

Mannoni, M. (1969), *The Child, his Illness, and the Family*, Tavistock.

Marcuse, H. (1955), *Eros and Civilisation*, Boston, Beacon Press.

Marx, K. (1910), *The Poverty of Philosophy* (trans. H. Quelch), Chicago.

Merleau-Ponty, M. (1962), *Phenomenology of Perception* (trans. C. Smith), Routledge & Kegan Paul.

Sartre, J.-P. (1960), Foreword to *The Traitor* by André Gorz, Calder.

17 Plowden children
P. S. Wilson

I had always thought that 'child-centred' was a label for educational arrangements aimed at freeing children from unnecessary constraints, particularly constraints upon what could or should be learned at school. I had thought, therefore, that a 'child-centred' school would be one where children found resources and expert help for learning whatever they chose to learn—within limits, no doubt, but ideally no narrower limits than those of reasonable safety to life and limb.

In practice, however, I have found that the term 'child-centred' is often used to label an entirely different state of affairs from the one I'd imagined. For example, I know many schools in which teachers view themselves as 'child-centred' although their children's freedom to learn is very tightly controlled indeed, in terms of mandatory syllabuses to be 'covered', prescribed amounts of different subjects to be 'done', 'basic' skills to be acquired first, and so on. Similarly I know of 'child-centred' schools in which children learn (or rather, 'do' schoolwork) not because they choose to, but because they are 'stimulated' into appropriate 'learning behaviour' by inducements which have nothing whatever to do with what they are supposed to be learning, but which reflect clearly their teachers' unshakeable resolve that these, and only these, shall be the sorts of tasks which may be performed by children in school.

My mistake, of course, lay in failing to realize that schools can be equally 'child-centred' yet totally different in every other respect, if their arrangements are based on totally different conceptions of what it is to be a 'child'. They can equally 'centre' education upon children, yet, if they view children in radically opposed ways, their versions of education or of what these children could valuably learn are bound to be mutually incompatible. It is this, in part at least,

which must explain the incompatibility between what I think of personally as 'child-centred education' and what I continually find going on under that label in schools. In this essay, then, I shall try to describe a view of children which, when education is 'centred' on it, generates a kind of schooling which is totally alien to the child-centred education which I summarily sketched in the first paragraph above.

It is a view which can be found in the Plowden Report. 'Underlying all educational questions,' the Report begins (p. 1), 'is the nature of the child himself' or, more picturesquely (p. 9), 'At the heart of the educational process lies the child.' Obviously, then, to educate the child, we must understand his nature. How are we to do this? Well, 'In the last fifty years . . . a number of general principles have been established' (p. 9). By whom? By experts—in other words, by those who have done the relevant research into 'the facts' about child-nature. What should be our strategy, then, as 'child-centred' educators? We get a clue on p. 196, for example: 'Teachers must rely both on their general knowledge of child development and on detailed observation of individual children for matching their demands to children's stages of development.' Thus, the Report implies, what we should do is to compare the children in our class with the children as described by the experts and then, having charted the respects in which our children are as it were OK or developing correctly according to the 'general principles', and also by contrast the areas in which they are defective or abnormal or not quite up to scratch, we should then set about devising methods of maintaining what's going along smoothly and servicing what needs treatment or repair. This strategy could be summed up in three simple postulates: (1) the nature of children is adequately describable in terms of general laws or principles, (2) these laws are discovered for us by child-nature experts, principally child psychologists, and (3) education normally consists in meeting

Source: *Hard Cheese*, no. 2, May 1973, pp. 8–18.

the psychological needs which the experts have discovered the children to have. (Abnormally, of course, the education has to be done by the experts themselves. On p. 214, for example, 'we are advised that if children have not learned to read by the age of nine they should be referred to an educational psychologist.')

These three postulates seem to me quite unwarranted and false. Before going on to explain why, however, it is worth noting in passing just how thin and sketchy, in fact, are the actual findings or 'general principles' upon which in practice the workability of the whole strategy depends. One of these principles, for example, is described on p. 9 as having to do with 'present-day concepts about critical or sensitive periods'; yet on p. 11 we are told that 'We have no exact knowledge about [these periods]' and on p. 12 that 'We do not yet know to what extent such critical periods occur in the development of children'. Another general principle is to do with 'developmental "sequence"' (p. 9) and, on p. 11, we are told that 'There seems good reason to suppose that Piaget's successive stages [of developmental "sequence"] depend on progressive maturation or at least progressive organization of the cerebral cortex'; yet, once again, on the same page we learn that 'We know practically nothing, however, about the development of the brain beyond [the age of two]'. A third general principle is given on p. 9 as relating to 'the complex and continuous interaction between the developing organism and its environment'; yet, as before, only a few pages later we discover that nothing much, really, is yet known about the complexities involved in the development, say, of intelligence: 'A particular environment may be highly suitable for a child with certain genes . . . We do not know if such interactions occur in the genesis, for example, of the variations in measured intelligence in our population' (p. 13).

Here are three fundamental 'general principles' of child-nature, then, relating respectively to critical periods in development, to the sequence of stages in development, and to the interaction of heredity and environment in development—but alas! it seems that we know virtually nothing for sure about them. How do we know them at all, in that case, one wonders? Certainly it seems highly improbable that workable educational policies could in practice be based on them.

I have not just picked out isolated examples of this apparent ignorance upon which teachers would have to depend, if they followed the Report's expert-centred strategy. (. . .) Look at the following instance: 'Parental personality, attitudes and modes of child rearing interact with the child's temperament, reinforcing or conflicting with the ways in which he prefers to respond. It is important that early learning should take into account the child's style of response. Little is known, however, of the way in which the different personalities of parent or teacher and child

interact, or of how different attitudes to or modes of rearing affect children of varying endowments' (p. 17). Well, if 'little is known', how on earth can teachers be guided by it? And, if they cannot be guided by it, why say that they ought to be?

Here is another example: 'The research evidence so far available is both too sparse and too heavily weighted by studies of special groups of children to be decisively in favour of nursery education for all. We rely, therefore, on the overwhelming evidence of experienced educators' (p. 119). Notice the strategy: educators' 'evidence' is to be relied on only when 'expert evidence' is unavailable. But what 'evidence' is there that sufficient 'expert evidence' ever will be, or could ever conceivably become, available? Meanwhile, with so great a need (according to the Report) of guidance and with so little help actually forthcoming from the 'guides', it is small wonder that the junior and infant heads who were asked how they achieved their educational aims were capable of 'little more than expressions of benevolent aspiration . . . little more than platitudes . . .' (p. 186). Small wonder, too, that although its basic strategy is to hand educational decisions over to child-nature theorists, the Report is at the same time profoundly ambivalent in its attitude to those theorists and their implied wisdom. On p. 187, for example, we are told that although such theorists 'seldom fear innovation . . . [their] ideas may founder because of their ignorance of what schools . . . are really like'. Yet on p. 121, as quoted above, we saw that the advice of 'experienced educators' was only heeded in default of our having decisive 'research evidence'. By contrast, yet again, on p. 201 we are told that 'great advances [in educational practice] appear to have been made without such theory, and research has still a long way to go before it can make a marked contribution'. Yet, by p. 236, we are being assured all over again that the 'great advances' or 'revolution' in mathematics teaching have only been possible because of the contribution of theory and research.

I shall not pursue these contradictions and ambivalences any further. My point was simply that the Plowden strategy is to base educational practice upon a certain theoretical view of children and their 'nature', namely, that children's education is the product of their maturation and of their learning, both of which are determined by certain 'general principles' of developmental need which are discovered by experts and which must be applied to particular cases by the teachers of the children concerned. As the Report puts it: 'Our study of children's development has emphasized the importance of maturation to learning. The corollary is not to make the teacher's role passive but to underline the importance of diagnosing children's needs and potentialities' (p. 311). It turns out, however, as the above examples illustrate, that this theoretical view is largely empty— a set of ideal principles which is promised for us when enough research has been done, but which in the meantime we have not in fact yet got. Children's 'developmental needs', upon the knowledge of which (as we have seen) the teacher is made dependent for his 'diagnoses' of his pupils' educational requirements, remain obscure. The evidence is 'too sparse'; 'little is known'; 'we have no exact knowledge'; 'we do not yet know . . .'

So, we are left with the three methodological postulates which I listed earlier. Not only is the educational strategy to which they give rise unworkable (because the experts can't yet tell us what they say we need to know); the postulates themselves, I asserted earlier, are unwarranted and false. Why is this?

At first sight the three elements of the strategy sound very plausible. Put them together and they make an appealing 'commonsense' sort of argument which would go something like this: 'We wouldn't dream of deciding for ourselves whether a child has, say, appendicitis or brain damage or a dietary deficiency. Well then, in exactly the same way, we should not expect to be able to see for ourselves what a child's educational deficiencies or needs are. Just as we need to consult experts in physiology, medicine and so on in order to get a reliable diagnosis of bodily health and illness, so, in like manner, we ought to admit our need of "mental" experts (i.e. psychologists etc.) in searching for diagnoses of children's educational needs. The fact that the "mental" experts don't actually know much yet (in the way of reliable evidence about intellectual, social and emotional growth) is irrelevant to the argument. It's just a temporary difficulty which will easily be put right, as more research findings become available. Meanwhile it is obvious, surely, that the right way to proceed in education is to be guided by the experts. Without expert research findings about the general laws of children's developing natures, we just wouldn't know how to devise efficient methods for "child-centred" education. It would all be merely guesswork.'

What is wrong with this plausible argument is its basic assumption that mental growth is exactly the same sort of thing as physical growth, only immaterial; or, to put it another way, that children are just material objects with an extra 'immaterial' bit attached to them, namely, their minds. It is because the Report conceives of the 'general principles' of development in the same terms as physical laws that, in spite of the total lack of agreement as to the content of those principles, it retains both its faith in their eventual discovery and also its determination that teachers should show the same respect for psychology that the surgeon shows for anatomy and physiology or the engineer for maths and physics. The three postulates of the Plowden strategy, in other words, make no sense except in terms of a basic assumption that minds and their education are of fundamentally the same character as bodies and their movement and growth. No one would suppose that the nature of children is adequately describable in terms of 'general principles' (postulate (1)), unless those 'natures' were seen as being fundamentally the same as the natures of physical objects. No one would suppose that the 'developmental needs' of children could ever be discovered by child psychologists (postulate (2)), unless psychology were seen as being fundamentally the same sort of study as physics. No one would suppose that 'education' is the meeting of developmental needs (postulate (3)), unless education were seen as being fundamentally the same sort of thing as processes of inanimate physical change and animate physical growth.

This basic physicalistic assumption runs right through the Report. Take p. 9, for example: the commonest method of studying physical growth, we are told, is 'by measuring the maturity of the skeleton . . . From birth onwards . . . bones undergo a sequence of changes [which] . . . is practically the same in everybody'. Now comes the jump in the argument, from physical changes to personal achievements: 'similar considerations apply to . . . motor development, and it is highly probable that they also apply to emotional and intellectual development.' Children's skills, emotions and intellects, in other words, are assumed to develop in just the same sort of way as their bones grow; their minds are assumed to be the same sort of things as their bodies (only invisible, of course); their thoughts and feelings thus become, theoretically, an immaterial skeleton upon which their education should hang, I suppose, like invisible flesh.

But this is absurd. Minds are conscious; children are aware of themselves and others. Skeletons, by contrast, are not aware of themselves or others, however well-fleshed. No physical object (such as a shinbone) sees itself as a physical object; but all persons (including children) see themselves and others as persons (such as children). Moreover, how a child sees himself and others makes all the difference in the world to what he actually is and may become. Of course there are 'general principles' determining the growth and change of physical things like rocks, trees and skeletons, but no general principles determine the developments and achievements of which persons are capable. It is characteristic of minds to be infinitely variable, to be able always to see and make differences, to construct laws rather than just to be subject to them.

Physical laws are generalizations. Such generalizations often work out all right for physical objects, because physical objects aren't themselves in the habit of making generalizations. But, in the case of children and their education, generalizations are not all right at all, since it is not generalizations but actual individuals whom we are employed to teach in school. In the first place, then, no generalizations ever adequately describe children (since any one of those children, at any time, may describe himself quite differently); in the second place, though, even if generalizations were indeed adequate, nothing would follow from them about how those children should be educated (since any one of those children, at any time, may have views of his own about how he should be educated). Compare with this, however, another passage on p. 9 of the Report: some statistical diagrams are given and we are then told that 'Girls begin puberty on average two years earlier than boys . . . This simple fact has implications for co-education . . . What the diagrams do not show, however, is the wide variations in rate of growth in any group of normal boys and girls . . . The normal range [of age of puberty], comprising 95 per cent of all girls, runs from 10.0 to 15.0 years; for 99 per cent of girls it is from 9.0 to 16.0 years.' So what is the 'simple fact'? If there is one, it can only be that statistical generalizations about puberty are quite useless as a guide to the 'developmental needs' of any actual individual. And even if they were not useless, what would be their 'implications for co-education'? Clearly, nothing at all. The educational values of co-education are something to be argued about whatever the age, or the variations in age, at which children reach puberty; moreover, they are something to be argued about by the 'normal boys and girls' (and the abnormal ones), too, as well as by the growth experts, and the parents, and the teachers, and everybody else concerned.

Take another example: 'Long term studies of the measured intelligence of individual children throughout the whole growing period make it seem likely that children differ in their rates of attaining their adult ability just as they do in attaining their adult height' (pp. 9–10). But how can this be so? In the first place, if 'there are no very precise criteria for determining what constitutes the exercise of intelligence' (p. 21), how can we measure the attainment of it? 'Intelligence' is not a physically measurable thing like height, so how can we know that children 'attain' it 'just as they do' their height? In the second place, though, even if children did indeed grow in intelligence as they do in height, they certainly don't necessarily stop growing when they reach 'adult ability' in the same way as they stop growing when they reach 'adult height'. A person may go on 'growing in intelligence' to the end of his days. Moreover he can 'grow' in some ways but diminish in others, which would be most puzzling if 'intelligence' were subject to the same kind of growth laws as height. (. . .)

Take another example (p. 14): 'Adverse environmental conditions may slow down physical growth, and throw the child off his "programmed curve", that is, off the curve that would be followed by someone of his genotype under optimal environmental conditions . . . The degree to which similar considerations apply to intellectual and emotional development is unknown'. This displays the full syndrome; first we get the assumption that physical and mental 'growth curves' follow the same sort of 'programme' and that this is genotypically determined. Then we are told that actually we know nothing yet about the latter 'growth curve', but of course the implication which we are expected to draw is that this gap in our knowledge is merely temporary and will be filled in due course by appropriate 'research'. What else could we conclude? Well, only that this whole enterprise of viewing persons as invisible physical objects, and education as invisible physical growth, is a fiasco.

Turn on a few pages: 'The emotional aspects of the child's development, like the intellectual, follow a regular sequence based on the interaction between maturational and biological factors on the one hand and experience and learning within the cultural setting on the other . . . Emotional life provides the spur and in many ways gives meaning to experience' (p. 22). So this is what a child's 'nature' is—to be a mere focus for the interaction of genetic and environmental forces or 'spurs' whose 'meaning' is constructed entirely for him by others (his 'setting') and whose 'regular sequence' of development must remain therefore for ever firmly outside his control. His own consciousness of what is happening to him is irrelevant. As he grows, he merely 'internalizes' the external 'controls': 'The child is at first dominated by his needs and impulses. Much early learning is concerned with helping him to . . . build up inner controls . . . within a context of parental and social expectations . . .' (p. 23). Poor little devil! He can't beat them, so he must join them: 'Out of an externally imposed rule of what is permitted arises a sense of what ought to be done and an internal system of control' (p. 25). He might as well be, then, the inanimate object or the quasi-mindless organism which in fact this view of his 'nature' takes him to be, for all the difference it would make. He is lumbered—not just with his determining 'genotype', but with a determining environment as well: 'Unlike the genetic factors, the environmental factors are, or ought to be, largely within our control' (p. 26), but never within his.

And so the Report goes on, describing in detail this overwhelming effort by parents, teachers, experts, everybody, to determine the child's nature for him as inexorably as the laws of chemistry, anatomy and physiology determine his physical growth: 'The outlook and aspirations of their own parents; the opportunities and handicaps of the neighbourhood in which they live; the skill of their teachers [in diagnosing "needs"] and the resources of the schools they go to [in repairing "deficits"]; their genetic inheritance; and other factors still unmeasured and unknown surround the children with a seamless web of circumstance' (p. 50). 'A seamless web of circumstance'—how very apt a phrase! It so perfectly explains the nonentity to which the child has been reduced, in the Report's strategy for him. Over him, as the presiding entity-in-chief, the *mens rationis* of the whole system, rules the child psychologist, dispensing to 'parents and teachers a fuller understanding of the needs of children and an appreciation of the range of behaviour that may properly be regarded as normal . . .' (p. 79). (. . .)

Human beings, then, are not just a focus of interaction or a 'product' of their genotype as 'processed' by their 'cultural setting'. (. . .) What people themselves think about their endowments and their environments makes a difference to them, whereas no stone or rocket could ever conceivably, of itself, make a difference to its rolling downhill or its firing off to the moon. The same goes for plants, insects and animals: what they become is not 'up to them' in the sense in which it is 'up to' a human being. What a cucumber or a police dog becomes is 'up to' causal variables—its stock or breeding, its nutrition and diet, the climate and the regime to which the gardener or the dog-handler subjects it. Yet it is in these sorts of terms, as plants or animals subject entirely to causal laws, that the Report continually describes children. I have given enough examples already, but just look at this one more: there is a strong association, the Report says, 'between the circumstances which affect the nutritional conditions underlying progress in physical development and those other conditions which nourish, as it were, intellectual and emotional growth' (p. 15). But this views knowledge as though it were some kind of invisible food. It gives rise to what Freire calls the 'digestion' model of education— 'mind' as a sort of digestive tract, assimilating invisible nutriment. What sort of education would this be? We could leave the children to forage about for their own 'food': this would be 'discovery based' education, I suppose. Or we could give some children 'compensatory' doses of 'enrichment' like sickly chrysanthemums, either by direct instruction or else by one of the Report's favourite devices, the 'carefully structured environment'. In either case though, whichever we did, the result for the children would be the same: we would be treating them as no more than a focus of external forces, passive objects incapable of becoming anything for themselves. At no time, on this view, could a child's own thoughts or feelings about himself or about his education be taken seriously. To try to take them seriously would be like asking the chrysanthemum whether it actually wanted to win the prize for which we were 'enriching' it, or like asking the police dog what it thought about the laws which we were busy training it to enforce. With this view of children, in practice we could no more 'centre' education upon the child than we could centre our training upon the dog or our composting upon the chrysanthemum. This is why, as I said at the beginning, to me this is not in any real sense 'child-centred' education at all. In fact, it is centred on child psychologists.

To make sense to me, child-centredness would have to be centred on the child as a person, rather than as a bundle of electro-chemical drives and deficits maturing in a nutrient liquid (or 'culture') of social variables. It would have to treat seriously a child's views both of himself and of his education. It would have to start with the child as the person you find him to be in ordinary life, not the child as a theoretical fiction or hypothetical entity in a set of expert statistics. Now, the main characteristic of a person—whether child or adult—is that he is or is capable of being exceptional. He can always, as we say, 'take exception to things'. Always, in other words, he can make out a more or less reasonable case for things being other than what they seem. He can construct a view of the world; he can make laws, interpret them, apply them; he can find out how to use them to his advantage; he can also respect laws— something which, by contrast, no law can do for him: the law, as we say, 'is no respecter of persons'.

Persons, then, are not just subject to law; they couldn't be. They can 'take exception' and 'make exceptions'; plants and machines can't. For a person, 'the facts' and the laws which describe them are always open to being interpreted or 'seen' in some alternative way. 'The facts' are never something entirely fixed, then, or settled once and for all— unless one's existence has 'in fact' become entirely machine-like, vegetable-like or like that of a fully domesticated animal. Short of that quasi-mindless condition, what we call 'the facts' are always matters which are open to reasonable agreement and disagreement. And 'the facts' about children, therefore, the 'laws' of their development—these too are inescapably provisional and negotiable, if children are persons, not mindless organisms or states of merely physical existence. Moreover, if that is so, then children are as entitled as anyone else, however expert, to have views of themselves and of their educational development, views which therefore should be considered as seriously as we consider our own or anyone else's, whenever decisions affecting them as persons are being made (which is all the time). When I want to know 'the facts' about some mindless object—such as a motor car engine which won't start—then I consult the experts' manual, try to recall whatever I once thought I knew about the laws which describe the relevant physical processes, and in the meantime proceed forthwith to tinker about with the engine until I find out what's wrong. By contrast, when I want to know 'the facts' about a person, the first thing I should do is to ask him, not to look up manuals of psychology or statistical tables. Of course he may be wrong about himself— that's not the point: anybody may be wrong; it's a risk you take in being human. The point is that, as a person, he is entitled to the serious consideration of his view as I am to mine or anyone else is to his. The fact that he may be a child is again totally irrelevant to his entitlement to views of his own which count. Why should only adults be entitled to have serious views of children? If children are persons, not just developing organisms and focuses of interaction, then they are as entitled to have their views counted as 'serious' as we are to have ours. (. . .)

Section V Curriculum and cultural reproduction

18 The organization child: experience management in a nursery school*

Rosabeth Moss Kanter

Intentionally or unintentionally, child-rearing practices in a society reflect the character of that society, not only in the explicit standards and demands communicated but also in the kinds of experiences chosen to convey them. There is a relationship between the structure of education and the major institutional forms of a society. If American society conducts a preponderance of its activity through formal organizations, then it is not surprising that even very young children[1] should be provided with the experiences of formal organizations, in the form of nursery schools. It is these experiences which comprise one of the several social worlds of the child, to which he orients his behavior and through which he fulfills his psychic needs. By offering a social world which has the phenomenological impact of a bureaucracy, in the experiences it provides, in the truths and meanings it advances, and in the kinds of interpersonal relationships it promotes, a nursery school can produce children whose world orientations are adjusted and attuned to bureaucratic life.

But nursery schools, like families, generally are not run by the personnel departments of large bureaucracies;[2] they are run by mothers, by teachers, and by others with a concern for the psychological health and normal growth to maturity of their children. Thus, to the extent that the experiences they offer the children reflect larger societal conditions, it is because the notions of health and the views of maturity informing their activities in turn support and reflect these wider social patterns. Educational ventures, then, may mirror and prepare people for structural conditions in their society in implementing theories of health and maturity which themselves attain prominence due to their 'fit' with that same society.

This paper, consequently, hopes to demonstrate: (1) that in an organizational society, a popular psychological ideology supports the defining of

bureaucracy-like experiences as promoting health and maturity; (2) that the practices of one nursery school translate into concrete form these experiences; and (3) that the behavior of the children in that school reflects their experience of a phenomenologically bureaucratic world.

The theses advanced here are derived from seven months of participant-observation in a nursery school in a mid-western town in 1964–5. There were three classes of about 20 children each, each run by a head teacher and one or more assistants. The children generally came from professional families. The teachers were college graduates with majors in psychology or elementary education; some of the assistants were education majors at a nearby college. Two classes of four-year-olds met three times a week for about two-and-one-half hours; one class of three-year-olds met twice a week for the same length of time. Observational material was supplemented by informal interviews with the teachers, attendance at counselling sessions and other functions for parents, and a questionnaire returned by the parents.

The framework was developed to account for the congruence of societal and ideological forces operating in a single case. It must be seen both as a model which generalizes on the basis of ideal types and as a case study bound by its historical time, the early 1960s. It is not a description of empirical reality expected to be true for all nursery schools, but rather a description of how certain factors worked together in one situation. It is presented to stimulate further thought and research on the relationship of structure and processes within educational organizations to wider societal trends.

The organizational society and concepts of psychological health

(. . .) Along with changes in society toward bureaucracy as the dominant social pattern and the bureaucrat

Source: *Sociology of Education*, 45 (2), 1972, pp. 186–212.

as the dominant social type concomitant changes in child-rearing have taken into account the shift in adult roles. Increasingly, more permissive, love-oriented techniques which emphasize social adjustment have been substituted for strict independence demands at early ages, which formerly stressed self-reliance and achievement.[3] Miller and Swanson (1958) have tied these changes directly to parents' conceptions of adult roles, to their bureaucratic as opposed to entrepreneurial orientations. Miller and Swanson define entrepreneurs as people holding jobs affected by the risks of the market place, with income dependent on enterprise and judgment. Bureaucrats, on the other hand, hold jobs characterized by lack of control of the means of production, specialization, wages or salary, and relative security. For the bureaucrat, then, innovation, independence, and risk-taking are no longer salient features of adult enterprise. Miller and Swanson (1958:55) found significant differences in the child-rearing practices of entrepreneurs and bureaucrats, indicating lowered achievement, independence, and self-reliance training for the children of bureaucrats, along with increased permissiveness. Thus, the expectations held for the child's adult roles in bureaucracies help shape his training. (. . .) Adjustment and 'belonging' rather than competition are stressed by bureaucratic parents.

The changes noted in child-rearing in a bureaucratic society also have been incorporated into the school system. Whyte (1956:432–4) has documented the bureaucratic emphasis in the schools to which the 'organization man' sends his children. These schools are marked by a noticeably permissive atmosphere, a stress on adjustment, a reduction of academic competition, and a desire by parents to have their children taught to be 'good citizens' who will get along well with other people. (. . .)

One major conception of mental health informing these changes, one set of psychological premises through which parents and educators choose and justify their acts, is neo-Freudian ideology—Freud and the neo-Freudians as they have been translated to the general public and popularized.[4] According to LaPiere (1959), the neo-Freudian ethic has replaced the Protestant ethic as the dominant conceptualization of the mature man; man's growth is measured by his social adjustment and interpersonal skill rather than by his individualistic accomplishments (taken by the Puritans as evidence of his worth in the eyes of God). On the other hand, the changes in child-rearing also are related to increasing bureaucratization of the adult world. These trends, bureaucratization of society and popularization of neo-Freudian ideology, provide the background for conceptions of psychological maturity. On the one hand, individual behavior can be measured against the needs and norms of bureaucratic organization,[5] and those who cannot adjust to bureaucracy can be considered 'abnormal' or 'immature.' At the same time, individual behavior can be measured against the explicitly psychological,

health-oriented standards of the neo-Freudians.[6] It can be shown that in a number of respects these two ideals for health and maturity are mutually reinforcing (see Kanter, 1968).

In a general sense, the goal of mature human development for Freud's transformers is rationality. Man is inherently irrational, but through various growth processes he can come to know and control his unconscious impulses. By striving to achieve mastery over his own irrationality, he can achieve a kind of rationality. Bureaucracy, in much the same way, can be seen as seeking to overcome irrationality, through a combination of knowing (i.e. becoming aware of recurrent problems and providing institutionalized means for their resolution) and self-control. Bureaucracy, of course, has as a defining characteristic its emphasis on rational control. Here is found a rational-legalistic basis of power, specific assignment of responsibility, investment of power in roles rather than persons, reliance on formal rules and procedures, and the basing of decisions on scientific and therefore standardized principles (Gerth and Mills, 1958: 196–244). While individual role incumbents certainly bring with them personal, emotional, and irrational considerations, the structural arrangements are such that these presumably have little effect on routine functioning. According to Merton (1957: 196): 'The structure is one which approaches the complete elimination of personalized relationships and nonrational considerations (hostility, anxiety . . .).' Thus, the central goal for both a healthy man and a 'healthy' organization is rationality or rational control. For a Freudian, the healthy man is rational because control of his mental life by the 'higher psychical agencies' is governed by the 'reality principle' (Freud, 1929). The bureaucrat is rational because 'he must constantly attend to the reality presented by his work if he is to perform it with precision and caution' (Miller and Swanson, 1958:208).

A second point of conceptual similarity of neo-Freudian ideology and the ideal typical bureaucratic organization lies in the attribution of responsibility for individual behavior. Neo-Freudian ideology shifts responsibility from the individual to society in many areas. The neo-Freudians translate the basic antagonism between man's natural impulses and the requirements of civilized life posited by Freud (1929) into the responsibility of society for producing the mature man. It is society's duty to replace man's unconscious antisocial impulses (which are no fault of his own) with civilized social tendencies. Society can work in the interests of man, and it is up to society to do so. To paraphrase a common saying, there are no intentionally bad children, only bad socializing agents: 'Society has failed the neurotic, never vice versa' (LaPiere, 1959:53). Fromm (1956) even has proposed that we consider societies unhealthy, rather than the people in them. Apparent individual neurosis might be in fact a 'socially patterned defect'

(Fromm, 1956:15). Personal accountability thereby is diminished. Neo-Freudian ideology further reduces individual accountability because of the relation of guilt to neurosis; guilt is held to be at the root of many neurotic difficulties. The healthy individual, however, is removed from the tyranny of a punitive superego (Jones, 1951:202), and free from the responsibility for conforming to its overly harsh, unnecessarily strict, and nearly impossible demands. Because guilt is considered unhealthy, and failure to meet certain demands might generate guilt, the area of personal accountability of the mature man should be 'reasonable' in terms of man's limitations—and thereby it is diminished and limited by the neo-Freudians.

At the same time, bureaucratic organization shifts much responsibility from the individual to the organization. For example, an organization may use tests to assign people to offices, so that failure in role-performance becomes attributable to a mistaken assignment by the organization rather than the personal fault of the individual. The personal worth of the individual rarely is at stake. Since only a segment of his personality is involved in his specialized role, feelings of complete personal responsibility for role performance in its widest sense, feelings which might generate guilt, are unnecessary. In addition, bureaucratic organization may take a statistical rather than a personal view of failure—that there will be a certain percentage of imperfect goods manufactured, a certain turnover rate, etc.; this is seen as being inherent in the organization. Bureaucracy limits the individual's sphere of decision-making, so that he is responsible only in a very narrow area of competence. It limits his personal accountability by giving him clearly-defined rules and routines to follow; mistakes can be attributed to poor rules set down by the organization or to the fact that rules do not cover all contingencies, and not to the individual. Since the organization makes rules to cover every envisioned situation, precluding 'the necessity for the issuance of specific instructions for each specific case' (Merton, 1957:196), it is taking responsibility for the person's behavior out of his hands. Thus, it appears to a bureaucratic society that behavior is a function of the organizational setting in which one works, just as certain other kinds of psychological behavior are explained by the culture and social structure into which one is born. The individual cannot be held completely accountable, and that, according to neo-Freudian ideology, is as it should be.

Third, both neo-Freudian ideology and bureaucratic organization emphasize security. Security is the 'magic word' in the neo-Freudian view of existence (LaPiere, 1959:92). Only with the knowledge that his world will stay fairly constant and predictable can man function as a 'calm complacent adult.' (This is, of course, connected with the notion that tension reduction is a primary motive in behavior and Freud's idea of the centrality of the 'pleasure principle' in human actions.) At the same time, the ideal typical bureaucracy, in order to secure rational control and reliability, is built on security, routinization, fixity of procedure, and constancy of stimuli and response. By such mechanisms as the regularization of promotion, the instituting of tenure and seniority, and generally fixed wages and salary which are unrelated to financial fluctuations and only slightly related to individual performance, the organization eliminates sources of uncertainty and inconstancy. According to Merton (1957:196): 'Most bureaucratic offices involve the expectation of life-long tenure, in the absence of disturbing factors which may decrease the size of the organization. Bureaucracy maximizes vocational security.' Finally, there are few risks for individuals associated with the bureaucratic organization; clear rules and procedures eliminate uncertainty and insecurity even in decision-making. Bureaucracies, as well as neo-Freudian ideology, find security a positive goal.

The neo-Freudian ethic considers individualistic, achievement-oriented people psychologically abnormal. LaPiere (1959:34) has written: 'To Marx men of enterprise are the villains of history, the capitalistic exploiters of the downtrodden, productive masses. To Freud, on the other hand, men of enterprise are neither heroes nor villains—they are neurotic.' Bureaucratic organization concurrently may tend to devalue men of individualistic enterprise. The stress for appropriate bureaucratic behavior is on reliability rather than innovation. The organization wants personnel who will perform faithfully the jobs given them in the tried-and-true way rather than challenge the established procedures. The organization cannot afford risk-takers; the immediate costs might be too great.

Freud himself theorized that there should be a balance between external control and freedom with regard to man's impulse life and, hence, his behavior. In *New Introductory Lectures on Psychoanalysis*, Freud has stated (cited in Wolman 1960:277):

> The child has to learn to control its instincts.
> To grant it complete freedom so that it obeys all
> its impulses without any restriction is impossible.
> The function of education therefore is to inhibit,
> forbid, and suppress, and it has at all times
> carried out this function to admiration. But we
> have learned from analysis that it is the very
> suppression of instincts that involves the danger
> of neurotic illness. Education has therefore to
> stem its way between the Scylla of giving the
> instincts free play and the Charybdis of frustrating
> them.

Large formal organizations also in a sense attempt a balance between control and freedom. On the one hand, control over the individual's impulsive behavior is secured by some of the rational means outlined earlier, and especially by uncertainty reduction, giving the individual a fixed set of expectations for his behavior. In Merton's terms, 'Specific procedural devices foster objectivity and restrain the "quick passage of impulse into action" ' (1957:195). That is, in a general procedural sense behavior is restricted and channelled in various ways. On the other hand, the individual is relatively free from coercion; his commitment to the organization is a calculative one (Etzioni, 1961:3–23) which balances the gains of membership against the costs of participation. Force is not exercised. As March and Simon (1958:84) have pointed out, people will continue to participate in the bureaucratic organization only as long as the inducements offered them are as great or greater than the contribution they are asked to make.

Finally, both neo-Freudian ideology and bureaucratic organization devalue and de-emphasize conflict. In the ideology, interpersonal conflict, especially competition and rivalry, are at the root of many neurotic difficulties. According to Horney (1937:284) individual competition leads to a diffuse hostile tension and fear of failure which may form the basis of a neurosis. The neurotic 'constantly measures himself against others' (Horney, 1937:188); he wishes to be exceptional and superior, seeking his own success at the expense of other people. (Horney 1937:192) has argued: 'Hostility is inherent in every intense competition, since the victory of one of the competitors implies the defeat of the other.' Competition generates anxiety not only for the 'loser,' but also for the 'winner,' since there is always the fear that someone even more skilled will appear and in turn be triumphant (Horney, 1937:207). Viewing the healthy man as non-competitive is congruent with bureaucratic organization, which negatively evaluates competition. For the smooth running of the organization, team work and loyalty to the system are stressed above individual rivalry, with system rewards often replacing individual rewards. Merton (1957:201) has noted:

> Another feature of the bureaucratic structure . . . [is that] functionaries have a sense of a common destiny for all who work together. They share the same interests, especially since there is relatively little competition insofar as promotion is in terms of seniority. In-group aggression is thus minimized and this arrangement is therefore conceived to be positively functional for the bureaucracy.

Competition is thus both unhealthy for the individual, according to the neo-Freudians, and unhealthy for the bureaucratic organization.

What emerges as the central psychological problem for both the neo-Freudian and for the bureaucratic organization is control of human emotional irrationality. This is defined by the neo-Freudians in terms of anxiety. Horney (1937:41) has termed anxiety 'the dynamic center of neurosis.' Sullivan (1955) believes that a person spends much of his lifetime and a great deal of his energy in avoiding more anxiety than he

already has, and, if possible, ridding himself of some of this anxiety.

And what experiences produce anxiety in the neo-Freudian ethic? Precisely those which are largely *limited* at the middle and lower ranks of bureaucratic organization. Central sources of trauma in neo-Freudian ideology are the antitheses of some bureaucratic forms. At least seven kinds of experience are considered to be traumatic, stimulating anxiety and therefore generating neurosis: *uncertainty* (lack of definition of the situation and of role relationships and requirements); *strangeness* (constant intrusion of unfamiliar stimuli); *mystery* (the a-rational, non-scientific unknown); *coercion* (being forced to do things 'against one's will'); personal *accountability* (guilt-induction, punitive self-assignment of responsibility); *unpleasantness* (necessity of performing unmotivated behavior); and external peer *conflict* (competitive, nonharmonious, non-status-equal relationships). But it is just these conditions which are mitigated in bureaucratic social systems, which stress instead clear rules for decision-making, fixity of procedures, constancy of stimuli, a rational-scientific world-view; calculative involvement, non-coercive means of social control, narrowing of personal accountability, non-competitive working relations, democratic norms, and interpersonal harmony. Attempts to eliminate these 'traumatic' conditions, then, in order to promote the neo-Freudian view of health, can lead to the establishment of bureaucratic norms.

The healthy, mature, well-adjusted man, in short, according to an extreme version of neo-Freudian ideology, is the man who, coincidentally, is attuned to bureaucracy: the man who does not experience such 'traumas' as uncertainty, guilt, and competition; the man who prefers certainty, security, limited responsibility, conformity, and no-conflict situations; the 'other-directed man' acting out the 'social ethic.' Organizational rationalization is presumed to make man rational, in this view, and bureaucratic forms become connected with conceptions of psychological maturity.

Thus, it is proposed that the conception of psychological health advanced by a particular pervasive school of thought and implemented by various social institutions has had the unintended consequence of spreading bureaucratic experiences. The psychic manifestations of a bureaucratic society are more pervasive than simply the number of formal organizations bearing bureaucratic structures would indicate. Many organizations which are not formally bureaucratic, which lack such defining characteristics as elaborate hierarchy, career involvement, and specialized official duties still may implement bureaucratic norms in their management of personal experience, in the phenomenological impact of their social arrangements (Gerth and Mills, 1958:194–244). A people-processing organization such as a nursery school, eager to implement the most advanced conceptions of mental health and maturity, anxious to provide the 'right kind' of experience for its children, unintentionally may establish bureaucratic conditions in order to do so. And for the children in such an organization, these phenomenologically-bureaucratic conditions represent their social world, the world to which they adjust their social behavior and through which they fulfill their psychic needs.

Thus far I have described the set of social and ideological circumstances which have combined to generate a nursery school such as the one I studied. Within the school these very general social trends are given specific form, in a set of arrangements and relationships which define one social world an American middle-class child might encounter.

The nursery school as an organizational experience

Nursery schools, compared to other kinds of schools, have a rather large amount of freedom of choice. Nursery school is not required under law, and there is no particular set of tasks that it must perform. To at least one of the parents whose children attended the school described here, the purpose of nursery school was nothing more than 'giving children an opportunity to play with their own age group.' For others, the goal is a very vague one: 'more knowledge about the world.' Many of the parents felt that the nursery school had fulfilled its responsibilities if their children returned home 'kind, courteous, and cheerful.'

Given this wide latitude, the nursery school implemented its conception of an appropriate set of experiences for the child. This involved dealing with the children and structuring the environment in such a way as to limit the seven experiences seen as 'anxiety-producing,' and, as a result, creating a world which was phenomenologically rather more like a bureaucratic organization than a nursery school, with its non-instrumental emphasis, need be.

Limiting uncertainty

Uncertainty can be mitigated by the provision of procedures and routines, by clearly defining relationships, expectations, and appropriate behavior. While formal routines and clearly-defined procedures are not a necessary feature of an organization oriented around play, the nursery school instituted definite routines. (. . .)

By means of the routine, activities clearly were circumscribed in time and space, with clear beginnings and endings, and the child's behavior was structured via the equipment available. A sense of specialization pervaded the routine; places, toys, and time periods all had particular activities associated with them. And, events to follow were as familiar as events that had already occurred, for they were regular in their form.

Play activity itself was circumscribed and given a place in the larger pattern of events that comprised the organization. Play illusions would be supported only when the situation was defined as 'playing' and discouraged when the context was different. For example, while playing in the school's sandbox, children often would give one of the teachers a gift of sand pie. The teachers would accept with gratitude, pretend to eat the pie, and proclaim it delicious. The same activity at any other time, however, would meet with disapproval. At snack time, when 'real' things were available to eat, the teachers would not support make-believe. Play thus was compartmentalized, and the distinction between play, a small part of the school's activity, and reality, the larger organizational context, made clear.

Delineation of role relationships also reduced uncertainty and showed the child his place in the organization. The most important role distinction was teacher-child. Teachers were socially distinguished from children not only by their adult stature and bearing, but also by their control of certain resources and their relative freedom with regard to participation in expressive songs and games. The teachers themselves informally distinguished their roles and status from the child's; they generally used a different tone of voice and vocabulary when speaking to a child than when speaking to another teacher or adult.

The teachers also imposed structure on the nursery school situation in other ways, by the institutionalization of certain practices, by asking that things have names in the 'real world,' and by attempts at organizing play. Possibly the most important institutionalized practice was Clean Up Time. A chord on the piano announced it, and the children would put their toys away with a great deal of enthusiasm. The insistence that things be identified in the 'real' (adult) world imposed the teachers' definition of reality on the child. For example, a child wrapped a scarf around his hand one day saying, 'Look, I have a new hand.' The teacher responded, 'No, that looks to me like a bandage,' rejecting the child's view of reality and substituting her own. And finally, the teachers also introduced games to the children, games with rules and procedures, and without fantasy or illusion.

Thus, the nursery school had a series of uncertainty-reducing mechanisms with a bureaucratic flavor: a formal and generally invariant routine; specialization of activities with respect to time and place; delineation of role and relationships; models of appropriate behavior; institutionalized and structured practices and procedures; and imposition of organization on even 'free' expressive behavior.

Limiting strangeness

Strangeness was handled by attempting to minimize change: easing the transition from familiar surroundings (the home) to initially unfamiliar ones (the nursery school), introducing any new or different routines, songs, and games slowly so as to avoid sudden intrusion of strange stimuli, and consistently and continually emphasizing familiar aspects of the organization through ritual. The goal was security.

Rituals of various kinds helped to emphasize the familiar. Nursery school rituals involved doing certain things over and over and over without thinking about them; within the ritual itself, key elements were repeated automatically. (. . .)

The familiar also was emphasized in other ways. Stories that the children liked were read over and over again, with the children often anticipating the words and chanting them with the teacher. Unimportant arrangements easily became traditional, part of the culture. Toys consisted primarily of familiar objects; a major play setting was the doll-house, which carefully duplicated aspects of the homes the children had left. Changes in routine were minimal. The children thus could come to depend upon the familiar and traditional, the security of the known.

Limiting mystery

In managing the experience of its children, the nursery school also attempted to eliminate the mysterious, magical, frightening, fantastic, the in-explicable, illogical, unknown. Instead the world was presented as rational, as mundane. It was the world of science, of twentieth century rationality, of pragma-tism, that was given to the children, not the world of fantasy, fairy stories, and miraculous occurrences. Stories, records, and games sought not to stretch their imagination or credulity, but rather to stress what an eminently logical world this is. Supernatural beings, including God, did not populate the world of this nursery school. The teachers viewed fairy tales as 'disturbing information' with which the children would not be able to cope, and in addition, as functionless, since they did not portray the 'real world.' (. . .)

Limiting coercion

While the nursery school had a rationalized culture and a routinized structure in which power was associated with certain roles, it at the same time attempted to moderate the exercise of authority so as to minimize coercion. The aim was to provide structure for the child without forcing him to 'do things against his will.' The teachers made use of two general strategies to limit coercion: (1) by permitting the child as much freedom of behavior as possible within the general procedural rules and routines— (e.g. it did not matter what a child did as long as he was in the proper place at the proper time); and (2) by a disguised use of power in those cases when they felt it necessary to control behavior. Reasons for an exercise of authority were phrased in terms of their benefit to the child; if, for example, one child were distracting another and the teacher wished him to stop, she never indicated this directly but instead would ask him to 'move forward so he could see better.' To remove a child from a room, the teacher would not send him out as punishment but ask him to 'do her a favor' and go help the other teacher. This meant in effect that there was an apparent absence of standards for behavior, except enabling the routine to operate smoothly, and an absence of punishments or perceived negative sanctions. In addition, non-scheduled activities generally were suppressed by the lack of access to them; since certain things were available only at certain times, the children generally found it easier to engage in the current group activity than to fail to, and thus, the teachers need not use their authority.

Limiting accountability

In order to limit accountability, and hence avoid what they defined as the experience of self-punishing guilt, the teachers first defined as little as possible as deviant or non-permissible and, secondly, promoted the view that any undesirable behaviors were un-intentional. The child was not considered responsible for any deviant or anti-social acts. Aggression by one child against another—kicking, pushing out of line— was attributed to carelessness or accident; a child would be admonished with: 'You'll be more careful next time, won't you?' Breaking one of the few rules that did exist in the school was attributed to poor memory. 'You forgot this time, next time you'll remember.' When an argument or fight developed between two children, the teachers would solve the dispute by separating them, rarely by admonishing them. Furthermore, there were no perceived negative consequences stemming from deviance as the only 'punishment' used was isolation from the group, often seen as a privilege by the children. In fact, isolation usually was used to ensure control over the rest of the children rather than to indicate deviant status. In short, there were only three kinds of situations in which the issue of accountability could arise: aggression against another, the breaking of a pro-cedural rule, or a threat to group control; in none of these did the child behind it suffer loss of esteem or face the consequences of his acts.

Limiting unpleasantness

This nursery school, probably in common with many others, wanted to eliminate for the child the necessity to engage in unmotivated behaviors. The teachers attempted to make everything fun for the children, even potentially unpleasant events, by making them into games or insisting on their pleasurable aspects. In talking to the children, the teachers consistently maintained that everything was wonderful, promoting a kind of 'fun philosophy.' For example, if a child should comment that working with clay was messy, the teacher would reply that in spite of this it 'felt good.' Only pleasant beliefs about the world and about themselves were encouraged, even in insignificant areas; the child was never asked to face unpleasant facts. Negative evaluations simply did not exist. To tell a child that his artistic output was 'wonderful'—and no other kind of remark ever was observed—was meant to motivate him to further endeavors, and to sustain positive self-concepts. (As in the case of limiting coercion, we can note an apparent absence of standards for behavior, such as the notion that some artistic efforts may be less 'wonderful' than others.) At the same time, unpleasantness was eliminated from tasks and teacher demands by turning them into games, with pleasure again seen to be a prime motivating principle. For example, elaborate transition games were used to move the children from one room to another, so that the potentially unpleasant situation of leaving an enjoyable activity and walking quietly to another room was turned into fun. In fact, games often were used as a device to get the children quiet. And finally, tasks such as cleaning up also were imbued with game-like qualities, with the spirit of fun. 'See how many blocks you can carry to the closet.' Holding the door for others or carrying a wastebasket for example, were designated 'honors.' Limiting unpleasantness meant, in a sense, that the organization had taken over the job of providing motivation for the children.

Limiting peer conflict

A final goal of the nursery school was to eliminate competitive, non-harmonious, non-status-equal relationships and replace them with harmonious, democratic groups in which the children worked together well and no child was favored. To this end, the school deemphasized competition. There were no gold stars, no prizes, and no winners—in fact, there were no achievements and no basis for differential rewards. There were no real rewards available that were not administered routinely to everyone. Instead, the teachers substituted explicit democratic norms of sharing and equality. The school was oriented around the principle that no child was better than any other, or possibly more accurately, that no child was any worse or less deserving. Hence, everyone had his turn as door-opener, wastebasket carrier, Farmer (in Farmer in the Dell) or 'leader,' in a game involving a leader. In fact, status seeking, or pushing to become 'leader,' often resulted in that person losing his turn. Skill differences among the children, in addition, were not recognized formally. When there was differential treatment, it, in the manner of bureaucracy, was accorded to a role and not to a person: Birthday Child, Farmer in the Dell. The teachers also attempted to maintain strict equality with respect to privileges and possessions. By providing a large number of toys and a variety of activities, the teachers hoped to avoid conflicts over scarce resources. But when such difficulties did arise the teachers limited conflict by using an impersonal principle, the norm of

sharing. Toys were shared; turns were shared: there were no monopolies formally acknowledged on anything, again regardless of skill differences. (. . .) In their limiting conflict the teachers revealed not only the dominating emphasis on smooth interpersonal relations characteristic of an organizational society but in addition the universalistic orientations also characteristic of bureaucratic organizations.

The nursery school, in summary, was an organizational experience in which a standard routine and a set of procedures involving temporal and spatial specialization were followed (. . .) In attempting to implement popularized neo-Freudian ideas about eliminating experiences incompatible with psychological health and maturity, the school had created a world phenomenologically resembling the large-scale formal organization. In fact, even though the expressed goal of the school involved promoting the growth of the children, the teachers spent more time managing the smooth running of the organization, just as in a bureaucracy, than they did dealing with the children's individual psychological needs.[7]

How might the recipient of such experiences behave? How might a child adjust his behavior to the world or organizations? How might he work within its constraints to fulfill his own needs?

The organization child

A composite picture of the children in the nursery school studied I call the 'organization child.'[8] There are several reasons for this: this ideal type describes a group of children within a formal organization; the formal organization is itself a reflection of views characteristic of an organizational or bureaucratic society; this child displays patterns of behavior well-suited to some of the demands and constraints of organizational life; and often he exhibits a striking similarity to adult 'organization men,' especially in his play.

The organization child, like the organization man, is asked to accept organizational reality as given, adjust to routine, take on a limited rather than a diffuse obligation to the organization, and guide his behavior by impersonal, universalistic principles. How did these factors enter into the behavior of the children in the nursery school?

Orientation to organizational reality

The organization child behaved as if he were more concerned with the aspects of his environment defined as 'real' by the school than the things he himself created. The nursery school emphasized concrete matters such as routines, limiting uncertainty, strangeness, and mystery, and the routine transcended in importance products of a child's individual imagination or his personal whim. Given all of this, the organization had more reality than any individual; it was permanent and unchanging, whereas the individual was temporary and variable; thus, the individual had to adapt to the reality of the organization, its rational, routinized character, and what he did by or for himself when there were no expectations was less 'real' than what the organization asked him to do.

The child oriented himself to this kind of reality, then, and was more comfortable in situations where the organization provided expectations and guides than with situations requiring his own structuring. He thus was oriented, like a bureaucrat, to the reliable performance of structured roles rather than to imagination; the child here exhibited a rationalization of his world analagous to the rationalization in bureaucracy. For example, most of the children in the school favored programmed activities, or ones in which structure predominated, over free play and fantasy: they might play rather listlessly during a free play period but throw themselves enthusiastically into Clean Up Time. Little pretending actually occurred in play. In fact, play generally was non-binding, minimally involving, and easily interrupted by the teacher; it was as though the children had a notion of what and who were really important.

The experiential world of the child as mediated by the school was a rational mundane place in which miraculous and inexplicable things did not occur. Before he could play he needed reasons for things; play situations generally had to make sense, to match reality as he knew it. (. . .)

Finally, the distinction between play and reality was very clear to the organization child. The children easily could effect the transition from play roles to organizational roles, and they managed with no difficulty to keep them separate and straight. During a costume party, for example, one girl introduced herself to me with, 'My name is Queen Esther. My real name is Annie.'

The routinization of play

In a nursery school characterized by a relatively great amount of structuring of relationships and reality orientation on the part of the children, it is not surprising that play itself became a matter of routine. Definite ways to play were acknowledged. There were 'rules' for the procedural conduct of play, just as there are rules in any organized situation. When asked why she was doing a particular thing, one girl responded, 'Because that's *how you play*.' The children had a technique for play, just as they had techniques for painting or riding tricycles, and just as the bureaucrat relied on techniques to perform his job. There was a continuity of the roles adopted in play and a persistence of certain structural patterns. It was important what things are called, how they were allocated, and who was 'allowed' to take which play roles. That is, for a large number of the children in a large number of situations, the conduct of play and the adoption of roles were not considered a matter of

personal choice or preference; they were rather, given by the organization of the play situation.

'How you play' involved naming the play, designating objects in terms of it, assigning roles, and allocating equipment and territories. This organized structuring became an end in itself, so that it was unimportant what the specific play situation was as long as it was set up properly. The children spent a relatively great deal of time organizing and relatively little time actually carrying out any activity for which they had so carefully designed and organized a structure. (. . .) Finally, the children appeared constrained by the structure they set up; they did not feel free to innovate or to exercise personal whim. They exhibited bureaucratic commitment to a line of action and to a routine.

The discouragement of personal responsibility

The aspects of the school concerned with limiting coercion, accountability, and unpleasantness could be associated with this third important aspect of the organization child. Since the child was not forced to do anything against his will, and neither punished for antisocial acts nor considered to have intended them, the source of responsibility for behavior was removed from the individual and placed squarely in the hands of the organization. If the teacher said that some aggressive act was an 'accident,' the child need not believe that he was at all responsible. In fact, the child became very adept at insisting, 'I didn't mean it!' and thereby removing himself from responsibility. This also enabled him to continue to do as he pleased. Further, the school took on the job of providing motivation *for* the child by making things 'fun.' The organization child, therefore, need experience no inner compulsions to be moral, to participate, to cooperate, or to keep the enterprise as a whole running smoothly; it was his responsibility only to look out for himself. This was the four-year-old equivalent of the 'minimum acceptable performance.' For example, the children often followed only the most general procedural requirement, such as presence in a particular room at a particular time, but they then participated in group activities or paid attention to the teacher only if they 'felt like it.'

The maintenance of ascendancy

Given an organizational form characterized by the elimination of competition and norms of sharing and equality, in what ways could a child establish a superior social position if he desired ascendancy? The organization child was found to develop four kinds of adaptive ascendancy-maintaining techniques: 'conversion,' the game of 'one-upmanship,' valuation of private resources, and manipulation of democratic norms. 'Conversion' refers to the taking over of attitudes and perspectives of authority figures— the teachers in the nursery school. Since there were no ascendant roles available for the child, he could identify with the teacher and act as she would toward other children, thus establishing a quasi-ascendancy. This was noted, for example, when children pointed out 'the rules' or the 'correct' way of doing things to others and insisted they be obeyed to the letter. 'Telling on' someone to the teacher was another conversion response.

Another frequent ascendancy-maintaining pattern was the game of 'one-upmanship.' When children desired recognition of their feats or possessions or that they be accorded credit for their uniqueness and superiority, a game of the following form ensued: Child 1: You know what I have? I have an X. Child 2 replies: Oh yeh, well I have a *bigger* X ... or a newer X, or several Xs, or a Y. The ultimate in one-upmanship was exhibited by one aggressive boy. The children's current game was revealing how high they could count. There were shouts of, 'I can count to a hundred!' 'I can count to a thousand!' but this boy managed to get the last word. He claimed he could count to infinity.

Associated with one-upmanship was the valuation of private property, territory, and one's niche in the organization. Just as for adults, the size and location of one's 'place' were symbols of prestige, means by which ascendancy could be indicated and maintained. Valued places included particular spots in games or being next to the teacher.

A final technique was manipulation of norms of sharing and equality. This was accomplished by overt acceptance and recognition of the universalistic norms but adapting them so as to maintain personal control of the situation. For example, a child might bring a possession from home and overtly share it with others, but remind them constantly of his munificence. Even though the norm of sharing was in operation, the children were dependent on the owner and obliged to recognize his superior position if they want to 'share' his possession. Similarly, the leader in a play situation could bow to the norm of equality by allowing others to have positions officially equal to his but still retain control by taking a slightly *more* equal position. For example, one boy usually held the position of highest authority when his group played, but occasionally others would want to be leader. He could officially consent to this but retain control by saying, 'Okay, Eric—you can be the *chief*, Larry—you can be the *head*, and I'll be the *boss*!' Now the others carried out the boy's orders not as subordinates but as equals. Similar manipulations in other situations also represented ways of getting ahead or maintaining ascendancy given the constraints of an overtly noncompetitive situation.

Thus, the organization child was oriented to organizational reality, his play was highly routinized, he had little personal responsibility, and he had developed adaptive techniques for the maintenance of ascendancy.

Conclusion

There are trends and counter-trends and exceptions to trends—this is recognized. Even while this was being written, the ideas and institutions themselves were changing. What was true in 1964 may be no longer true today. But this paper is an attempt to detail what happens when certain trends coincide in one concrete organization at one time in history, and to make sense out of the behavior in this organization by seeing it as a function of this coincidence of trends. Other nursery schools exist, utilizing other theories—Montessori schools, for example. There are other explanations for the individual pieces of behavior I describe, just as there are other determinants of behavior than those I mention. But when all of the pieces that I found together at one time and in one place are added up, a model such as that proposed here is needed to adequately conceptualize the whole. (...)

Notes

* Revision of Working Paper no. 16, Center for Research on Social Organization, University of Michigan. An earlier version was read at the 1966 Meeting of the American Sociological Association.
1 Nursery schools are generally for three- and four-year-olds, but I have heard of two-year-olds attending.
2 In fact, there is a larger corporation in Boston that is attempting to run a nursery school for the children of workers, but the personnel department is not in charge.
3 See Stendler (1965), Wolfenstein (1953), and Bronfenbrenner (1964).
4 What I am loosely calling neo-Freudian ideology, LaPiere (1959) calls 'the Freudian ethic.' 'Freudian' is something of a misnomer, since Freud's own writings maintain a radical bent and a skepticism about the ability of society ever to meet individual needs (see Rieff, 1959). Freud shows a fundamental ambivalence toward work, authority, and other social facts, and this does not quite coincide with acceptance of bureaucratic trends (see Riesman, n.d.:174–302). It is rather the neo-Freudians (Horney, Fromm, Sullivan) who transform this somewhat radical position into a more conservative acceptance of the bureaucratic-welfare society, as pointed out by Marcuse (1962:217–51). For this reason the ideology will be termed neo-Freudian. Of course, even in this case it has been distorted and exaggerated in the process of popularization.
5 The statements about bureaucracy apply primarily to the middle and lower levels of bureaucratic organization. Some of these propositions would not hold true for the upper levels of bureaucracy. Weber, for example, saw the very top levels of bureaucracies as peopled not with bureaucrats but with charismatic or traditional leaders, that is, men whose power base was other than legal-rationalistic. Miller and Swanson (1958) and others define the men at the upper levels of

large-scale organizations as entrepreneurs and propose that their situation and hence their orientations are much more entrepreneurial than bureaucratic. The discussion to follow, then, and comments throughout this paper, refer primarily to middle and low-level bureaucrats, the vast ranks of organizations, and not to the men or the situation at the top.

6 The ideology here is defined as consisting predominantly of the works of Horney, Fromm, and Sullivan. Some 'levelling' and 'sharpening' has occurred in the process of translating their ideas into a popular ideology, and these writers themselves might not completely agree with all the conclusions drawn from their work.

7 One could argue, as I suppose the teachers would, that smooth running of the organization itself promoted growth. This, of course, involves again a set of assumptions about the nature of psychological health and personal growth and what experiences encourage this.

8 The designation 'organization child' has antecedents. Whyte (1957) refers to 'organization children,' and Olson and Daley (1963:432) use the title also.

References

Bronfenbrenner, Urie, 1964, 'The changing American child: a speculative analysis', in Neil Smelser and William T. Smelser, eds, *Personality and Social Systems*, New York, Wiley, pp. 347–57.

Etzioni, Amitai, 1961, *A Comparative Analysis of Complex Organizations*, New York, Free Press.

Freud, Sigmund, 1929, *Civilization and Its Discontents*, trans. and ed. James Strachey, New York, Norton (1962).

Fromm, Erich, 1956, *The Sane Society*, Routledge & Kegan Paul.

Gerth, Hans, and Mills, C. Wright, 1958, *From Max Weber: Essays in Sociology*, New York, Oxford University Press (Routledge & Kegan Paul, 1948).

Horney, Karen, 1937, *The Neurotic Personality of Our Times*, New York, Norton.

Jones, Ernest, 1951, *Essays in Applied Psychoanalysis*, vol. 1, Hogarth Press.

Kanter, Rosabeth Moss, 1968, 'Neo-Freudian views of maturity and bureaucratic norms', in J. Alan Winter, Jerome Rabow, and Mark Chesler, eds, *Vital Problems for American Society*, New York, Random House, pp. 378–82.

LaPiere, Richard T., 1959, *The Freudian Ethic*, New York, Duell, Sloan & Pearce.

March, James G., and Simon, H. A., *Organizations*, New York, Wiley.

Marcuse, Herbert, 1962, *Eros and Civilization: A Philosophical Inquiry into Freud*, New York, Vintage.

Merton, Robert K. 1957, 'Bureaucratic structure and personality', in Robert K. Merton, ed., *Social Theory and Social Structure*, Chicago, Free Press, pp. 195–207.

Miller, Daniel R., and Swanson, G. E., 1958, *The Changing American Parent*, New York, Wiley.

Olson, Philip, and Daley, Carleton, 1963, 'The education of the "individual" ', in Philip Olson, ed., *America as a Mass Society*, New York, Free Press, pp. 419–34.

Rieff, Philip, 1959, *Freud: The Mind of the Moralist*, New York, Viking Press.

Riesman, David, n.d., *Selected Essays from Individualism Reconsidered*, New York, Doubleday Anchor.

Stendler, Ceilia B., 1950, 'Sixty years of child training practices', *Pediatrics*, 36:122–34.

Sullivan, Henry Stack, 1955, *Interpersonal Theory of Psychiatry*, New York, Norton.

Whyte, William H., Jr, 1956, *The Organization Man*, New York, Doubleday Anchor.

Wolfenstein, Martha, 1953, 'Trends in infant care', *American Journal of Orthopsychiatry*, 23: 120–30.

Wolman, Benjamin H., 1960, *Contemporary Theories and Systems in Psychology*, New York, Harper.

19 Commonsense categories and curriculum thought*

Michael W. Apple

(. . .) there's the King's Messenger' [said the Queen]. 'He's in prison now, being punished: and the trial doesn't even begin till next Wednesday: and of course the crime comes last of all.'

'Suppose he never commits the crime?' said Alice.

'That would be all the better, wouldn't it?' the Queen said, as she turned the plaster round her finger with a bit of ribbon.

Alice felt there was no denying *that*. 'Of course it would be all the better,' she said: 'but it wouldn't be all the better his being punished.'

'You're wrong *there*, at any rate,' said the Queen. 'Were *you* ever punished?'

'Only for faults,' said Alice.

'And you were all the better for it, I know!' the Queen said triumphantly.

'Yes, but then I *had* done the things I was punished for,' said Alice: 'that makes all the difference.'

'But if you *hadn't* done them,' the Queen said, 'that would have been better still; better, and better, and better!'—Lewis Carroll, *Through the Looking-Glass*

My orientation here will be to explore critically certain aspects of social institutions—particularly the school—and our ways of talking about and engaging in research about them. This will be done with a view toward building the sort of perspective and forms of knowledge that will enable educators to construct more just institutions of schooling.

I am particularly interested in exploring the ethical dimensions of our accepted ways of viewing students. Educational questions are, at least partly,

moral questions. For one thing they assume choices as to the relevant realms of expertise educators should use to comprehend children and schools. As Blum puts it, 'All inquiry [and especially educational inquiry I might add] displays a moral commitment in that it makes reference to an authoritative election concerning how a phenomenon ought to be understood.'[1] Furthermore, if conceptions of 'the moral' concern questions of oughtness or goodness, then it should be clear that educational questions are moral questions on this criterion as well. Finally, by the very fact that school people influence students, their acts cannot be interpreted fully without the use of an ethical rubric.

However, there are a number of factors that cause educators to perceive their problems in ways significantly different from this. Because this causal nexus is exceptionally complex, this paper cannot hope to explore all aspects of the difficulty. To do so would require an extensive investigation of the relationship between science, ideology, and educational thought[2] and an analysis of the reduction of conceptions of humans and institutions to technical considerations in advanced industrial societies.[3] Hopefully, this essay will serve as a stimulus for further inquiry into these areas and especially into the ways by which school people pass over the ethical and, as we shall see, political implications of their acts.

The investigation to be sketched out in what follows is theoretic. However, its implications for the day to day density of classroom life are exceptionally important. I am using the idea of a theoretic investigation in a rather specific way in this analysis. I wish to begin to explore ways of illuminating some of the taken-for-granted or commonsense assumptions which underpin the curriculum field. This type of orientation has been noted most clearly by Douglas in his statement concerning the differences between a naturalistic and a theoretical stance. He puts it this way:[4]

Source: J. B. Macdonald and E. Zaret, eds, *Schools in Search of Meaning*, Washington, Association for Supervision and Curriculum Development, 1975, pp. 116–29, 131–44.

There are different ways to make use of commonsense experience. . . . There is, especially, a fundamental distinction between taking the *natural* (or *naturalistic*) stance and taking the *theoretic* stance, as the phenomenological philosophers have long called them. Taking the natural stance consists primarily in *taking the standpoint of common sense*, of *acting within* common sense, whereas taking the theoretic stance consists in *standing back from common sense* and *studying common sense to determine its nature.*

That is, for Douglas and myself, one must bracket any commitment to the utility of employing our taken-for-granted perspectives so that these common-sense presuppositions themselves can become subject to investigation. In this way our commonsense pre-suppositions can be used as *data* to focus upon the latent significance of much that we unquestioningly do in schools. This is particularly important because they provide the basic logic which organizes our activity and often act as tacit guidelines for determining the success or failure of our educational procedures.

It is not the case, however, that these ideological configurations have been constructed consciously. The very fact that they have grown from common-sense presuppositions makes them even more difficult to deal with. They are difficult to question, that is, because they rest upon assumptions that are un-articulated and that seem essential in making some headway in education. But other things contribute to the lack of critical insight. In the field of education these configurations are academically and socially respectable and are supported by the prestige of a process that 'shows every sign of being valid scholar-ship, complete with tables of numbers, copious foot-notes, and scientific terminology.' Furthermore, the altruistic and humanitarian elements of these positions are quite evident, so it is hard to conceive of them as principally functioning to detract from our ability to solve social or educational problems.[5]

However, an investigation into the history of many ameliorative reform movements that were supported by research and perspectives similar to those we will consider here documents the rather interesting fact that often the ameliorative reforms had quite problematic results. Frequently they ultimately even ended up harming the individuals upon whom they focused. Platt's treatment of the reform of the juvenile justice system in the latter part of the last century is instructive here.

In attempting to create more humane conditions for 'wayward' youth, these reforms created a new category of deviance called 'juvenile delinquency' and in the long run served to abridge the civil and con-stitutional rights of youth.[6] In many ways, we have yet to recover from these 'reforms.' As I shall argue in this paper, many of the seemingly ameliorative reforms school people propose in schools, and the assumptions that lie behind them, have the same effect—ultimately harming rather than helping, clouding over basic issues and value conflicts rather than contributing to our ability to face them honestly.

This is especially the case in the major topic of this paper, the process of using clinical, psychological, and therapeutic perspectives and labels in schools. These forms of language and the perspectives they embody may be interpreted not as 'helping,' but more critically as a mechanism by which schools engage in anonymizing and sorting out individuals into preordained social, economic, and educational slots.

The labeling process, thus, tends to function as a form of social control,[7] a 'worthy' successor to a long line of mechanisms in schools that sought to homogen-ize social reality, to eliminate disparate perceptions, and to use supposedly therapeutic means to create moral, valuative, and intellectual consensus.[8] The fact that this process can be deadening, that it results in the elimination of diversity, that it ignores the importance of conflict and surprise in human inter-action is too often lost in the background in our rush to 'help.'

There is nothing very odd about the fact that we usually do not focus on the basic sets of assumptions which we use. First, they are normally known only tacitly, remain unspoken, and are very difficult to formulate explicitly. Second, these basic rules are so much a part of us that they do not have to be expressed. By the very fact that they are *shared* assumptions, the product of specific groups of people, and are commonly accepted by most educators (if not most people in general), they only become problematic when an individual violates them[9] or else when a previously routine situation becomes significantly altered. However, if we are to be true to the demands of rigorous analysis, it is a critical inquiry into just such things as the routine grounds of our day to day experience that is demanded.

On the necessity of critical awareness

The curriculum field, and education as a whole, has been quite ameliorative in its orientation. This is understandable given the pressures on and interest by the field to serve schools and their ongoing pro-grams and concerns. The marked absorption in amelioration, however, has had some rather detri-mental effects. Not only has it caused us to ignore questions and research that might contribute in the long run to our basic understanding of the process of schooling,[10] but such an orientation neglects the crucial role critical reflection must play if a field is to remain vital.

A critically reflective mode is important for a number of reasons. First, curriculum specialists help establish and maintain institutions that affect students and others in a myriad of ways. Because of these effects, they must be aware of the reasons and intentions that guide them. This is especially true of ideological and political purposes, both manifest and latent.[11] Since schools as institutions are so interconnected with other political and economic institutions which dominate a collectivity and since schools often unquestioningly act to distribute knowledge and values through both the overt and hidden curricula that often act to support these same institutions, it is a necessity for educators to engage in searching analyses of the ways in which they allow values and commitments unconsciously to work through them.

Second, it is important to argue that the very activity of rational investigation requires a critical style. The curriculum field has been much too accepting of forms of thought that do not do justice to the complexity of inquiry and thus the field has not really changed its basic perspective for decades. It has been taken with the notions of systematicity, certainty, and control as the ideals of programmatic and conceptual activity, in its treatment of research and people. This is strongly mirrored in the behavioral objectives movement and in the quest for taxonomies which codify 'cognitive,' 'affective,' and 'psychomotor' behavior. These activities find their basis in a conception of rationality that is less than efficacious today. Not only is it somewhat limiting,[12] but it also is historically and empirically inaccurate.

Our taken-for-granted view posits a conception of rationality based upon ordering beliefs and concepts in tidy logical structures and upon the extant intellectual paradigms which seem to dominate the field of curriculum at a given time. Yet, any serious conception of rationality must be concerned not with the specific intellectual positions a professional group or individual employs at any given time, but instead *with the conditions on which and the manner in which this field of study is prepared to criticize and change those accepted doctrines.*[13] In this way, intellectual flux, not 'intellectual immutability,' is the expected and normal occurrence. What has to be explained is *not* why we should change our basic conceptual structure, but rather the stability or crystallization of the forms of thought a field has employed over time.[14]

The crystallization and lack of change of fundamental perspectives is not a new problem in the curriculum field by any means. In fact, a major effort was made in the 1940s[15] to identify and deal with just such a concern. The fact that many curriculum specialists are unaware of the very real traditions of grappling with the field's tendency toward hardening its positions obviously points to the necessity of greater attention being given to historical scholarship in the curriculum field.

This intellectual conservatism often coheres with a social conservatism as well. It is not the case that a critical perspective is 'merely' important for illuminating the stagnation of the curriculum field. What is even more crucial is the fact that means must be found to illuminate the concrete ways in which the curriculum field supports the widespread interests in technical control of human activity, in rationalizing, manipulating, and bureaucratizing individual action, and in eliminating personal style and political diversity. These are interests that dominate advanced industrial societies and they contribute quite a bit to the suffering of minorities and women, the alienation of youth, the malaise and meaninglessness of work for a large proportion of the population, and the increasing sense of powerlessness and cynicism that seems to dominate our society. Curriculum specialists and other educators need to be aware of all of these outcomes, yet there is little in-depth analysis of the role our commonsense thought plays in causing us to be relatively impotent in the face of these problems.

Many educators consistently attempt to portray themselves as being 'scientific,' by referring to the 'scientific' (or technical) and therefore neutral status of their activity to give it legitimacy. They are thereby ignoring the fact that a good deal of social science research is currently being strongly criticized for its support of bureaucratized assumptions and institutions that deny dignity and significant choice to individuals and groups of people. This criticism cannot be shunted aside easily by educators, for unlike many other people, their activity has a direct influence on the present and future of masses of children. By being the primary institution through which individuals pass to become 'competent' adults, schools give children no choice about the means by which they are distributed into certain roles in society. As we shall see, 'neutral scientific' terminology acts as a veneer to cover this fact, and, thus, becomes more ideological than helpful.[16]

Perhaps one of the fundamental reasons the field has stagnated both socially and intellectually involves our lack of concern for less positivistic scholarship. We have been less than open to forms of analysis that would effectively counterbalance our use of rubrics embodying the interests of technical control and certainty. This lack of openness has caused us to be inattentive to the functions of the very language systems we employ and has led us to disregard fields whose potency lies in their concern for a critical perspective. This will require a closer examination.

Are things as they seem?

Let us focus first on the linguistic tools we employ to talk about 'students' in schools. My basic point will be that much of our language, while seemingly neutral, is not neutral in its impact nor is it unbiased in regard to existing institutions of schooling. An underlying thesis of this argument, and one which can only be treated in less depth than it merits, is that our accepted faith that the extension of 'neutral techniques of science and technology' will provide solutions to all of the dilemmas we confront is misplaced and that such a faith tends to obscure the fact that much of educational research serves and justifies already existing technical control systems that accept the distribution of power in American society as given.[17] Much of the discussion here will be stimulated by the insights derived from recent reconstructed Marxist scholarship, particularly the potent notion that our basic perspectives often hide our 'real' relationships with other persons with whom we have real and symbolic contact. The analysis will employ arguments from research on the process of labeling to bring this initial point home. (. . .)

There are a number of reasons why reconstructed Marxist scholarship has not found a serious place in Anglo-Western educational investigation. While, historically, orthodox Marxism had an effect in the 1930s on such educators as Brameld, Counts, and others, the movement lost its potency due to the political situation evolving later.

To this problem, of course, can be added the overly deterministic and dogmatic interpretations of applying Marxist analysis by even many later 'Marxists.' Part of the problem of applying critical insights to advanced industrial societies like our own is to free these insights from their embeddedness in such dogmatism.[18] It should not have to be said, but unfortunately it must, that the rigidly controlled nature of a number of modern societies bears little relation to the uniquely cogent analyses found in the Marxist tradition itself. Our neglect of this scholarly tradition says more about the fear laden past of American society than it does about the merits of the (all too often unexplored) tradition of critical analysis.

Yet, there are other more basic and less overtly political explanations for the atrophy and lack of acceptance of a Marxist intellectual tradition in places like the United States. The atomistic and strict empiricist frame of mind so prevalent in our thought has difficulty with the critically oriented notion of the necessity of a plurality of ways of looking at the world. On this, critical scholarship holds a position quite similar to that of phenomenology in that the 'truth' of something can only be seen through the use of the totality of perspectives one can bring to bear upon it.[19]

Also, the tendency in Western industrialized societies to strictly separate value from fact would make it difficult to accept a position which holds that most social and intellectual categories are themselves *valuative* in nature and may reflect ideological commitments, a fact that will be of exceptional import in this discussion. Furthermore, the long tradition of individualism and a strongly utilitarian frame of mind would no doubt cause one to look less than positively upon both a more social conception of man and an ideal commitment that is less apt to be immediately ameliorative and more apt to raise basic questions about the very framework of social life that is accepted as given by a society.[20]

In opposition to the atomistic assumptions that predominate in our commensense thought, a critical viewpoint usually sees any object 'relationally.'

This is an important key to understanding the type of analysis one might engage in from a reconstructed perspective. This implies two things. First, any subject matter under investigation must be seen in relation to its historical roots—how it evolved, from what conditions it arose—and its latent contradictions and tendencies in the future. In the highly complicated world of critical analysis, existing structures are actually in something like continual motion. Change and development are the norm and any institutional structure is 'merely' a stage in process.[21] Thus, institutional reification becomes problematic, as do the patterns of thought that support this lack of institutional change. Second, anything being examined is defined not only by its obvious characteristics, but by its less overt ties to other factors. It is these ties or relationships that make the subject what it is and give it its primary meaning.[22] In this way, our ability to illuminate the interdependence and interaction of factors is considerably expanded.

To accept this relational view is obviously to go against our traditional concept that what we see is as it appears. In fact, the argument is that our very taken-for-granted perceptions mislead us here and that this is a rather grave limitation on our thought and action. That is, anything is a good deal more than it appears,[23] especially when one is dealing with complex and interrelated institutions including the school. It is this very point that will enable us to make progress in uncovering some of the functions of educational language. (. . .)

The intent of such a critique and of critical scholarship in general, then, is twofold. First, it aims at illuminating the tendencies for unwanted and often unconscious domination, alienation, and repression within certain existing cultural, political, educational, and economic institutions. Second, through exploring the negative effects and contradictions of much that unquestioningly goes on in these institutions, it seeks to 'promote conscious emancipatory activity.'[24] That is, it examines what is supposed to be happening in, say, schools, if one takes the language and slogans of many school people seriously; and, it then shows how these things *actually* work in a manner that is destructive of ethical rationality and personal political and institutional power. Once this actual functioning is held up to scrutiny, it attempts to point to concrete activity that will lead to challenging this taken-for-granted activity.

An example of some aspects of the approach we have been discussing might be an analysis of the major concepts and procedures which dominate educational activity today, with systems management offering a good instance. By linking this taken-for-granted procedure to its historical precedents and showing the latent tendencies within it, and at the same time exploring the relationships or ties that educational systems analysis has to a conservative institutional and ideological framework, hidden social and valuative commitments are made clear.[25]

It may very well be the case that until such commitments are uncovered, the field of curriculum itself will make little headway in creating educational institutions that are humanly responsive. A similar instance involves the linguistic categories curriculum specialists and other educators employ to order, guide, and give meaning to their work.

Institutional language and ethical responsibility

One of the most potent issues raised by critical scholarship over the years is the tendency for us to hide what are profound interrelations between persons through the use of a 'neutral' commodity language.[26] That is, educators have developed categories and modes of perception which reify or 'thingify' individuals so that they (the educators) can confront students as institutional abstractions rather than concrete persons. Given the complexity of mass education this is understandable. However, the implications of the growth of this form of language are profound and must be examined in depth.

In order to accomplish this, one fact must be made clear. The categories that curriculum workers and other educators employ are themselves social constructs. They also imply the notion of the power of one group to 'impose' these social constructions on others. For example, the categories by which we differentiate 'smart' from 'stupid' children, 'academic' from 'nonacademic' areas, 'play' from 'learning' activity, and even 'students' from 'teachers,' are all commonsense constructions *which grow out of the nature of existing institutions*.[27] As such they must be treated as historically conditioned data, not absolutes. This is not to say that they are necessarily wrong; rather it points to the necessity of understanding them for what they are—categories that developed out of specific social and historical situations which conform to a specific framework of assumptions and institutions, the use of which categories brings with it the logic of the institutional assumptions as well.

As I mentioned, the field itself has a tendency to 'disguise' relations between people as relations between things or abstractions.[28] Hence, ethical issues such as the profoundly difficult problem concerning the ways by which one person may seek to influence another are not usually treated as important considerations. It is here that the abstract categories that grow out of institutional life become quite serious. If an educator may define another as a 'slow learner,' a 'discipline problem,' or other general category, he or she may prescribe general 'treatments' that are seemingly neutral and helpful. However, by the very fact that the categories themselves are based upon institutionally defined abstractions (the commonsense equivalent of statistical averages), the educator is freed from the more difficult task of examining the institutional context that caused these abstract labels to be placed upon a concrete individual in the first place. Thus, the understandable attempt to reduce complexity leads to the use of 'average treatments' applied to fillers of abstract roles. This preserves the anonymity of the intersubjective relationship between 'educator' and 'pupil' which is so essential if institutional definitions of situations are to prevail. It, thereby, protects both the existing institution and the educator from self-doubt and from the innocence and reality of the child.

This has important implications for educational scholarship. By using official categories and constructs such as those defined by and growing out of existing institutional practices—examples might be studies of the 'slow learner,' 'discipline problems,' and 'remediation'—curriculum researchers may be lending the rhetorical prestige of science to what may be questionable practices of an educational bureaucracy.[29] That is, there is no rigorous attempt to examine *institutional* culpability. The notion of imputing culpability is of considerable moment to our analysis. Scott makes this point rather clearly in his discussion of the effects of labeling someone as different or deviant.[30]

> Another reaction that commonly occurs when a deviant label is applied is that within the community a feeling arises that 'something ought to be done about *him*.' Perhaps the most important fact about this reaction in our society is that almost all of the steps that are taken are *directed solely at the deviant*. Punishment, rehabilitation, therapy, coercion, and other common mechanisms of social control are things that are done to him, implying that the causes of deviance reside within the person to whom the label has been attached, and that the solutions to the problems that he presents can be achieved by doing something to him. This is a curious fact, particularly when we examine it against the background of social science research on deviance that so clearly points to the crucial role played by ordinary people in determining who is labeled a deviant and how a deviant behaves. *This research suggests that none of the corrective measures that are taken can possibly succeed in the intended way unless they are directed at those who confer deviant labels as well as those to whom they are applied.*

In clearer language, in the school students are the persons expressly focused upon. Attention is primarily paid to their specific behavioral, emotional, or educational 'problems,' and, thus, there is a strong inclination to divert attention both from the inadequacies of the educational institution itself[31] and what bureaucratic, social, and economic conditions caused the necessity of applying these constructs originally. (. . .)

Mercer attributes this overdistribution of the mental retardate designation to the diagnostic, evaluative, and testing 'machinery' of the school.[32] Based as it is on statistical formulations that conform to problematic institutional assumptions concerning normality and deviance drawn from existing and often biased economic and political structures, it plays a large part in the process of channeling certain types of students into preexisting categories. The painful fact that this supposedly helpful machinery of diagnosis and remediation does not meet the reality of the child is given further documentation by Mehan's[33] important study of supposedly 'normal' young children's reconstruction of the meaning of a testing situation and the evaluative instruments themselves. In essence, what he found was that, even in the most personally administered diagnostic testing, 'testers' were apt to use speculative and inaccurate labels to summarize even more speculative and inaccurate results. The school tests actually *obscured* the children's real understanding of the materials and tasks, did not capture the children's varied abilities to reason adequately, and did not show 'the negotiated, contextually bound measurement decisions that the tester makes while scoring children's behavior as "correct" or "incorrect".' While this was especially true of 'nonmodal' children (in this case, Spanish-speaking) it was also strikingly true for all other students as well.

If this research is correct, given the intense pressure for 'accountability' today, the dominance of a process-product testing mentality, hence, will no doubt lead to even more problematic, anonymous, and socially and economically biased institutions due to the labels that stem from the testing process itself. The importance given to testing in schools cannot be underestimated in other ways. The labels that come from these 'diagnoses' and assessments are not easily shaken off, and are in fact used by other institutions to continue the definitional ascription given by the school.

That is, not only does the school perform a central function of assigning labels to children in the process of sorting them and then distributing different knowledge, dispositions, and views of self to each of these labeled groups, but, just as important, the school occupies *the* central position in a larger network of other institutions. The labels imputed by the public schools are borrowed by legal, economic, health, and community institutions to define the individual in his or her contact with them as well.[34]

(. . .) The only serious way to make sense out of the imputation of labels in schools is to analyze the assumptions that underlie the definitions of competence these entail; and this can only be done in terms of an investigation of those who are in a position to *impose* these definitions.[35] Thus, the notion of *power* (what economic group or social class actually has it and how it is really being used) becomes critical if we are to understand why certain forms of social meanings—the authoritative election Blum talks of in the quote on the first page of this essay—are used to select and organize the knowledge and perspectives educators employ to compre-

hend, order, and control activity in educational institutions.

One important latent function of schooling seems to be the distribution of forms of consciousness, often quite unequally, to students. Sociologically, then, through their appropriation of these dispositions and outlooks, students are able to be sorted into the various roles sedimented throughout the fabric of an advanced industrial society. The process of labeling occupies a subtle but essential place in this sorting. Because the designations, categories, and linguistic tools employed by educators, and especially by most members of the curriculum field of a behavioral persuasion, are perceived by them to have 'scientific' status, there is little or no realization that the very language that they resort to is ideally suited to maintain the bureaucratic rationality that has dominated schooling for so long a time.[36]

Edelman makes a similar point in discussing the way the distinctive language system of the 'helping professions' is used to justify and marshal public support for professional practices that have profound political and ethical consequences.[37]

> Because the helping professions define other people's statuses (and their own), the special terms they employ to categorize clients and justify restrictions of their physical movements and of their moral and intellectual influence are especially revealing of the political functions language performs and of the multiple realities it helps create. Language is both a sensitive indicator and a powerful creator of background assumptions about people's levels of competence and merit. Just as any single numeral evokes the whole number scheme in our minds, so a term, a syntactic form, or a metaphor with political connotations can evoke and justify a power hierarchy in the person who used it and the groups that respond to it.

Edelman's basic argument is not merely that the language forms educators and others use 'arrange' their reality, but also that these forms covertly justify status, power, and authority. In short, one must examine the contradiction between a perspective that is there to help and at the same time actually serves the existing distribution of power in institutions and society.[38] This contradiction is difficult to miss in the language employed by school people.

Perhaps this argument is best summarized by quoting again from Edelman:[39]

> In the symbolic worlds evoked by the language of the helping professions, speculations and verified fact readily merge with each other. Language dispels the uncertainty in speculation, changes facts to make them serve status distinctions and reinforce ideology. The names for forms of mental illness, forms of delinquency, and for educational capacities are the basic terms. Each of them

normally involves a high degree of unreliability in diagnosis, in prognosis, and in the prescription of rehabilitative treatments; but also entails unambiguous constraints upon clients, especially their confinement and subjection to the staff and the rules of a prison, school, or hospital. *The confinement and constraints are converted into liberating and altruistic acts by defining them as education, therapy, or rehabilitation. The arbitrariness and speculation in the diagnosis and the prognosis, on the other hand, are converted into clear and specific perceptions of the need for control* [by the 'helping group']. Regardless of the arbitrariness or technical unreliability of professional terms, their political utility is manifest; they marshal popular support for professional discretion, concentrating public attention upon procedures and rationalizing in advance any failures of the procedures to achieve their formal objectives.

That is, the supposedly neutral language of an institution, even though it rests upon highly speculative data and may be applied without actually being appropriate, provides a framework that legitimates control of major aspects of an individual's or a group's behavior. At the same time, by sounding scientific and 'expert,' it contributes to the quiescence of the public by focusing attention on its 'sophistication' not on its political or ethical results. Thus, historically outmoded, and socially and politically conservative (and often educationally disastrous) practices are not only continued, but are made to sound as if they were actually more enlightened and ethically responsive ways of dealing with children.

As in other institutions where there is little choice about whether an individual (student, patient, inmate) may come or go as he or she pleases, by defining students through the use of such a quasi-scientific and quasi-clinical and therapeutic terminology and hence 'showing' that students cannot be fully responsible for a large part of their activity within that institution (they are not adults; they have not reached a certain developmental stage; they have limited attention spans), educators need not face the often coercive aspects of their own activity.[40] Therefore, the ethical question of the nature of control in school settings does not have to be responded to. The clinical perspectives, the treatment language, the 'helping' labels, all define it out of existence.

In what can almost act as a summary of this part of this essay, then, it is possible to argue that these criticisms are actually generic to clinical perspectives and helping labels[41] themselves as they function in education. The assumptions in which they are grounded are themselves open to question. These viewpoints are distinguished by a number of striking characteristics, each of which when combined with the others seems logically to lead to a conservative stance toward existing institutional arrangements.

The first characteristic is that the researcher or practitioner studies or deals with those individuals who have already been labeled as different or deviant by the institution. In doing this, he or she adopts the values of the social system that defined the person as deviant. Furthermore, he or she assumes that the judgments made by the institution and based on these values are the valid measures of normality and competence without seriously questioning them.

Second, these clinical and helping perspectives have a strong tendency to perceive the difficulty as a problem with the individual, as something the individual rather than the institution lacks. Thus, combined with the assumption that the official definition is the only right definition, almost all action is focused on changing the individual rather than the defining agent, the larger institutional context. Third, researchers and practitioners who accept the institutional designations and definitions tend to assume that all of the people within these categories are the same. There is an assumption of homogeneity. In this way, individual complexity is automatically flattened.

Also, it can well be argued that there are strong motivations for use already built into these labels and the processes and expertise behind them. That is, the 'professional helpers' who employ the supposedly diagnostic and therapeutic terminologies *must* find (and hence create) individuals who fit the categories, otherwise the expertise is useless. This is probably a general educational fact. Once a 'new' (but always limited) tool or perspective for 'helping' children is generated, it tends to expand beyond the 'problem' for which it was initially developed. The tools (here diagnostic, therapeutic, and linguistic) also have the effect of redefining past issues in these other areas into problems the tool is capable of dealing with.[42] The best example is behavior modification. While applicable to a limited range of difficulties in schools, it becomes both a diagnostic language and a form of 'treatment' for a wider range of 'student problems.' Thus, for instance, its increasing use and acceptance in ghetto schools and elsewhere with 'disruptive' children, or with entire classes as is becoming more the case, really acts as a cloak to cover the political fact that the nature of the existing educational institutions is unresponsive to a large portion of students. In addition, its treatment language acts to hide the alienating wage-product relationship that has been established and called education. Finally, the perspective, by defining itself clinically, covers the very real moral questions that must be raised concerning the appropriateness of the technique itself in dealing with students who have no choice about being in the institution.

Labeling: part of a complex avoidance process

(...) The orientations which so predominate curriculum theory, and indeed have consistently dominated it in the past, effectively obscure and often deny the profound ethical issues educators face. They transform these dilemmas into engineering problems or puzzles that are amenable to technical 'professional' solutions. Perhaps the best example is the field's nearly total reliance on perspectives drawn from the psychology of learning. The terminology drawn from this psychology and its allied fields is quite inadequate since it neglects or at best tends to draw attention from the basically political and moral character of social existence and human development.

The language of reinforcement, learning, negative feedback, and so forth is a rather weak tool for dealing with the continual encroachment of chaos upon order, with the creation and recreation of personal meaning and interpersonal institutions, and with notions such as responsibility and justice in conduct with others. In essence, the language of psychology as it is exercised in curriculum 'deethicizes and depoliticizes human relations and personal conduct.'[43]

For example, much of our busy endeavor to define operational objectives and to state student 'outcomes' in behavioral terms may be interpreted as exactly that—busywork, if I may use commonsense terminology for the moment. That is, because of the field's preoccupation with the wording of its goal statements and 'output measures,' attention is diverted from the crucial political and moral implications of our activity as educators. In this way means are turned into ends and children are transformed into manipulable and anonymous abstractions called 'learners.' Speaking of the field of sociology, though quite the same things could be said about a large portion of curricular language and research, Friedrichs articulates part of the problem clearly.[44]

> What sociologists appear completely unaware of is the long-run impact of coming to *conceive* of one's fellows as manipulable. Language—and the choice among symbols it entails—pervades all meaningful social action, either overtly or covertly, consciously or unconsciously. The symbolic manipulation of man cannot be wholly isolated from the rest of a person's symbolically mediated relationships with others. As man's intellectual life more and more demands such symbolic manipulation, he runs the increasing risk of conceiving man in other areas of his life in terms that invite or are particularly amenable to a means-ends relationship rather than those that support an attitude toward others as ends in themselves.

Thus, the manipulative ethos of a larger society is found within curriculum discourse in the basic behavioral and treatment language and categories used for even conceiving of educational relationships. It thereby creates and reinforces patterns of interaction that not only reflect but actually embody the interests in certainty and control that dominate the consciousness of advanced industrial societies.

Furthermore, it should be clear that no single attribute of an individual can be employed to define that person.[45] Nor is it the case that any one model or language system can exhaust the complexity of an individual's response to his or her situation. The propensity of curriculum specialists and other educators to define the student as 'learner' and thus to design an environment which corresponds to this one attribute of being human is but one example of this sort of category error in educational thought.

As a final part of this section, let me attempt through alternative examples to show that these conceptions, categories, and labels are, in fact, commonsensical and ideological not preordained or 'natural.' In our society, a high premium is put on intelligence. Schools are obviously organized around and value such a concept. The fact that they limit it to quite constructed and mostly verbal versions of it is important but not the point here. Rather, we should note that it is possible to describe other conceptions around which our educational and social institutions could be organized and our technology designed. For instance, envision a society in which physical *grace* not our overly constricted definitions of competence and intelligence was the most valued characteristic.[46] Those who were clumsy or merely reached lower categories of grace might then be discriminated against. The culture's educational structure would categorize individuals according to their 'capacity for grace.' The technology would be so designed that it would require elegance in motion for it to be employed.

Besides physical grace (which is really not too outlandish a concept) one could also point to the possibility of valuing, say, moral excellence. After all, this type of dispositional element is one of the things that education is all about, isn't it? However, as the literature on the hidden curriculum strongly suggests, the basic regularities of schools excel in teaching the opposite. For example, because of the dominance of evaluation—both public and private, of oneself and one's peers—in school settings, subterfuge, hiding one's real feelings, joy at someone else's failure, and so forth, are quite effectively taught. This occurs merely by the student's living within an institution and having to cope with its density, power, and competitiveness.[47]

The implications of these counterexamples are rather significant for they indicate that a serious attempt at changing the accepted commonsense conceptions of competence in *practice* may need to change the basic regularities of the institutional structure of schooling itself. The regularities themselves are the 'teaching devices' that communicate lasting norms and dispositions to students, that instruct children in 'how the world really is.' It is important to notice the critical implications of each of these alternative conceptions for the business, advertising, and other institutions of the larger society as well. They act as potent reminders that criticism of many of the characteristics of schools and social, political, and cultural criticism must go hand in hand. Schools do not exist in a vacuum.

For instance, much of the labeling process that I have been examining here has at its roots a concern for efficiency. That is, schools as agents of social control in some sense need to operate as efficient organizations and labeling helps a good deal in this.[48] As much activity as possible must be rationalized and made goal specific so that cost effectiveness and smoothness of operation are heightened and 'waste,' inefficiency, and uncertainty are eliminated. Furthermore, conflict and argumentation over goals and procedures must be minimized so as not to jeopardize existing goals and procedures. After all, there is a good deal of economic and psychological investment in these basic institutional regularities. Techniques for the control and manipulation of difference must be developed, then, in order to prevent disorder of any significant sort from encroaching on institutional life. If significant difference (either intellectual, aesthetic, valuative, or normative) is found, it must be redefined into categories that can be handled by existing bureaucratic assumptions. The fact that these assumptions are relatively unexamined and are, in fact, *self-confirming* as long as educators employ categories that grow out of them is forgotten.

However, to point to the schools as the originators of this concern for efficiency above all else in education is too limited an appraisal. The roots of this technocratic perspective lie in a taken-for-granted ideology that provides the constitutive framework for thought and action in all advanced industrial societies, an instrumental ideology that places efficiency, standardized technique, growth, and consensus at its very heart. Consequently, the caughtness of schools and especially the curriculum field in what Kliebard has called a factory model[49] is part of a larger social problem concerning the lack of responsiveness of our major institutions to human needs and sentiment. To lose sight of this is to miss much of the real problem. There are questions, though, that can be asked within an educational framework that could challenge portions of this ideology. A few of these questions will be pointed to in the final part of this analysis.

Toward asking some salient questions

This essay has sought to raise a number of questions regarding some of the taken-for-granted underpinnings shared by groups of school people. It would not be complete without at least pointing out a direction that curriculum scholarship and practice could take if the field is to be reconstructed. While the specific path suggested here is tentative, the author has few doubts that the general direction is appropriate.

Our movement should be progressively away from the current 'quasi-scientific' and engineering framework that now guides most of the field's endeavors and should consistently move toward a political and ethical structure. While there is certainly a need for technical expertise in the field—after all, curriculum specialists are called upon to assist in the designing and creating of concrete environments based on our differing educational visions—all too often a technical and efficiency perspective supplies the problems, and other considerations such as those analyzed in this paper are afterthoughts, if they are indeed considered at all. A more appropriate relationship might require that educational engineering and technical competence be secured firmly within a framework that continually seeks to be self-critical and places one person's responsibility to treat another person ethically and justly at the center of its deliberations.[50]

Habermas extends these arguments and their implications for the reconstruction of curriculum research and practice. He holds that the controlling and bureaucratized institutions of advanced industrial society require increasing scientific and technical knowledge. The research communities, for example, generate new rationalities and techniques that make further control and domination of individuals and groups by an instrumental and technical ideology possible. However, while these communities produce data that support existing institutionalized rubrics and mechanisms for control, they are also in an increasingly pivotal strategic position. Because the basic social norms that ideally guide the various 'scientific' communities rest strongly upon a foundation of open and honest communication,[51] there is a potential within these groups for the recognition of the unnecessary control and domination that exist in many of the institutions of society. In addition, the turning around of even a small portion of the community of educational scholars and practitioners to recognize the quasi-neutral perspectives that dominate their rationality, language, and investigations would have the positive effect of illuminating the way educational and other forms of social research miss the ethical and political meaning of their work.[52] In other words, the development of a critical perspective within the educational community can 'contribute to the creation of alternative programs of research and development' that challenge the commonsense assumptions that underpin the field.

Just as important, in this way . . .[53]

Knowledge can be generated that relates to the needs of the peoples who are trying to build social community, resist cultural manipulation, facilitate decentralization movements, and in general contribute to the actualization of human needs that are otherwise ignored. By reorienting the scientific community, or at least a significant section of it, critical theory can become a material force for change by counteracting the current drift of science toward the formation and implementation of state policy.

It should be clear, therefore, that these arguments imply[54] that advocacy models of research and practice are critically needed if substantial progress is to be made.

Reality, however, has to be faced here. To most people, the very idea of regaining any real control over social institutions and personal development is abstract and 'nonsensical.' In general, people see society's economic, social, and educational institutions as basically self-directing, with little need for their participation and with little necessity for them to communicate and argue over the ends and means of these same institutions. Even though the disintegration of aspects of family life, schools, or work, is

often evident, the basic categories of industrialized logic have become so commonsensical that people no longer even see a need for emancipation, other than an anomic sense that pervades certain segments of the population. This makes the development of a *critical* curriculum community, for example, all the more essential since it is here that a part of the systematic criticism of the basic categories that grow out of and help produce problematic institutions can originate. That is, one of the fundamental conditions of emancipation is the ability to 'see' the actual functionings of institutions in all their positive *and* negative complexity, to illuminate the contradictions of extant regularities,[55] and, finally, to assist others in 'remembering' the possibilities of spontaneity and choice. (. . .)

Notes

* A briefer version of portions of this essay was presented at the conference, 'Toward the Reconstruction of the Curriculum Field', Philadelphia, Pennsylvania, 10–11 May 1973.

1 Alan F. Blum, 'Sociology, wrongdoing, and akrasia: an attempt to think Greek about the problem of theory and practice', in Robert A. Scott and Jack D. Douglas, eds, *Theoretical Perspectives on Deviance*, New York, Basic Books, 1972, p. 343.

2 See Jürgen Habermas, *Knowledge and Human Interests*, Boston, Beacon Press, 1971; Peter Berger and Thomas Luckman, *The Social Construction of Reality*, New York, Doubleday, 1966; Penguin, 1971.

3 See, for example, Hannah Arendt, *The Human Condition*, New York, Doubleday, 1958; Albrecht Wellmer, *Critical Theory of Society*, New York, Herder & Herder, 1971.

4 Jack D. Douglas, *American Social Order*, New York, Free Press, 1971, pp. 9–10. Douglas' stress.

5 William Ryan, *Blaming the Victim*, New York, Random House, 1971, pp. 21–2.

6 Anthony Platt, *The Child Savers: the Invention of Delinquency*, University of Chicago Press, 1969.

7 Edwin M. Schur, *Labeling Deviant Behavior*, New York, Harper & Row, 1971, p. 33.

8 On the dominance of a social control ethic in schools, see Clarence Karier, Paul Violas, and Joel Spring, *Roots of Crisis*, Chicago, Rand McNally, 1973; Barry Franklin, 'The curriculum field and the problem of social control, 1918–1938: a study in critical theory', unpublished doctoral thesis, University of Wisconsin, Madison, 1974.

9 Douglas, op. cit., p. 181. I have explored one of these *basic* or, as I have called them, *constitutive* rules—that of consensus—elsewhere. See Michael W. Apple, 'The hidden curriculum and the nature of conflict', *Interchange*, 2 (4), 1971, 27–40. See also the discussion of interpretive and normative rules in Aaron Cicourel, 'Basic and normative rules in the negotiation of status and role', in H. P. Dreitzel, ed., *Recent Sociology*, no. 2, New York, Macmillan, 1970, pp. 4–45.

10 Herbert M. Kliebard, 'Persistent curriculum issues in historical perspective', in E. C. Short, ed., *The Search for Valid Content for Curriculum Courses*, The University of Toledo, 1970, p. 33.

11 I am using the concept of ideology here to refer to commonsense views of the world held by specific groups, not merely as 'politically' biased views. This follows from Harris' statement that 'Ideologies are not disguised descriptions of the world, but rather real descriptions of the world from a specific viewpoint, just as all descriptions of the world are from a particular viewpoint.' See Nigel Harris, *Beliefs in Society: the Problem of Ideology*, Watts, 1968, p. 22.

12 See Susanne Langer's articulate treatment of the necessity of discursive and nondiscursive forms of rationality in her *Philosophy in a New Key*, New York, Mentor Books, 1951.

13 Stephen Toulmin, *Human Understanding: the Collective Use and Evolution of Concepts*, Princeton University Press, 1972, p. 84.

14 ibid., p. 96.

15 Alice Miel, *Changing the Curriculum: A Social Process*, New York, Appleton-Century, 1946.

16 Michael W. Apple, 'The process and ideology of valuing in educational settings', in M. W. Apple, M. J. Subkoviak and H. S. Lufler, Jr, eds, *Educational Evaluation: Analysis and Responsibility*, Berkeley, Calif., McCutchan, 1974.

17 Such a statement obviously needs justification, more than is possible in a paper of this length. Provocative and insightful discussions of the problem can be found in Trent Schroyer, 'Toward a critical theory for advanced industrial society', in H. P. Dreitzel, ed., *Recent Sociology*, no. 2, pp. 210–34; Alvin W. Gouldner, *The Coming Crisis of Western Sociology*, New York, Basic Books, 1970.

18 See, for example, the well written portrayal of Marx's own lack of rigid dogmatism in Michael Harrington, *Socialism*, New York, Bantam Books, 1972. For a reappraisal of Marx's supposed economic determinism, one that argues against such an interpretation, see Bertell Ollman, *Alienation: Marx's Conception of Man in Capitalist Society*, Cambridge University Press, 1971.

19 Aron Gurwitsch, *The Field of Consciousness*, Duquesne University Press, 1964, p. 184.

20 Charles Taylor, 'Marxism and empiricism', in Bernard Williams and Alan Montefiore, eds, *British Analytical Philosophy*, Routledge & Kegan Paul; New York, Humanities Press, 1966 pp. 227–46.

21 B. Ollman, op. cit., p. 18.
22 ibid., p. 15. This position has been given the name of a 'philosophy of internal relations.' Oddly, such a view has had an extensive history of American thought, even somewhat in educational thought. See, for example, the work of Whitehead such as *Process and Reality*.
23 ibid., p. 90.
24 Trent Schroyer, *The Critique of Domination*, New York, Braziller, 1973, pp. 30–1.
25 See M. W. Apple, 'The adequacy of systems management procedures in education', in Albert H. Yee, ed., *Perspectives on Management Systems Approaches in Education*, Englewood Cliffs, N.J., Educational Technology Press, 1973, pp. 3–31.
26 Shlomo Avineri, *The Social and Political Thought of Karl Marx*, Cambridge University Press, 1968, p. 117. Avineri puts it this way, 'Ultimately, a commodity is an objectified expression of an intersubjective relationship.'
27 Michael F. D. Young, Introduction to M. F. D. Young, ed., *Knowledge and Control*, Macmillan, 1971, p. 2.
28 On the relationship between this transformation of human interaction into other reified forms and an ideological, political, and economic framework, see Ollman, op. cit., pp. 198–9.
29 Douglas, op. cit., pp. 70–1.
30 Robert A. Scott, 'A proposed framework for analyzing deviance as a property of social order', in Scott and Douglas, eds, op. cit., p. 15. My stress.
31 Bonnie Freeman, 'Labeling Theory and Bureaucratic Structures in Schools', unpublished paper, University of Wisconsin, Madison, 1973.
32 Jane R. Mercer, *Labeling the Mentally Retarded*, University of California Press, 1973, pp. 96–123.
33 Hugh Mehan, 'Assessing children's school performance', in H. P. Dreitzel, ed., *Childhood and Socialization* (*Recent Sociology*, no. 5), New York, Macmillan, 1973, pp. 240–64. (See also *The Process of Schooling*, no. 15.) For further discussion of how dominant modes of educational evaluation and assessment ignore the concrete reality of students and function in a conservative political and epistemological manner, see Apple, 'The process and ideology of valuing in educational settings'.
34 Mercer, op. cit., p. 96.
35 Michael F. D. Young, 'Curriculum and the social organization of knowledge', in Richard Brown, ed., *Knowledge, Education and Cultural Change*, Tavistock, 1973, p. 350.
36 See Freeman, op. cit.; Herbert M. Kliebard, 'Bureaucracy and curriculum theory', in V. Haubrich, ed., *Freedom, Bureaucracy, and Schooling*, Washington, DC, Association for Supervision and Curriculum Development, 1971, pp. 74–93.
37 Murray Edelman, 'The Political Language of the Helping Professions', unpublished paper, University of Wisconsin, Madison, 1973, pp. 3–4.
38 ibid., p. 4.
39 ibid., pp. 7–8. My stress.
40 Erving Goffman, *Asylums*, New York, Doubleday, 1961, p. 115.
41 Jane R. Mercer, 'Labeling the mentally retarded', in Earl Rubington and Martin S. Weinberg, eds, *Deviance: the Interactionist Perspective*, New York, Macmillan, 1968. For a more complete treatment of the conservative posture of clinical and helping viewpoints, see Apple, 'The process and ideology of valuing in educational settings'.
42 An interesting point should be made here. Persons employing clinical perspectives in dealing with health or deviance are apt to label people as 'sick' rather than 'well' in most instances to avoid the danger of what might happen to the 'patient' if they are wrong. Here, one more motivation for 'finding' individuals to fit institutional categories can be uncovered. See Thomas Scheff, *Being Mentally Ill: a Sociological Theory*, Chicago, Aldine, 1966, pp. 105–6.
43 Thomas S. Szasz, *Ideology and Insanity*, New York, Doubleday, 1970, p. 2.
44 Robert W. Friedrichs, *A Sociology of Sociology*, New York, Free Press, 1970, pp. 172–3.
45 Ollman, op. cit., p. 111. For a less Marxist, but no less critical, phenomenological approach to this position see Abraham Heschel, *Who Is Man?*, Stanford University Press, 1965.
46 Lewis A. Dexter, 'On the politics and sociology of stupidity in our society', in Howard S. Becker, ed., *The Other Side*, New York, Free Press, 1964, pp. 37–49.
47 See Jules Henry, *Culture Against Man*, New York, Random House, 1963; Philip Jackson, *Life in Classrooms*, New York, Holt, Rinehart & Winston, 1968. Goffman's notion of 'secondary adjustments' is quite helpful in interpreting parts of the hidden curriculum (op. cit., p. 189).
48 Schur, op. cit., p. 96.
49 Kliebard, op. cit.
50 This is obviously a difficult analytic issue as well as a moral concern. A good place to begin would be the impressive work of John Rawls. See especially *A Theory of Justice*, Harvard University Press, 1971.
51 See Norman Storer, *The Social System of Science*, New York, Holt, Rinehart & Winston, 1966.
52 Schroyer, *The Critique of Domination*, pp. 165–6.
53 ibid., p. 172.
54 See, for example, Michael W. Apple and Thomas Brady, 'Toward increasing the potency of student rights claims', in V. F. Haubrich and M. W. Apple, eds, *Schooling and the Rights of Children*, Berkeley, Calif., McCutchan, 1975.
55 Schroyer, *The Critique of Domination*, p. 248.

20 Curriculum change: limits and possibilities*

Michael F. D. Young

I am concerned with the problem of change in education—with developing a theory or theories that may enable those involved in education to become aware of ways of changing their or their pupils' or students' educational experience, even if this leads us to conceive of teachers' struggles as not independent from other struggles in the work places and communities where people live.[1] I want to do this through a critical examination of two contrasting conceptions of the curriculum, which are well expressed by Maxine Greene (1971). She describes the dominant view of the curriculum of educational philosophers such as Hirst and Peters[2] in terms of 'a structure of socially prescribed knowledge, external to the knower, there to be mastered', which she compares with her own phenomenological view of the curriculum as 'a possibility for the learner as an existing person mainly concerned with making sense of his own life-world'.[3]

For the present purposes I shall call these two views 'curriculum as fact' and 'curriculum as practice'.[4] The 'curriculum as fact'—or commodity-view[5] of knowledge has been rightly criticized as both dehumanizing, and mystifying education, mostly by marxist and phenomenologically inspired sociologists and philosophers—Paulo Freire and Maxine Greene are but two. These critiques, as expressed in the view of 'curriculum as practice' do not start from the structure of knowledge but the intentions and actions of men. I shall want to argue that such a view, as a kind of over-reaction to the pervasiveness of subjects, forms of knowledge and objectives, can itself be a form of mystification. I shall suggest that 'curriculum as fact' needs to be seen as more than mere illusion, a superficial veneer on teachers' and pupils' classroom practice, but as a historically specific social reality expressing particular production relations among men.[6] It is mystifying in the way it presents the curriculum as having a life of its own, and obscures

Source: *Educational Studies*, 1 (2), June 1975, pp. 129–38.

the human relations in which it as any conception of knowledge is embedded, leaving education as neither understandable nor controllable by men. The alternative conception of 'curriculum as practice' can equally mystify to the extent that it reduces the social reality of 'curriculum' to the subjective intentions and actions of teachers and pupils. This limits us from understanding the historical emergence and persistence of particular conceptions of knowledge and *particular* conventions (school subjects for example). In that we are limited from being able to situate the problems of contemporary education historically, we are again limited from understanding and control.

Before exploring these contrasting views in more detail, I should like to take an example—mathematics, as an unlikely case to illustrate the distinction between theories of knowledge that I wish to make. To do this I shall draw on a discussion by David Bloor (1973), who begins by quoting from G. H. Hardy's *A Mathematician's Apology*: '317 is a prime, not because we think so, or because our minds are shaped in one way rather than another, but *because it is so* because mathematical reality is built that way'. Hardy exemplifies the kind of realist theory of knowledge which posits a realm of truth independent of man; such a theory underlies what I have referred to as the view of 'curriculum as fact'. Bloor contrasts Hardy with Wittgenstein (1967) who in discussing logical inferences involved in simple number sequences, writes as follows: 'with endless practice, with merciless exactitude; that is why it is inexorably insisted that we shall all say "two" after "one", "three" after "two" and so on'. For Wittgenstein, it is *we* not mathematics who are inexorable, Bloor remarks. 'Our children', Wittgenstein writes, 'are not only given practice in calculation but are also trained to adopt a particular attitude towards a mistake in calculating'—the feeling, Bloor suggests that the calculation goes its own way, even if we as calculators may lapse. This seems to me a profound insight into how our concepts of knowledge are related to our ideas about teaching and learning. This, as Bloor points out, is not a theory which denies the social reality of mathematics. It recognizes that mathematics is an invention not a discovery, but that it, like all inventions, can come to have a life of its own, to be re-ified, and therefore experienced as external to men. The question, which I shall return to, of how particular forms of reification[7] emerge and persist is not adequately dealt with, either by dismissing the problem as theories such as Hardy's do, nor by treating the rules of mathematics, or any form of knowing, as mere convention or usage, as Wittgenstein might be interpreted as doing.

Let us now return to the first of my two views of curriculum, 'curriculum as fact'.

Most writing and research concerned with curriculum unavoidably treats it as in some way a topic, thus affirming rather than explaining it as a social reality. It becomes something to be preserved or brought up to date—as in grammar schools, modified or made more relevant for the so-called less able, broadened or integrated for those who specialize too soon, and so on. We can also trace a range of administrative practices, which though doubtless starting with a concern about what should be happening to pupils and students, in effect sustain the idea of the curriculum as something to be studied, reorganized and analysed—we find deputy head teachers and vice-principals for curriculum, professors, journals, degrees and departments, and of course the final academic accolade of all otherwise unrecognized activity, attempts to develop curriculum 'theory'. Parallel to this we find new special interests like the sociology and psychology of the curriculum in which the two disciplines apply their respective vocabularies—for sociology it has been stratification and integration, and, for psychology, mental development and stages of learning. I would suggest that in each case, problems are created, such as the separation and hierarchies between different areas of enquiry in sociology, which our methods do not enable us to solve, for our starting points have been knowledge and curricula, rather than their production in teachers' and pupils' practice. Academic theorists, often in search of a spurious scientism, can be far more naïve than teachers. They present curriculum as a reality to which the language of cause and effect, resistance and change, is appropriate, and we discover articles with absurd titles like 'How does the curriculum change?' This is not so different from politicians' talk of 'the National Interest' or 'the Economy', in which an ideology is mistaken for the set of social relations it seeks to legitimate. These social relations between teachers and taught and the assumptions about knowledge and curriculum embedded in them become masked or even subsumed by the language of curriculum theory. A parallel might be drawn with classical economics which took prices and wages as its topics, thus masking the production relations between owners and employees. This conception of 'curriculum as fact', with its underlying theory of knowledge as external to the knower, both teacher and student, embodied in syllabuses and text-books, is widely held and has profound implications for our conceptions of teaching and learning. To say 'I teach history, or physics' implies a body of knowledge to be transferred from the teacher who has it to the pupil who has not, whether by rote and test or enquiry and project. Though this applies most obviously to secondary schools, the notion of a body of knowledge, though not formalized as a set of 'subjects' is no less involved in saying 'I teach 4th year juniors.' This is the framework that has been taken as given by most of those who have theorized about educational or curriculum change. It is teachers as well as philosophers who see teaching as initiating children into 'worthwhile' activities—and so long as the idea of initiation, with the knowledge and the worthwhile presupposed, and with its unavoidably hierarchical relations, is not questioned, educational philosophy merely confirms what every teacher and pupil knows, and the only possible explanations of pupil failure are either in terms of 'bad teaching' or in terms of social or psychological characteristics of the pupil. Nell Keddie (1971) suggests what is involved in such a conception of curriculum and teaching. She argues that becoming initiated into the teachers' form of knowledge, or, as we more normally describe it, becoming an educational success, is premised precisely on pupils *not* questioning the grounds of teachers' knowledge. I would like to illustrate the way in which I see notions of teaching as 'knowledge to be transmitted' are involved in teacher-pupil interaction, by referring to a transcript I made from a first year science class in a large East London Comprehensive School. I think it also illustrates how, with such a conception of knowledge prevailing, passivity is almost forced on, in this case, a remarkably reluctant pupil.

(Teacher and pupils have a worm in front of them)
T: Have you ever seen examples of when it [soil] is produced?
B: No.
T: Earth on the grass.
B: No I just seen holes on the grass.
T: Have you ever seen anything else that might tell you there was a worm on the grass?
B: Yeah, they're what's called again, the holes they make are called
T: Have you seen those little piles?
B: Piles?
T: Have you seen those little heaps of
B: Leaves
T: On the grass, little
B: Holes.
T: Em?

B: Dots.
T: Have you seen have you ever come
B: I've seen holes
T: Do you know something called a cast?

If you should see this as just an example of 'bad teaching', I would suggest you might ask similar questions about any example of what you would consider 'good teaching'. I would want to argue that the assumptions about knowledge as external, to-be-transmitted, are no less a feature of 'good' teaching than 'bad', and that they are integral for both teachers and pupils in creating a sense of pupils as 'not knowing' at least till his 'knowledge' is confirmed by the teacher.

If we turn specifically to what Banks has called 'mainstream' or 'traditional' sociology of education,[8] we find a conception of 'curriculum as fact' as no less pervasive. Most writers, from Durkheim to Parsons and Banks conceive of education *as* cultural transmission, or socialization into skills and values. Thus the teacher's problem, which he hardly needed the sociologist to tell him, is already defined—how is he or she to devise more effective ways of transmitting these skills, whatever they are to as many pupils as possible? All such sociological theory can do is to offer a range of explanations, from cultural inadequacy or lack of innate ability of the pupils to some reference to 'the structure of our society', to account to teachers why, according to conventional academic standards, they are so often unsuccessful.

The school curriculum becomes presented as a set of gateways to a world of adult competence, though educationalists are inclined to find all kinds of justification for the very tenuous relationships between school defined 'competence' and what anyone needs to survive in or understand, let alone change, the world they are supposedly being prepared for. It is, predominantly, a subject-ordered world—even when presented as integrated studies—on what grounds, one might ask, can we distinguish the new 'integrations' from the old 'subjects'? Take geography and chemistry for example; they are undoubtedly ways of producing, anyway for teachers, a sense of integration of a very disparate set of themes and topics, so that as with Nuffield Secondary Science, it is possible to say 'it's a bit short on chemistry'. However, this sense of integration is also produced, to take an example, by those who teach environmental studies or material science, and it would be extremely difficult to claim, except in terms of custom and tradition, any distinctiveness about the second examples of integration. There is a more important point; integration in both cases produces an ordering of the world through which the learner has to find his way, rather than involving the learner in the process of integration himself. Where pupils reject the discontinuity between their knowledge of the world and what they experience as school orderings, subjects, topics, etc., they invariably become

described as less-able or non-academic. Such descriptions depend for their plausibility on a view of 'curriculum as fact', which tells us what 'able' and 'academic' refer to. That this view of curriculum is also presupposed by the proposals for 'curricula for the less-able' is illustrated for example by the Schools Council's project 'Mathematics for the majority'. The difference is that while knowledge is still seen as external to both teacher and pupils, it involves not only ideas about what counts as mathematics, but about the supposed relevance of certain mathematical practices for pupils' lives outside of school.

More generally then, I would suggest that the prevailing notions of curriculum to which I have referred express a power relation between teacher and learner, and a relatively passive model of the teacher as reproducing the knowledge produced elsewhere by others. One way in which this passivity is displayed is the way outside bodies such as University Exam Boards are able, almost without question, to define what counts as knowledge in the schools. Even bodies such as the CSE boards and the Schools Council are, more often than not, felt as external constraints on the work of classroom teachers—you have only to talk to teachers who have tried to obtain Schools Council support for local development projects, or in many areas, to develop Mode 3 schemes with minimal formal examinations, to be aware that 'teacher control' of these organizations is more of a constitutional rhetoric than a reality.

To sum up this section—I have suggested that a view of 'curriculum as fact' expresses many of the prevailing assumptions or theories of practitioners, both teachers and pupils. In that most of what passes for curriculum theory, whether of that name or derived from philosophy, psychology or sociology, confirms such assumptions, it can do little more than redescribe a world that teachers and pupils already know. Paradoxically, it confirms for teachers both the irrelevance of theory for practical change in schools, and their own insignificance as theorists: teachers have theories of knowledge, teaching and curriculum, which I shall argue later are crucially important for the possibilities of change, but they lack the abstract elegance and empty clarity of philosophy, the conceptual obscurity of sociology, and the mindless banalities of the curriculum taxonomies. As a theory, therefore, 'curriculum as fact' fails according to the criteria I started with, in 'not enabling people to become aware of changing their world', for that would be about enabling teachers and pupils to theorize, rather than to learn that others theorize about their practice. 'Curriculum as fact' presents education as a thing, hiding the social relations between human beings who collectively produce it—what then of the view of 'curriculum as practice', the theory which informs the critique of prevailing ideas such as those I have referred to?

The basic premise of a view of 'curriculum as practice'[9] is not a structure of knowledge, but how men collectively attempt to order their world and in the process produce knowledge. In education the focus has been on teachers' and pupils' classroom practices, and how educational realities such as subjects, curriculum and ability are not external or attributes of pupils, but products of these practices, and the assumptions about knowledge, learning and teaching which are embedded in them.[10] From this view, teachers' practices are seen as crucial in sustaining or challenging prevailing views of knowledge and curriculum which thus ceases to be treated as distinct from the variety of ranking activities through which teachers produce marks, discipline, and children of differing abilities.[11] The implication that follows is that a critical examination of assumptions underlying teachers' activities will enable them to implement change almost at will. Such a theory, while valuable in challenging the view of 'curriculum as fact' and teachers as passive reproducers, is misleading both theoretically and practically in locating the possibilities of change in education solely within teachers' practices. Teachers are thereby given a kind of spurious autonomy and independence from the wider contexts of which their activity is a part, and thus have no way of understanding their own failures except in terms of personal inadequacy.

A view of 'curriculum as practice' involves a radically different view of knowledge to that referred to in Hardy's mathematics—no longer can knowledge be viewed almost as private property handed down from the academic 'discoverers', for the teacher to distribute or 'transmit'. Knowledge becomes that which is accomplished in the collaborative work of teachers and pupils. Theoretically this has profound implications for existing school hierarchies, and for how we organize educational practice. What might be involved for example, in seeing education as the collaborative production of history or science, when we normally think of teaching as the transmission of knowledge, however we dress it up as enquiry or projects? The problem is not just that such possibilities may seem exciting to some but threatening to others, but that they remain possibilities 'in theory', generated as they are from a view of curriculum *as* teachers' practice. In other words such a view of curriculum can itself be seen as an ideology in treating teachers' practices as some independent reality. Radical changes based on a theory of 'curriculum as practice' are likely to face very quickly the practical experience that curriculum is not *just* teachers' and pupils' practice—that it involves also the views about what education should be of parents, employers, administrators and so on. If there was a situation in a school or group of schools where teachers began with pupils a critical examination and reformulation of current practice, then I would suggest that in their attempts to implement alternatives, they would *practically* be taken far outside the context of the classroom, and *theoretically* to trying to develop a theory more adequate for understanding their

situation than that of 'curriculum as practice'.

I would like to illustrate these general points by two specific examples from science education, which I would argue have a more general relevance to the problems of a view of curriculum as practice. Innovation in science education has been virtually synonomous with the Nuffield/Schools Council Projects, which have tended without exception to sustain rather than challenge existing conceptions of school science and to perpetuate its stratification into 'pure' and 'applied' (Hardy, 1975). The attempts to introduce Project Technology largely through craft departments in schools is a case in point; as is in a different context the remark of a head of chemistry in a north of England comprehensive school that he thought he could get his environmental science syllabus through for CSE 'if the highest Grade he asked for was Grade 3'.

At a meeting of the British Association in September 1974, Professor Jevons was quoted as saying that in science education 'we are up against something in the cognitive structure of science itself', and that therefore science was not appropriate 'to meet the more radical ideals of education': a very clear example of the mode of reasoning underlying the view of 'curriculum as fact' and the kind of teaching that it implies. If, however, we go back a century we can see how our conceptions of school science as a body of knowledge enshrined in textbooks, syllabuses and labs, gradually gained ascendancy over quite different possibilities. A recent study (Layton, 1973) brings this out well by describing the fate of a movement during the early days of school science called by its founder Richard Dawes, the 'Science of common things'. In the work of this movement, pupils' experiences of the natural world, in their work, their homes and their daily lives formed the basis of the development of their enquiries in school science. A particular example Layton cites is the 'radical curriculum' of Arthur Rigg, Principal of Chester Training College, in which a major emphasis was placed on the kind of science and workshop skills relevant to an area where most people were employed in the cotton industry. This project was short lived, Layton suggests, because it undermined the separation of teachers from those they were to teach, and it was feared by the Inspectorate that those studying their own work context might come to see it too critically. Furthermore, it was felt that teachers emerging from such a course might become as one inspector put it, 'active emissaries of misrule'. Both Dawes and Rigg can be seen as working with notions of curriculum as *practice*, in which school and college science is the emergent product of teacher and student collaborative activities. In the particular context their proposals were perceived, by their opponents anyway, as raising questions of significance far outside the classroom or the lab; the powerlessness and ultimate demise of the movement can be seen in part as reflecting the limitations of a theory that restricts itself to what happens in the school. Though it is not possible to draw any direct parallels with science education today, what is emphasized is the historical emergence and political character of the most basic assumptions of what is now taken to be school science.

My second example illustrates the limits of a view of curriculum as practice, and suggests how examiners, outside the school context are involved in sustaining particular notions of school knowledge—it is taken from the Nuffield Science A level in which the typical practical test is replaced by a project to be devised and written up by the candidate and is allocated 15 per cent of the marks. In one case a girl chose to investigate problems of streamlining a boat, and in doing so, she drew on and learnt a considerable amount about viscosity—a standard school science topic at A level. In the context of her project, viscosity was not an external body of knowledge to be learnt because it was on the syllabus, but a way of understanding and transforming an aspect of her environment which was important to her outside school.[12] The teacher and pupil activity, both theoretical and practical became, in this instance the reality of science education. However, this *practice*, as a part of teachers' and pupils' activity on a physical science course was crammed in to one afternoon a week, while the rest of the time was used in the 'real' work of reproducing knowledge for the formal exams which count 85 per cent of the marks. It may be therefore that such liberalization tends to sustain rather than challenge, both for teachers and pupils, a view that knowledge of viscosity, like all *real* knowledge, is something to be learnt and reproduced rather than a way of understanding the world we are part of: thus a view of curriculum as fact rather than as practice is confirmed.

To summarize this section; I have argued that a view of curriculum as practice does challenge attempts to legitimate particular educational practice in terms of structures of knowledge, but that in replacing a notion of reality located in such structures by one located in teachers' classroom practice, it has serious weaknesses. Attempts by teachers to develop strategies in terms of such a theory will not only confront them with the limits on their possibilities of action, but also with the limits of a theory that cannot enable them to comprehend the character of such limits.

I would like to conclude by drawing together the themes of the two critiques in relation to my original problem—developing a theory or theories that may enable those of us involved in education to be aware of ways of transforming educational practice. Curriculum as fact, with its concepts of teaching, knowledge and ability, takes for granted just that which its task as a theory should be to explain. How did education formulated in terms of curricula originate and why does it prevail or persist? By failing to ask this question such a theory must be assuming, at least for advanced industrial societies, that the kind of educational practices which prevail are in a sense

necessary. This is a kind of end-of-history argument, in which the past as a dynamic of action and interests which produced the present is forgotten, and the future is viewed as some kind of universal present. The significance of this view of curriculum is the extent to which it is not just a theory produced by academics, but rather that it represents the way those involved in ordering our educational institutions, administrators, headmasters and teachers, actually conceive of education. In this way it represents part of the circumstances within which anyone concerned to change educational practice has to work. If it is a characteristic of any *critical* theory[13] that the starting point of its argument must be people's everyday views of the world, and if as I have suggested, the concept of education expressed in the idea of 'curriculum as fact' is such a view, then any theory concerned with the possibilities of change, cannot treat such a view as mere illusion, the irrelevant product of ivory tower academics. This then is the major weakness of the view of curriculum as practice. Though challenging prevailing conceptions of education, in treating them as conventions arbitrarily imposed on the real practices of men, it can mislead as to the possibilities of change by locating them primarily in teachers' practices. In doing so it directly contradicts the lived experience of those about whom it theorizes, contributing, paradoxically to the division between theory and practice, which its critique of structures of knowledge would seem to question.[14] In emphasizing the conventionality of prevailing hierarchies of knowledge—academic and non-academic, theoretical and practical, abstract and concrete, for example, it limits the possibility of understanding how these particular educational hierarchies (the separation of science from technology is but one) are embedded in historically specific sets of social relations both *in* and *of* education.[15] Convention implies that things could be otherwise (which is like equating the ordering of knowledge with customs of eating or greetings)—that school subjects like mathematics only persist through habit or custom, or because that is how those in power define what is conventional. What starts as a critique of the separation of knowledge from the knower, ends up in a contradiction by having to invoke the crudest of mechanistic relations between knowledge and social position which in effect explain nothing, and not surprisingly offer no strategies for change.

A theory that can provide for possibilities of change in education does not emerge either from the dominant view of 'curriculum as fact' or from a critique of such a view expressed in the idea of curriculum as practice. The first, by starting from a view of knowledge abstracted from men in history and from the teachers and pupils to whom it is addressed, denies them possibilities except within its framework and definitions. The second, in its concern to recognize teachers and pupils as conscious agents of change, as theorists in their own right, and to emphasize the human possibilities in all situations has also become abstracted from the constraints of teachers' lived experience. Possibilities may be recognized in *theory*, but their practical implementation is experienced as something quite remote. A *theoretical* critique of the *necessity* of hierarchies of knowledge and ability may be exciting in a seminar, but is not any good to those who experience such necessities as real in *practice*. The problem then is not to deny or accept these hierarchies as necessary but to try and reformulate them as not in the order of things but as the outcomes of the collective actions of men—and thus understandable and potentially changeable. This takes me to the three directions in which I see a critical theory which transcends the dichotomy of 'fact' and practice will need to develop.

1. The prescription to *start* from teachers' and pupils' practice, the theories that they evolve in their day to day practice, can itself remain mere theory. This will be so without a *practical* change in the relations between those who are currently labelled theorists and those about whom they theorize. This is not an anti-theory argument, for this could lead to an uncritical acceptance of any tradition and custom currently found in school. It is a recognition that the testing ground of a theory is not its conceptual clarity nor its ability to predict outcomes, criteria we have inherited from a narrow conception of philosophizing and a dubious scientism, but how such ideas are transformed into action in the practice of teachers and pupils that make up our schools.

2. Educational practice is often experienced and thought about as if it was either isolated or separate (Hextall & Sarup, 1975). I would want to emphasize that theories and innovations in education rarely challenge existing hierarchies within schools let alone without, and thus our own activity tends to create its own sense of autonomy. However, if questions about our assumptions about curriculum are to be more than just questions, political problems will inevitably be raised for teachers, and anyone involved in education. This suggests that prevailing notions about curricula, though sustained by those in formal education, are not sustained by them alone. A more adequate theory of curriculum as *practice*, would not restrict practice to that of teachers, nor of teachers' practice to their activities in the school and classroom. If the educational experience of both teachers

and pupils is to become a realistic possibility of human liberation, then this is going to involve many others who have no direct involvement with the school, and much action by teachers and pupils that would not be seen as either confined to school or in conventional terms necessarily educational at all.

3. Both views of curriculum I have referred to tend to obscure the political and economic character of education; this, as I have argued, sets limits on their possibilities as a theory of change. They also have in common with much educational writing a lack of any sense of history or of linking the present to the past, a fault also of much of what passes for 'history of education'. The nearest one gets is some kind of inevitable tradition or evolution. One crucial way of reformulating, and so potentially understanding and transcending the limits within which we work, is to see, as in Layton's example referred to earlier, how such limits are not given or fixed but produced through the conflicting actions and interests of men in history (Stead, 1974). The recent historical studies of the origins of psychological testing, and the way compulsory education was used to impose central control on grass-roots popular education movements (Karier, 1972) are an important example. They offer much more to a theory of the possibilities of change in education than the static analyses of the deschoolers and the critics of behavioural psychology. Similarly, studies of Trades Councils and Local School Boards at the turn of the century present a very different picture of working-class parental involvement when compared with the current Plowden-type dogmas, and also a very different strategy to the well-intentioned paternalism of the EPA Projects (Lynch, 1974).

These suggestions are no more than tentative directions as to how limits can become transformed into possibilities and possibilities made real in practice. They do argue for making more explicit the political character of education, and for a shift of responsibility to define education from colleges and offices to classrooms and communities. In doing so I see this as recognizing that much of what we hope can be realized in education will not take place in school, and as part of an attempt to enable all involved in education to learn about the world we live in and that it is our world to make.

Notes

* This paper was originally given as one of the Doris Lee Lectures on 20 February 1975 at the University of London Institute of Education.
1 A discussion of the limits and possibilities of community action is given by Dearlove (1974) and others in the symposium *Community Work One.*
2 Also of course most sociology, psychology and so-called curriculum 'theory'.
3 Some of the possibilities for theory of educational change

Maxine Greene develops in a more recent paper (1974).
4 This distinction is developed from ideas worked out with Geoff Whitty (Whitty & Young, 1975): of course if treated as a kind of mechanistic dichotomy it can become as misleading an oversimplification as Marx's famous 'base' and 'superstructure' (Williams, 1973). The intention of this paper is to suggest that a *critical* theory needs to see 'fact' and 'practice' as both theoretically *and* practically related.

5 The theoretical and practical importance of a critique of a commodity view of knowledge for educational change is pointed out by Whitty (1974).

6 I do not use the term 'production' in any narrow 'economistic' sense. Economic relations are as Ollman (1972) argues, even for Marx, but one aspect, albeit a critical one, of men's productive activity at any particular time.

7 I use the term 'reification' here in Marx's sense when he refers in *Capital* to how 'a definite social relation between men . . . assumes, in their eyes the fantastic form of a relation between things'. A very clear discussion of this aspect of Marx's work can be found in Geras (1971).

8 See Olive Banks' article in *Forum* (Banks, 1974) and my reply in the same journal (Young, 1975).

9 Two books which trace this idea of man as an active sense-maker in what are, in other ways, very diverse philosophical traditions are Roche (1973), and Bernstein (1971).

10 A recent example of a study which shows how the assigning of a quality like academic ability to a child can be viewed as the practical accomplishment of teachers is the work of Cicourel *et al.* (1974).

11 Very different and potentially exciting possibilities for conceiving of teachers' ranking practices are suggested by Hextall & Sarup (1975).

12 This example taken from an unpublished paper by Mr B. J. Hine of Queen Elizabeth's Girls' School, Barnet.

13 The clearest and most explicit formulation of the distinction between *critical* and traditional theory is to be found in Horkheimer (1972).

14 Bartholomew (1975) points out the necessity of seeing the problem of theory and practice as a problem of the division of labour between theorists and practitioners.

15 This distinction is explored by Holly (1975).

References

Banks, O. (1974), 'The "new" sociology of education', *Forum*, autumn.

Bartholomew, J. C. (1975), 'Theory and practice: an unaddressed issue?', *Education for Teaching*, May.

Bernstein, R. J. (1971), *Praxis and Action*, Duckworth.

Bloor, D. (1973), 'Wittgenstein and Mannheim on the sociology of mathematics', *Studies in the History and Philosophy of Science*, 4.

Cicourel, A. V. *et al.* (1974), *Language Use and School Performance*, Academic Press.

Dearlove J. (1974), 'The control of change and the regulation of community action', in *Community Work One*, ed. D. Jones and M. Mayo, Routledge & Kegan Paul.

Geras, N. (1971), 'Essence and appearance: aspects of fetishism in Marx's *Capital*', *New Left Review*, 65.

Greene, M. (1971), 'Curriculum and consciousness', *The Record*, F3 (2).

Greene, M. (1974), 'Countering privatism', *Educational Theory*, 24 (3).

Hardy, J. (1975), 'Ideology and Natural Science: possibilities for science educators?', paper presented to British Sociological Association, Sociology of Science Study Group, February 1975.

Hextall, I. and Sarup, M. (1975), 'School knowledge, evaluation and alienation', paper presented to the Annual Conference of the British Sociological Association.

Holly, D. (1975), 'Education and social relations of a capitalist society', paper presented to the British Sociological Association Annual Conference.

Horkheimer, M. (1972), *Critical Theory*, Herder & Herder.

Karier, C. (1972), 'Testing for order and control in the corporate liberal state',† *Educational Theory*, 22 (2).

Keddie, N. (1971), 'Classroom knowledge', in *Knowledge and Control*, ed. M. F. D. Young, Collier-Macmillan.

Layton, D. (1973), *Science for the People*, Allen & Unwin.

Lynch, G. (1974), 'Ideology and the social organization of educational knowledge in England and Scotland 1840–1920', MA dissertation, University of London, Institute of Education.

Ollman, B. (1972), *Alienation: Marx's Concept of Man in Capitalist Society*, Cambridge University Press.

Roche, M. (1973), *Phenomenology, Language and Social Science*, Routledge & Kegan Paul.

Stead, D. (1974), 'History as school knowledge', MA dissertation, University of London, Institute of Education.

Whitty, G. (1974), 'Sociology and the problems of radical educational change: towards a reconceptionalisation of the "new sociology of education"', in *Educability, Schools and Ideology*, ed. M. Flude and J. Ahier, Croom Helm.

Whitty, G. and Young, M. F. D. (1975), 'Sociology and the politics of school knowledge', *Teaching London Kids*, 6, September.

Williams, R. (1973), 'Base and superstructure in Marxist cultural theory', *New Left Review*, 82.

Wittgenstein, L. (1967), *Remarks on the Foundations of Mathematics*, Oxford, Basil Blackwell.

Young, M. F. D. (1975), 'Sociologists and the politics of comprehensive education', *Forum*, summer.

† In this volume.

21   Systems of education and systems of thought

Pierre Bourdieu

Speaking of the course of his intellectual development in *A World on the Wane*, Claude Lévi-Strauss describes the techniques and rites of philosophy teaching in France:[1]

> It was then that I began to learn how any problem, whether grave or trivial, can be resolved. The method never varies. First you establish the traditional 'two views' of the question. You then put forward a commonsense justification of the one, only to refute it by the other. Finally you send them both packing by the use of a third interpretation, in which both the others are shown to be equally unsatisfactory. Certain verbal manoeuvres enable you, that is, to line up the traditional 'antitheses' as complementary aspects of a single reality: form and substance, content and container, appearance and reality, essence and existence, continuity and discontinuity and so on. Before long the exercise becomes the merest verbalizing, reflection gives place to a kind of superior punning, and the 'accomplished philosopher' may be recognized by the ingenuity with which he makes ever-bolder play with assonance, ambiguity and the use of those words which sound alike and yet bear quite different meanings.
>
> Five years at the Sorbonne taught me little but this form of mental gymnastics. Its dangers are, of course, self-evident: the mechanism is so simple, for one thing, that there is no such thing as a problem which cannot be tackled. When we were working for our examinations and, above all, for that supreme ordeal, the *leçon* (in which the candidate draws a subject by lot, and is given only six hours in which to prepare a comprehensive survey of it), we used to set one another the bizarrest imaginable themes. . . . The method, universal in its application, encouraged the student to overlook the many possible forms and variants of thought, devoting himself to one particular unchanging instrument. Certain elementary adjustments were all that he needed . . .

This admirable ethnological description of the intellectual and linguistic patterns transmitted—implicitly rather than explicitly—by French education, has its counterpart in the description of the patterns that direct the thinking and behaviour of the Bororo Indians when they build their villages to a plan every bit as formal and fictitious as the dualistic organization of the *agrégation* exercises, patterns whose necessity or, to put it another way, whose function is recognized in this case by the ethnologist, probably because he is, at once, more detached and more intimately involved:[2]

> The wise men of the tribe have evolved a grandiose cosmology which is writ large in the lay-out of their villages and distribution of their homes. When they met with contradictions, those contradictions were cut across again and again. Every opposition was rebutted in favour of another. Groups were divided and re-divided, both vertically and horizontally, until their lives, both spiritual and temporal, became an escutcheon in which symmetry and asymmetry were in equilibrium . . .

As a social individual, the ethnologist is on terms of intimacy with his culture and therefore finds it difficult to think objectively about the patterns governing his own thought; the more completely those patterns have been mastered and have become a part of his make-up—and therefore coextensive and

Source: *International Social Science Journal*, 19 (3), 1967, pp. 338–52; also appeared in M. F. D. Young, ed., *Knowledge and Control: New Directions for the Sociology of Education*, Collier-Macmillan, 1971, pp. 189–207.

consubstantial with his consciousness—the more impossible is it for him to apply conscious thought to them. He may also be reluctant to admit that, even though acquired through the systematically organized learning processes of the school, and therefore generally explicit and explicitly taught, the patterns which shape the thinking of educated men in 'school-going' societies may fulfil the same function as the unconscious patterns he discovers, by analysing such cultural creations as rites or myths, among individuals belonging to societies with no educational institutions, or as those 'primitive forms of classification' which are not, and cannot be, the subject of conscious awareness and explicit, methodical transmission. Do the patterns of thought and language transmitted by the school, e.g., those which treatises of rhetoric used to call figures of speech and figures of thought, actually fulfil, at any rate among members of the educated classes, the function of the unconscious patterns which govern the thinking and the productions of people belonging to traditional societies, or do they, because of the conditions in which they are transmitted and acquired, operate only at the most superficial level of consciousness? If it be true that the specificity of societies possessing a scholarly, cumulative, accumulated culture lies, from the point of view that concerns us here, in the fact that they have special institutions to transmit, explicitly or implicitly, explicit or implicit forms of thought that operate at different levels of consciousness—from the most obvious which may be apprehended by irony or by pedagogical thinking to the most deeply buried forms which find expression in acts of cultural creation or interpretation, without being thought about specifically—the question then arises whether the sociology of the institutionalized transmission of culture is not, at any rate in one of its aspects, one of the paths and not the least important, to the sociology of knowledge.

The school and cultural integration

To appreciate how unusual this approach is, we need only note that Durkheim and, after him, most of the authors who have dealt with the sociology of education from an anthropological standpoint emphasize the school's 'moral' integration function, relegating to second place or passing over in silence what might be called the cultural (or logical) integration function of the educational institution. Is it not paradoxical that, in his writings on education, the author of *Formes primitives de classification* and *Formes élémentaires de la vie religieuse* should have failed to realize that, like religion in primitive societies, the culture that comes from schooling provides individuals with a common body of thought categories which make communication possible? It is perhaps less paradoxical that Durkheim, in his sociology of knowledge, should try to establish the social origin of logical categories without mentioning the role of

education, since he is concerned in the above-mentioned works with societies in which the transmission of these logical categories is not generally entrusted to an institution specially designed for the purpose, but it is none the less surprising that he should regard schooling as one of the most effective means of securing the 'moral' integration of differentiated societies and yet not realize that the school is tending, more and more completely and exclusively as knowledge advances, to assume a logical integration function. 'Programmed' individuals—endowed with a homogeneous programme of perception, thought and action—are the most specific product of an educational system. Those trained in a certain discipline or a certain school have in common a certain 'mentality' as the 'arts' or 'science' mentality or, in France, the *normalien* or *polytechnicien* mentality. Minds thus patterned in the same way are pre-disposed to immediate communication and understanding among themselves. As Henri-Irénée Marrou points out, this applies to individuals trained in the humanistic tradition; the traditional form of education makes sure that there is, 'among all minds, those of a given generation and those of a whole period of history, a fundamental homogeneity which makes communication and communion easier. . . . Within a classical culture, all men share the same treasury of admiration, patterns, rules and, above all, of examples, metaphors, images, words, a common idiom'.[3] The aphorisms, maxims and apologues of Graeco-Latin culture, like the metaphors and parallels inspired by Greek or Roman history, play a part comparable in all respects with that which traditional societies allot to proverbs, sayings and gnomic poems. If it be accepted that culture and, in the case in point, scholarly or academic culture, is a common code enabling all those possessing that code to attach the same meaning to the same words, the same types of behaviour and the same works and, conversely, to express the same meaningful intention through the same words, the same behaviour patterns and the same works, it is clear that the school, which is responsible for handing on that culture, is the fundamental factor in the cultural consensus in as far as it represents the sharing of a common sense which is the prerequisite for communication. Individuals owe to their schooling, first and foremost, a whole collection of commonplaces, covering not only common speech and language but also areas of encounter and agreement, common problems and common methods of approaching those common problems: educated people of a given period may disagree on the questions they discuss but are at any rate in agreement about discussing certain questions. A thinker is linked to his period, and identified in space and time, primarily by the conditioning background of problem approach in which and by which he thinks. Just as linguists have recourse to the criterion of inter-comprehension for determining linguistic areas, so intellectual and cultural areas and generations could be determined by identifying the sets of dominant conditioning questions which define the cultural field of a period. To conclude in all cases, on the basis of the manifest divergences which separate the intellectuals of a given period on what are sometimes known as the 'major problems of the day', that there is a deficiency of logical integration would be to allow ourselves to be misled by appearances; disagreement presupposes agreement on the areas of disagreement, and the manifest conflicts between trends and doctrines conceal from the people concerned in those conflicts the implied basic concurrence which strikes the observer alien to the system. The consensus in dissensus, which constitutes the objective unity of the intellectual field of a given period, i.e., participation in the intellectual background of the day—which is not to be confused with submission to fashion—is rooted in the academic tradition. Authors having nothing else at all in common are yet contemporary in the accepted questions on which they are opposed and by reference to which at least one aspect of their thought is organized: like the fossils that enable us to date prehistoric eras, the subjects of discussion—crystallized remains of the great debates of the day—indicate, though probably with certain shifts in time, the questions which directed and governed the thinking of an age. We might, for instance, in the recent history of philosophic thought in France, distinguish a period of dissertation on judgement and concept, a period of dissertation on essence and existence (or fear and anxiety) and finally, a period of dissertation on language and speech (or nature and culture). A comparative study of the commonest subjects of academic essays or treatises and of lectures in different countries at different periods would make an important contribution to the sociology of knowledge by defining the necessary frame of problematic reasoning, which is one of the most fundamental dimensions of the intellectual programming of a society and a period. This was what Renan foreshadowed when he wrote:[4]

Will it be believed that, at ceremonies similar to our prize-givings, when in our country oratory is essential, the Germans merely read out grammatical treatises of the most austere type, studded with Latin words? Can we conceive of formal public meetings taken up with readings of the following: On the nature of the conjunction; On the German period; On the Greek mathematicians; On the topography of the battle of Marathon; On the plain of Crissa; On the centuries of Servius Tullius; On the vines of Attica; Classification of prepositions; Clarification of difficult words in Homer; Commentary on the portrait of Thersites in Homer, etc.? This implies that our neighbours have a wonderful taste for serious things and perhaps, too, a certain capacity for facing up

bravely to boredom when circumstances require.

There may be coexisting in the thought of a given author, and *a fortiori* of a given period, elements which belong to quite different scholastic periods;[5] the cultural field is transformed by successive restructurations rather than by radical revolutions, with certain themes being brought to the fore while others are set to one side without being completely eliminated, so that continuity of communication between intellectual generations remains possible. In all cases, however, the patterns informing the thought of a given period can be fully understood only by reference to the school system, which is alone capable of establishing them and developing them, through practice, as the habits of thought common to a whole generation.

Culture is not merely a common code or even a common catalogue of answers to recurring problems; it is a common set of previously assimilated master patterns from which, by an 'art of invention' similar to that involved in the writing of music, an infinite number of individual patterns directly applicable to specific situations are generated. The *topoi* are not only commonplaces but also patterns of invention and supports for improvisation: these *topoi*—which include such particularly productive contrasting pairs as thought and action, essence and existence, continuity and discontinuity, etc.—provide bases and starting points for developments (mainly improvised), just as the rules of harmony and counterpoint sustain what seems to be the most inspired and the freest musical 'invention'. These patterns of invention may also serve to make up for deficiency of invention, in the usual sense of the term, so that the formalism and verbalism criticized by Lévi-Strauss are merely the pathological limit of the normal use of any method of thought. Mention may be made, in this context, of what Henri Wallon wrote about the function of thinking by pairs in children:[6]

contrasts of images or of speech result from such a natural and spontaneous association that they may sometimes override intuition and the sense of reality. They are part of the equipment constantly available to thought in the process of self-formulation and they may prevail over thinking. They come under the head of that 'verbal knowledge' whose findings, already formulated, are often merely noted, without any exercise of reflective intelligence and whose workings often outlast those of thought in certain states of mental debilitation, confusion or distraction . . .

Verbal reflexes and thinking habits should serve to sustain thought but they may also, in moments of intellectual 'low tension', take the place of thought; they should help in mastering reality with the minimum effort, but they may also encourage those who rely on them not to bother to refer to reality. For every period, besides a collection of common themes, a particular constellation of dominant patterns could probably be determined, with as many epistemological profiles (taking this in a slightly different sense from that given to it by Gaston Bachelard) as there are schools of thought. It may be assumed that every individual owes to the type of schooling he has received a set of basic, deeply interiorized master-patterns on the basis of which he subsequently acquires other patterns, so that the system of patterns by which his thought is organized owes its specific character not only to the nature of the patterns constituting it but also to the frequency with which these are used and to the level of consciousness at which they operate, these properties being probably connected with the circumstances in which the most fundamental intellectual patterns were acquired.

The essential point is probably that the patterns which have become second nature are generally apprehended only through a reflexive turning-back—which is always difficult—over the operations already carried out; it follows that they may govern and regulate mental processes without being consciously apprehended and controlled. It is primarily through the cultural unconscious which he owes to his intellectual training and more particularly, to his scholastic training, that a thinker belongs to his society and age—schools of thought may, more often than is immediately apparent, represent the union of thinkers similarly schooled.

An exemplary confirmation of this hypothesis is to be found in the famous analysis by Erwin Panofsky of the relationship between Gothic art and Scholasticism. What the architects of the Gothic cathedrals unwittingly borrowed from the schoolmen was a *principium importans ordinem ad actum* or a *modus operandi*, i.e., a 'peculiar method of procedure which must have been the first thing to impress itself upon the mind of the layman whenever it came in touch with that of the schoolman'.[7] Thus, for example, the principle of clarification (*manifestatio*), a scheme of literary presentation discovered by Scholasticism, which requires the author to make plain and explicit (*manifestare*) the arrangement and logic of his argument—we should say his plan—also governs the action of the architect and the sculptor, as we can see by comparing the Last Judgement on the tympanum of Autun Cathedral with the treatment of the same theme at Paris and Amiens where, despite a greater wealth of motifs, consummate clarity also prevails through the effect of symmetry and correspondance.[8] If this is so, it is because the cathedral-builders were subject to the constant influence—to the habit-forming force—of Scholasticism, which, from about 1130–40 to about 1270, 'held a veritable monopoly of education' over an area of roughly 100 miles around Paris.[9]

It is not very probable that the builders of Gothic

structures read Gilbert de la Porrée or Thomas Aquinas in the original. But they were exposed to the Scholastic point of view in innumerable other ways, quite apart from the fact that their own work automatically brought them into a working association with those who devised the liturgical and iconographic programs. They had gone to school; they listened to sermons; they could attend the public *disputationes de quolibet* which, dealing as they did with all imaginable questions of the day, had developed into social events not unlike our operas, concerts or public lectures; and they could come into profitable contact with the learned on many other occasions.

It follows, according to Panofsky, that the connection between Gothic art and Scholasticism is 'more concrete than a mere "parallelism" and yet more general than those individual (and very important) "influences" which are inevitably exerted on painters, sculptors or architects by erudite advisors'. This connection is 'a genuine cause-and-effect relation' which 'comes about by the spreading of what may be called, for want of a better term, a mental habit—reducing this overworked cliché to its precise Scholastic sense as "a principle that regulates the act"', *principium importans ordinem ad actum*'.[10] As a habit-forming force, the school provides those who have been subjected directly or indirectly to its influence not so much with particular and particularized patterns of thought as with that general disposition, generating particular patterns that can be applied in different areas of thought and action, which may be termed cultured *habitus*.

Thus, in accounting for the structural homologies that he finds between such different areas of intellectual activity as architecture and philosophical thought, Erwin Panofsky does not rest content with references to a 'unitarian vision of the world' or a 'spirit of the times'—which would come down to naming what has to be explained or, worse still, to claiming to advance as an explanation the very thing that has to be explained; he suggests what seems to be the most naïve yet probably the most convincing explanation. This is that, in a society where the handing on of culture is monopolized by a school, the hidden affinities uniting the works of man (and, at the same time, modes of conduct and thought) derive from the institution of the school, whose function is consciously (and also, in part, unconsciously) to transmit the unconscious or, to be more precise, to produce individuals equipped with the system of unconscious (or deeply buried) master-patterns that constitute their culture. It would no doubt be an over-simplification to end our efforts at explanation at this point, as though the school were an empire within an empire, as though culture had there its absolute beginning; but it would be just as naïve to disregard the fact that, through the very logic of its functioning, the school modifies the content and the spirit of the culture it transmits and, above all, that its express function is to transform the collective heritage into a common individual unconscious. To relate the works of a period to the practices of the school therefore gives us a means of explaining not only what these works consciously set forth but also what they unconsciously reveal in as much as they partake of the symbolism of a period or of a society.

Schools of thought and class cultures

Apart from collective representations, such as the representation of man as the outcome of a long process of evolution, or the representation of the world as governed by necessary and immutable laws instead of by an arbitrary and capricious fate or by a providential will, every individual unconsciously brings to bear general tendencies such as those by which we recognize the 'style' of a period (whether it be the style of its architecture and furniture, or its style of life) and patterns of thought which organize reality by directing and organizing thinking about reality and make what he thinks thinkable for him as such and in the particular form in which it is thought. As Kurt Lewin remarks, 'Experiments dealing with memory and group pressure on the individual show that what exists as "reality" for the individual is, to a high degree, determined by what is socially accepted as reality. . . . "Reality" therefore, is not an absolute. It differs with the group to which the individual belongs.'[11] Similarly, what is a 'topical question' largely depends on what is socially considered as such; there is, at every period in every society, a hierarchy of legitimate objects for study, all the more compelling for there being no need to define it explicitly, since it is, as it were, lodged in the instruments of thought that individuals receive during their intellectual training. What is usually known as the Sapir-Whorf hypothesis is perhaps never so satisfactorily applicable as to intellectual life; words, and especially the figures of speech and figures of thought that are characteristic of a school of thought, mould thought as much as they express it. Linguistic and intellectual patterns are all the more important in determining what individuals take as worthy of being thought and what they think of it in that they operate outside all critical awareness. 'Thinking . . . follows a network of tracks laid down in the given language, an organization which may concentrate systematically upon certain phases of reality, certain aspects of intelligence, and may systematically discard others featured by other languages. The individual is utterly unaware of this organization and is constrained completely within its unbreakable bounds.'[12]

Academic language and thought effect this organization by giving prominence to certain aspects of reality: thinking by 'schools' and types (designated by so many concepts ending in 'ism') which is a specific product of the school, makes it possible to organize things pertaining to the school, i.e., the universe of philosophical, literary, visual and musical works and, beyond or through them, the whole experience of reality and all reality. To use the terms of Greek tradition, the natural world becomes meaningful only when it has been subject to *diacrisis*—an act of separation introducing the 'limit' (*peras*) into indeterminate chaos (*apeiron*). The school provides the principle for such organization and teaches the art of effecting it. Basically, is taste anything other than the art of differentiating—differentiating between what is cooked and what is raw, what is insipid and what has savour, but also between the classical style and the baroque style or the major mode and the minor mode? Without this principle of separation and the art of applying it that the school teaches, the cultural world is merely an indeterminate, undifferentiated chaos; museum visitors not equipped with this basic stock of words and categories by which differences can be named and, thereby, apprehended—proper names of famous painters which serve as generic categories, concepts designating a school, an age, a 'period' or a style and rendering possible comparisons ('parallels') or contrasts—are condemned to the monotonous diversity of meaningless sensations. In the words of a workman from Dreux: 'When you don't know anything about it, it's difficult to get the hang of it. . . . Everything seems the same to me . . . beautiful pictures, beautiful paintings, but it's difficult to make out one thing from another'. And another workman, from Lille this time, comments: 'It's difficult for someone who wants to take an interest in it. All you can see are paintings and dates. To see the differences, you need a guide, otherwise everything looks the same'.[13] As the systems of typical pre-knowledge that individuals owe to the school grow richer (in other words, as the standard of education rises), familiarity with the organized universe of works becomes closer and more intense. The school does not merely provide reference marks: it also maps out itineraries, that is to say methods (in the etymological sense) or programmes of thought. The intellectual and linguistic master-patterns organize a marked-out area covered with compulsory turnings and one-way streets, avenues and blind alleys; within this area, thought can unfurl with the impression of freedom and improvisation because the marked-out itineraries that it is bound to follow are the very ones that it has covered many a time in the course of schooling. The order of exposition that the school imposes on the culture transmitted—which, most of the time, owes at least as much to school routines as to educational requirements—tends to gain acceptance, as being absolutely necessary, from those acquiring the culture through that order. By its orderly treatment of the works of culture the school hands on, at one and the same time, the rules establishing the orthodox manner of approaching works (according to their position in an established hierarchy) and the principles on which that hierarchy is founded. Because the order of acquisition tends to appear indissolubly associated with the culture acquired and because each individual's relationship with his culture bears the stamp of the conditions in which he acquired it, a self-taught man can be distinguished straightaway from a school-trained man. Having no established itineraries to rely on, the autodidact in Sartre's *La Nausée* sets about reading, in alphabetical order, every author possible. It is perhaps only in its decisive rigidity that this programme seems more arbitrary than the usual syllabus sanctioned by the school and based on a chronological order which, though apparently natural and inevitable, is in fact equally alien to considerations of logic and teaching; nevertheless, in the eyes of people who have gone through the ordered sequence of the *cursus*, a culture acquired by such a curious process would always contrast as sharply with an academic culture as a tangled forest with a formal garden.

Being responsible for instilling these principles of organization, the school must itself be organized to carry out this function. If it is to hand on this programme of thought known as culture, it must subject the culture it transmits to a process of programming that will make it easier to hand on methodically. Whenever literature becomes a school subject—as among the Sophists or in the Middle Ages—we find emerging the desire to classify, usually by genre and by author, and also to establish hierarchies, to pick out from the mass of works the 'classics' worthy of being preserved through the medium of the school. Collections of excerpts and textbooks are typical of such works designed to serve the school's allotted function of ordering and emphasizing. Having to prepare their pupils to answer academic questions, teachers tend to plan their teaching in accordance with the system of organization that their pupils will have to follow in answering those questions; in the extreme case, we have those prose composition manuals providing ready-made essays on particular subjects. In the organization of his teaching and sometimes of his whole work every teacher is obliged to make some concessions to the requirements of the educational system and of his own function. Gorgias's *Encomium of Helen* is perhaps the first historic example of a demonstration of professorial skill combined with something like a 'crib'; and surely many of Alain's essays are but consummate examples of what French students in *rhétorique supérieure* (the classical upper sixth), whom he taught for the best part of his life, call *topos*, i.e. lectures or demonstrations closely tailored to the letter and spirit of the syllabus and meeting perfectly, in themes, sources, style and even spirit, the examination requirements for admission to the École Normale Supérieure. The programme of thought and action that it is the school's function to impart thus owes a substantial number of its practical characteristics to the institutional conditions in which it is transmitted and to specifically academic requirements. We therefore cannot hope fully to understand each 'school of thought', defined by its subjection to one or other of these programmes, unless we relate it to the specific logic governing the operation of the school from which it derives.

It follows that the gradual rationalization of a system of teaching geared more and more exclusively to preparation for an increasing variety of occupational activities could threaten the cultural integration of the educated class if, so far as that class is concerned, education, and more particularly what is known as general culture, were not at least as much a matter for the family as for the school, for the family in the sense of parents and their progeny and also in that of the fields of knowledge (many scientists are married to women with an arts background) and if all types of training did not allot a place, always a fairly important one, to classical, liberal education. The sharing of a common culture, whether this involves verbal patterns or artistic experience and objects of admiration, is probably one of the surest foundations of the deep underlying fellow-feeling that unites the members of the governing classes, despite differences of occupation and economic circumstances. It is understandable that T. S. Eliot should regard culture as the key instrument in the integration of the elite:[14]

A society is in danger of disintegration when there is a lack of contact between people of different areas of activity—between the political, the scientific, the artistic, the philosophical and the religious minds. The separation cannot be repaired merely by public organization. It is not a question of assembling into committees representatives of different types of knowledge and experience, of calling in everybody to advise everybody else. The elite should be something different, something much more organically composed, than a panel of bonzes, caciques and tycoons. Men who meet only for definite serious purposes and on official occasions do not wholly meet. They may have some common concern very much at heart, they may, in the course of repeated contacts, come to share a vocabulary and an idiom which appear to communicate every shade of meaning necessary for their common purpose; but they will continue to retire from these encounters each to his private social world as well as to his solitary world. Everyone has observed that the possibilities of contented silence, of a mutual happy awareness when engaged upon a common task, or an underlying seriousness and significance in the enjoyment of a silly joke, are characteristics of any close personal intimacy; and the congeniality of any circle of friends depends upon a common social convention, a common ritual, and common pleasures of relaxation. These aids to intimacy are no less important for the communication of meaning in words than the possession of a common subject upon which the several parties are informed. It is unfortunate for a man when his friends and his business associates are two unrelated groups; it is also narrowing when they are one and the same group.

Intimacy and fellow-feeling, congeniality, based on a common culture are rooted in the unconscious and give the traditional elites a social cohesion and continuity which would be lacking in elites united solely by links of professional interest: 'They will be united only by a part, and that the most conscious part, of their personalities; they will meet like committees'.[15] It would not be difficult to find, within the ruling class, social units based on the 'intimacy' created by the same intellectual 'programming'—affinities of schooling play an extremely important part once a body can be recruited by co-option.

Unlike the traditional type of education, setting out to hand on the integrated culture of an integrated society—all-round education producing people equipped for their various roles in society in general—specialized education, imparting specific types of knowledge and know-how, is liable to produce as many 'intellectual clans' as there are specialized schools. To take the most obvious and crudest example, the relations between arts people and science people are often governed, in present-day society, by the very laws to be seen in operation in the contacts between different cultures. Misunderstandings, borrowings removed from their context and reinterpreted, admiring imitation and disdainful aloofness—these are all signs familiar to specialists on the situations that arise when cultures meet. The debate between the upholders of literary humanism and the upholders of scientific or technological humanism is usually conducted in relation to ultimate values—efficiency or disinterestedness, specialization or general liberal education—just because each type of schooling naturally tends to be shut into an autonomous and self-sufficient world of its own; and because any action for the handing on of a culture necessarily implies an affirmation of the value of the culture imparted (and, correlatively, an implicit or explicit depreciation of other possible cultures); in other words, any type of teaching must, to a large extent, produce a need for its own product and therefore set up as a value, or value of values, the culture that it is concerned with imparting, achieving this in and through the very act of imparting it.[16] It follows that individuals whose education condemns them to a kind of cultural hemiplegia, while at the same time encouraging them to identify their own worth with the worth of their culture, are inclined to feel uneasy in their contacts with people with an alien and sometimes rival culture; this uneasiness may be reflected in a compensatory enthusiasm serving as a means of exorcism (we need only think, for example, of the fetishism and Shamanism to be seen among certain specialists in the sciences of man with regard to the formalization of their findings) as well as in rejection and scorn.

The primary causes of the opposition between 'intellectual clans', of which people in general are aware, are never all to be found in the content of the cultures transmitted and the mentality that goes with them. What distinguishes, for example, within the large 'arts' group, a graduate of the École Normale Supérieure from a graduate of the École Nationale de l'Administration or, within the 'science' group, a graduate of the École Polytechnique from a graduate of the École Centrale is perhaps, quite as much as the nature of the knowledge they have acquired, the way in which that knowledge has been acquired, i.e. the nature of the exercises they have had to do, of the examinations they have taken, the criteria by which they have been judged and by reference to which they have organized their studies. An individual's contact with his culture depends basically on the circumstances in which he has acquired it, among other things because the act whereby culture is communicated is, as such, the exemplary expression of a certain type of relation to the culture. The formal lecture, for instance, communicates something other, and something more, than its literal content: it furnishes an example of intellectual prowess and thereby indissociably defines the 'right' culture and the 'right' relation to that culture; vigour and brilliance, ease and elegance are qualities of style peculiar to the act of communication which mark the culture communicated and gain acceptance at the same time as the culture from those receiving it in this form.[17] It could be shown in the same way how all teaching practices implicitly furnish a model of the 'right' mode of intellectual activity; for example, the very nature of the tests set (ranging from the composition, based on the technique of 'development', which is the predominant form in most arts examinations, to the 'brief account' required in advanced science examinations), the type of rhetorical and linguistic qualities required and the value attached to these qualities, the relative importance given to written papers and oral examinations and the qualities required in both instances, tend to encourage a certain attitude towards the use of language—sparing or prodigal, casual or ceremonious, complacent or restrained. In this way the canons governing school work proper, in composition or exposition, may continue to govern writings apparently freed from the disciplines of the school—newspaper articles, public lectures, summary reports and works of scholarship.

Taking it to be the fact that educated people owe their culture—i.e. a programme of perception, thought and action—to the school, we can see that, just as the differentiation of schooling threatens the cultural integration of the educated class, so the *de facto* segregation which tends to reserve secondary education (especially in the classics) and higher education almost exclusively to the economically and, above all, culturally most favoured classes, tends to create a cultural rift. The separation of those who, around the age of 10 or 11, embark on a school career that will last many years, from those who are shot straight into adult life, probably follows class divisions much more closely than in past centuries. Under the *ancien régime*, as Philippe Ariès points out, 'schooling habits differed not so much according to rank as according to function. Consequently, attitudes to life, like many other features of everyday life, differed not much more', notwithstanding 'the rigidly diversified social hierarchy'.[18] On the other hand, 'since the eighteenth century, the single school system has been replaced by a dual educational system, each branch of which is matched not to an age group but to a social class—the *lycée* or the *collège* (secondary schooling) for the middle classes and the elementary (or primary) school for the common people'.[19] Since then, the distinct quality of education has been matched by a duality of culture. 'The whole complexion of life', to quote Philippe Ariès again, 'has been changed by the difference in schooling given to middle class children and working class children'.[20] Culture, whose function it was if not to unify at least to make communication possible, takes on a differentiating function. 'It is not quite true,' writes Edmond Goblot, 'that the bourgeoisie exists only in the practice of society and not in law. The *lycée* makes it a legal institution. The *baccalauréat* is the real barrier, the official, State-guaranteed barrier, which holds back the invasion. True, you may join the bourgeoisie, but first you have to get the *baccalauréat*.'[21] The 'liberal' culture of the humanist traditions with Latin its keystone and the social 'signum' *par excellence*, constitutes the difference while at the same time giving it the semblance of legitimacy. 'When, instead of thinking of his individual interests, he (a member of the bourgeoisie) thinks of his class interests, he needs a culture that marks out an elite, a culture that is not purely utilitarian, a luxury culture. Otherwise, he would fast become indistinguishable from the section of the working classes that manages to gain an education by sheer hard work and intelligence and goes on to lay siege to the professions. The educational background of a middle class child who will not work, despite the educational resources of the *lycée*, will not bear comparison with that of a working class child who studies hard with nothing but the resources of the senior primary school. Even when schooling

leads nowhere professionally, therefore, it is still useful in maintaining the barrier.[22]

The school's function is not merely to sanction the *distinction*—in both senses of the word—of the educated classes. The culture that it imparts separates those receiving it from the rest of society by a whole series of systematic differences. Those whose 'culture' (in the ethnologists' sense) is the academic culture conveyed by the school have a system of categories of perception, language, thought and appreciation that sets them apart from those whose only training has been through their work and their social contacts with people of their own kind. Just as Basil Bernstein contrasts the 'public language' of the working classes, employing descriptive rather than analytical concepts, with a more complex 'formal language', more conducive to verbal elaboration and abstract thought, we might contrast an academic culture, confined to those who have been long subjected to the disciplines of the school, with a 'popular' culture, peculiar to those who have been excluded from it, were it not that, by using the same concept of culture in both cases, we should be in danger of concealing that these two systems of patterns of perception, language, thought, action and appreciation are separated by an essential difference. This is that only the system of patterns cultivated by the school, i.e. academic culture (in the subjective sense of personal cultivation or *Bildung* in German), is organized primarily by reference to a system of works embodying that culture, by which it is both supported and expressed. To speak of 'popular' culture suggests that the system of patterns that makes up the culture (in the subjective sense) of the working classes could or should, in circumstances that are never specified, constitute a culture (in the objective sense) by being embodied in 'popular' works, giving the populace expression in accordance with the patterns of language and thought that define its culture (in the subjective sense). This amounts to asking the populace to take over the intention and means of expression of academic culture (as the proletarian writers do, whether of middle class or working class extraction) to express experience structured by the patterns of a culture (in the subjective sense) to which that intention and those means are essentially alien. It is then quite obvious that 'popular' culture is, by definition, deprived of the objectification, and indeed of the intention of objectification, by which academic culture is defined. (...)

Notes

1 Hutchinson, 1961, pp. 54–5.
2 ibid., p. 230.
3 H.-I. Marrou, *Histoire de l'éducation dans l'antiquité*, sixth ed., Paris, Seuil, 1965, p. 333.
4 E. Renan, *L'Avenir de la science*, Paris, Calmann-Lévy, 1890, pp. 116–17.

5 Because of its own inertia, the school carries along categories and patterns of thought belonging to different ages. In the observance of the rules of the dissertation in three points, for example, French schoolchildren are still contemporaries of Saint Thomas. The feeling of the 'unity of European culture' is probably due to the fact

that the school brings together and reconciles—as it must for the purposes of teaching—types of thought belonging to very different periods.

6 H. Wallon, *Les Origines de la pensée chez l'enfant*, Paris, Presses Universitaires de France, 1945, vol. 1, p. 63.

7 *Gothic Architecture and Scholasticism*, New York, 1957, p. 28.

8 ibid., p. 40.

9 ibid., p. 23.

10 ibid., pp. 20–1.

11 K. Lewin, *Resolving Social Conflicts*, New York, Harper, 1948, p. 57.

12 B. L. Whorf, 'Language, mind and reality', in *Language, Thought, and Reality*, ed. Carroll and Carroll, MIT Press, 1956, p. 256.

13 Cf. P. Bourdieu and A. Darbel, with D. Schnapper, *L'Amour de l'art, les musées et leur public*, Paris, Éditions de Minuit, 1966, pp. 69–76.

14 *Notes towards a Definition of Culture*, Faber, 1962, pp. 84–5.

15 ibid., p. 47.

16 As disparagement of the rival culture is the most convenient and surest means of magnifying the culture being imparted and of reassuring the person imparting it of his own worth, the temptation to resort to this means is all the greater in France because of the teachers' leaning towards charismatic instruction (which leads them to feel that subjects and teachers are on competitive terms), and towards the charismatic ideology that goes with it, which encourages them to regard intellectual careers as personal vocations based upon 'gifts' so obviously mutually exclusive that possession of one rules out possession of the other: to proclaim that you are no good at science is one of the easiest ways of assuring others and yourself that you are gifted on the literary side.

17 Although there is no necessary link between a given content and a given way of imparting it, people who have acquired them together tend to regard them as inseparable. Thus, some people regard any attempt to rationalize teaching as threatening to desacralize culture.

18 *L'Enfant et la vie familiale sous l'Ancien Régime*, Paris, Plon, 1960, p. 375.

19 ibid.

20 ibid., p. 376.

21 *La Barrière et le niveau, étude sociologique sur la bourgeoisie française*, Alcan, 1930, p. 126.

22 ibid., pp. 125–6.

Section VI Consciousness and change

22 Base and superstructure in Marxist cultural theory

Raymond Williams

Any modern approach to a Marxist theory of culture must begin by considering the proposition of a determining base and a determined superstructure. From a strictly theoretical point of view this is not, in fact, where we might choose to begin.[1] It would be in many ways preferable if we could begin from a proposition which originally was equally central, equally authentic: namely the proposition that social being determines consciousness. It is not that the two propositions necessarily deny each other or are in contradiction. But the proposition of base and superstructure, with its figurative element, with its suggestion of a definite and fixed spatial relationship, constitutes, at least in certain hands, a very specialized and at times unacceptable version of the other proposition. Yet in the transition from Marx to Marxism, and in the development of mainstream Marxism itself, the proposition of the determining base and the determined superstructure has been commonly held to be the key to Marxist cultural analysis.

Now it is important, as we try to analyse this proposition, to be aware that the term of relationship which is involved, that is to say 'determines', is of great linguistic and real complexity. The language of determination and even more of determinism was inherited from idealist and especially theological accounts of the world and man. It is significant that it is in one of his familiar inversions, his contradictions of received propositions, that Marx uses the word 'determines'. He is opposing an ideology that had been insistent on the power of certain forces outside man, or, in its secular version, on an abstract determining consciousness. Marx's own proposition explicitly denies this, and puts the origin of determination in men's own activities. Nevertheless, the particular history and continuity of the term serves to remind us that there are, within ordinary use—

Source: *New Left Review*, 82, December 1973, pp. 3–16.

and this is true of most of the major European languages—quite different possible meanings and implications of the word 'determine'. There is, on the one hand, from its theological inheritance, the notion of an external cause which totally predicts or prefigures, indeed totally controls a subsequent activity. But there is also, from the experience of social practice, a notion of determination as setting limits, exerting pressures.

Now there is clearly a difference between a process of setting limits and exerting pressures, whether by some external force or by the internal laws of a particular development, and that other process in which a subsequent content is essentially prefigured, predicted and controlled by a pre-existing external force. Yet it is fair to say, looking at many applications of Marxist cultural analysis, that it is the second sense, the notion of prefiguration, prediction or control, which has often explicitly or implicitly been used.

Superstructure: qualifications and amendments

The term of relationship is then the first thing that we have to examine in this proposition, but we have to do this by going on to look at the related terms themselves. 'Superstructure' has had most attention. People commonly speak of 'the superstructure', although it is interesting that originally, in Marx's German, the term is in one important use plural. Other people speak of the different activities 'inside' the superstructure or superstructures. Now already in Marx himself, in the later correspondence of Engels, and at many points in the subsequent Marxist tradition, qualifications have been made about the determined character of certain superstructural activities. The first kind of qualification had to do with delays in time, with complications, and with certain indirect or relatively distant relationships. The simplest notion of a superstructure, which is still by no means entirely abandoned, had been the reflection, the imitation or the reproduction of the reality of the base in the superstructure in a more or less direct way. Positivist notions of reflection and reproduction of course directly supported this. But since in many real cultural activities this relationship cannot be found, or cannot be found without effort or even violence to the material or practice being studied, the notion was introduced of delays in time, the famous lags; of various technical complications; and of indirectness, in which certain kinds of activity in the cultural sphere—philosophy, for example— were situated at a greater distance from the primary economic activities. That was the first stage of qualification of the notion of superstructure: in effect, an operational qualification. The second stage was related but more fundamental, in that the process of the relationship itself was more substantially looked at. This was the kind of reconsideration which gave rise to the modern notion of 'mediation', in which something more than simple reflection or reproduction—indeed something radically different from either reflection or reproduction—actively occurs. In the later twentieth century there is the notion of 'homologous structures', where there may be no direct or easily apparent similarity, and certainly nothing like reflection or reproduction, between the superstructural process and the reality of the base, but in which there is an essential homology or correspondence of structures, which can be discovered by analysis. This is not the same notion as 'mediation', but it is the same kind of amendment in that the relationship between the base and the superstructure is not supposed to be direct, nor simply operationally subject to lags and complications and indirectnesses, but that of its nature it is not direct reproduction.

These qualifications and amendments are important. But it seems to me that what has not been looked at with equal care, is the received notion of the base. And indeed I would argue that the base is the more important concept to look at if we are to understand the realities of cultural process. In many uses of the proposition of base and superstructure, as a matter of verbal habit, 'the base' has come to be considered virtually as an object, or in less crude cases, it has been considered in essentially uniform and usually static ways. 'The base' is the real social existence of man. 'The base' is the real relations of production corresponding to a stage of the development of material productive forces. 'The base' is a mode of production at a particular stage of its development. We make and repeat propositions of this kind, but the usage is then very different from Marx's emphasis on productive activities, in particular structural relations, constituting the foundation of all other activities. For while a particular stage of the development of production can be discovered and made precise by analysis, it is never in practice either uniform or static. It is indeed one of the central propositions of Marx's sense of history that there are deep contradic-

tions in the relationships of production and in the consequent social relationships. There is therefore the continual possibility of the dynamic variation of these forces. Moreover, when these forces are considered, as Marx always considers them, as the specific activities and relationships of real men, they mean something very much more active, more complicated and more contradictory than the developed metaphorical notion of 'the base' could possibly allow us to realize.

Base and productive forces

So we have to say that when we talk of 'the base', we are talking of a process and not a state. And we cannot ascribe to that process certain fixed properties for subsequent deduction to the variable processes of the superstructure. Most people who have wanted to make the ordinary proposition more reasonable have concentrated on refining the notion of superstructure. But I would say that each term of the proposition has to be revalued in a particular direction. We have to revalue 'determination' towards the setting of limits and the exertion of pressure, and away from a predicted, prefigured and controlled content. We have to revalue 'superstructure' towards a related range of cultural practices, and away from a reflected, reproduced or specifically dependent content. And, crucially, we have to revalue 'the base' away from the notion of a fixed economic or technological abstraction, and towards the specific activities of men in real social and economic relationships, containing fundamental contradictions and variations and therefore always in a state of dynamic process.

It is worth observing one further implication behind the customary definitions. 'The base' has come to include, especially in certain twentieth-century developments, a strong and limiting sense of basic industry. The emphasis on heavy industry, even, has played a certain cultural role. And this raises a more general problem, for we find ourselves forced to look again at the ordinary notion of 'productive forces'. Clearly what we are examining in the base is primary productive forces. Yet some very crucial distinctions have to be made here. It is true that in his analysis of capitalist production Marx considered 'productive work' in a very particular and specialized sense corresponding to that mode of production. There is a difficult passage in the *Grundrisse* in which he argues that while the man who makes a piano is a productive worker, there is a real question whether the man who distributes the piano is also a productive worker; but he probably is, since he contributes to the realization of surplus value. Yet when it comes to the man who plays the piano, whether to himself or to others, there is no question: he is not a productive worker at all. So piano-maker is base, but pianist superstructure. As a way of considering cultural activity, and incidentally the economics of modern cultural activity, this is very clearly a dead-end. But for any theoretical clarification it is crucial to recognize that Marx was there engaged in an analysis of a particular kind of production, that is capitalist commodity production. Within his analysis of that mode, he had to give to the notion of 'productive labour' and 'productive forces' a specialized sense of primary work on materials in a form which produced commodities. But this has narrowed remarkably, and in a cultural context very damagingly, from his more central notion of *productive forces*, in which, to give just brief reminders, the most important thing a worker ever produces is himself, himself in the fact of that kind of labour, or the broader historical emphasis of men producing themselves, themselves and their history. Now when we talk of the base, and of primary productive forces, it matters very much whether we are referring, as in one degenerate form of this proposition became habitual, to primary production within the terms of capitalist economic relationships, or to the primary production of society itself, and of men themselves, material production and reproduction of real life. If we have the broad sense of productive forces, we look at the whole question of the base differently, and we are then less tempted to dismiss as superstructural, and in that sense as merely secondary, certain vital productive social forces, which are in the broad sense, from the beginning, basic.

Uses of totality

Yet, because of the difficulties of the ordinary proposition of base and superstructure, there was an alternative and very important development, an emphasis primarily associated with Lukàcs, on a social 'totality'. The totality of social practices was opposed to this layered notion of a base and a consequent superstructure. This totality of practices is compatible with the notion of social being determining consciousness, but it does not understand this process in terms of a base and a superstructure. Now the language of totality has become common, and it is indeed in many ways more acceptable than the notion of base and superstructure. But with one very important reservation. It is very easy for the notion of totality to empty of its essential content the original Marxist proposition. For if we come to say that society is composed of a large number of social practices which form a concrete social whole, and if we give to each practice a certain specific recognition, adding only that they interact, relate and combine in very complicated ways, we are at one level much more obviously talking about reality, but we are at another level withdrawing from the claim that there is any process of determination. And this I, for one, would be very unwilling to do. Indeed, the key question to ask about any notion of totality in cultural theory is this: whether the notion of totality includes the notion of intention. For if totality is simply concrete, if it is simply the recognition of a large variety of mis-

cellaneous and contemporaneous practices, then it is essentially empty of any content that could be called Marxist. Intention, the notion of intention, restores the key question, or rather the key emphasis. For while it is true that any society is a complex whole of such practices, it is also true that any society has a specific organization, a specific structure, and that the principles of this organization and structure can be seen as directly related to certain social intentions, intentions by which we define the society, intentions which in all our experience have been the rule of a particular class. One of the unexpected consequences of the crudeness of the base/superstructure model has been the too easy acceptance of models which appear less crude—models of totality or of a complex whole— but which exclude the facts of social intention, the class character of a particular society and so on. And this reminds us of how much we lose if we abandon the superstructural emphasis altogether. Thus I have great difficulty in seeing processes of art and thought as superstructural in the sense of the formula as it is commonly used. But in many areas of social and political thought—certain kinds of ratifying theory, certain kinds of law, certain kinds of institutions, which after all in Marx's original formulations were very much part of the superstructure—in all that kind of social apparatus, and in a decisive area of political and ideological activity and construction, if we fail to see a superstructural element we fail to recognize reality at all. These laws, constitutions, theories, ideologies, which are claimed as natural, or as having universal validity or significance, simply have to be seen as expressing and ratifying the domination of a particular class. Indeed the difficulty of revising the formula of base and superstructure has had much to do with the perception of many militants—who have to fight such institutions and notions as well as fighting economic battles—that if these institutions and their ideologies are not perceived as having that kind of dependent and ratifying relationship, if their claims to universal validity or legitimacy are not denied and fought, then the class character of the society can no longer be seen. And this has been the effect of some versions of totality as the description of cultural process. Indeed I think that we can properly use the notion of totality only when we combine it with that other crucial Marxist concept of 'hegemony'.

The complexity of hegemony

It is Gramsci's great contribution to have emphasized hegemony, and also to have understood it at a depth which is, I think, rare. For hegemony supposes the existence of something which is truly total, which is not merely secondary or superstructural, like the weak sense of ideology, but which is lived at such a depth, which saturates the society to such an extent, and which, as Gramsci put it, even constitutes the limit of common sense for most people under its sway, that it corresponds to the reality of social experience very much more clearly than any notions derived from the formula of base and superstructure. For if ideology were merely some abstract imposed notion, if our social and political and cultural ideas and assumptions and habits were merely the result of specific manipulation, of a kind of overt training which might be simply ended or withdrawn, then the society would be very much easier to move and to change than in practice it has ever been or is. This notion of hegemony as deeply saturating the consciousness of a society seems to be fundamental. And hegemony has the advantage over general notions of totality, that it at the same time emphasizes the facts of domination.

Yet there are times when I hear discussions of hegemony and feel that it too, as a concept, is being dragged back to the relatively simple, uniform and static notion which 'superstructure' in ordinary use had become. Indeed I think that we have to give a very complex account of hegemony if we are talking about any real social formation. Above all we have to give an account which allows for its elements of real and constant change. We have to emphasize that hegemony is not singular; indeed that its own internal structures are highly complex, and have continually to be renewed, recreated and defended; and by the same token, that they can be continually challenged and in certain respects modified. That is why instead of speaking simply of 'the hegemony', 'a hegemony', I would propose a model which allows for this kind of variation and contradiction, its sets of alternatives and its processes of change.

But one thing that is evident in some of the best Marxist cultural analysis is that it is very much more at home in what one might call *epochal* questions than in what one has to call *historical* questions. That is to say, it is usually very much better at distinguishing the large features of different epochs of society, as between feudal and bourgeois, or what might be, than at distinguishing between different phases of bourgeois society, and different moments within the phases: that true historical process which demands a much greater precision and delicacy of analysis than the always striking epochal analysis which is concerned with main lineaments and features.

Now the theoretical model which I have been trying to work with is this. I would say first that in any society, in any particular period, there is a central system of practices, meanings and values, which we can properly call dominant and effective. This implies no presumption about its value. All I am saying is that it is central. Indeed I would call it a corporate system, but this might be confusing, since Gramsci uses 'corporate' to mean the subordinate as opposed to the general and dominant elements of hegemony. In any case what I have in mind is the central, effective and dominant system of meanings and values, which are not merely abstract but which are organized and lived. That is why hegemony is not to be understood at the level of mere opinion or mere manipulation. It is a whole body of practices and expectations; our assignments of energy, our ordinary understanding of the nature of man and of his world. It is a set of meanings and values which as they are experienced as practices appear as reciprocally confirming. It thus constitutes a sense of reality for most people in the society, a sense of absolute because experienced reality beyond which it is very difficult for most members of the society to move, in most areas of their lives. But this is not, except in the operation of a moment of abstract analysis, in any sense a static system. On the contrary we can only understand an effective and dominant culture if we understand the real social process on which it depends: I mean the process of incorporation. The modes of incorporation are of great social significance, and incidentally in our kind of society have considerable economic significance. The educational institutions are usually the main agencies of the transmission of an effective dominant culture, and this is now a major economic as well as cultural activity; indeed it is both in the same moment. Moreover, at a philosophical level, at the true level of theory and at the level of the history of various practices, there is a process which I call the *selective tradition*: that which, within the terms of an effective dominant culture, is always passed off as 'the tradition', '*the* significant past'. But always the selectivity is the point; the way in which from a whole possible area of past and present, certain meanings and practices are chosen for emphasis, certain other meanings and practices are neglected and excluded. Even more crucially, some of these meanings and practices are reinterpreted, diluted, or put into forms which support or at least do not contradict other elements within the effective dominant culture. The processes of education; the processes of a much wider social training within institutions like the family; the practical definitions and organisation of work; the selective tradition at an intellectual and theoretical level: all these forces are involved in a continual making and remaking of an effective dominant culture, and on them, as experienced, as built into our living, its reality depends. If what we learn there were merely an imposed ideology, or if it were only the isolable meanings and practices of the ruling class, or of a section of the ruling class, which gets imposed on others, occupying merely the top of our minds, it would be—and one would be glad—a very much easier thing to overthrow.

It is not only the depths to which this process reaches, selecting and organizing and interpreting our experience. It is also that it is continually active and adjusting; it isn't just the past, the dry husks of ideology which we can more easily discard. And this can only be so, in a complex society, if it is something more substantial and more flexible than any abstract imposed ideology. Thus we have to recognize the alternative meanings and values, the alternative opinions and attitudes, even some alternative senses of the world, which can be accommodated and tolerated within a particular effective and dominant culture. This has been much under-emphasized in our notions of a superstructure, and even in some notions of hegemony. And the under-emphasis opens the way for retreat to an indifferent complexity. In the practice of politics, for example, there are certain truly incorporated modes of what are nevertheless, within those terms, real oppositions, that are felt and fought out. Their existence within the incorporation is recognizable by the fact that, whatever the degree of internal conflict or internal variation, they do not in practice go beyond the limits of the central effective and dominant definitions. This is true, for example, of the practice of parliamentary politics, though its internal oppositions are real. It is true about a whole range of practices and arguments, in any real society, which can by no means be reduced to an ideological cover, but which can nevertheless be properly analysed as in my sense corporate, if we find that, whatever the degree of internal controversy and variation, they do not exceed the limits of the central corporate definitions.

But if we are to say this, we have to think again about the sources of that which is not corporate; of those practices, experiences, meanings, values which are not part of the effective dominant culture. We can express this in two ways. There is clearly something that we can call alternative to the effective dominant culture, and there is something else that we can call oppositional, in a true sense. The degree of existence of these alternative and oppositional forms is itself a matter of constant historical variation in real circumstances. In certain societies it is possible to find areas of social life in which quite real alternatives are at least left alone. (If they are made available, of course, they are part of the corporate organization.) The existence of the possibility of opposition, and of its articulation, its degree of openness, and so on, again depends on very precise social and political forces. The facts of alternative and oppositional forms of social life and culture, in relation to the effective and dominant culture, have then to be recognized as subject to historical variation, and as having sources which are very significant, as a fact about the dominant culture itself.

Residual and emergent cultures

I have next to introduce a further distinction, between *residual* and *emergent* forms, both of alternative and of oppositional culture. By 'residual' I mean that some experiences, meanings and values which cannot be verified or cannot be expressed in the terms of the dominant culture, are nevertheless lived and practised on the basis of the residue—cultural as well as social— of some previous social formation. There is a real case of this in certain religious values, by contrast with the very evident incorporation of most religious meanings and values into the dominant system. The

same is true, in a culture like Britain, of certain notions derived from a rural past, which have a very significant popularity. A residual culture is usually at some distance from the effective dominant culture, but one has to recognize that, in real cultural activities, it may get incorporated into it. This is because some part of it, some version of it—and especially if the residue is from some major area of the past— will in many cases have had to be incorporated if the effective dominant culture is to make sense in those areas. It is also because at certain points a dominant culture cannot allow too much of this kind of practice and experience outside itself, at least without risk. Thus the pressures are real, but certain genuinely residual meanings and practices in some important cases survive.

By 'emergent' I mean, first, that new meanings and values, new practices, new significances and experiences, are continually being created. But there is then a much earlier attempt to incorporate them, just because they are part—and yet not part—of effective contemporary practice. Indeed it is significant in our own period how very early this attempt is, how alert the dominant culture now is to anything that can be seen as emergent. We have then to see, first, as it were a temporal relation between a dominant culture and on the one hand a residual and on the other hand an emergent culture. But we can only understand this if we can make distinctions, that usually require very precise analysis, between residual-incorporated and residual not incorporated, and between emergent-incorporated and emergent not incorporated. It is an important fact about any particular society, how far it reaches into the whole range of human practices and experiences in an attempt at incorporation. It may be true of some earlier phases of bourgeois society, for example that there were some areas of experience which it was willing to dispense with, which it was prepared to assign as the sphere of private or artistic life, and as being no particular business of society or the state. This went along with certain kinds of political tolerance, even if the reality of that tolerance was malign neglect. But I am sure it is true of the society that has come into existence since the last war, that progressively, because of developments in the social character of labour, in the social character of communications, and in the social character of decision, it extends much further than ever before in capitalist society into certain hitherto resigned areas of experience and practice and meaning. Thus the effective decision, as to whether a practice is alternative or oppositional, is often now made within a very much narrower scope. There is a simple theoretical distinction between alternative and oppositional, that is to say between someone who simply finds a different way to live and wishes to be left alone with it, and someone who finds a different way to live and wants to change the society in its light. This is usually the difference between individual and small-group solutions to social crisis and those solutions which properly belong to political and ultimately revolutionary practice. But it is often a very narrow line, in reality, between alternative and oppositional. A meaning or a practice may be tolerated as a deviation, and yet still be seen only as another particular way to live. But as the necessary area of effective dominance extends, the same meanings and practices can be seen by the dominant culture, not merely as disregarding or despising it, but as challenging it.

Now it is crucial to any Marxist theory of culture that it can give an adequate explanation of the sources of those practices and meanings. We can understand, from an ordinary historical approach, at least some of the sources of residual meanings and practices. These are the results of earlier social formations, in which certain real meanings and values were generated. In the subsequent default of a particular phase of a dominant culture, there is then a reaching back to those meanings and values which were created in real societies in the past, and which still seem to have some significance because they represent areas of human experience, aspiration and achievement, which the dominant culture undervalues or opposes, or even cannot recognize. But our hardest task theoretically, is to find a non-metaphysical and a non-subjectivist explanation of emergent cultural practice. Moreover, part of our answer to this question bears on the process of persistence of residual practices.

Class and human practice

We do have indeed one source to hand from the central body of Marxist theory. We have the formation of a new class, the coming to consciousness of a new class. This remains, without doubt, quite centrally important. Of course, in itself, this process of formation complicates any simple model of base and superstructure. It also complicates some of the ordinary versions of hegemony, although it was Gramsci's whole object to see and to create by organization the hegemony of a proletarian kind which is capable of challenging the bourgeois hegemony. We have then one central source of new practice, in the emergence of a new class. But we have also to recognize certain other kinds of source, and in cultural practice some of these are very important. I would say that we can recognize them on the basis of this proposition: that no mode of production, and therefore no dominant society or order of society, and therefore no dominant culture, in reality exhausts human practice, human energy, human intention. Indeed it seems to me that this emphasis is not merely a negative proposition, allowing us to account for certain things which happen outside the dominant mode. On the contrary, it is a fact about the modes of domination that they select from and consequently exclude the full range of human practice. The difficulties of human practice outside or against the dominant mode are, of course, real. It depends very much whether it is in an area in

which the dominant class and the dominant culture have an interest and a stake. If the interest and the stake are explicit, many new practices will be reached for, and if possible incorporated, or else extirpated with extraordinary vigour. But in certain areas, there will be in certain periods practices and meanings which are not reached for. There will be areas of practice and meaning which, almost by definition from its own limited character, or in its profound deformation, the dominant culture is unable in any real terms to recognize. This gives us a bearing on the observable difference between, for example, the practices of a capitalist state and a state like the contemporary Soviet Union in relation to writers. Since from the whole Marxist tradition literature was seen as an important activity, indeed a crucial activity, the Soviet state is very much sharper in investigating areas where different versions of practice, different meanings and values, are being attempted and expressed. In capitalist practice, if the thing is not making a profit, or if it is not being widely circulated, then it can for some time be overlooked, at least while it remains alternative. When it becomes oppositional in an explicit way, it does, of course, get approached or attacked.

I am saying then that in relation to the full range of human practice at any one time, the dominant mode is a conscious selection and organization. At least in its fully formed state it is conscious. But there are always sources of real human practice which it neglects or excludes. And these can be different in quality from the developing and articulate interests of a rising class. They can include, for example, alternative perception of others, in immediate personal relationships, or new perceptions of material and media, in art and science, and within certain limits these new perceptions can be practised. The relations between the two kinds of source—the class and the excluded human area—are by no means necessarily contradictory. At times they can be very close, and on the relations between them, much in political practice depends. But culturally and as a matter of theory the areas can be seen as distinct.

Now if we go back to the cultural question in its most usual form—what are the relations between art and society, or literature and society?—in the light of the preceding discussion, we have to say first that there are no relations between literature and society in that abstracted way. The literature is there from the beginning as a practice in the society. Indeed until it and all other practices are present, the society cannot be seen as fully formed. A society is not fully available for analysis until each of its practices is included. But if we make that emphasis we must make a corresponding emphasis: that we cannot separate literature and art from other kinds of social practice, in such a way as to make them subject to quite special and distinct laws. They may have quite specific features as practices, but they cannot be separated from the general social process. Indeed one way of emphasizing this is to say, to insist, that literature is not restricted to operating in any one of the sectors I have been seeking to describe in this model. It would be easy to say, it is a familiar rhetoric, that literature operates in the emergent cultural sector, that it represents the new feelings, the new meanings, the new values. We might persuade ourselves of this theoretically, by abstract argument, but when we read much literature, over the whole range, without the sleight-of-hand of calling Literature only that which we have already selected as embodying certain meanings and values at a certain scale of intensity, we are bound to recognize that the act of writing, the practices of discourse in writing and speech, the making of novels and poems and plays and theories, all this activity takes place in all areas of the culture.

Literature appears by no means only in the emergent sector, which is always, in fact, quite rare. A great deal of writing is of a residual kind, and this has been deeply true of much English literature in the last half-century. Some of its fundamental meanings and values have belonged to the cultural achievements of long-past stages of society. So widespread is this fact, and the habits of mind it supports, that in many minds 'literature' and 'the past' acquire a certain identity, and it is then said that there is now no literature: all that glory is over. Yet most writing, in any period, including our own, is a form of contribution to the effective dominant culture. Indeed many of the specific qualities of literature, its capacity to embody and enact and perform certain meanings and values, or to create in single particular ways what would be otherwise merely general truths, enable it to fulfil this effective function with great power. To literature, of course, we must add the visual arts and music, and in our own society the powerful arts of film and of broadcasting. But the general theoretical point should be clear. If we are looking for the relations between literature and society, we cannot either separate out this one practice from a formed body of other practices, nor when we have identified the particular practice can we give it a uniform, static and ahistorical relation to some abstract social formation. The arts of writing and the arts of creation and performance, over their whole range, are parts of the cultural process in all the different ways, the different sectors, that I have been seeking to describe. They contribute to the effective dominant culture and are a central articulation of it. They embody residual meanings and values, not all of which are incorporated, though many are. They express also and significantly some emergent practices and meanings, yet some of these may eventually be incorporated, as they reach people and begin to move them. Thus it was very evident in the sixties, in some of the emergent arts of performance, that the dominant culture reached out to transform them or seek to transform them. In this process, of course, the dominant culture itself changes, not in its central formation, but in many of its articulated features. But then in a modern society it must always change in this way, if it is to remain dominant, if it is still to be felt as in real ways central in all our many activities and interests.

Critical theory as consumption

What then are the implications of this general analysis for the analysis of particular works of art? This is the question towards which most discussion of cultural theory seems to be directed: the discovery of a method, perhaps even a methodology, through which particular works of art can be understood and described. I would not myself agree that this is the central use of cultural theory, but let us for a moment consider it. What seems to me very striking is that nearly all forms of contemporary critical theory are theories of *consumption*. That is to say, they are concerned with understanding an object in such a way that it can profitably or correctly be consumed. The earliest stage of consumption theory was the theory of 'taste', where the link between the practice and the theory was direct in the metaphor. From taste you got the more elevated notion of 'sensibility', in which it was the consumption by sensibility of elevated or insightful works that was held to be the essential practice of reading, and critical activity was then a function of this sensibility. There were then more developed theories, in the 1920s with Richards, and later in New Criticism, in which the effects of consumption were studied directly. The language of the work of art as object then became more overt. 'What effect does this work ("the poem" as it was ordinarily described) have on me?' Or, 'what impact does it have on me?', as it was later to be put in a much wider area of communication studies. Naturally enough, the notion of the work of art as *object*, as *text*, as an isolated artifact, became central in all these later consumption theories. It was not only that the practices of *production* were then overlooked, though this fused with the notion that most important literature anyway was from the past. The real social conditions of production were in any case neglected because they were believed to be at best secondary. The true relationship was always between the taste, the sensibility or the training of the reader and this isolated work, this object 'in itself as it really is', as most people commonly put it. But the notion of the work of art as object had a further large theoretical effect. If you ask questions about the work of art seen as object, they may include questions about the components of its production. Now, as it happened, there was a use of the formula of base and superstructure which was precisely in line with this. The components of a work of art were the real activities of the base, and you could study the object to discover these components. Sometimes you even studied the components and then projected the object. But in any case the relationship that was looked for was one between an object and its components. But this was not only true of Marxist suppositions of a base and a superstructure. It was true also of various kinds of psychological theory, whether in the form of archetypes, or the images of the collective unconscious, or the myths and symbols which were seen as the *components* of particular works of art. Or again there was biography, or psycho-biography and its like, where the components were in the man's life and the work of art was an object in which components of this kind were discovered. Even in some of the more rigorous forms of new criticism and of structuralist criticism, this essential procedure of regarding the work as an object which has to be reduced to its components, even if later it may be reconstituted, came to persist.

Objects and practices

Now I think the true crisis in cultural theory, in our own time, is between this view of the work of art as object and the alternative view of art as a practice. Of course it is at once objected that the work of art *is* an object: that various works have survived from the past, particular sculptures, particular paintings, particular buildings, and these are objects. This is of course true, but the same way of thinking is applied to works which have no such specific material existence. There is no *Hamlet*, no *Brothers Karamazov*, no *Wuthering Heights*, in the sense that there is a particular great painting. There is no *Fifth Symphony*, there is no work in the whole area of music and dance and performance, which is an object in any way comparable to those works in the visual arts which have survived. And yet the habit of treating all such works as objects has persisted because this is a basic theoretical and practical presupposition. But in literature, especially in drama, in music and in a very wide area of the performing arts, what we have are not objects but *notations*. These notations have to be interpreted in an active way, according to particular conventions. But indeed this is true over an even wider field. The relationship between the making of a work of art and the reception of a work of art, is always active, and subject to conventions, which in themselves are forms of social organization and relationship, and this is radically different from the production and consumption of an object. It is indeed an activity and a practice, and in its accessible forms, although it may in some arts have the character of a material object, it is still only accessible through active perception and interpretation. This makes the case of notation, in arts like drama and literature and music, only a special case of a much wider truth.

What this can show us here about the practice of analysis is that we have to break from the notion of isolating the object and then discovering its components. On the contrary we have to discover the nature of a practice and then its conditions. Often these two processes may in part resemble each other: in many other cases they are of radically different kinds. And I would conclude with an observation on

the way this distinction bears on the Marxist tradition of the relation between primary economic and social practices, and cultural practices. If we suppose that what is produced in cultural practice is a series of objects, we shall, as in most current forms of sociological-critical procedure, set about discovering their components. Within a Marxist emphasis these components will be from what we have been in the habit of calling the base. We shall isolate certain features which we can so to say recognize *in component form*, or we will ask what processes of transformation or mediation these components have gone through before they arrived in this accessible state. But I am saying that we should look not for the components of a product but for the conditions of a practice. When we find ourselves looking at a particular work, or group of works, often realizing, as we do so, their essential community as well as their irreducible individuality, we should find ourselves attending first to the reality of their practice and the conditions of the practice as it was then executed. And from this I think we ask essentially different questions. Take for example the way in which an object is related to a genre, in orthodox criticism. We identify it by certain leading features, we then assign it to a larger category, the genre, and then we may find the components of the genre in a particular social history (although in some variants of Marxist criticism not even that is done, and the genre is supposed to be some permanent category of the mind). It is not that way of proceeding that seems to be required. The recognition of the relation of a collective mode and an individual project—and these are the only categories that we can initially presume—is a recognition of related practices. That is to say, the irreducibly individual projects that particular works are, may come in experience and in analysis to show resemblances which allow us to group them into collective modes. These are by no means always genres. They may exist as resemblances within and across genres. They may be the practice of a group in a period, rather than the practice of a phase in a genre. But as we discover the nature of a particular practice, and the nature of the relation between an individual project and a collective mode, we find that we are analysing, as two forms of the same process, both its active composition and its conditions of composition, and in either direction this is a complex of extending active relationships. This means, of course, that we have no built-in procedure of the kind which is indicated by the fixed character of an object. We have the principles of the relations of practices, within a discoverably intentional organization, and we have the available hypotheses of dominant, residual and emergent. But what we are actively seeking is the true practice which has been alienated to an object, and the true conditions of practice—whether as literary conventions or as social relationships—which have been alienated to components or to mere background. As a general proposition this is only an emphasis, but it seems to me to suggest at once the point of break and the point of departure, in practical and theoretical work, within an active and self-renewing Marxist cultural tradition.

Note

1 Revised text of a lecture given in Montreal, April 1973.

23 The new forms of control

Herbert Marcuse

A comfortable, smooth, reasonable, democratic un-freedom prevails in advanced industrial civilization, a token of technical progress. Indeed, what could be more rational than the suppression of individuality in the mechanization of socially necessary but painful performances; the concentration of individual enter-prises in more effective, more productive corporations; the regulation of free competition among unequally equipped economic subjects; the curtailment of prerogatives and national sovereignties which impede the international organization of resources. That this technological order also involves a political and intellectual coordination may be a regrettable and yet promising development.

The rights and liberties which were such vital factors in the origins and earlier stages of industrial society yield to a higher stage of this society: they are losing their traditional rationale and content. Freedom of thought, speech, and conscience were—just as free enterprise, which they served to promote and protect—essentially *critical* ideas, designed to replace an obsolescent material and intellectual culture by a more productive and rational one. Once institutionalized, these rights and liberties shared the fate of the society of which they had become an integral part. The achievement cancels the premises.

To the degree to which freedom from want, the concrete substance of all freedom, is becoming a real possibility, the liberties which pertain to a state of lower productivity are losing their former content. Independence of thought, autonomy, and the right to political opposition are being deprived of their basic critical function in a society which seems increasingly capable of satisfying the needs of the individuals through the way in which it is organized. Such a society may justly demand acceptance of its principles and institutions, and reduce the opposition to the discussion and promotion of alternative policies *within* the status quo. In this respect, it seems to make little difference whether the increasing satisfaction of needs is accomplished by an author-itarian or a non-authoritarian system. Under the conditions of a rising standard of living, non-con-formity with the system itself appears to be socially useless, and the more so when it entails tangible economic and political disadvantages and threatens the smooth operation of the whole. Indeed, at least in so far as the necessities of life are involved, there seems to be no reason why the production and distribution of goods and services should proceed through the competitive concurrence of individual liberties.

Freedom of enterprise was from the beginning not altogether a blessing. As the liberty to work or to starve, it spelled toil, insecurity, and fear for the vast majority of the population. If the individual were no longer compelled to prove himself on the market, as a free economic subject, the disappearance of this kind of freedom would be one of the greatest achieve-ments of civilization. The technological processes of mechanization and standardization might release individual energy into a yet uncharted realm of freedom beyond necessity. The very structure of human existence would be altered; the individual would be liberated from the work world's imposing upon him alien needs and alien possibilities. The individual would be free to exert autonomy over a life that would be his own. If the productive apparatus could be organized and directed toward the satisfac-tion of the vital needs, its control might well be centralized; such control would not prevent individual autonomy, but render it possible.

This is a goal within the capabilities of advanced industrial civilization, the 'end' of technological rationality. In actual fact, however, the contrary trend operates: the apparatus imposes its economic

Source: *One-Dimensional Man: Studies in the Ideology of Advanced Industrial Society*, Routledge & Kegan Paul, 1964, pp. 1–18.

and political requirements for defense and expansion on labor time and free time, on the material and intellectual culture. By virtue of the way it has organized its technological base, contemporary industrial society tends to be totalitarian. For 'totalitarian' is not only a terroristic political co-ordination of society, but also a non-terroristic economic-technical coordination which operates through the manipulation of needs by vested interests. It thus precludes the emergence of an effective opposition against the whole. Not only a specific form of government or party rule makes for totalitarianism, but also a specific system of production and distribution which may well be compatible with a 'pluralism' of parties, newspapers, 'countervailing powers,' etc.

Today political power asserts itself through its power over the machine process and over the technical organization of the apparatus. The government of advanced and advancing industrial societies can maintain and secure itself only when it succeeds in mobilizing, organizing, and exploiting the technical, scientific, and mechanical productivity available to industrial civilization. And this productivity mobilizes society as a whole, above and beyond any particular individual or group interests. The brute fact that the machine's physical (only physical?) power surpasses that of the individual, and of any particular group of individuals, makes the machine the most effective political instrument in any society whose basic organization is that of the machine process. But the political trend may be reversed; essentially the power of the machine is only the stored-up and projected power of man. To the extent to which the work world is conceived of as a machine and mechanized accordingly, it becomes the *potential* basis of a new freedom for man.

Contemporary industrial civilization demonstrates that it has reached the stage at which 'the free society' can no longer be adequately defined in the traditional terms of economic, political, and intellectual liberties, not because these liberties have become insignificant, but because they are too significant to be confined within the traditional forms. New modes of realization are needed, corresponding to the new capabilities of society.

Such new modes can be indicated only in negative terms because they would amount to the negation of the prevailing modes. Thus economic freedom would mean freedom *from* the economy—from being controlled by economic forces and relationships; freedom from the daily struggle for existence, from earning a living. Political freedom would mean liberation of the individuals *from* politics over which they have no effective control. Similarly, intellectual freedom would mean the restoration of individual thought now absorbed by mass communication and indoctrination, abolition of 'public opinion' together with its makers. The unrealistic sound of these propositions is indicative, not of their utopian character, but of the strength of the forces which prevent their realization. The most effective and enduring form of warfare against liberation is the implanting of material and intellectual needs that perpetuate obsolete forms of the struggle for existence.

The intensity, the satisfaction and even the character of human needs, beyond the biological level, have always been preconditioned. Whether or not the possibility of doing or leaving, enjoying or destroying, possessing or rejecting something is seized as a *need* depends on whether or not it can be seen as desirable and necessary for the prevailing societal institutions and interests. In this sense, human needs are historical needs and, to the extent to which the society demands the repressive development of the individual, his needs themselves and their claim for satisfaction are subject to overriding critical standards.

We may distinguish both true and false needs. 'False' are those which are superimposed upon the individual by particular social interests in his repression: the needs which perpetuate toil, aggressiveness, misery, and injustice. Their satisfaction might be most gratifying to the individual, but this happiness is not a condition which has to be maintained and protected if it serves to arrest the development of the ability (his own and others) to recognize the disease of the whole and grasp the chances of curing the disease. The result then is euphoria in unhappiness. Most of the prevailing needs to relax, to have fun, to behave and consume in accordance with the advertisements, to love and hate what others love and hate, belong to this category of false needs.

Such needs have a societal content and function which are determined by external powers over which the individual has no control; the development and satisfaction of these needs is heteronomous. No matter how much such needs may have become the individual's own, reproduced and fortified by the conditions of his existence; no matter how much he identifies himself with them and finds himself in their satisfaction, they continue to be what they were from the beginning—products of a society whose dominant interest demands repression.

The prevalence of repressive needs is an accomplished fact, accepted in ignorance and defeat, but a fact that must be undone in the interest of the happy individual as well as all those whose misery is the price of his satisfaction. The only needs that have an unqualified claim for satisfaction are the vital ones—nourishment, clothing, lodging at the attainable level of culture. The satisfaction of these needs is the prerequisite for the realization of *all* needs, of the unsublimated as well as the sublimated ones.

For any consciousness and conscience, for any experience which does not accept the prevailing societal interest as the supreme law of thought and behavior, the established universe of needs and satisfactions is a fact to be questioned—questioned in terms of truth and falsehood. These terms are historical throughout, and their objectivity is historical. The judgment of needs and their satisfaction, under the given conditions, involves standards of *priority*—standards which refer to the optimal development of the individual, of all individuals, under the optimal utilization of the material and intellectual resources available to man. The resources are calculable. 'Truth' and 'falsehood' of needs designate objective conditions to the extent to which the universal satisfaction of vital needs and, beyond it, the progressive alleviation of toil and poverty, are universally valid standards. But as historical standards, they do not only vary according to area and stage of development, they also can be defined only in (greater or lesser) *contradiction* to the prevailing ones. What tribunal can possibly claim the authority of decision?

In the last analysis, the question of what are true and false needs must be answered by the individuals themselves, but only in the last analysis; that is, if and when they are free to give their own answer. As long as they are kept incapable of being autonomous, as long as they are indoctrinated and manipulated (down to their very instincts), their answer to this question cannot be taken as their own. By the same token, however, no tribunal can justly arrogate to itself the right to decide which needs should be developed and satisfied. Any such tribunal is reprehensible, although our revulsion does not do away with the question: how can the people who have been the object of effective and productive domination by themselves create the conditions of freedom?

The more rational, productive, technical, and total the repressive administration of society becomes, the more unimaginable the means and ways by which the administered individuals might break their servitude and seize their own liberation. To be sure, to impose Reason upon an entire society is a paradoxical and scandalous idea—although one might dispute the righteousness of a society which ridicules this idea while making its own population into objects of total administration. All liberation depends on the consciousness of servitude, and the emergence of this consciousness is always hampered by the predominance of needs and satisfactions which, to a great extent, have become the individual's own. The process always replaces one system of preconditioning by another; the optimal goal is the replacement of false needs by true ones, the abandonment of repressive satisfaction.

The distinguishing feature of advanced industrial society is its effective suffocation of those needs which demand liberation—liberation also from that which is tolerable and rewarding and comfortable—while it sustains and absolves the destructive power and repressive function of the affluent society. Here, the social controls exact the overwhelming need for the production and consumption of waste; the need for stupefying work where it is no longer a real necessity; the need for modes of relaxation which soothe and prolong this stupefaction; the need for maintaining such deceptive liberties as free competition at admin-istered prices, a free press which censors itself, free choice between brands and gadgets.

Under the rule of a repressive whole, liberty can be made into a powerful instrument of domination. The range of choice open to the individual is not the decisive factor in determining the degree of human freedom, but *what* can be chosen and what *is* chosen by the individual. The criterion for free choice can never be an absolute one, but neither is it entirely relative. Free election of masters does not abolish the masters or the slaves. Free choice among a wide variety of goods and services does not signify freedom if these goods and services sustain social controls over a life of toil and fear—that is, if they sustain alienation. And the spontaneous reproduction of superimposed needs by the individual does not establish autonomy; it only testifies to the efficacy of the controls.

Our insistence on the depth and efficacy of these controls is open to the objection that we overrate greatly the indoctrinating power of the 'media,' and that by themselves the people would feel and satisfy the needs which are now imposed upon them. The objection misses the point. The preconditioning does not start with the mass production of radio and television and with the centralization of their control. The people enter this stage as preconditioned receptacles of long standing; the decisive difference is in the flattening out of the contrast (or conflict) between the given and the possible, between the satisfied and the unsatisfied needs. Here, the so-called equalization of class distinctions reveals its ideological function. If the worker and his boss enjoy the same television program and visit the same resort places, if the typist is as attractively made up as the daughter of her employer, if the Negro owns a Cadillac, if they all read the same newspaper, then this assimilation indicates not the disappearance of classes, but the extent to which the needs and satisfactions that serve the preservation of the Establishment are shared by the underlying population.

Indeed, in the most highly developed areas of contemporary society, the transplantation of social into individual needs is so effective that the difference between them seems to be purely theoretical. Can one really distinguish between the mass media as instruments of information and entertainment, and as agents of manipulation and indoctrination? Between the automobile as nuisance and as convenience? Between the horrors and the comforts of functional architecture? Between the work for national defense and the work for corporate gain? Between the private pleasure and the commercial and political utility involved in increasing the birth rate?

We are again confronted with one of the most vexing aspects of advanced industrial civilization: the rational character of its irrationality. Its productivity and efficiency, its capacity to increase and spread comforts, to turn waste into need, and destruction into construction, the extent to which this civilization transforms the object world into an extension of man's mind and body makes the very notion of alienation questionable. The people recognize themselves in their commodities; they find their soul in their automobile, hi-fi set, split-level home, kitchen equipment. The very mechanism which ties the individual to his society has changed, and social control is anchored in the new needs which it has produced.

The prevailing forms of social control are technological in a new sense. To be sure, the technical structure and efficacy of the productive and destructive apparatus has been a major instrumentality for subjecting the population to the established social division of labor throughout the modern period. Moreover, such integration has always been accompanied by more obvious forms of compulsion: loss of livelihood, the administration of justice, the police, the armed forces. It still is. But in the contemporary period, the technological controls appear to be the very embodiment of Reason for the benefit of all social groups and interests—to such an extent that all contradiction seems irrational and all counteraction impossible.

No wonder then that, in the most advanced areas of this civilization, the social controls have been introjected to the point where even individual protest is affected at its roots. The intellectual and emotional refusal 'to go along' appears neurotic and impotent. This is the socio-psychological aspect of the political event that marks the contemporary period: the passing of the historical forces which, at the preceding stage of industrial society, seemed to represent the possibility of new forms of existence.

But the term 'introjection' perhaps no longer describes the way in which the individual by himself reproduces and perpetuates the external controls exercised by his society. Introjection suggests a variety of relatively spontaneous processes by which a Self (Ego) transposes the 'outer' into the 'inner.' Thus introjection implies the existence of an inner dimension distinguished from and even antagonistic to the external exigencies—an individual consciousness and an individual unconscious *apart from* public opinion and behavior.[1] The idea of 'inner freedom' here has its reality: it designates the private space in which man may become and remain 'himself.'

Today this private space has been invaded and whittled down by technological reality. Mass production and mass distribution claim the *entire* individual, and industrial psychology has long since ceased to be confined to the factory. The manifold processes of introjection seem to be ossified in almost mechanical reactions. The result is, not adjustment but *mimesis*: an immediate identification of the individual with *his* society and, through it, with the society as a whole.

This immediate, automatic identification (which may have been characteristic of primitive forms of association) reappears in high industrial civilization; its new 'immediacy,' however, is the product of a sophisticated, scientific management and organization. In this process, the 'inner' dimension of the mind in which opposition to the status quo can take root is whittled down. The loss of this dimension, in which the power of negative thinking—the critical power of Reason—is at home, is the ideological counterpart to the very material process in which advanced industrial society silences and reconciles the opposition. The impact of progress turns Reason into submission to the facts of life, and to the dynamic capability of producing more and bigger facts of the same sort of life. The efficiency of the system blunts the individuals' recognition that it contains no facts which do not communicate the repressive power of the whole. If the individuals find themselves in the things which shape their life, they do so, not by giving, but by accepting the law of things—not the law of physics but the law of their society.

I have just suggested that the concept of alienation seems to become questionable when the individuals identify themselves with the existence which is imposed upon them and have in it their own development and satisfaction. This identification is not illusion but reality. However, the reality constitutes a more progressive stage of alienation. The latter has become entirely objective; the subject which is alienated is swallowed up by its alienated existence. There is only one dimension, and it is everywhere and in all forms. The achievements of progress defy ideological indictment as well as justification; before their tribunal, the 'false consciousness' of their rationality becomes the true consciousness.

This absorption of ideology into reality does not, however, signify the 'end of ideology.' On the contrary, in a specific sense advanced industrial culture is *more* ideological than its predecessor, inasmuch as today the ideology is in the process of production itself.[2] In a provocative form, this proposition reveals the political aspects of the prevailing technological rationality. The productive apparatus and the goods and services which it produces 'sell' or impose the social system as a whole. The means of mass transportation and communication, the commodities of lodging, food, and clothing, the irresistible output of the entertainment and information industry carry with them prescribed attitudes and habits, certain intellectual and emotional reactions which bind the consumers more or less pleasantly to the producers and, through the latter, to the whole. The products indoctrinate and manipulate; they promote a false consciousness which is immune against its falsehood. And as these beneficial products become available to more individuals in more social classes, the indoctrination they carry ceases to be publicity; it becomes a way of life. It is a good way of life—much better than before—and as a good way of life, it militates against qualitative change. Thus emerges a pattern of *one-dimensional thought and behavior* in which ideas, aspirations, and objectives that, by their content, transcend the established universe of discourse and action are either repelled or reduced to terms of this universe. They are redefined by the rationality of the given system and of its quantitative extension.

The trend may be related to a development in scientific method: operationalism in the physical, behaviorism in the social sciences. The common feature is a total empiricism in the treatment of concepts; their meaning is restricted to the representation of particular operations and behavior. The operational point of view is well illustrated by P. W. Bridgman's analysis of the concept of length:[3]

> We evidently know what we mean by length if we can tell what the length of any and every object is, and for the physicist nothing more is required. To find the length of an object, we have to perform certain physical operations. The concept of length is therefore fixed when the operations by which length is measured are fixed: that is, the concept of length involves as much and nothing more than the set of operations by which length is determined. In general, we mean by any concept nothing more than a set of operations; *the concept is synonymous with the corresponding set of operations*.

Bridgman has seen the wide implications of this mode of thought for the society at large:[4]

> To adopt the operational point of view involves much more than a mere restriction of the sense in which we understand 'concept,' but means a far-reaching change in all our habits of thought, in that we shall no longer permit ourselves to use as tools in our thinking concepts of which we cannot give an adequate account in terms of operations.

Bridgman's prediction has come true. The new mode of thought is today the predominant tendency in philosophy, psychology, sociology, and other fields. Many of the most seriously troublesome concepts are being 'eliminated' by showing that no adequate account of them in terms of operations or behavior can be given. The radical empiricist onslaught thus provides the methodological justification for the debunking of the mind by the intellectuals—a positivism which, in its denial of the transcending elements of Reason, forms the academic counterpart of the socially required behavior.

Outside the academic establishment, the 'far-reaching change in all our habits of thought' is more serious. It serves to coordinate ideas and goals with those exacted by the prevailing system, to enclose them in the system, and to repel those which are irreconcilable with the system. The reign of such a one-dimensional reality does not mean that materialism rules, and that the spiritual, metaphysical, and bohemian occupations are petering out. On the contrary, there is a great deal of 'Worship together this week,' 'Why not try God,' Zen, existentialism, and beat ways of life, etc. But such modes of protest and transcendence are no longer contradictory to the status quo and no longer negative. They are rather the ceremonial part of practical behaviorism, its harmless negation, and are quickly digested by the status quo as part of its healthy diet.

One-dimensional thought is systematically promoted by the makers of politics and their purveyors of mass information. Their universe of discourse is populated by self-validating hypotheses which, incessantly and monopolistically repeated, become hypnotic definitions or dictations. For example, 'free' are the institutions which operate (and are operated on) in the countries of the Free World; other transcending modes of freedom are by definition either anarchism, communism, or propaganda. 'Socialistic' are all encroachments on private enterprises not undertaken by private enterprise itself (or by government contracts), such as universal and comprehensive health insurance, or the protection of nature from all too sweeping commercialization, or the establishment of public services which may hurt private profit. This totalitarian logic of accomplished facts has its Eastern counterpart. There, freedom is the way of life instituted by a communist regime, and all other transcending modes of freedom are either capitalistic, or revisionist, or leftist sectarianism. In both camps, non-operational ideas are non-behavioral and subversive. The movement of thought is stopped at barriers which appear as the limits of Reason itself.

Such limitation of thought is certainly not new. Ascending modern rationalism, in its speculative as well as empirical form, shows a striking contrast between extreme critical radicalism in scientific and philosophic method on the one hand, and an uncritical quietism in the attitude toward established and functioning social institutions. Thus Descartes' *ego cogitans* was to leave the 'great public bodies' untouched, and Hobbes held that 'the present ought always to be preferred, maintained, and accounted best.' Kant agreed with Locke in justifying revolution *if and when* it has succeeded in organizing the whole and in preventing subversion.

However, these accommodating concepts of Reason were always contradicted by the evident misery and injustice of the 'great public bodies' and the effective, more or less conscious rebellion against them. Societal conditions existed which provoked and permitted real dissociation from the established state of affairs; a private as well as political dimension was present in which dissociation could develop into effective opposition, testing its strength and the validity of its objectives.

With the gradual closing of this dimension by the society, the self-limitation of thought assumes a larger significance. The interrelation between scientific-philosophical and societal processes, between theoretical and practical Reason, asserts itself 'behind the back' of the scientists and philosophers. The society bars a whole type of oppositional operations and behavior; consequently, the concepts pertaining to them are rendered illusory or meaningless. Historical transcendence appears as metaphysical transcendence, not acceptable to science and scientific thought. The operational and behavioral point of view, practiced as a 'habit of thought' at large, becomes the view of the established universe of discourse and action, needs and aspirations. The 'cunning of Reason' works, as it so often did, in the interest of the powers that be. The insistence on operational and behavioral concepts turns against the efforts to free thought and behavior *from* the given reality and *for* the suppressed alternatives. Theoretical and practical Reason, academic and social behaviorism meet on common ground: that of an advanced society which makes scientific and technical progress into an instrument of domination.

'Progress' is not a neutral term; it moves toward specific ends, and these ends are defined by the possibilities of ameliorating the human condition. Advanced industrial society is approaching the stage where continued progress would demand the radical subversion of the prevailing direction and organization of progress. This stage would be reached when material production (including the necessary services) becomes automated to the extent that all vital needs can be satisfied while necessary labor time is reduced to marginal time. From this point on, technical progress would transcend the realm of necessity, where it served as the instrument of domination and exploitation which thereby limited its rationality; technology would become subject to the free play of faculties in the struggle for the pacification of nature and of society.

Such a state is envisioned in Marx's notion of the 'abolition of labor.' The term 'pacification of existence' seems better suited to designate the historical alternative of a world which—through an international conflict which transforms and suspends the contradictions within the established societies—advances on the brink of a global war. 'Pacification of existence' means the development of man's struggle with man and with nature, under conditions where the competing needs, desires, and aspirations are no longer organized by vested interests in domination and scarcity—an organization which perpetuates the destructive forms of this struggle.

Today's fight against this historical alternative finds a firm mass basis in the underlying population, and finds its ideology in the rigid orientation of thought and behavior to the given universe of facts. Validated by the accomplishments of science and technology, justified by its growing productivity, the status quo defies all transcendence. Faced with the possibility of pacification on the grounds of its technical and intellectual achievements, the mature industrial society closes itself against this alternative. Operationalism, in theory and practice, becomes the theory and practice of *containment*. Underneath its obvious dynamics, this society is a thoroughly static system of life: self-propelling in its oppressive productivity and in its beneficial coordination. Containment of technical progress goes hand in hand with its growth in the established direction. In spite of the political fetters imposed by the status quo, the more technology appears capable of creating the conditions for pacification, the more are the minds and bodies of man organized against this alternative.

The most advanced areas of industrial society exhibit throughout these two features: a trend toward consummation of technological rationality, and intensive efforts to contain this trend within the established institutions. Here is the internal contradiction of this civilization: the irrational element in its rationality. It is the token of its achievements. The industrial society which makes technology and science its own is organized for the ever-more-effective domination of man and nature, for the ever-more-effective utilization of its resources. It becomes irrational when the success of these efforts opens new dimensions of human realization. Organization for peace is different from organization for war; the institutions which served the struggle for existence cannot serve the pacification of existence. Life as an end is qualitatively different from life as a means.

Such a qualitatively new mode of existence can never be envisaged as the mere by-product of economic and political changes, as the more or less spontaneous effect of the new institutions which constitute the necessary prerequisite. Qualitative change also involves a change in the *technical* basis on which this society rests—one which sustains the economic and political institutions through which the 'second nature' of man as an aggressive object of administration is stabilized. The techniques of industrialization are political techniques; as such, they prejudge the possibilities of Reason and Freedom.

To be sure, labor must precede the reduction of labor, and industrialization must precede the development of human needs and satisfactions. But as all freedom depends on the conquest of alien necessity, the realization of freedom depends on the *techniques* of this conquest. The highest productivity of labor can be used for the perpetuation of labor, and the most efficient industrialization can serve the restriction and manipulation of needs.

When this point is reached, domination—in the guise of affluence and liberty—extends to all spheres of private and public existence, integrates all authentic opposition, absorbs all alternatives. Technological rationality reveals its political character as it becomes the great vehicle of better domination, creating a truly totalitarian universe in which society and nature, mind and body are kept in a state of permanent mobilization for the defense of this universe.

Notes

1 The change in the function of the family here plays a decisive role: its 'socializing' functions are increasingly taken over by outside groups and media. See my *Eros and Civilization*, Boston, Beacon Press, 1955, pp. 96ff.

2 Theodor W. Adorno, *Prismen, Kulturkritik und Gesellschaft*, Frankfurt, Suhrkamp, 1955, p. 24f.

3 *The Logic of Modern Physics*, New York, Macmillan, 1928, p. 5. The operational doctrine has since been refined and qualified. Bridgman himself has extended the concept of 'operation' to include the 'paper-and-pencil' operations of the theorist (in Philipp J. Frank, *The Validation of Scientific Theories*, Boston, Beacon Press, 1954, ch. II). The main impetus remains the same: it is 'desirable' that the paper-and-pencil operations 'be capable of eventual contact, although perhaps indirectly, with instrumental operations.'

4 op. cit., p. 31.

24 The intellectuals

Antonio Gramsci

The formation of the intellectuals

Are intellectuals an autonomous and independent social group, or does every social group have its own particular specialised category of intellectuals? The problem is a complex one, because of the variety of forms assumed to date by the real historical process of formation of the different categories of intellectuals.

The most important of these forms are two:

1 Every social group, coming into existence on the original terrain of an essential function in the world of economic production, creates together with itself, organically, one or more strata of intellectuals which give it homogeneity and an awareness of its own function not only in the economic but also in the social and political fields. The capitalist entrepreneur creates alongside himself the industrial technician, the specialist in political economy, the organisers of a new culture, of a new legal system, etc. It should be noted that the entrepreneur himself represents a higher level of social elaboration, already character-ised by a certain directive [*dirigente*] and technical (i.e. intellectual) capacity: he must have a certain technical capacity, not only in the limited sphere of his activity and initiative but in other spheres as well, at least in those which are closest to economic production. He must be an organiser of masses of men; he must be an organiser of the 'confidence' of investors in his business, of the customers for his product, etc.

If not all entrepreneurs, at least an *élite* amongst them must have the capacity to be an organiser of society in general, including all its complex organism of services, right up to the state organism, because of the need to create the conditions most favourable to the expansion of their own class; or at the least they must possess the capacity to choose the deputies (specialised employees) to whom to entrust this activity of organising the general system of relation-ships external to the business itself. It can be observed that the 'organic' intellectuals which every new class creates alongside itself and elaborates in the course of its development, are for the most part 'specialisations' of partial aspects of the primitive activity of the new social type which the new class has brought into prominence.[1]

Even feudal lords were possessors of a particular technical capacity, military capacity, and it is precisely from the moment at which the aristocracy loses its monopoly of technico-military capacity that the crisis of feudalism begins. But the formation of intellectuals in the feudal world and in the preceding classical world is a question to be examined separately: this formation and elaboration follows ways and means which must be studied concretely. Thus it is to be noted that the mass of the peasantry, although it performs an essential function in the world of pro-duction, does not elaborate its own 'organic' intel-lectuals, nor does it 'assimilate' any stratum of 'traditional' intellectuals, although it is from the peasantry that other social groups draw many of their intellectuals and a high proportion of traditional intellectuals are of peasant origin.

2 However, every 'essential' social group which emerges into history out of the preceding economic structure, and as an expression of a development of this structure, has found (at least in all of history up to the present) categories of intellectuals already in existence and which seemed indeed to represent an historical continuity uninterrupted even by the most complicated and radical changes in political and social forms.

The most typical of these categories of intellectuals is that of the ecclesiastics, who for a long time (for a whole phase of history, which is partly characterised by this very monopoly) held a monopoly of a number

Source: *Selections from the Prison Notebooks of Antonio Gramsci*, ed. and trans. by Q. Hoare and G. Nowell Smith, Lawrence & Wishart, 1971, pp. 5–16.

of important services: religious ideology, that is the philosophy and science of the age, together with schools, education, morality, justice, charity, good works, etc. The category of ecclesiastics can be considered the category of intellectuals organically bound to the landed aristocracy. It had equal status juridically with the aristocracy, with which it shared the exercise of feudal ownership of land, and the use of state privileges connected with property.[2] But the monopoly held by the ecclesiastics in the superstructural field[3] was not exercised without a struggle or without limitations, and hence there took place the birth, in various forms (to be gone into and studied concretely), of other categories, favoured and enabled to expand by the growing strength of the central power of the monarch, right up to absolutism. Thus we find the formation of the *noblesse de robe*, with its own privileges, a stratum of administrators, etc. scholars and scientists, theorists, non-ecclesiastical philosophers, etc.

Since these various categories of traditional intellectuals experience through an '*esprit de corps*' their uninterrupted historical continuity and their special qualification, they thus put themselves forward as autonomous and independent of the dominant social group. This self-assessment is not without consequences in the ideological and political field, consequences of wide-ranging import. The whole of idealist philosophy can easily be connected with this position assumed by the social complex of intellectuals and can be defined as the expression of that social utopia by which the intellectuals think of themselves as 'independent', autonomous, endowed with a character of their own, etc.

One should note however that if the Pope and the leading hierarchy of the Church consider themselves more linked to Christ and to the apostles than they are to senators Agnelli and Benni, the same does not hold for Gentile and Croce, for example: Croce in particular feels himself closely linked to Aristotle and Plato, but he does not conceal, on the other hand, his links with senators Agnelli and Benni, and it is precisely here that one can discern the most significant character of Croce's philosophy.

What are the 'maximum' limits of acceptance of the term 'intellectual'? Can one find a unitary criterion to characterise equally all the diverse and disparate activities of intellectuals and to distinguish these at the same time and in an essential way from the activities of other social groupings? The most widespread error of method seems to me that of having looked for this criterion of distinction in the intrinsic nature of intellectual activities, rather than in the ensemble of the system of relations in which these activities (and therefore the intellectual groups who personify them) have their place within the general complex of social relations. Indeed the worker or proletarian, for example, is not specifically characterised by his manual or instrumental work, but by performing this work in specific conditions and in specific social relations (apart from the consideration that purely physical labour does not exist and that even Taylor's phrase of 'trained gorilla' is a metaphor to indicate a limit in a certain direction: in any physical work, even the most degraded and mechanical, there exists a minimum of technical qualification, that is, a minimum of creative intellectual activity). And we have already observed that the entrepreneur, by virtue of his very function, must have to some degree a certain number of qualifications of an intellectual nature although his part in society is determined not by these, but by the general social relations which specifically characterise the position of the entrepreneur within industry.

All men are intellectuals, one could therefore say: but not all men have in society the function of intellectuals.[4]

When one distinguishes between intellectuals and non-intellectuals, one is referring in reality only to the immediate social function of the professional category of the intellectuals, that is, one has in mind the direction in which their specific professional activity is weighted, whether towards intellectual elaboration or towards muscular-nervous effort. This means that, although one can speak of intellectuals, one cannot speak of non-intellectuals, because non-intellectuals do not exist. But even the relationship between efforts of intellectual-cerebral elaboration and muscular-nervous effort is not always the same, so that there are varying degrees of specific intellectual activity. There is no human activity from which every form of intellectual participation can be excluded: *homo faber* cannot be separated from *homo sapiens*. Each man, finally, outside his professional activity, carries on some form of intellectual activity, that is, he is a 'philosopher', an artist, a man of taste, he participates in a particular conception of the world, has a conscious line of moral conduct, and therefore contributes to sustain a conception of the world or to modify it, that is, to bring into being new modes of thought.

The problem of creating a new stratum of intellectuals consists therefore in the critical elaboration of the intellectual activity that exists in everyone at a certain degree of development, modifying its relationship with the muscular-nervous effort towards a new equilibrium, and ensuring that the muscular-nervous effort itself, in so far as it is an element of a general practical activity, which is perpetually innovating the physical and social world, becomes the foundation of a new and integral conception of the world. The traditional and vulgarised type of the intellectual is given by the man of letters, the philosopher, the artist. Therefore journalists, who claim to be men of letters, philosophers, artists, also regard themselves as the 'true' intellectuals. In the modern world, technical education, closely bound to industrial labour even at the most primitive and unqualified level, must form the basis of the new type of intellectual.

On this basis the weekly *Ordine Nuovo* worked to

develop certain forms of new intellectualism and to determine its new concepts, and this was not the least of the reasons for its success, since such a conception corresponded to latent aspirations and conformed to the development of the real forms of life. The mode of being of the new intellectual can no longer consist in eloquence, which is an exterior and momentary mover of feelings and passions, but in active participation in practical life, as constructor, organiser, 'permanent persuader' and not just a simple orator (but superior at the same time to the abstract mathematical spirit); from technique-as-work one proceeds to technique-as-science and to the humanistic conception of history, without which one remains 'specialised' and does not become 'directive' (specialised and political).

Thus there are historically formed specialised categories for the exercise of the intellectual function. They are formed in connection with all social groups, but especially in connection with the more important, and they undergo more extensive and complex elaboration in connection with the dominant social group. One of the most important characteristics of any group that is developing towards dominance is its struggle to assimilate and to conquer 'ideologically' the traditional intellectuals, but this assimilation and conquest is made quicker and more efficacious the more the group in question succeeds in simultaneously elaborating its own organic intellectuals.

The enormous development of activity and organisation of education in the broad sense in the societies that emerged from the medieval world is an index of the importance assumed in the modern world by intellectual functions and categories. Parallel with the attempt to deepen and to broaden the 'intellectuality' of each individual, there has also been an attempt to multiply and narrow the various specialisations. This can be seen from educational institutions at all levels, up to and including the organisms that exist to promote so-called 'high culture' in all fields of science and technology.

School is the instrument through which intellectuals of various levels are elaborated. The complexity of the intellectual function in different states can be measured objectively by the number and gradation of specialised schools: the more extensive the 'area' covered by education and the more numerous the 'vertical' 'levels' of schooling, the more complex is the cultural world, the civilisation, of a particular state. A point of comparison can be found in the sphere of industrial technology: the industrialisation of a country can be measured by how well equipped it is in the production of machines with which to produce machines, and in the manufacture of ever more accurate instruments for making both machines and further instruments for making machines, etc. The country which is best equipped in the construction of instruments for experimental scientific laboratories and in the construction of instruments with which to test the first instruments, can be regarded as the most complex in the technical-industrial field, with the highest level of civilisation, etc. The same applies to the preparation of intellectuals and to the schools dedicated to this preparation; schools and institutes of high culture can be assimilated to each other. In this field also, quantity cannot be separated from quality. To the most refined technical-cultural specialisation there cannot but correspond the maximum possible diffusion of primary education and the maximum care taken to expand the middle grades numerically as much as possible. Naturally this need to provide the widest base possible for the selection and elaboration of the top intellectual qualifications—i.e. to give a democratic structure to high culture and top-level technology—is not without its disadvantages: it creates the possibility of vast crises of unemployment for the middle intellectual strata, and in all modern societies this actually takes place.

It is worth noting that the elaboration of intellectual strata in concrete reality does not take place on the terrain of abstract democracy but in accordance with very concrete traditional historical processes. Strata have grown up which traditionally 'produce' intellectuals and these strata coincide with those which have specialised in 'saving', i.e. the petty and middle landed bourgeoisie and certain strata of the petty and middle urban bourgeoisie. The varying distribution of different types of school (classical and professional) over the 'economic' territory and the varying aspirations of different categories within these strata determine, or give form to, the production of various branches of intellectual specialisation. Thus in Italy the rural bourgeoisie produces in particular state functionaries and professional people, whereas the urban bourgeoisie produces technicians for industry. Consequently it is largely northern Italy which produces technicians and the South which produces functionaries and professional men.

The relationship between the intellectuals and the world of production is not as direct as it is with the fundamental social groups but is, in varying degrees, 'mediated' by the whole fabric of society and by the complex of superstructures, of which the intellectuals are, precisely, the 'functionaries'. It should be possible both to measure the 'organic quality' [*organicità*] of the various intellectual strata and their degree of connection with a fundamental social group, and to establish a gradation of their functions and of the superstructures from the bottom to the top (from the structural base upwards). What we can do, for the moment, is to fix two major superstructural 'levels': the one that can be called 'civil society', that is the ensemble of organisms commonly called 'private', and that of 'political society' or 'the State'. These two levels correspond on the one hand to the function of 'hegemony' which the dominant group exercises throughout society and on the other hand to that of 'direct domination' or command exercised through the State and 'juridical' government. The functions in question are precisely organisational and connective. The intellectuals are the dominant group's 'deputies' exercising the subaltern functions of social hegemony and political government. These comprise:

1 The 'spontaneous' consent given by the great masses of the population to the general direction imposed on social life by the dominant fundamental group; this consent is 'historically' caused by the prestige (and consequent confidence) which the dominant group enjoys because of its position and function in the world of production.

2 The apparatus of state coercive power which 'legally' enforces discipline on those groups who do not 'consent' either actively or passively. This apparatus is, however, constituted for the whole of society in anticipation of moments of crisis of command and direction when spontaneous consent has failed.

This way of posing the problem has as a result a considerable extension of the concept of the intellectual, but it is the only way which enables one to reach a concrete approximation of reality. It also clashes with preconceptions of caste. The function of organising social hegemony and state domination certainly gives rise to a particular division of labour and therefore to a whole hierarchy of qualifications in some of which there is no apparent attribution of directive or organisational functions. For example, in the apparatus of social and state direction there exist a whole series of jobs of a manual and instrumental character (non-executive work, agents rather than officials or functionaries). It is obvious that such a distinction has to be made just as it is obvious that other distinctions have to be made as well. Indeed, intellectual activity must also be distinguished in terms of its intrinsic characteristics, according to levels which in moments of extreme opposition represent a real qualitative difference—at the highest level would be the creators of the various sciences, philosophy, art, etc., at the lowest the most humble 'administrators' and divulgators of pre-existing, traditional, accumulated intellectual wealth.[5]

In the modern world the category of intellectuals, understood in this sense, has undergone an unprecedented expansion. The democratic-bureaucratic system has given rise to a great mass of functions which are not all justified by the social necessities of production, though they are justified by the political necessities of the dominant fundamental group. Hence Loria's conception of the unproductive 'worker' (but unproductive in relation to whom and to what mode of production?), a conception which could in part be justified if one takes account of the fact that these masses exploit their position to take for themselves a large cut out of the national income. Mass formation has standardised individuals both psychologically and in terms of individual qualification and has produced the same phenomena as with other standardised masses: competition which makes necessary organisations for the defence of pro-fessions, unemployment, over-production in the schools, emigration, etc.

The different position of urban and rural-type intellectuals

Intellectuals of the urban type have grown up along with industry and are linked to its fortunes. Their function can be compared to that of subaltern officers in the army. They have no autonomous initiative in elaborating plans for construction. Their job is to articulate the relationship between the entrepreneur and the instrumental mass and to carry out the immediate execution of the production plan decided by the industrial general staff, controlling the elementary stages of work. On the whole the average urban intellectuals are very standardised, while the top urban intellectuals are more and more identified with the industrial general staff itself.

Intellectuals of the rural type are for the most part 'traditional', that is they are linked to the social mass of country people and the town (particularly small-town) petite bourgeoisie, not as yet elaborated and set in motion by the capitalist system. This type of intellectual brings into contact the peasant masses with the local and state administration (lawyers, notaries, etc.). Because of this activity they have an important politico-social function, since professional mediation is difficult to separate from political. Furthermore: in the countryside the intellectual (priest, lawyer, notary, teacher, doctor, etc.), has on the whole a higher or at least a different living standard from that of the average peasant and consequently represents a social model for the peasant to look to in his aspiration to escape from or improve his condition. The peasant always thinks that at least one of his sons could become an intellectual (especially a priest), thus becoming a gentleman and raising the social level of the family by facilitating its economic life through the connections which he is bound to acquire with the rest of the gentry. The peasant's attitude towards the intellectual is double and appears contradictory. He respects the social position of the intellectuals and in general that of state employees, but sometimes affects contempt for it, which means that his admiration is mingled with instinctive elements of envy and impassioned anger. One can understand nothing of the collective life of the peasantry and of the germs and ferments of development which exist within it, if one does not take into consideration and examine concretely and in depth this effective subordination to the intellectuals. Every organic development of the peasant masses, up to a certain point, is linked to and depends on movements among the intellectuals.

With the urban intellectuals it is another matter. Factory technicians do not exercise any political function over the instrumental masses, or at least this is a phase that has been superseded. Sometimes, rather, the contrary takes place, and the instrumental masses, at least in the person of their own organic intellectuals, exercise a political influence on the technicians.

The central point of the question remains the distinction between intellectuals as an organic category of every fundamental social group and intellectuals as a traditional category. From this distinction there flow a whole series of problems and possible questions for historical research.

The most interesting problem is that which, when studied from this point of view, relates to the modern political party, its real origins, its developments and the forms which it takes. What is the character of the political party in relation to the problem of the intellectuals? Some distinctions must be made:

1 The political party for some social groups is nothing other than their specific way of elaborating their own category of organic intellectuals directly in the political and philosophical field and not just in the field of productive technique. These intellectuals are formed in this way and cannot indeed be formed in any other way, given the general character and the conditions of formation, life and development of the social group.[6]

2 The political party, for all groups, is precisely the mechanism which carries out in civil society the same function as the State carries out, more synthetically and over a larger scale, in political society. In other words it is responsible for welding together the organic intellectuals of a given group—the dominant one—and the traditional intellectuals. The party carries out this function in strict dependence on its basic function, which is that of elaborating its own component parts—those elements of a social group which has been born and developed as an 'economic' group—and of turning them into qualified political intellectuals, leaders [*dirigenti*] and organisers of all the activities and functions inherent in the organic development of an integral society, both civil and political. Indeed it can be said that within its field the political party accomplishes its function more completely and organically than the State does within its admittedly far larger field. An intel-

lectual who joins the political party of a particular social group is merged with the organic intellectuals of the group itself, and is linked tightly with the group. This takes place through participation in the life of the State only to a limited degree and often not at all. Indeed it happens that many intellectuals think that they *are* the State, a belief which, given the magnitude of the category, occasionally has important consequences and leads to unpleasant complications for the fundamental economic group which *really* is the State.

That all members of a political party should be regarded as intellectuals is an affirmation that can easily lend itself to mockery and caricature. But if one thinks about it nothing could be more exact. There are of course distinctions of level to be made. A party might have a greater or lesser proportion of members in the higher grades or in the lower, but this is not the point. What matters is the function, which is directive and organisational, i.e. educative, i.e. intellectual. A tradesman does not join a political party in order to do business, nor an industrialist in order to produce more at lower cost, nor a peasant to learn new methods of cultivation, even if some aspects of these demands of the tradesman, the industrialist or the peasant can find satisfaction in the party.[7]

For these purposes, within limits, there exists the professional association, in which the economic-corporate activity of the tradesman, industrialist or peasant is most suitably promoted. In the political party the elements of an economic social group get beyond that moment of their historical development and become agents of more general activities of a national and international character. This function of a political party should emerge even more clearly from a concrete historical analysis of how both organic and traditional categories of intellectuals have developed in the context of different national histories and in that of the development of the various major social groups within each nation, particularly those groups whose economic activity has been largely instrumental. (. . .)

Notes

1 Mosca's *Elementi di Scienza Politica* (new expanded edition, 1923) are worth looking at in this connection. Mosca's so-called 'political class' is nothing other than the intellectual category of the dominant social group. Mosca's concept of 'political class' can be connected with Pareto's concept of the *élite*, which is another attempt to interpret the historical phenomenon of the intellectuals and their function in the life of the state and of society. Mosca's book is an enormous hotch-potch, of a sociological and positivistic character, plus the tendentiousness of immediate politics which makes it less indigestible and livelier from a literary point of view.

2 For one category of these intellectuals, possibly the most important after the ecclesiastical for its prestige and the social function it performed in primitive societies, the category of *medical men* in the wide sense, that is all those who 'struggle' or seem to struggle against death and disease, compare the *Storia della medicina* of Arturo Castiglioni. Note that there has been a connection between religion and medicine, and in certain areas there still is: hospitals in the hands of religious orders for certain organisational functions, apart from the fact that wherever the doctor appears, so does the priest (exorcism, various forms of assistance, etc.). Many great religious figures were and are conceived of as great 'healers': the idea of miracles, up to the resurrection of the dead. Even in the case of kings the belief long survived that they could heal with the laying on of hands, etc.

3 From this has come the general sense of 'intellectual' or 'specialist' of the word '*chierico* (clerk, cleric) in many languages of romance origin or heavily influenced, through church Latin, by the romance languages, together with its correlative '*laico*' (lay, layman) in the sense of profane, non-specialist.

4 Thus, because it can happen that everyone at some time fries a couple of eggs or sews up a tear in a jacket, we do not necessarily say that everyone is a cook or a tailor.

5 Here again military organisation offers a model of complex gradations between subaltern officers, senior officers and general staff, not to mention the NCOs, whose importance is greater than is generally admitted. It is worth observing that all these parts feel a solidarity and indeed that it is the lower strata that display the most blatant *esprit de corps*, from which they derive a certain 'conceit' which is apt to lay them open to jokes and witticisms.

6 Within productive technique those strata are formed which can be said to correspond to NCOs in the army, that is to say, for the town, skilled and specialised workers and, for the country (in a more complex fashion) share-cropping and tenant farmers—since in general terms these types of farmer correspond more or less to the type of the artisan, who is the skilled worker of a mediaeval economy.

7 Common opinion tends to oppose this, maintaining that the tradesman, industrialist or peasant who engages in 'politicking' loses rather than gains, and is the worst type of all—which is debatable.

25 A few notions about the word 'concientization'*

Paulo Freire

What then is conciêntização?

One of the characteristics of man is that *man is only himself man*. Man alone is able to look at the world and objective reality from a distance. This is precisely the *human praxis*: the action-reflection of man on the world, on reality. Nevertheless, in approaching the world, objective reality does not present itself to him as a cognisant object of his critical conscience. In other words, in man's spontaneous approach to the world, the attitude he takes is not a critical one, or, in more sophisticated terms, it is not an epistemological attitude. That is, at this first stage, man's attitude is not the one of a knowing subject; it is not an intentionally curious attitude, but the naïve attitude of somebody who *experiences* something. Note that I do not say 'experiments' but 'experiences'. The first term expresses the attitude of somebody who intentionally searches for something with curiosity, while the second expresses the spontaneity of one who finds something without searching for it.

At this level, man, in approaching reality, simply experiences himself with that reality which is with him. Thus his mind does not yet take a critical stand. This does not mean that, at this level of spontaneity, man does not have a consciousness of the world and reality. The epistemological intention—'intendre'—is there, and it is already a kind of knowledge; it makes his consciousness to be a consciousness of something. As the Brazilian philosopher Fiori says: 'A consciousness of nothing is nothing of consciousness.'

At this level of spontaneity there is a consciousness of reality, but, as yet, not a critical attitude, there is a perception of reality which includes a certain kind of knowledge of it. The Greeks called this 'doxa'—simple opinion or belief. Knowledge that remains at the level of 'doxa' and does not go further to reach

Source: *Hard Cheese*, no. 1, 1971, pp. 23-8.

the level of 'opus', the intrinsic reason why of reality (as Mao Tse Tung would put it), does not reach the stage of full knowledge; it is not the 'logos' of reality.

It is enough, to be a man, to have consciousness of world and man—to apprehend the reality of the dialectical relations between man and world. These are so intimate that in fact we should not speak about man and world but about man and man-world. This first level of apprehension of reality is the 'praise de conciênce'. This consciousness of reality exists precisely because men, as beings in time and space, are with and in the world, knowing it and being part of it.

This 'praise de conciênce' is not conciêntização as yet. Conciêntização is the deepening of the praise de conscience, it is the critical development of the 'praise de conciênce'. Conciêntização implies going through the spontaneous stage of apprehension of reality into a critical stage in which reality becomes a cogniscible object towards which man takes an epistemological attitude, man searching for deeper knowledge. Thus conciêntização becomes a *test* of reality. The more one acquires conciêntização (conciêntizasizes oneself), the more one discovers reality, the more one penetrates the phenomenological essence of the object one has in front of oneself in order to analyse it. For this very reason conciêntização is not a falsely intellectual attitude towards reality. Conciêntização cannot exist without or outside praxis, that is outside action-reflection. The two unities express the permanently dialectical characteristic of the way man is and the way he transforms the world.

Conciêntização, then, is a 'historical commitment'. There cannot be a conciêntização without a 'commitment' with history. Hence conciêntização is a historic conscience as well, it is a critical insertion in history. It implies that men take the role of agents, makers and remakers of the world; it demands that men create their existence with the elements that life offers them. This is the reason why the more they are concientized the more they exist, not just live. Man, as a historical being, a maker of history, will be more a subject of the historical process the more he discovers himself as the object of it.

In asserting that conciêntização is a historical commitment—and this requires transforming the world not just adapting to it—I want to emphasize that the simple praise de conscience of an oppressing situation, for instance, does not yet mean the overcoming of it. The first step is to discover oneself as oppressed but one is not free yet. To discover one's oppression is the beginning of a process of liberation when it becomes a historical commitment—which means engagement. Engagement, though, would be more than commitment; it would be the critical insertion into history to create history, to make history. Therefore, the realization of oppression, if it does not lead to engage people in the process of transforming the oppressing reality, is not conciêntização.

Conciêntização implies that in discovering myself oppressed I know that I will be liberated only if I try to transform the oppressing situation in which I find myself. And I cannot transform that situation just in my head—that would be idealism, a way of thinking which believes that conscience can transform reality just by thinking. In this instance the structures would go on the same and my freedom would not begin to grow. Conciêntização, then, implies a critical insertion in the praxis and the process of historical change. Conciêntização invites us to take a utopian attitude to the world, an attitude that makes the concientized man a utopian factor in the process of history.

Utopian, to my way of thinking, is not that which cannot be real, it is not idealism. Utopia is the dialectical process of denouncing and announcing— denouncing the oppressing structure and announcing the humanizing structure. It is therefore a historical commitment and engagement. Utopia is an act of knowing critically. I cannot denounce an oppressing structure if I do not penetrate into it and know it. Nor can I announce what I do not know. Between the time of announcing and the beginning of what is announced there is a gap, not so much temporal as critical. The announcing is not a project, but a pre-project which becomes a project only in historical praxis. Acting the pre-project becomes project. Praxis and not only words make the announcing an essential element of conciêntização. That is the meaning of historical engagement inspired by a prophetic, utopian, but critical hope. Only those who are continually denouncing and announcing, committed and engaged in the transformation of the world, are utopian and create hope. The oppressors cannot be utopian and cannot create hope. What is the future of the oppressor but the preservation of his oppressing present? What denouncing can the oppressors do but the denouncing of those who denounce them? What can their announcing be, but the announcing of their myths? What can be the hope of the oppressors if they cannot create a future?

Conciêntização implies utopia. If we are not utopian we will easily become bureaucratic and dehumanizing. This is the risk revolutions run when they become static and institutionalized. Revolution must be permanent and it must be *Cultural Revolution*—a continuous cultural self-criticism of men in society and the world. *Conciêntização is a permanent critical approach to reality in order to discover it and discover the myths that deceive us and help to maintain the oppressing dehumanizing structures.*

Where can we find the process, the how of conciêntização?

The how of conciêntização implies a basic starting-point: the distinction between education as an instrument of domination and education as an instrument of liberation.

Systematic education for conformity is characterized by being the transmission of knowledge in which the educator transfers his thirst for knowledge to those being educated. Despite an apparent active methodology, those being educated receive knowledge in a passive way. Conciêntização is not viable here. It nevertheless appears to a certain extent in students' reactions to it precisely because the 'intention'— 'intendre'—of human consciousness cannot be completely eradicated by the domesticating education we have.

Concientizing education—for liberation—instead of being an act of transferring knowledge is an act of knowing. It therefore implies, in its process, that educators and learners all become learners assuming the same attitude as cognitive subjects discovering knowledge through one another and through the objects they try to know. It is not a situation where one knows and others do not; it is rather the search, by all, at the same time to discover something by the act of knowing which cannot exhaust all the possibilities in the relation between object and subject. In other words, education for liberation tries to make history— not just receiving or reading history.

Let us return to the question of myths and slogans. The phenomenon of the permanence of the myths of the old structures and the phenomenon of the reactivation of new structures must be taken into account and understood as far as possible. Without the critical grasping of this phenomenon we cannot understand how, for instance, after the transformation of a political structure, or any infrastructure, men go on thinking the same way they thought before the transformation. The dialectical understanding of this explains the unviability of a mechanistic explanation of social change. This was a problem for Lenin after the Soviet Revolution. It is the problem that Castro is having with peasants, though less now than before. This was and still is Mao's problem. His answer to the problem has been the most genial one in this century: *Cultural Revolution*. Cultural action, cultural revolution, is the way in which we attack culturally our own culture. It is to take culture as always problematic and to question it without accepting the myths that ossify it and ossify us.

While education for conformity emphasizes its praxis as an inversion and domesticates people by reinforcing mythical introspection, education for freedom intends to catch the inversion of that praxis in the act of inversion in order to prevent it. How does one do this? By making problematic the power of inversion of the praxis of education, or life, we must try and make an object of knowing the very inversion and its domesticating power. Thus, the act of knowing illuminates praxis which is the source of our knowledge. This implies a continuous dynamic questioning of culture. If we do not do this, culture becomes static in the form of myths. We would thus fall into an elitist situation which would be no longer liberating or humanizing.

How do we make a type of cultural action or education for freedom when we find people subjected to the so-called media of communication (which are means of indoctrination without communication)? We have to give the word 'communication' its true meaning and liberate it from the danger of being mistaken as an invasion of slogans. Cultural action is a kind of action that intends to expose the mythification of reality. We have to make—and help others to make—problematic the myth power of the slogans which domesticate us.

Let us, for example, analyse the extreme situation of peasants in north-east Brazil. Their conscience is oppressed to the extreme of making them unable to see reality as something produced by the structure created by man. But they are rational beings and need an explanation of the situation in which they find themselves. How does he question himself? What are the reasons he gives himself? How does his oppressed conscience analyse the situations?

He tries to find the cause, the origin of the situation, in superior entities more powerful than man. One of these entities is God; God is responsible for the situation; he knows best; he is powerful; man can do nothing. Fortunately many Christians do not think that way any more. Nevertheless that is the way of thinking of the oppressed masses. Thus, God being made responsible for the state of oppression, a number of myths have to be created in order to rationalize the dominating structures. If God is not made responsible, then it is fate. Consciousness at this level is extremely fatalistic and therefore they remain inactive. *We can do nothing*.

A second way of rationalizing is also a myth maintained by the dominating structures: *The Ontological Inability of the Oppressed*. The oppressed conscience analyses itself and discovers its incapacity to overcome the situation, hence thinking it is essentially incapable. In some countries whites say that negroes are created inferior by God in order to be subjected to them. This is the image of the colonial creator by the colonizers. The oppressor dictates the image of the oppressed. There is nothing to do beyond this situation for the oppressed conscience.

For the critical conscience, for the man who is becoming concientized, there is something not reached as yet, but which we must do: we must make the project real, we must create the historic future. In order to do this the situation which dehumanizes men has to be transformed. It is not with aspirins that we will change extreme situations but rather through men changing history.

The more we analyse the perception of the oppressing reality and its causes, the more we expose it, the more it will be challenged. We will have to opt either to be committed or not, but we have to know why. Conciêntização leaves nobody inactive. It is a process in which some commit themselves and others feel guilty if they do not do it. Conciêntização makes me realize that my brothers who do not eat or laugh, who do not sing, do not love, who live under oppression, suffer and are hated, and who are less and less every day, are the victims of structures that create that extreme situation. Then, either I commit myself to the historic process with all the risks, and this is not easy, or I remain outside, uncommitted, and feel guilty because I do not do what I know I should. This feeling takes peace away so then I try to buy it with generosities, trying to compensate for my lack of commitment and trying to buy my peace. *Peace* however cannot be bought or sold. Peace must be lived; it cannot be lived outside a commitment with others. This commitment with others cannot exist outside the transformation of the structures which have created the dehumanizing situation. There is only one way to buy peace: *to make peace in union with others*.

It is extremely interesting to notice that these two basic attitudes appear in all the courses I have directed—some of only two days, like this one. Many times I have been violently attacked because many people listening feel exposed and think that I am exposing them. Their reaction is always to attack not the things said—they know they are true—but the person who says them. This process is very interesting, even beautiful to watch, because it shows the power of conciêntização.

This process also takes place with oppressed people. There are many among them that flee from freedom. Oppression is such a deep strong reality that it produces fear of freedom. Fear of freedom exists when one sees a threat, even in talking about it. Freedom is never a gift. It is something difficult because nobody can give freedom to somebody else and nobody makes himself free either. Men are made free in communion with others through a situation we have to change. We have to make our freedom together with others—'We' not 'I'.

Summing up what I have said, we can say that conciêntização is a painful business, it is disturbing in its beginning as if we were born again. Conciêntização is a call to be new every day and to give witness to utopia, thus engendering hope and peace.

Conciêntização is not, it cannot be, an imposition, a manipulation. I cannot impose my opinions on others. I can only invite others to share them, discuss them. Love is not just a free act, it is an act for the sake of freedom, ordered and geared towards freedom, a maker of freedom. Love which cannot produce freedom is not love. There is a difference between love and pathology of love. We cannot identify love with sadism and masochism. I only love others if I love them as people—in their being, in growing and changing, falling and rising up again, allowing them to be themselves and, helping them to be themselves. Anything else is a mistaken love. I cannot, for example, force my children to say 'Good night' if they do not want to. I will never impose on them anything in the name of civilization thinking that I love them in doing so. Above all one must avoid the possibility of this becoming a 'banking concept of education' in which one only teaches.

Other works of Freire

The Pedagogy of the Oppressed, Sheed & Ward, 1972; Penguin, 1972.
Education as Cultural Action, Penguin, 1972.

Note

* This is an edited version of a translated transcript of a talk given by Freire in Rome in 1970. Translation by Manuel Vaquerizo.

Index